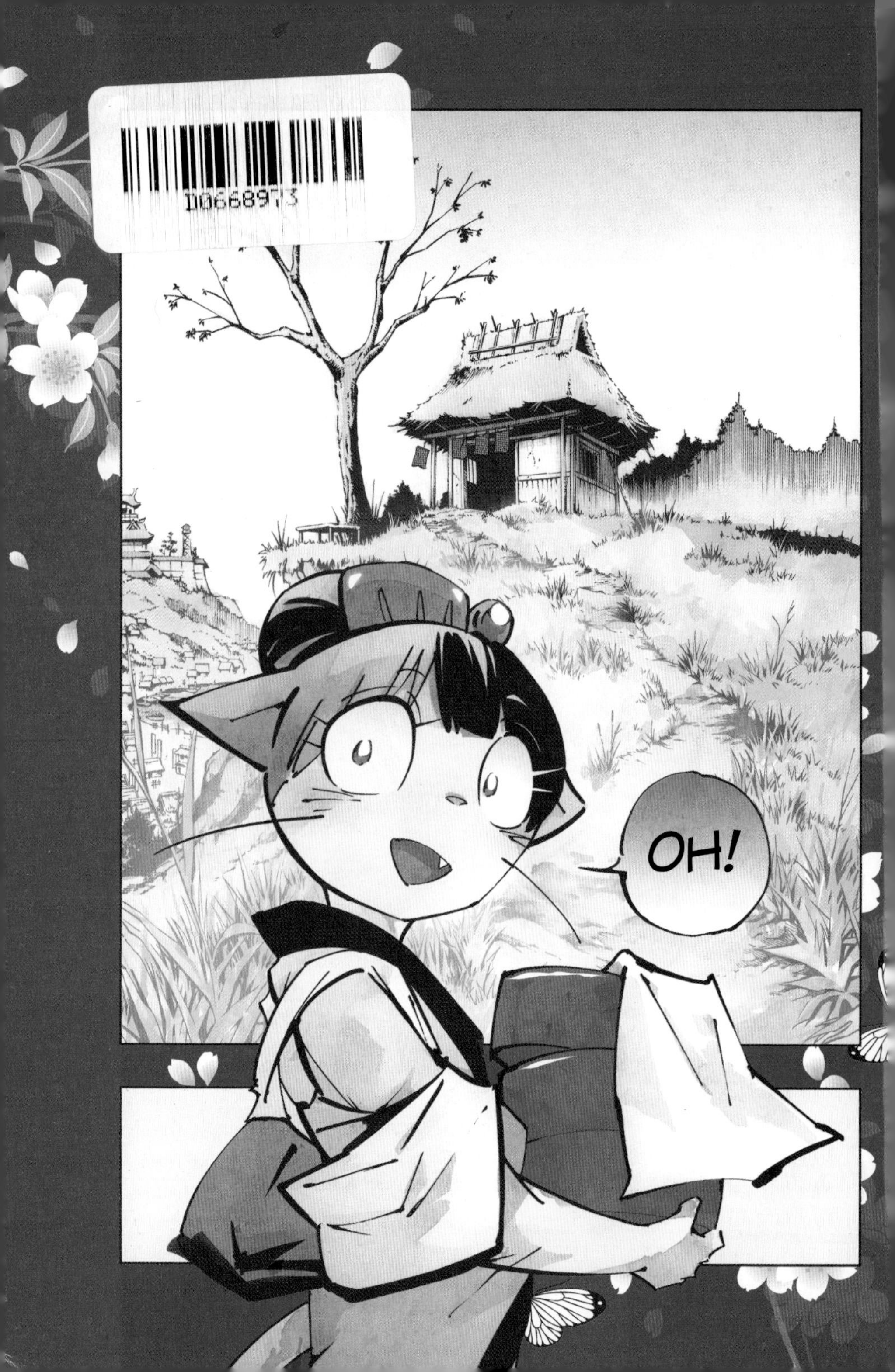
OH!

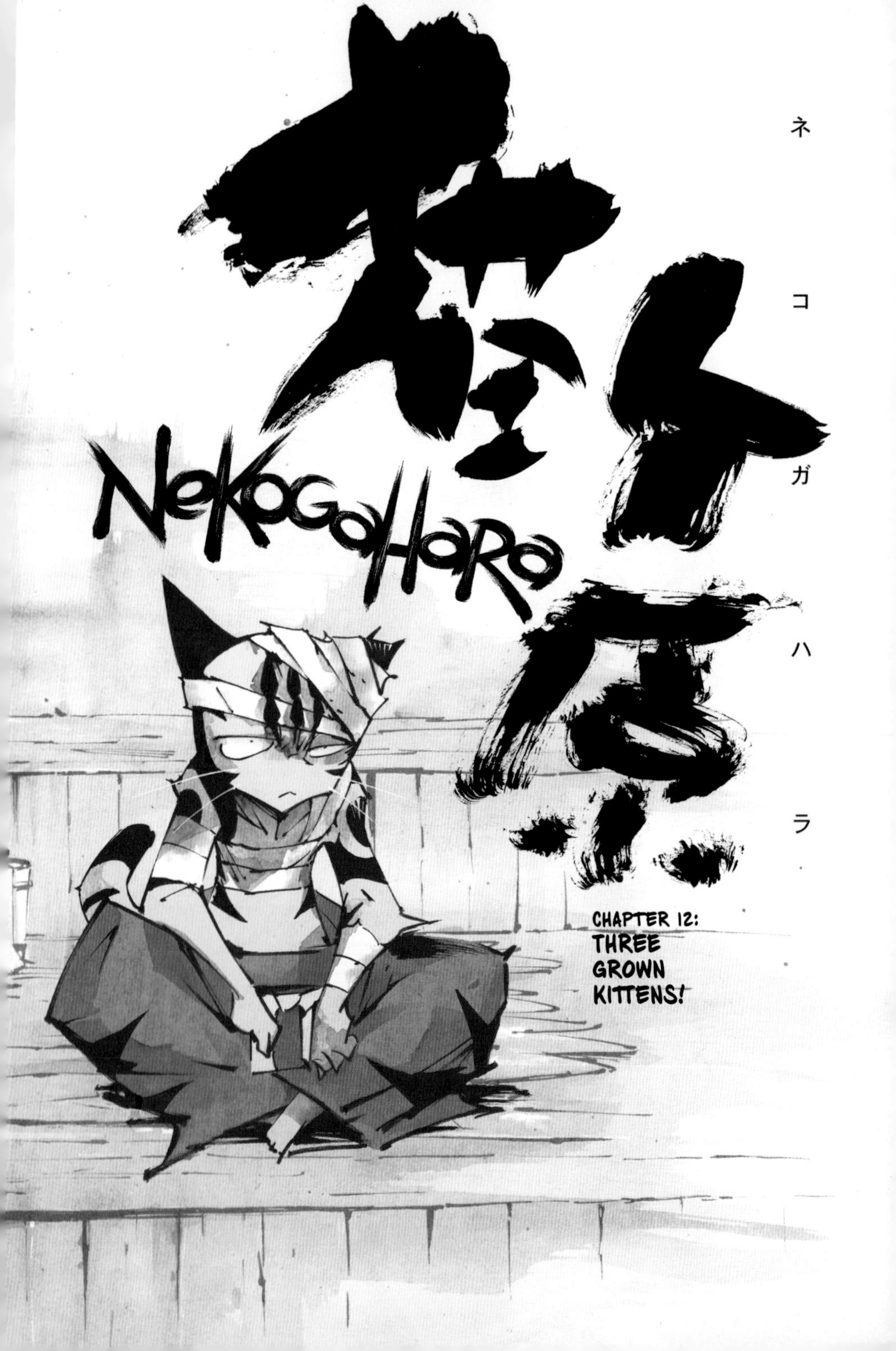
NekoGaHara
ネコガハラ

Chapter 12: Three Grown Kittens!

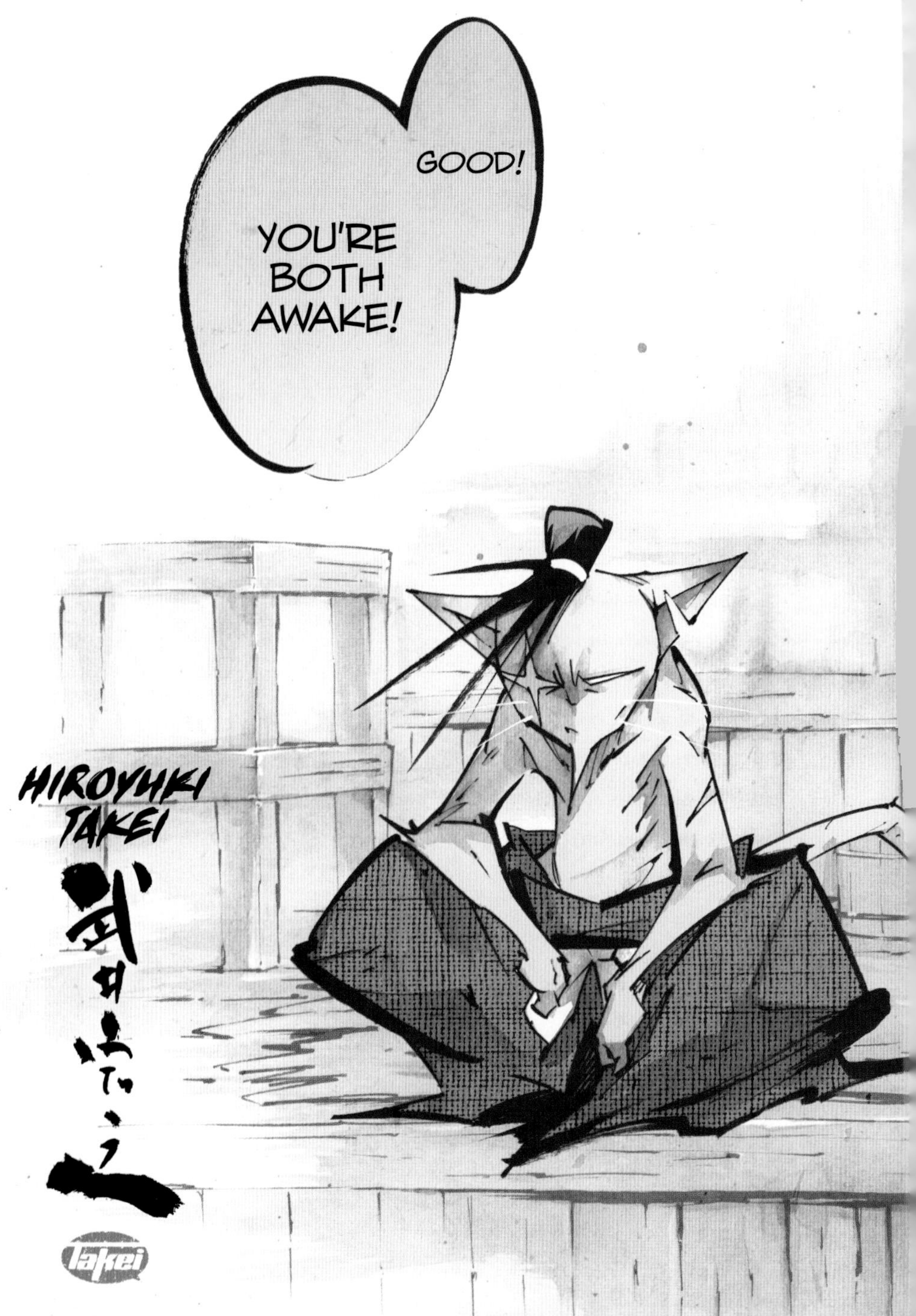
GOOD!
YOU'RE BOTH AWAKE!
HIROYUKI TAKEI
Takei

NEKOGAHARA VOLUME THREE CONTENTS

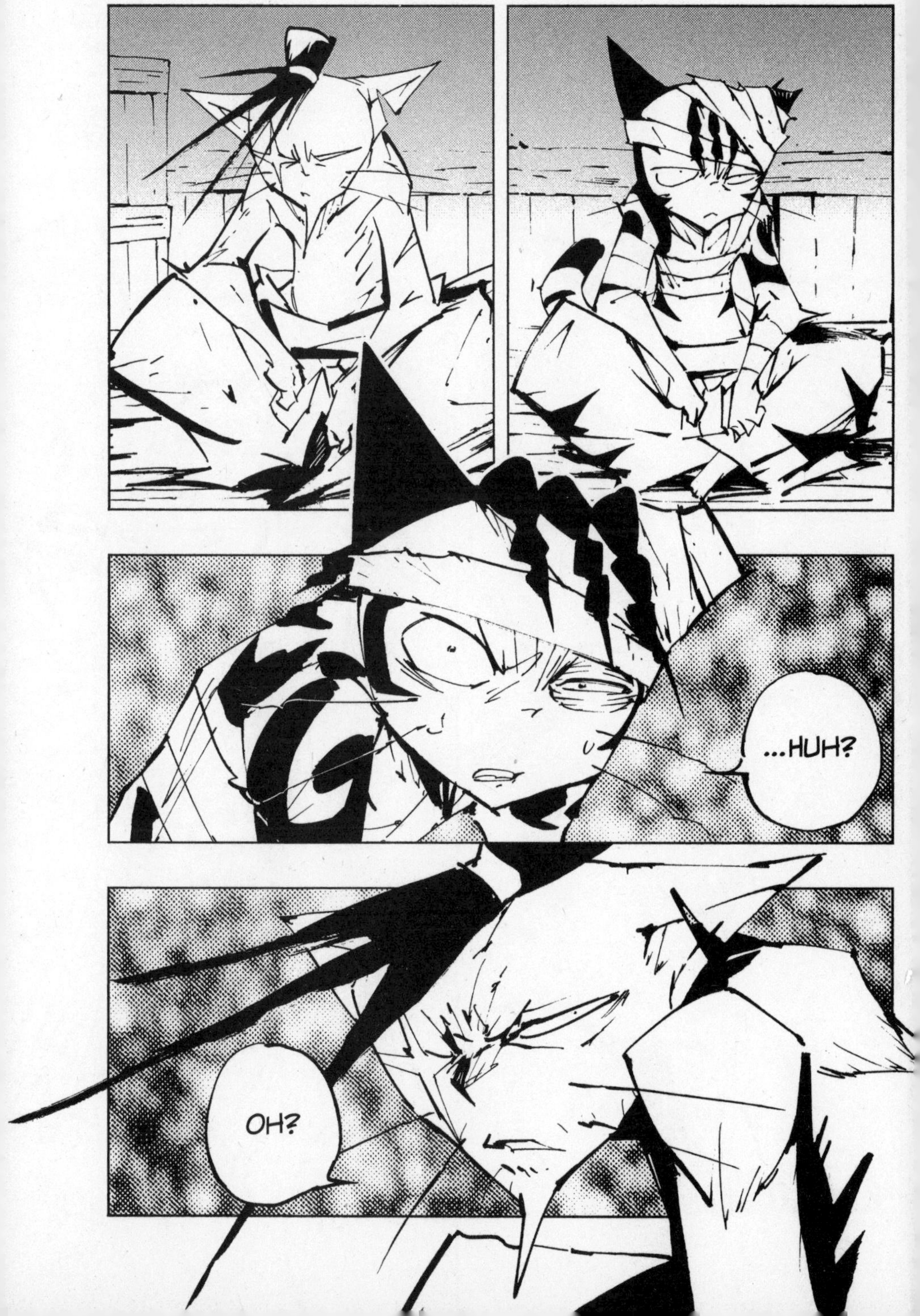
...HUH?
OH?

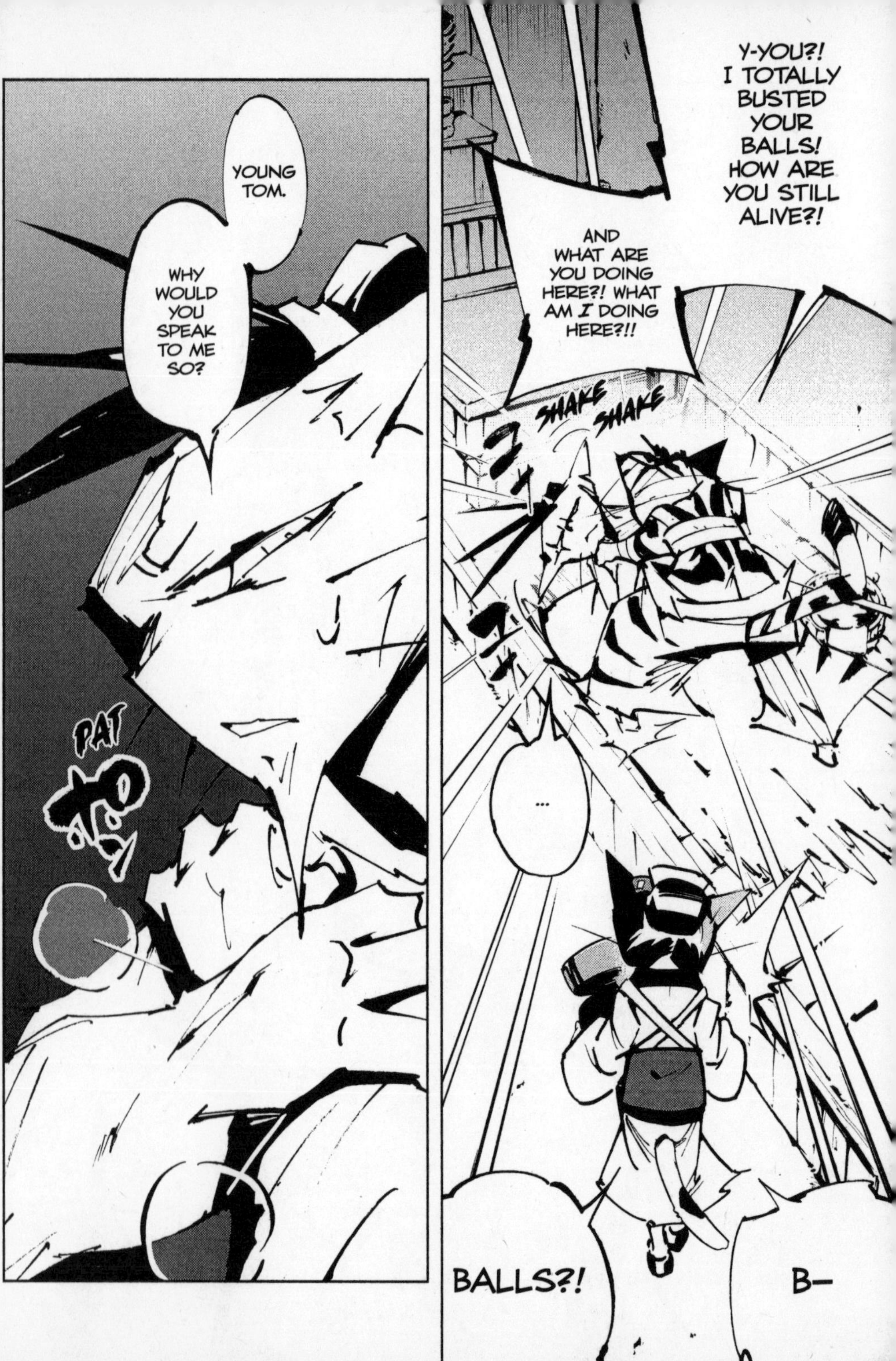
Y-YOU?! I TOTALLY BUSTED YOUR BALLS! HOW ARE YOU STILL ALIVE?!
AND WHAT ARE YOU DOING HERE?! WHAT AM I DOING HERE?!!
SHAKE
SHAKE
...
B—
BALLS?!
YOUNG TOM.
WHY WOULD YOU SPEAK TO ME SO?
PAT

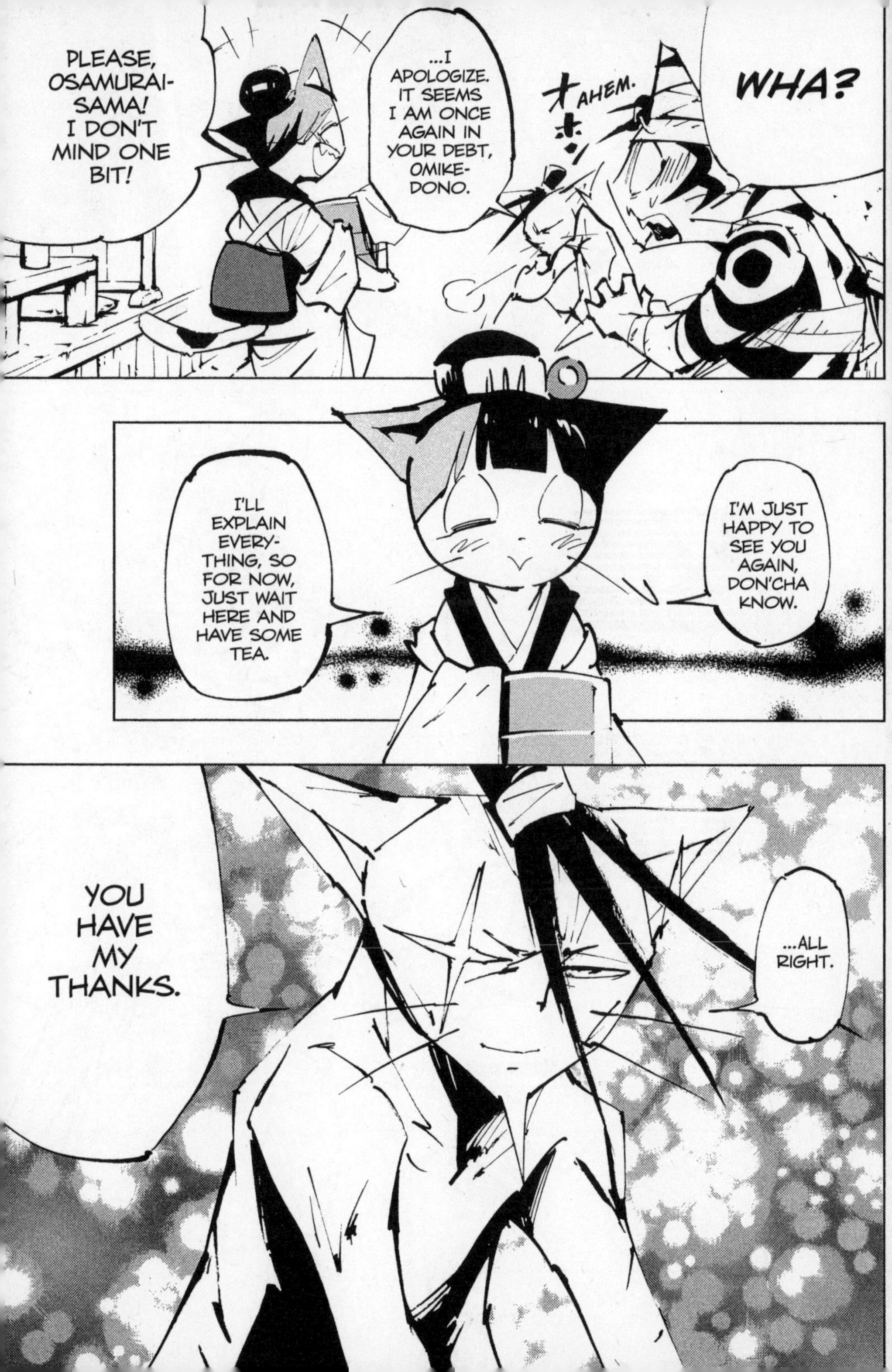
WHA?
AHEM.
...I APOLOGIZE. IT SEEMS I AM ONCE AGAIN IN YOUR DEBT, OMIKE-DONO.
PLEASE, OSAMURAI-SAMA! I DON'T MIND ONE BIT!
I'M JUST HAPPY TO SEE YOU AGAIN, DON'CHA KNOW.
I'LL EXPLAIN EVERY-THING, SO FOR NOW, JUST WAIT HERE AND HAVE SOME TEA.
...ALL RIGHT.
YOU HAVE MY THANKS.

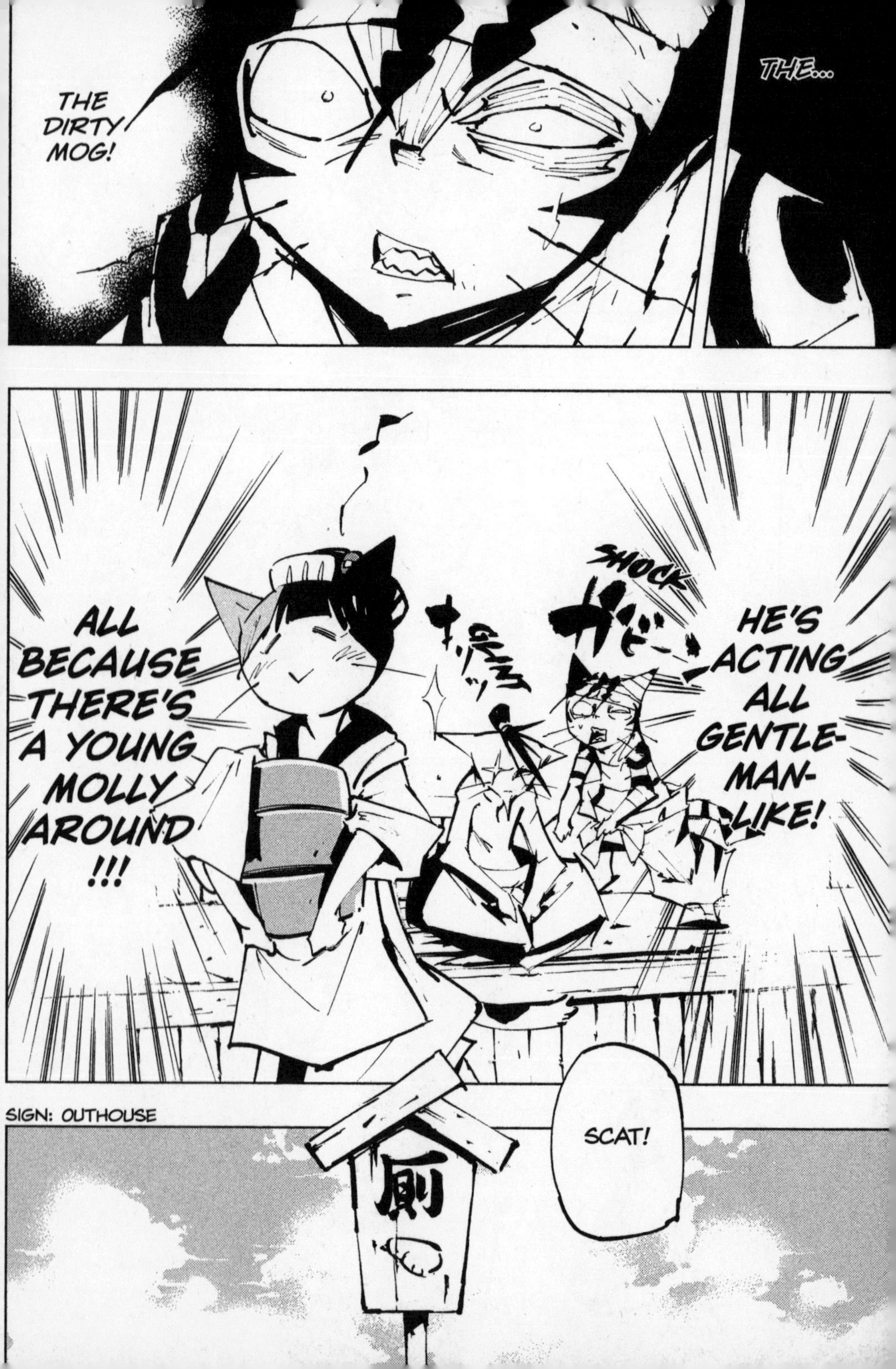
THE...
THE DIRTY MOG!
HE'S ACTING ALL GENTLE-MAN-LIKE!
SHOCK
GLEAM
ALL BECAUSE THERE'S A YOUNG MOLLY AROUND !!!
SIGN: OUTHOUSE
SCAT!
厠

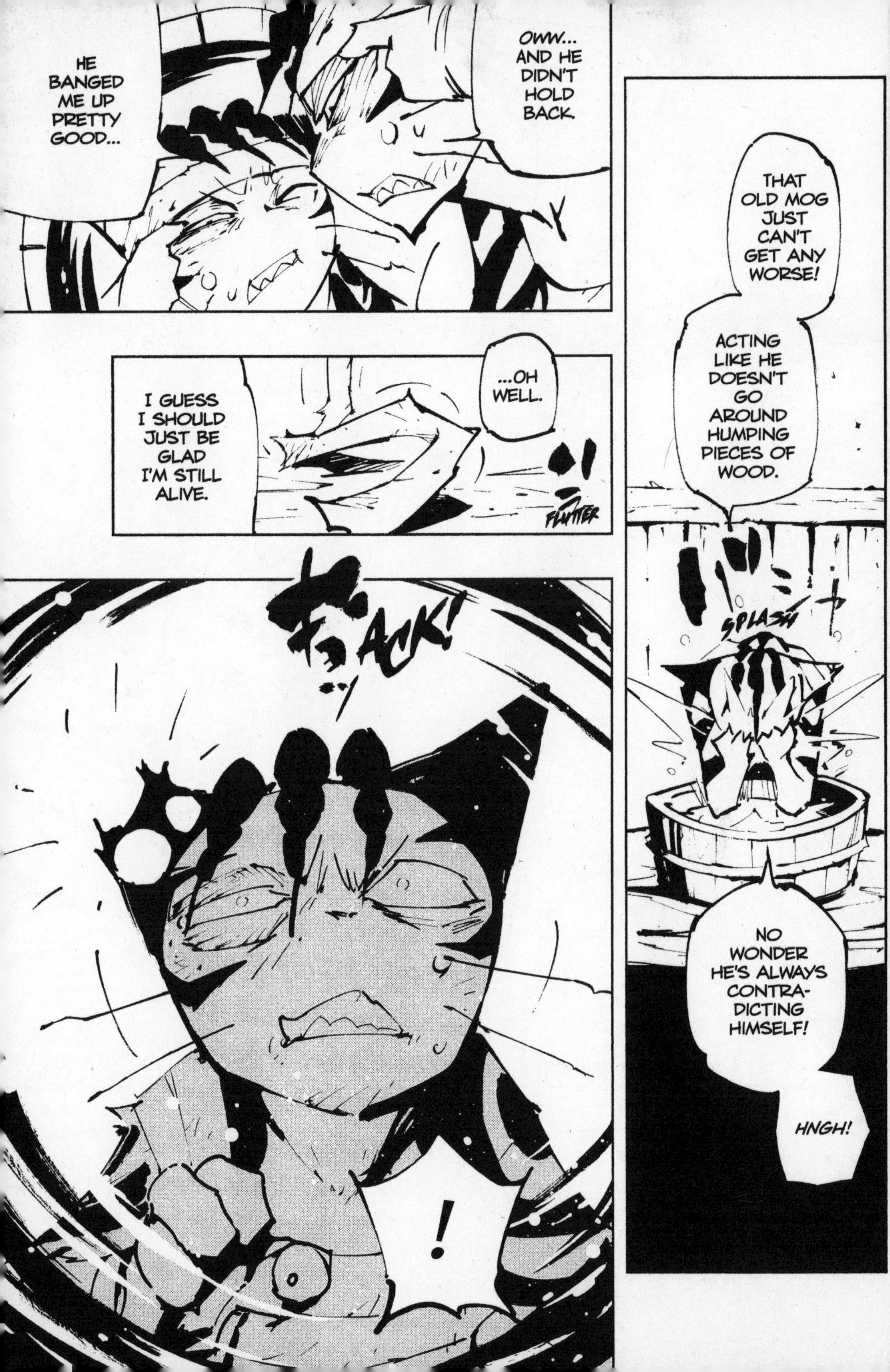
THAT OLD MOG JUST CAN'T GET ANY WORSE!
ACTING LIKE HE DOESN'T GO AROUND HUMPING PIECES OF WOOD.
SPLASH
NO WONDER HE'S ALWAYS CONTRA-DICTING HIMSELF!
HNGH!
OWW... AND HE DIDN'T HOLD BACK.
HE BANGED ME UP PRETTY GOOD...
...OH WELL.
FLUTTER
I GUESS I SHOULD JUST BE GLAD I'M STILL ALIVE.
THACK!
!

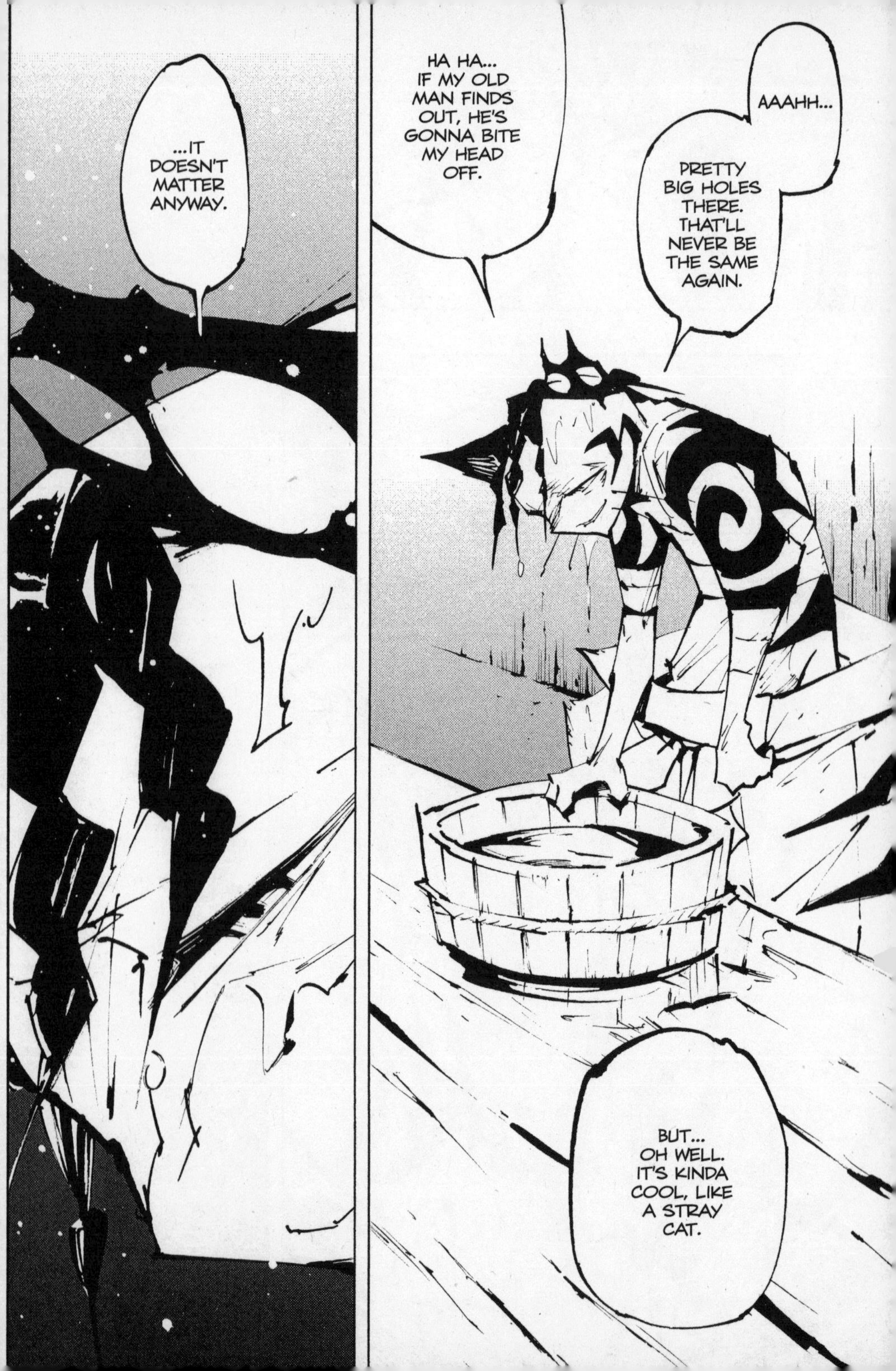
AAAHH...
PRETTY BIG HOLES THERE. THAT'LL NEVER BE THE SAME AGAIN.
HA HA... IF MY OLD MAN FINDS OUT, HE'S GONNA BITE MY HEAD OFF.
BUT... OH WELL. IT'S KINDA COOL, LIKE A STRAY CAT.
...IT DOESN'T MATTER ANYWAY.

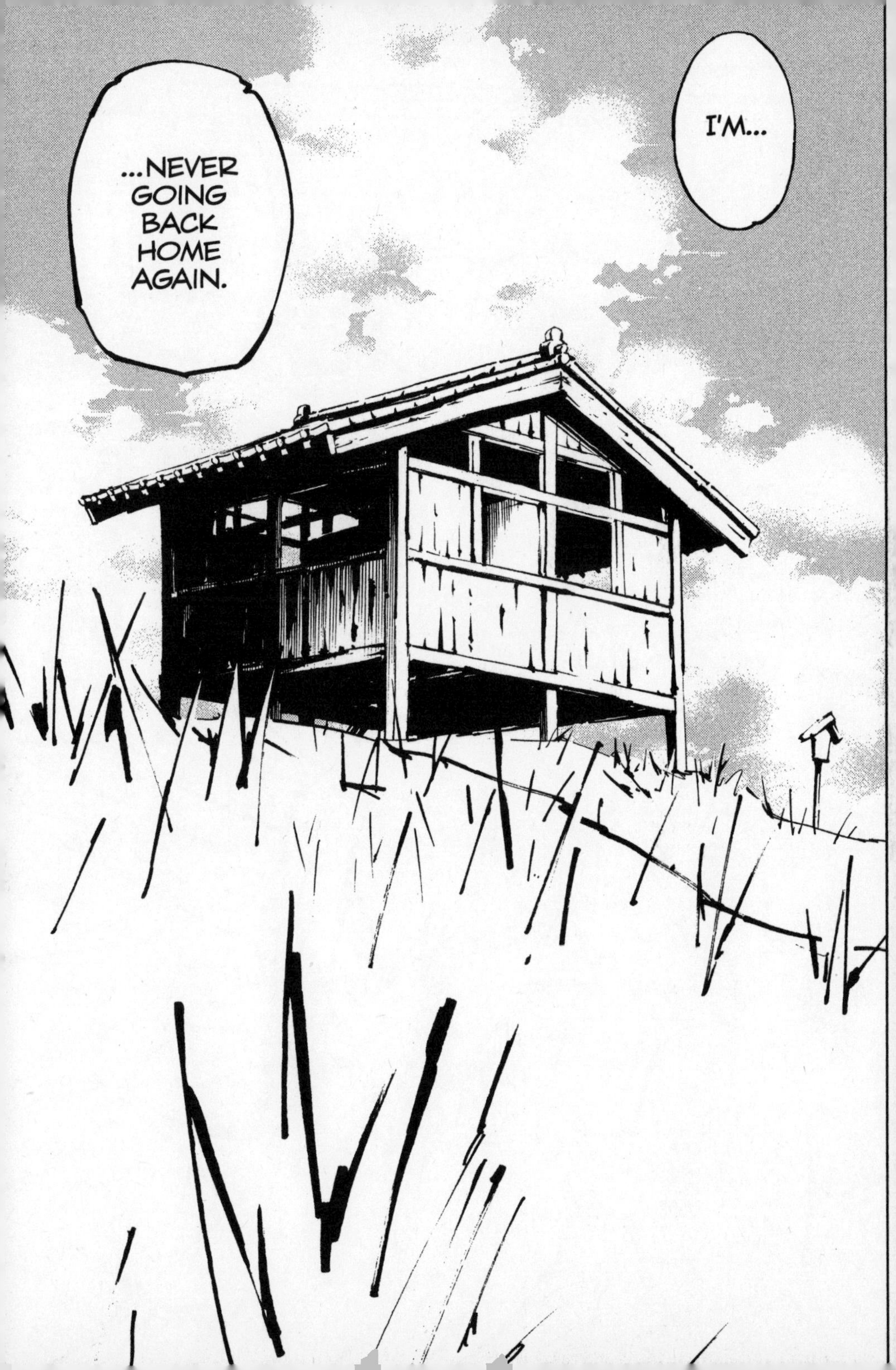
I'M...
...NEVER GOING BACK HOME AGAIN.

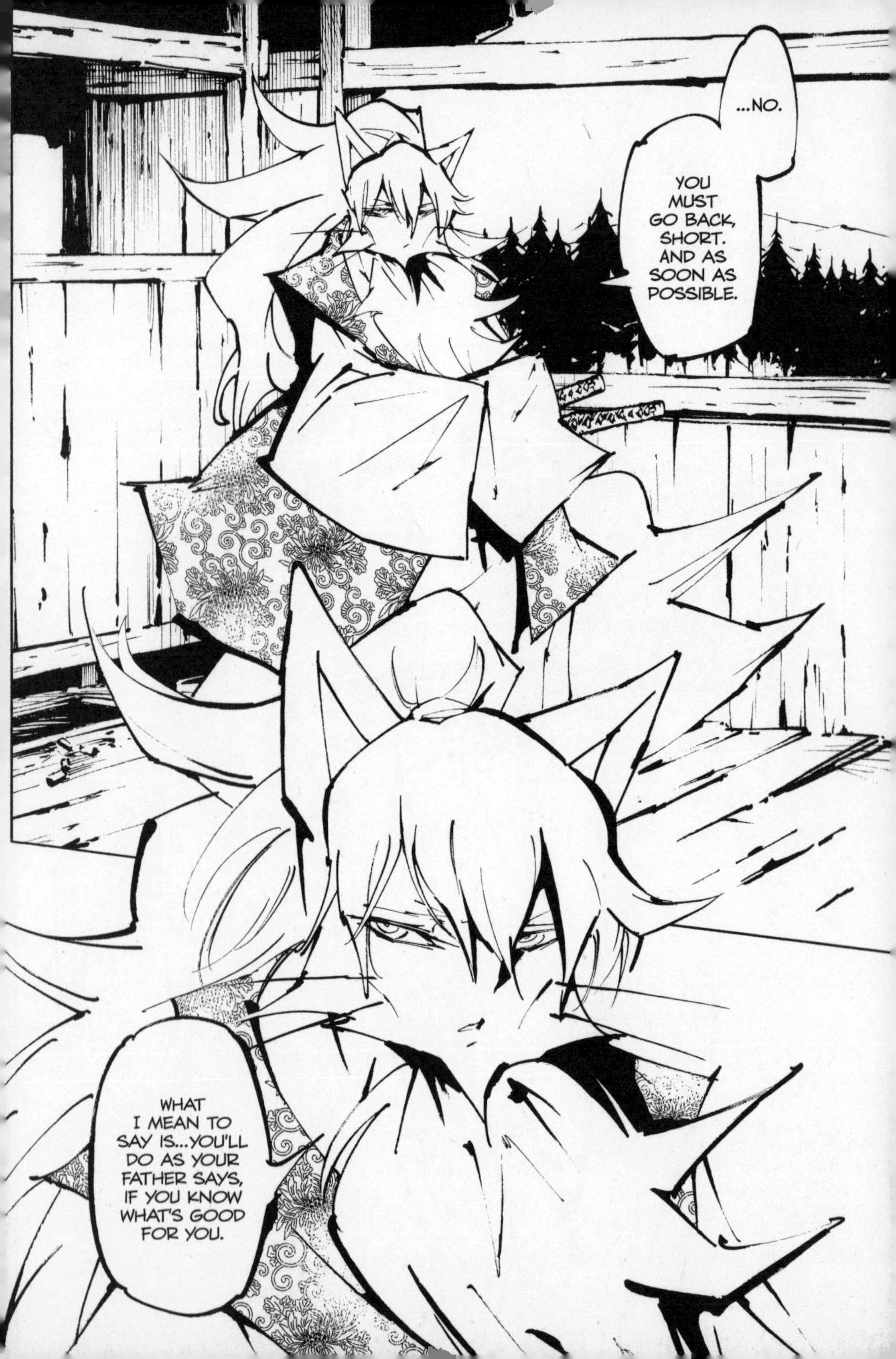
...NO.
YOU MUST GO BACK, SHORT. AND AS SOON AS POSSIBLE.
WHAT I MEAN TO SAY IS...YOU'LL DO AS YOUR FATHER SAYS, IF YOU KNOW WHAT'S GOOD FOR YOU.

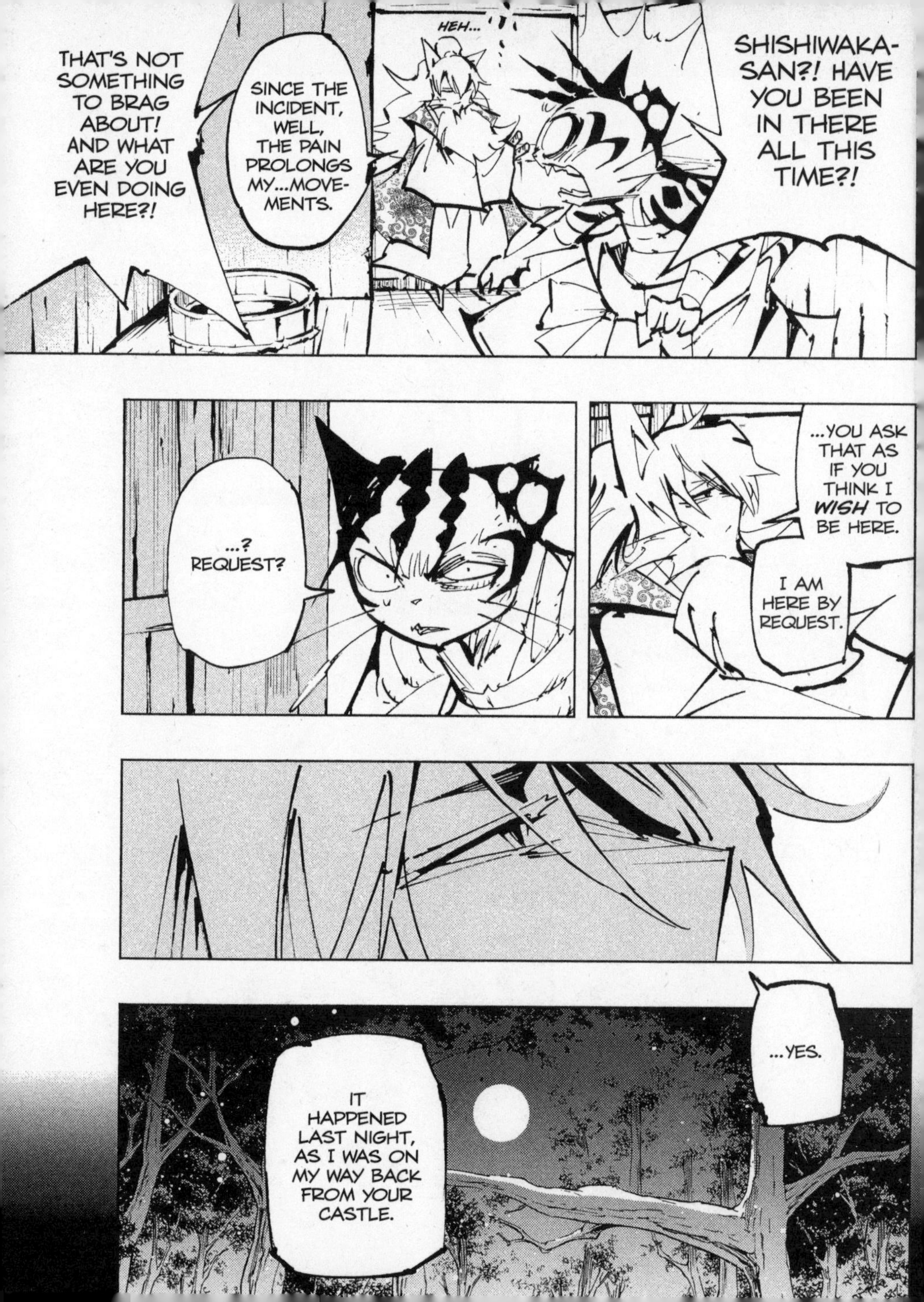
SHISHIWAKA-SAN?! HAVE YOU BEEN IN THERE ALL THIS TIME?!
HEH...
SINCE THE INCIDENT, WELL, THE PAIN PROLONGS MY...MOVEMENTS.
THAT'S NOT SOMETHING TO BRAG ABOUT! AND WHAT ARE YOU EVEN DOING HERE?!
...YOU ASK THAT AS IF YOU THINK I *WISH* TO BE HERE.
I AM HERE BY REQUEST.
...? REQUEST?
...YES.
IT HAPPENED LAST NIGHT, AS I WAS ON MY WAY BACK FROM YOUR CASTLE.

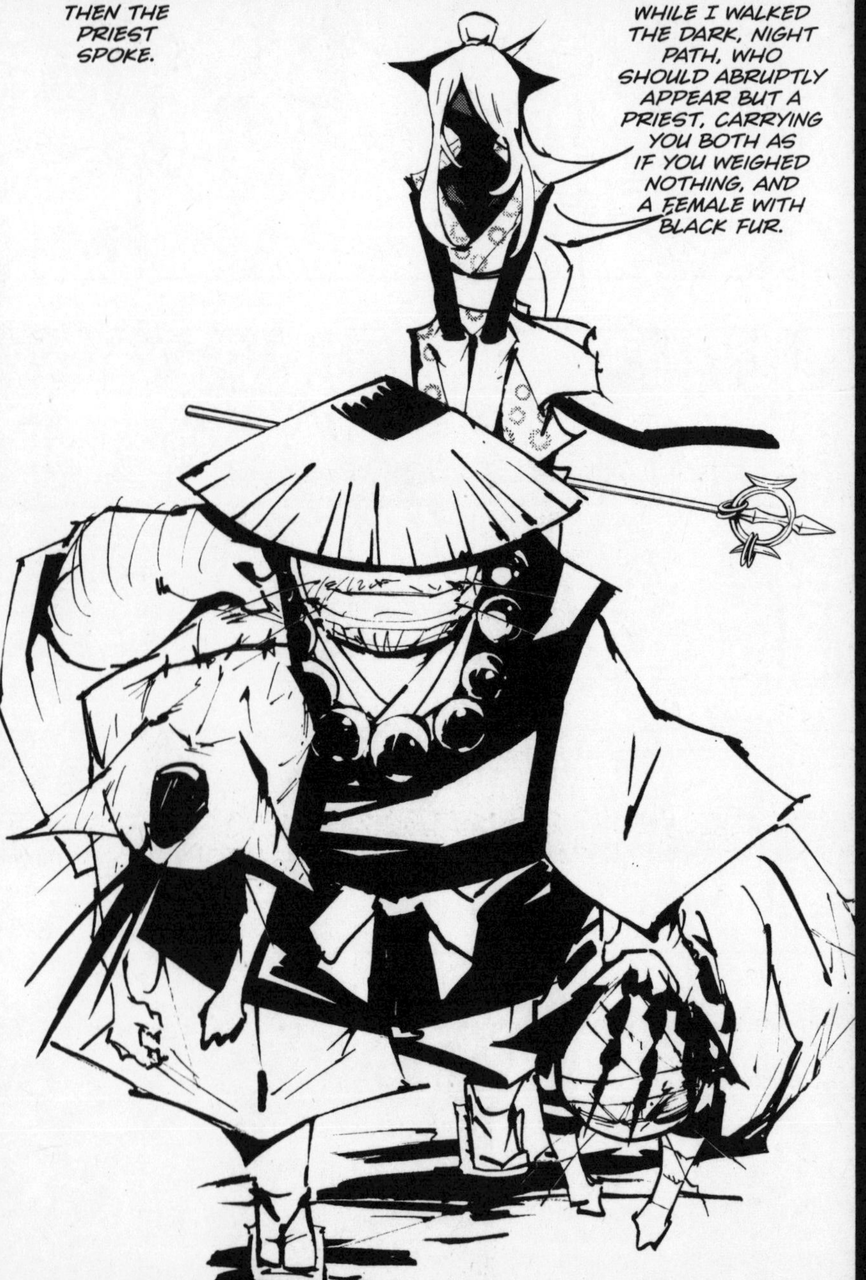
WHILE I WALKED THE DARK, NIGHT PATH, WHO SHOULD ABRUPTLY APPEAR BUT A PRIEST, CARRYING YOU BOTH AS IF YOU WEIGHED NOTHING, AND A FEMALE WITH BLACK FUR.
THEN THE PRIEST SPOKE.

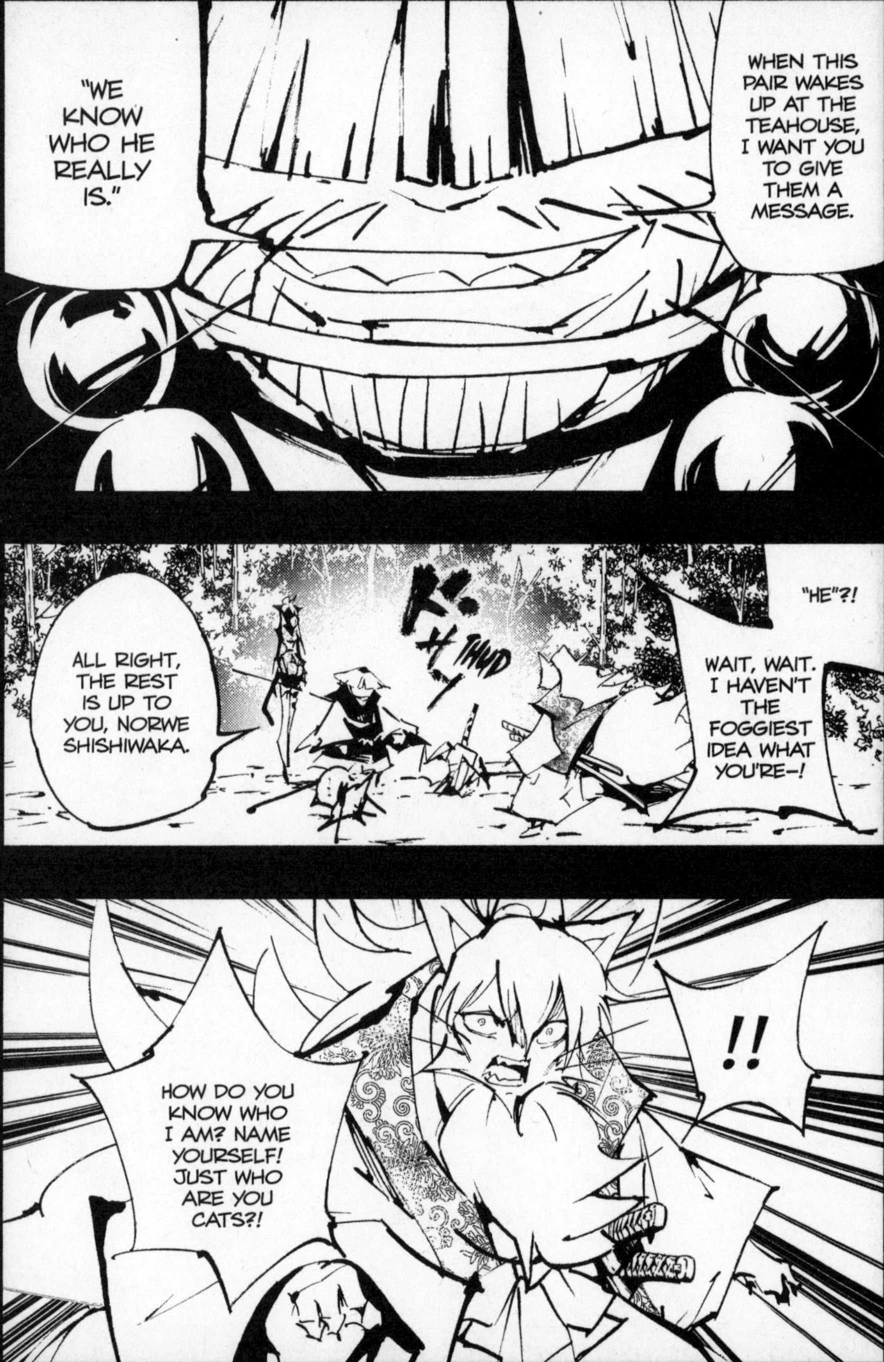
WHEN THIS PAIR WAKES UP AT THE TEAHOUSE, I WANT YOU TO GIVE THEM A MESSAGE.
"WE KNOW WHO HE REALLY IS."
"HE"?!
WAIT, WAIT. I HAVEN'T THE FOGGIEST IDEA WHAT YOU'RE-!
THUD
ALL RIGHT, THE REST IS UP TO YOU, NORWE SHISHIWAKA.
!!
HOW DO YOU KNOW WHO I AM? NAME YOURSELF! JUST WHO ARE YOU CATS?!

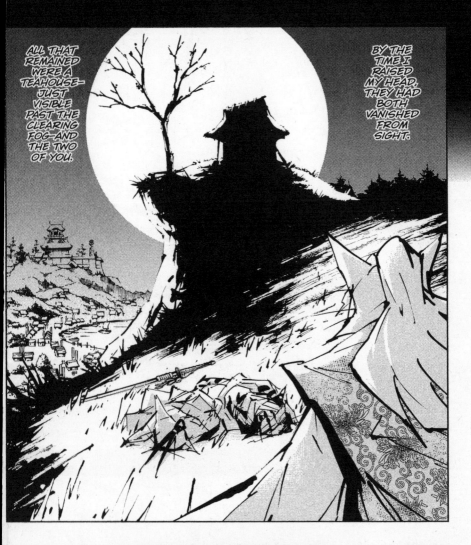

BY THE TIME I RAISED MY HEAD, THEY HAD BOTH VANISHED FROM SIGHT.
ALL THAT REMAINED WERE A TEAHOUSE—JUST VISIBLE PAST THE CLEARING FOG—AND THE TWO OF YOU.

...IT WAS AS IF I WERE IN A DREAM.
IF I COULD HAVE IT MY WAY, I WOULD WAKE UP TO FIND THAT YESTERDAY ***HAD*** ALL BEEN A DREAM.

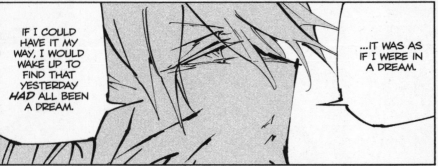

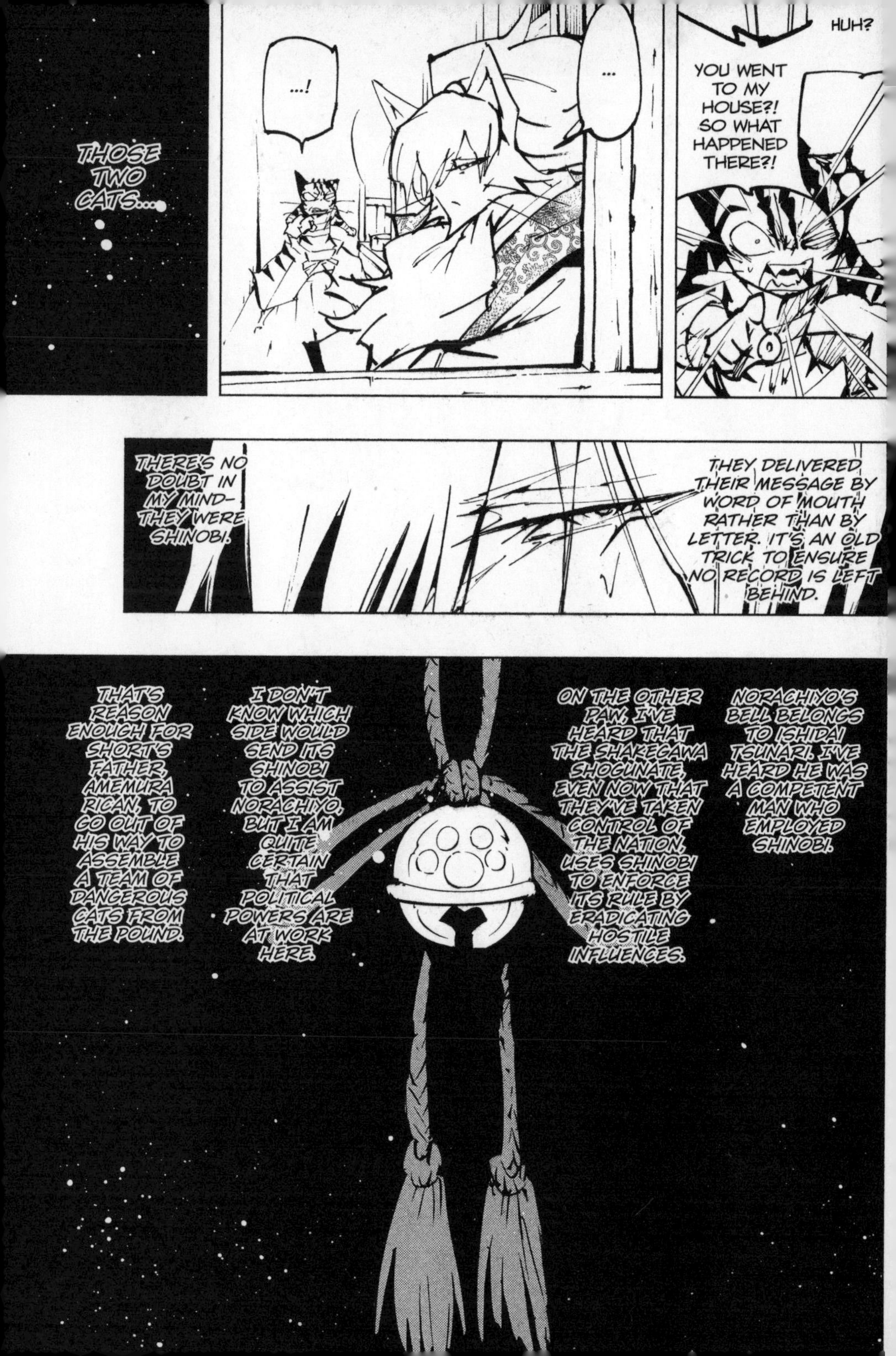
HUH?
YOU WENT TO MY HOUSE?! SO WHAT HAPPENED THERE?!
...
...!
THOSE TWO CATS...
THEY DELIVERED THEIR MESSAGE BY WORD OF MOUTH RATHER THAN BY LETTER. IT'S AN OLD TRICK TO ENSURE NO RECORD IS LEFT BEHIND.
THERE'S NO DOUBT IN MY MIND– THEY WERE SHINOBI.
NORACHIYO'S BELL BELONGS TO ISHIDAI TSUNARI. I'VE HEARD HE WAS A COMPETENT MAN WHO EMPLOYED SHINOBI.
ON THE OTHER PAW, I'VE HEARD THAT THE SHAKEGAWA SHOGUNATE, EVEN NOW THAT THEY'VE TAKEN CONTROL OF THE NATION, USES SHINOBI TO ENFORCE ITS RULE BY ERADICATING HOSTILE INFLUENCES.
I DON'T KNOW WHICH SIDE WOULD SEND ITS SHINOBI TO ASSIST NORACHIYO, BUT I AM QUITE CERTAIN THAT POLITICAL POWERS ARE AT WORK HERE.
THAT'S REASON ENOUGH FOR SHORT'S FATHER, AMEMURA RICAN, TO GO OUT OF HIS WAY TO ASSEMBLE A TEAM OF DANGEROUS CATS FROM THE POUND.

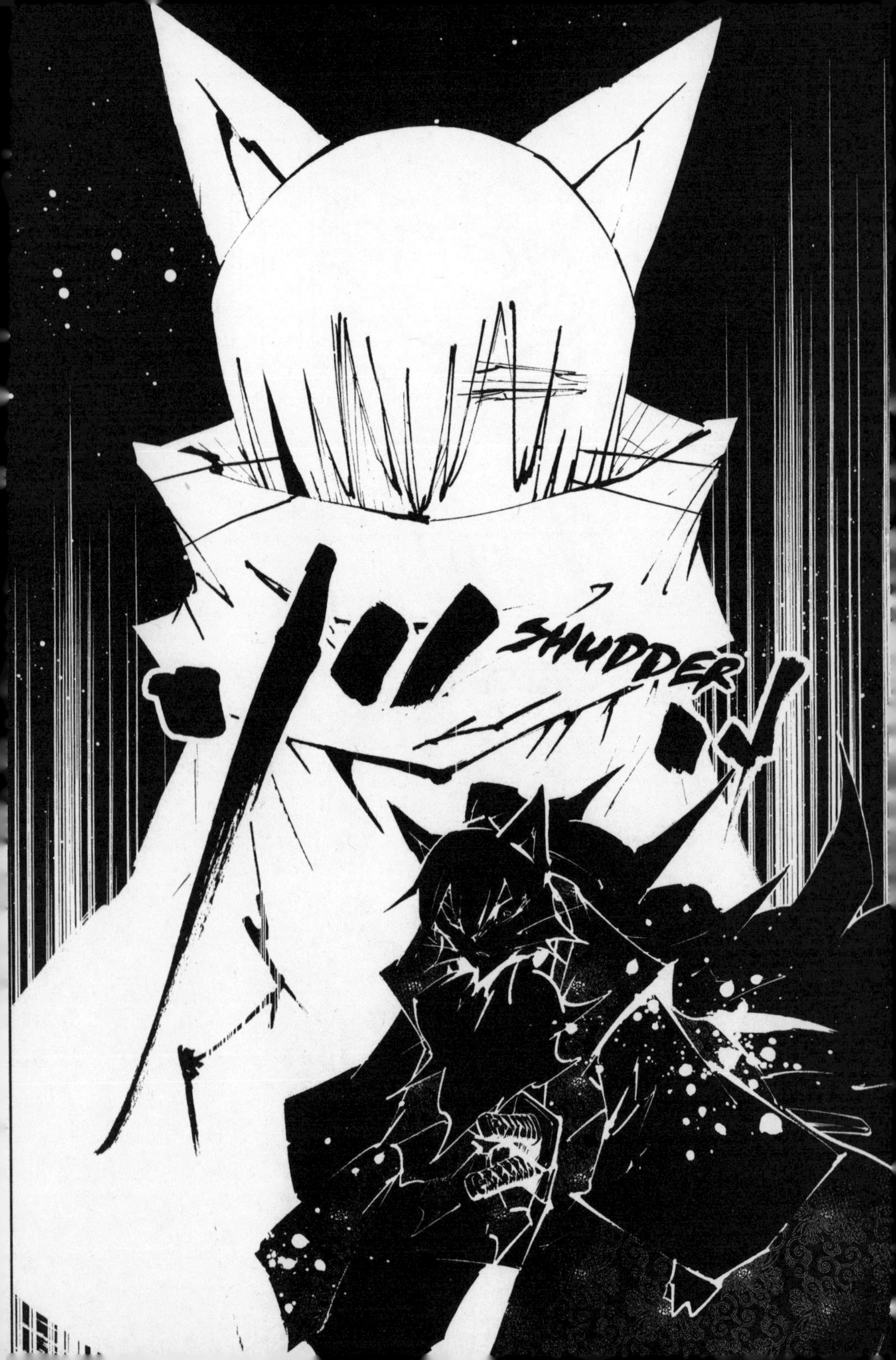
SHUDDER

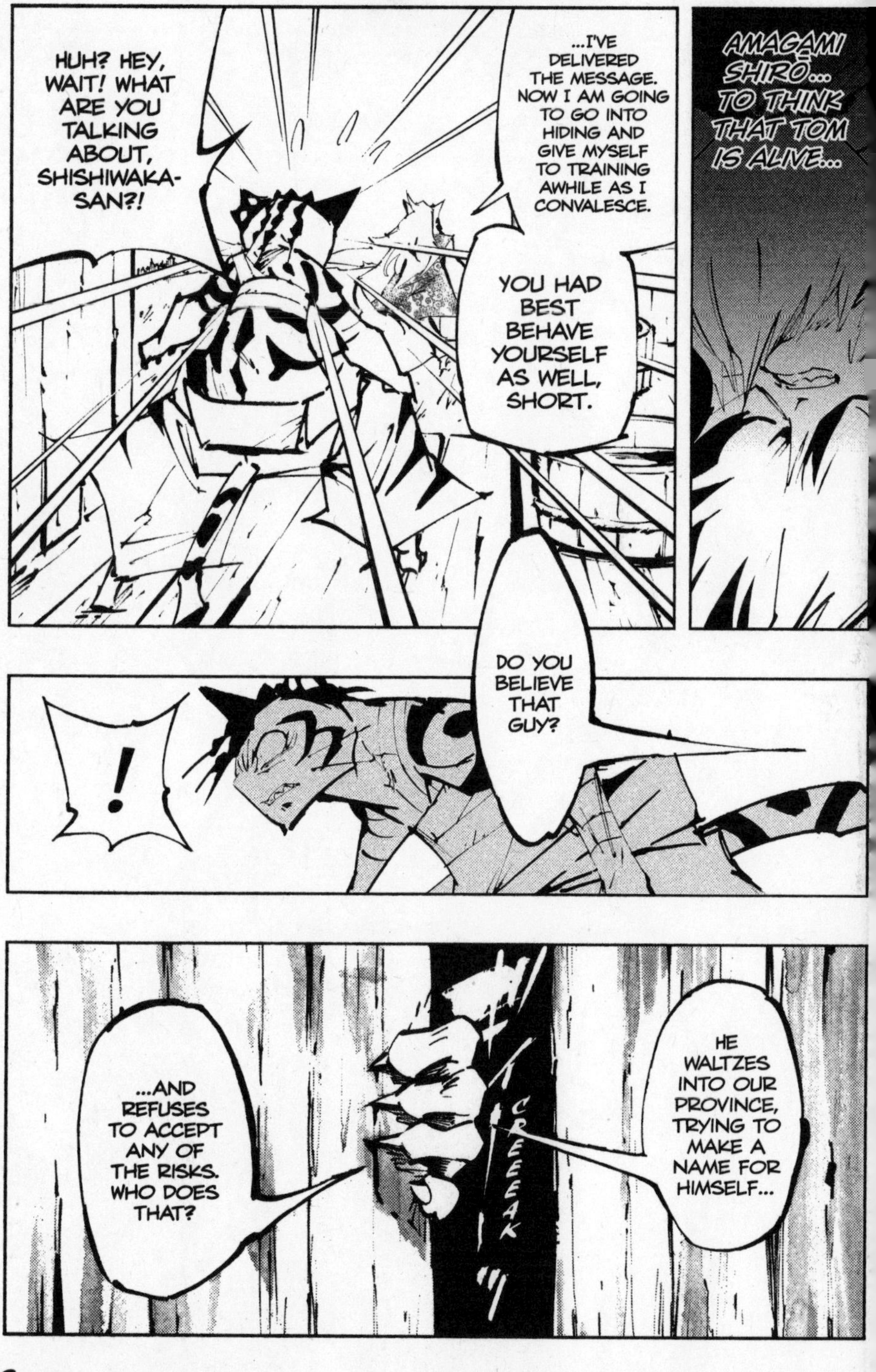
AMAGAMI SHIRŌ... TO THINK THAT TOM IS ALIVE...
...I'VE DELIVERED THE MESSAGE. NOW I AM GOING TO GO INTO HIDING AND GIVE MYSELF TO TRAINING AWHILE AS I CONVALESCE.
YOU HAD BEST BEHAVE YOURSELF AS WELL, SHORT.
HUH? HEY, WAIT! WHAT ARE YOU TALKING ABOUT, SHISHIWAKA-SAN?!
DO YOU BELIEVE THAT GUY?
!
HE WALTZES INTO OUR PROVINCE, TRYING TO MAKE A NAME FOR HIMSELF...
CREEEAK
...AND REFUSES TO ACCEPT ANY OF THE RISKS. WHO DOES THAT?

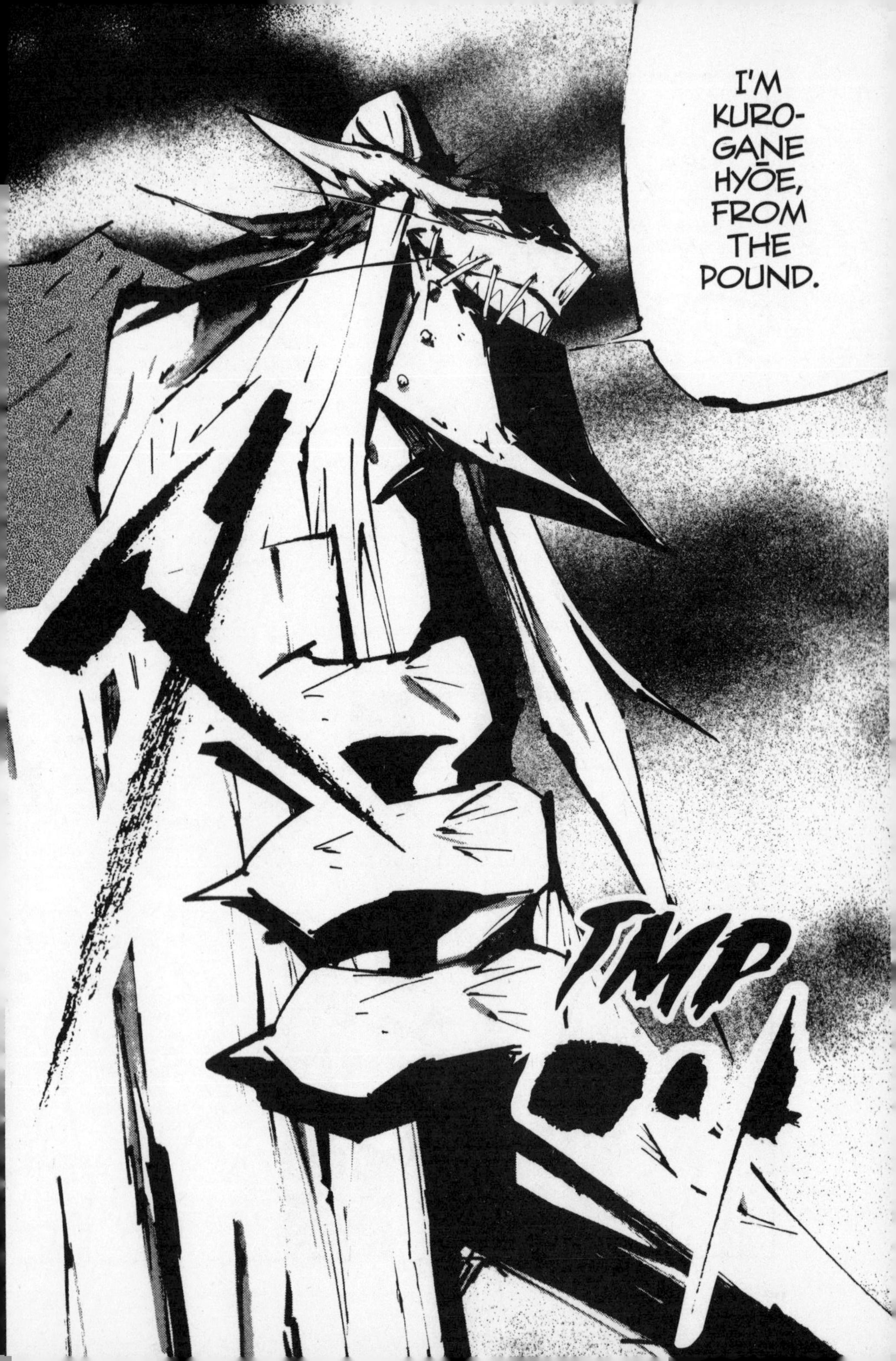
I'M KURO-GANE HYŌE, FROM THE POUND.
TMP

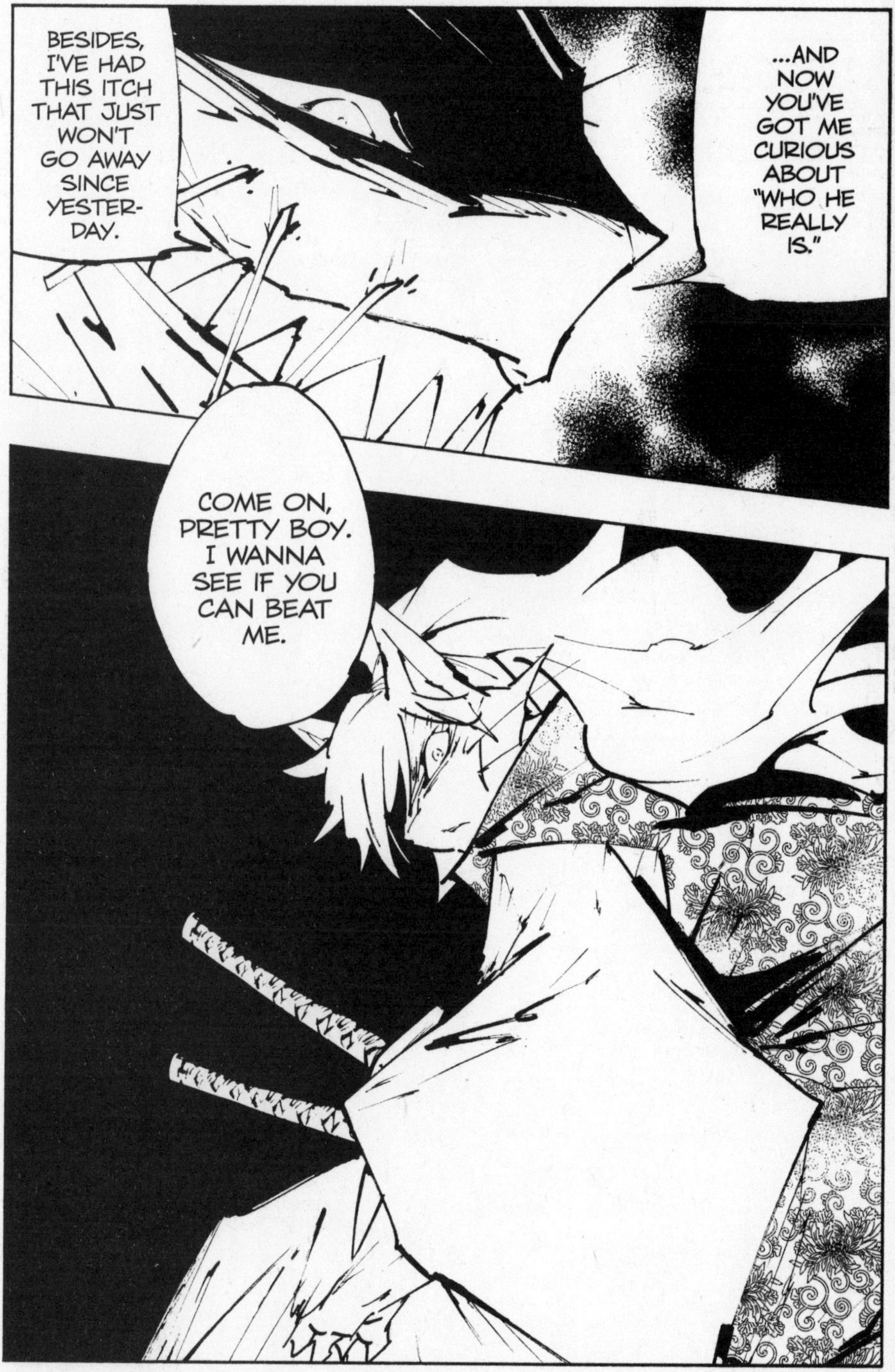
BESIDES, I'VE HAD THIS ITCH THAT JUST WON'T GO AWAY SINCE YESTER-DAY.
...AND NOW YOU'VE GOT ME CURIOUS ABOUT "WHO HE REALLY IS."
COME ON, PRETTY BOY. I WANNA SEE IF YOU CAN BEAT ME.

猫ヶ原

NeKoGaHaRa

ネコガハラ

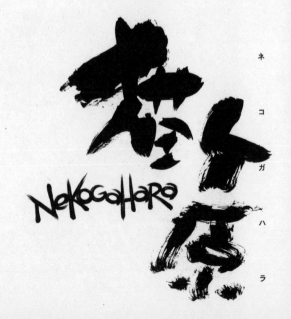

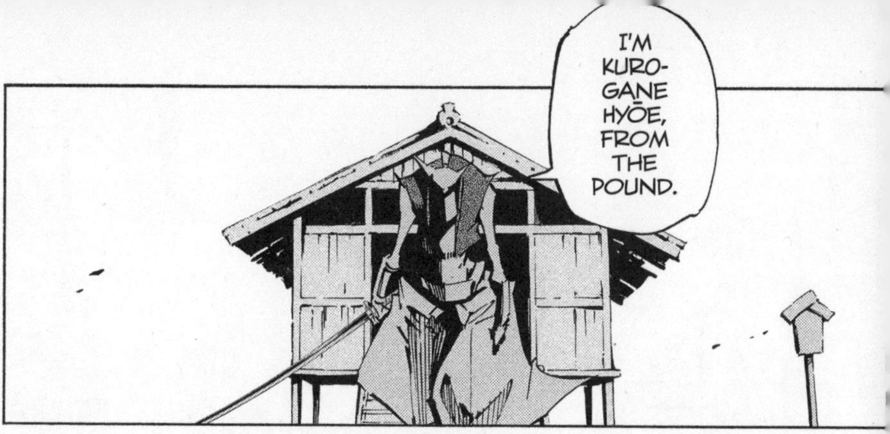
I'M KURO-GANE HYŌE, FROM THE POUND.

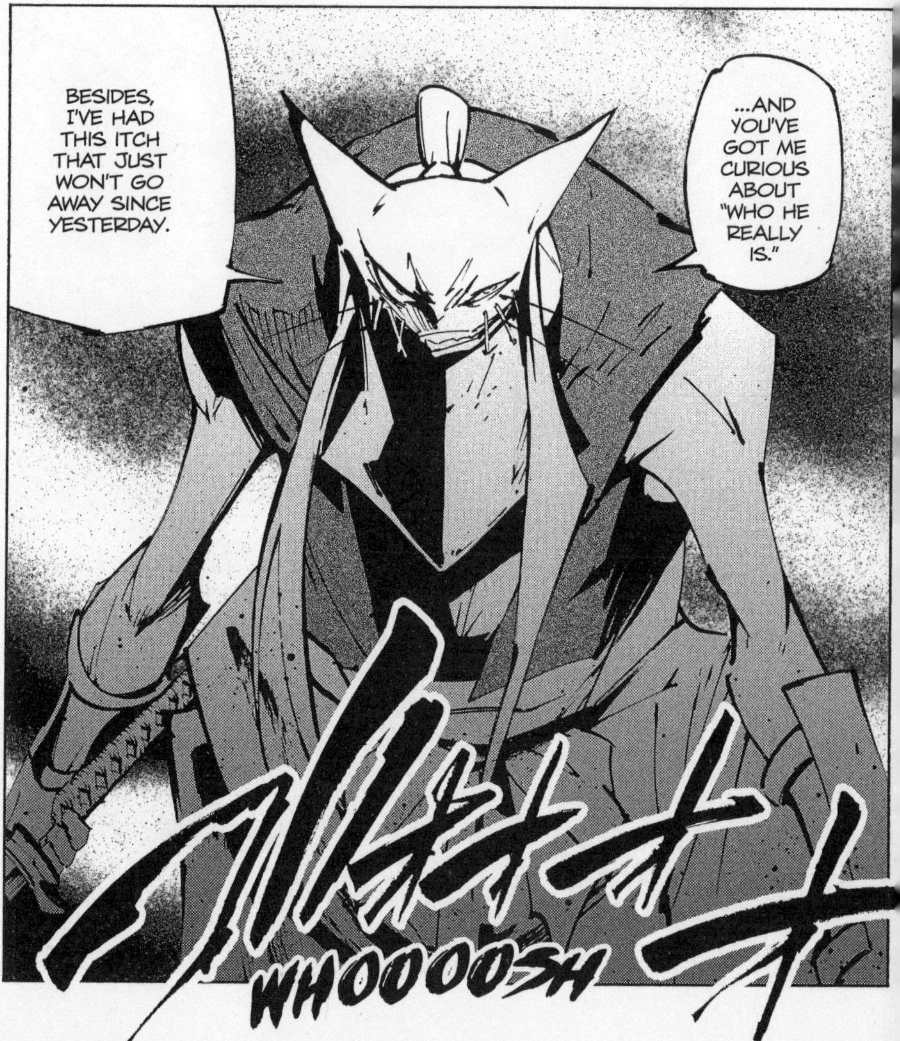
...AND YOU'VE GOT ME CURIOUS ABOUT "WHO HE REALLY IS."
BESIDES, I'VE HAD THIS ITCH THAT JUST WON'T GO AWAY SINCE YESTERDAY.
WHOOOOSH

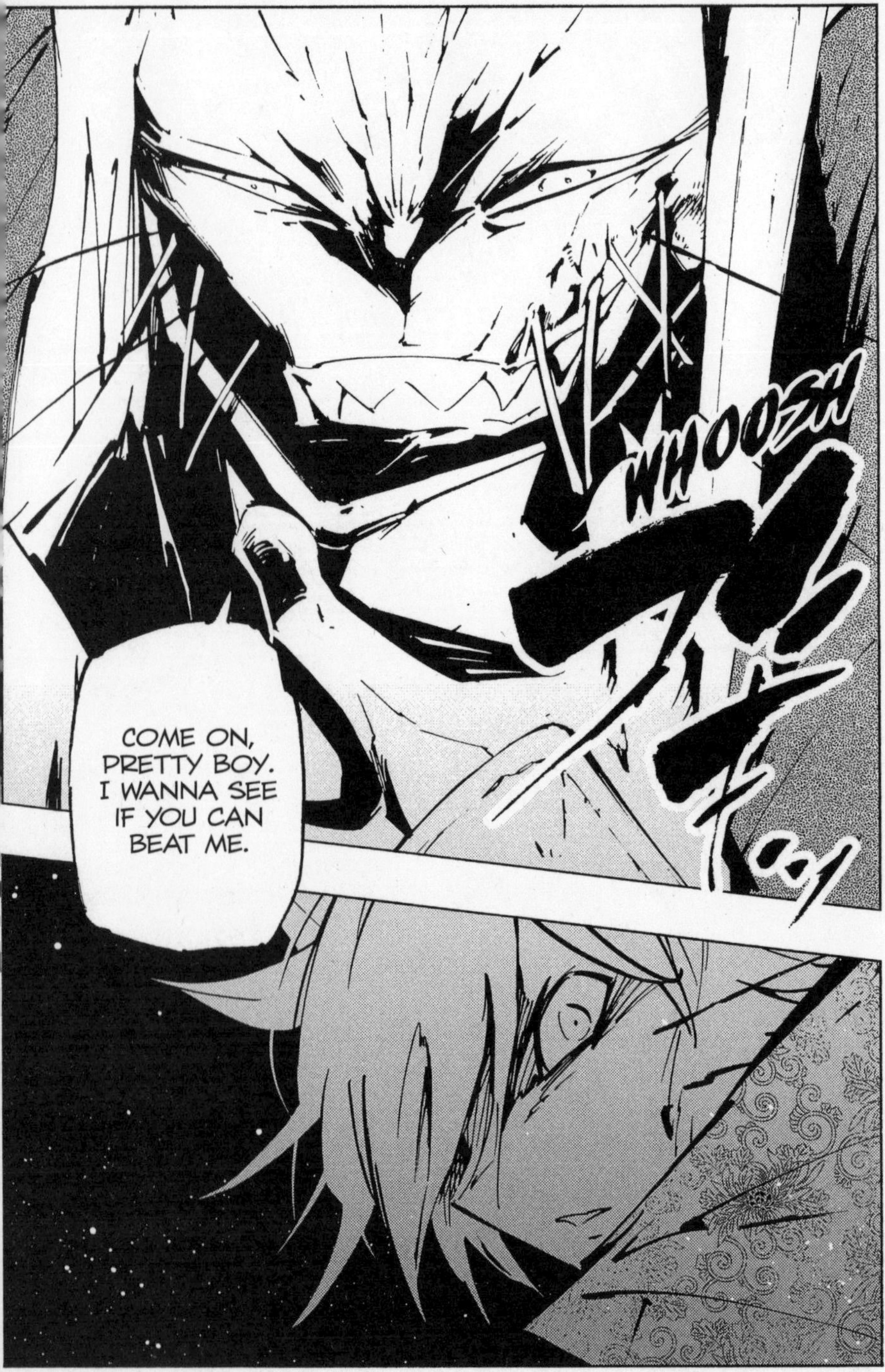
WHOOOSH
COME ON, PRETTY BOY. I WANNA SEE IF YOU CAN BEAT ME.

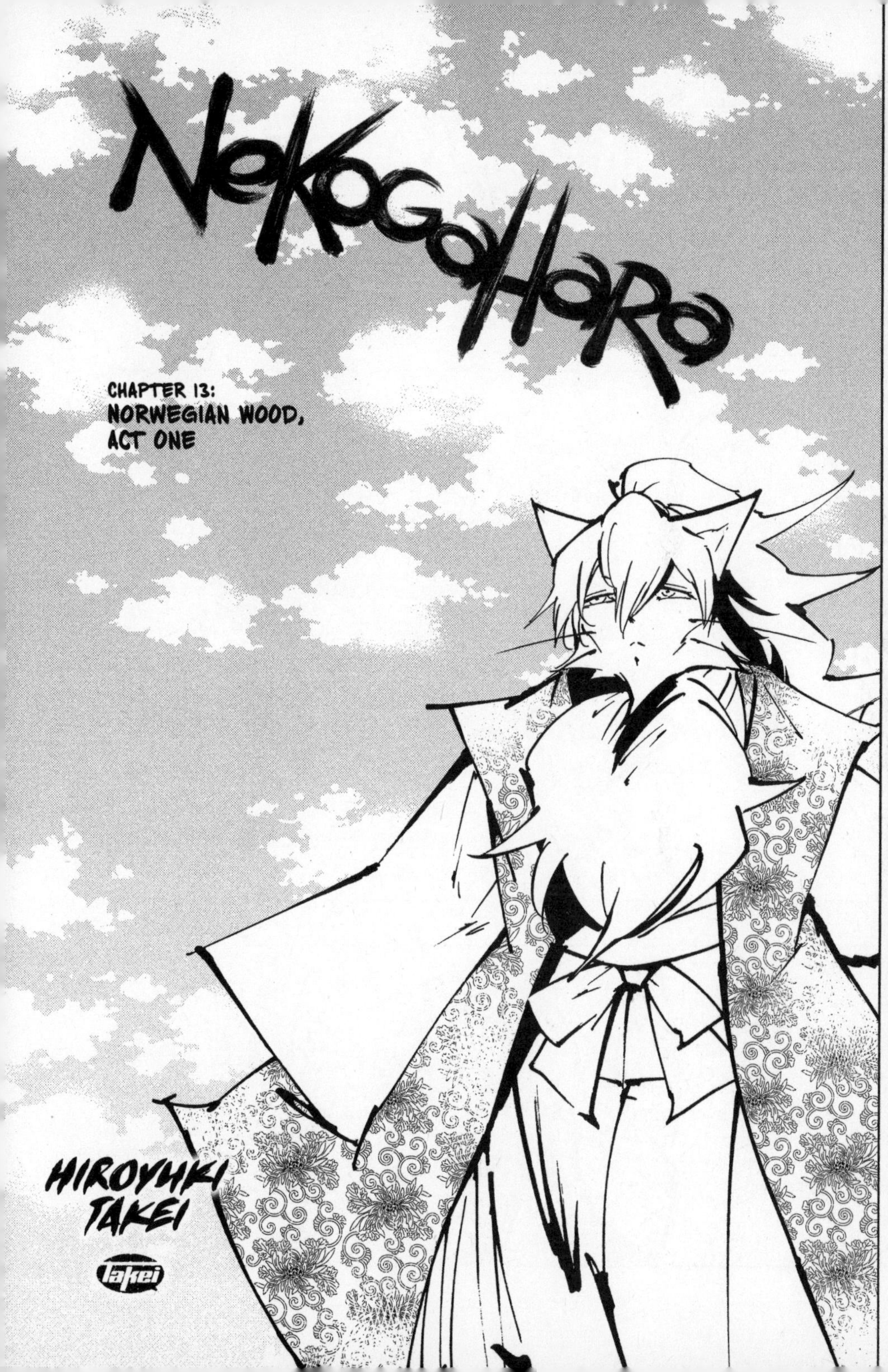
NEKOGAHARA
CHAPTER 13:
NORWEGIAN WOOD,
ACT ONE
HIROYUKI
TAKEI
Takei

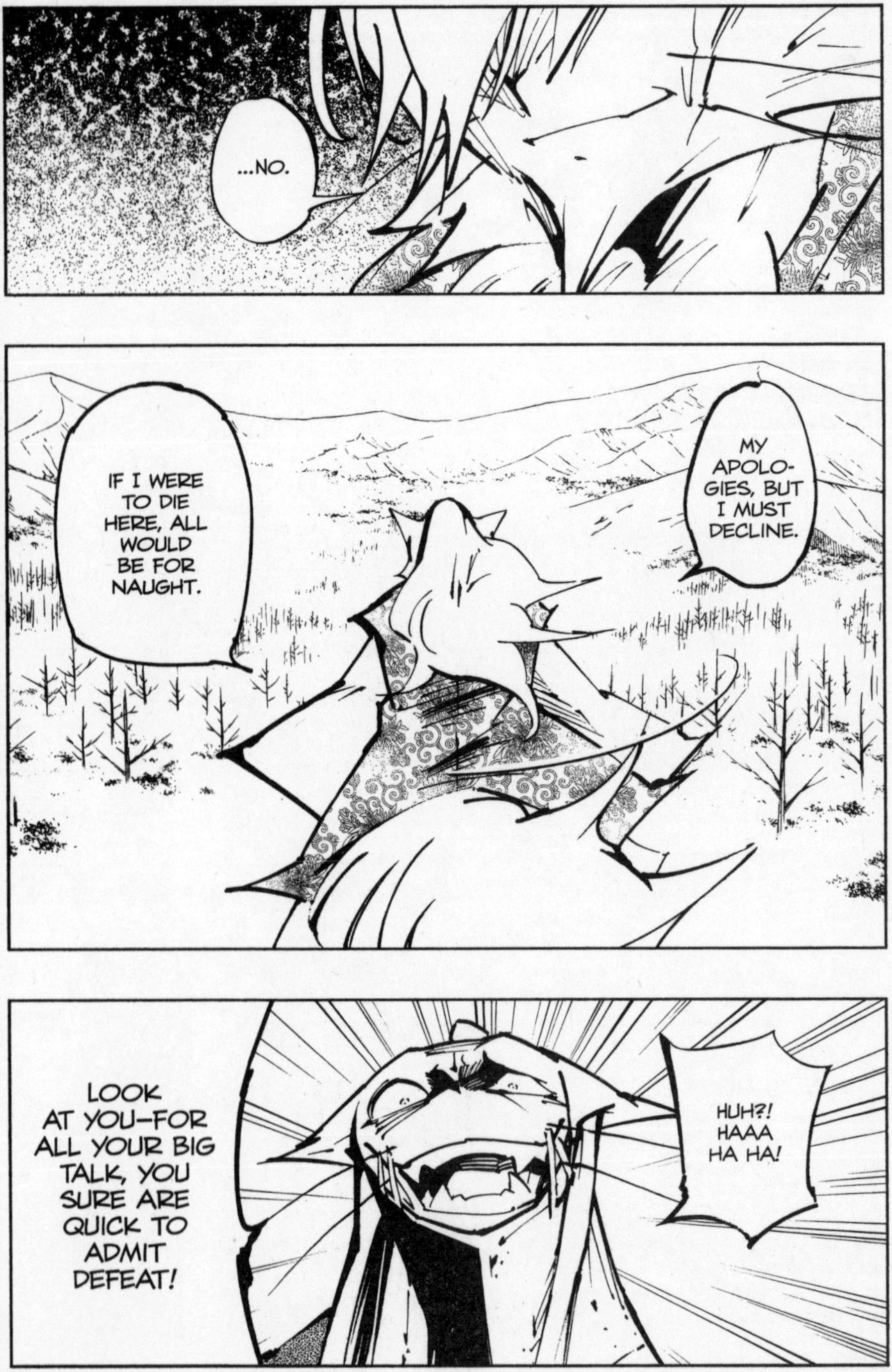
...NO.
MY APOLO-GIES, BUT I MUST DECLINE.
IF I WERE TO DIE HERE, ALL WOULD BE FOR NAUGHT.
HUH?! HAAA HA HA!
LOOK AT YOU–FOR ALL YOUR BIG TALK, YOU SURE ARE QUICK TO ADMIT DEFEAT!

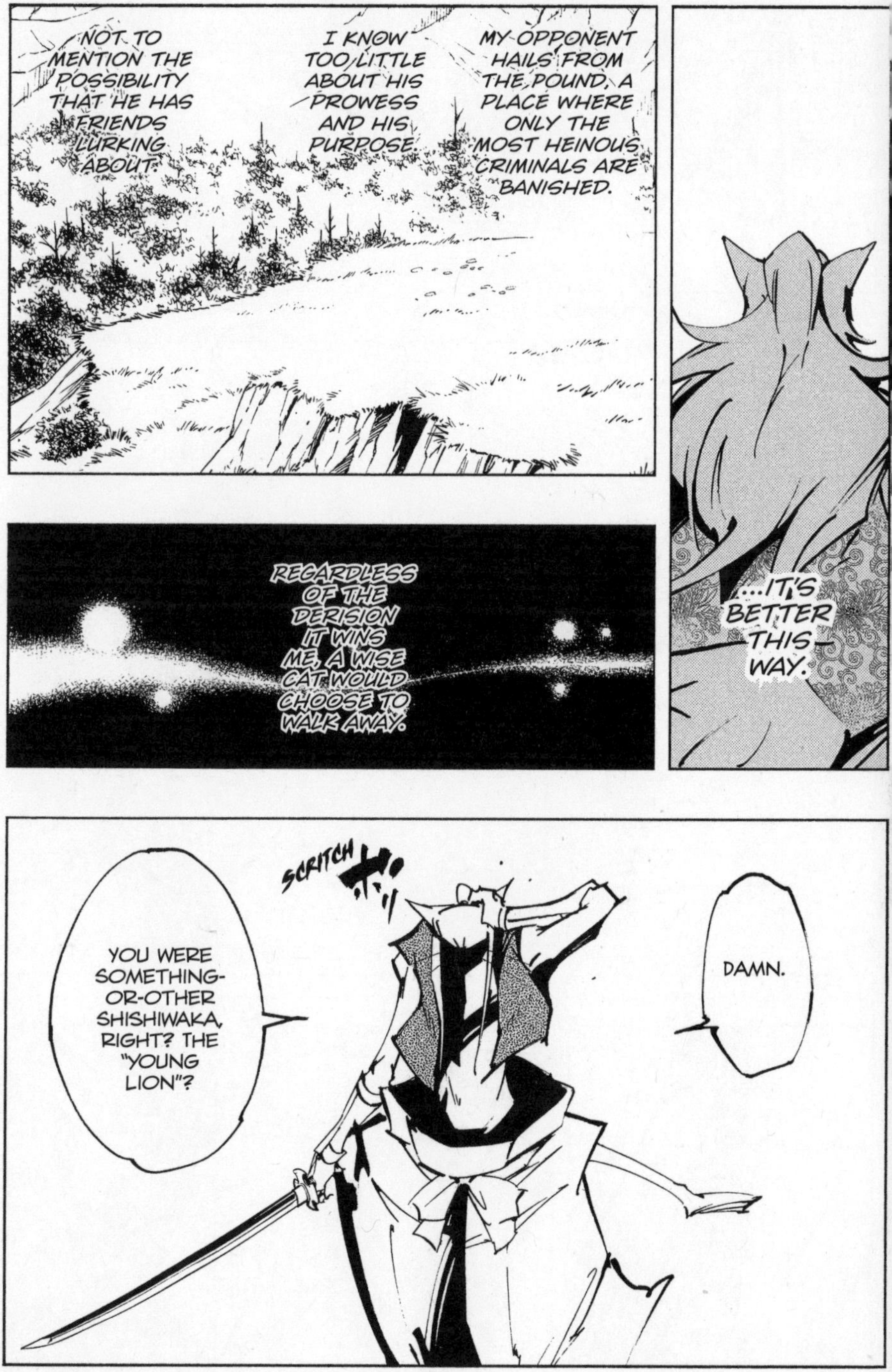
...IT'S BETTER THIS WAY.
MY OPPONENT HAILS FROM THE POUND, A PLACE WHERE ONLY THE MOST HEINOUS CRIMINALS ARE BANISHED.
I KNOW TOO LITTLE ABOUT HIS PROWESS AND HIS PURPOSE.
NOT TO MENTION THE POSSIBILITY THAT HE HAS FRIENDS LURKING ABOUT.
REGARDLESS OF THE DERISION IT WINS ME, A WISE CAT WOULD CHOOSE TO WALK AWAY.
DAMN.
SCRITCH
YOU WERE SOMETHING-OR-OTHER SHISHIWAKA, RIGHT? THE "YOUNG LION"?

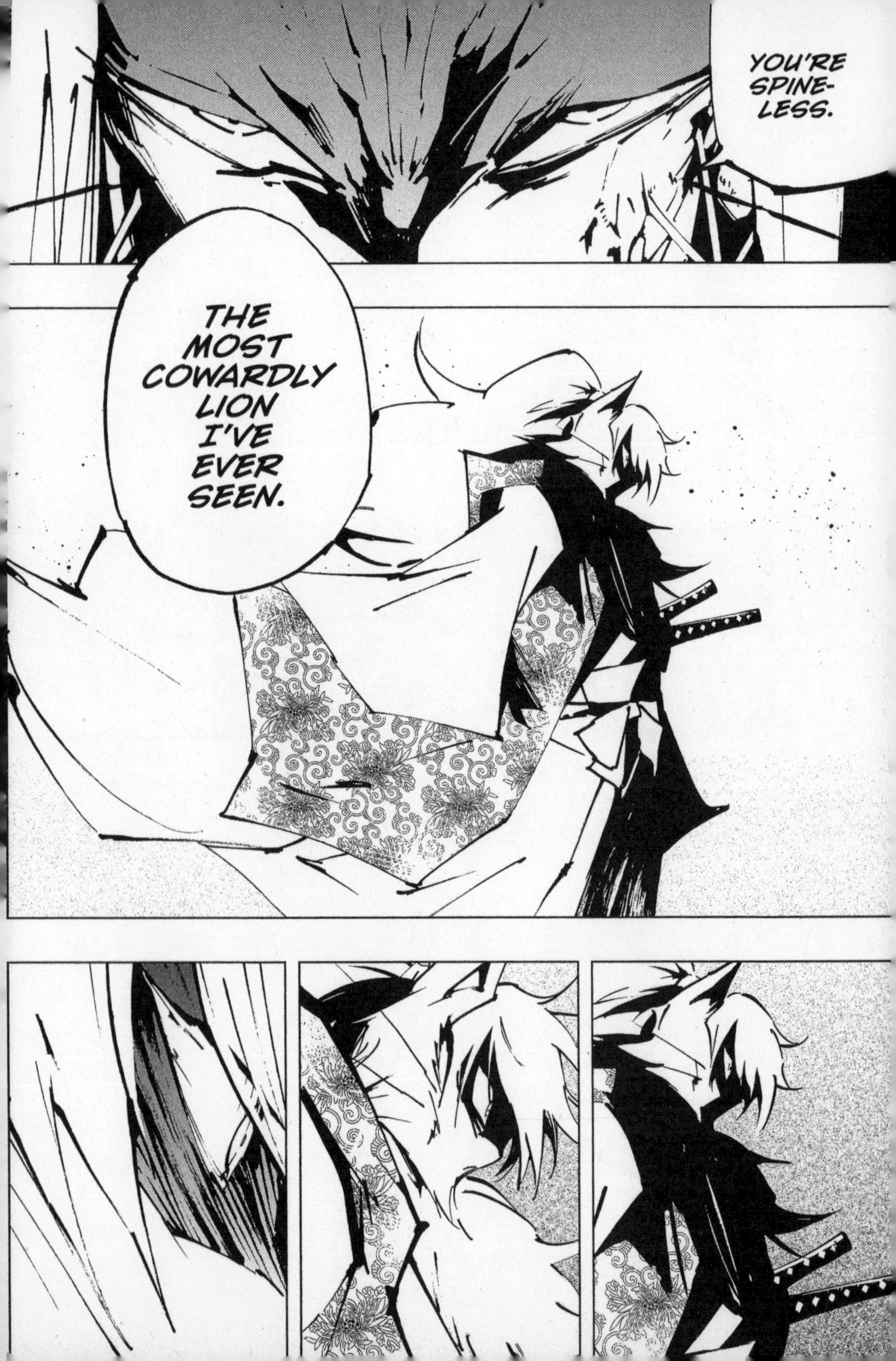
YOU'RE SPINE-LESS.
THE MOST COWARDLY LION I'VE EVER SEEN.

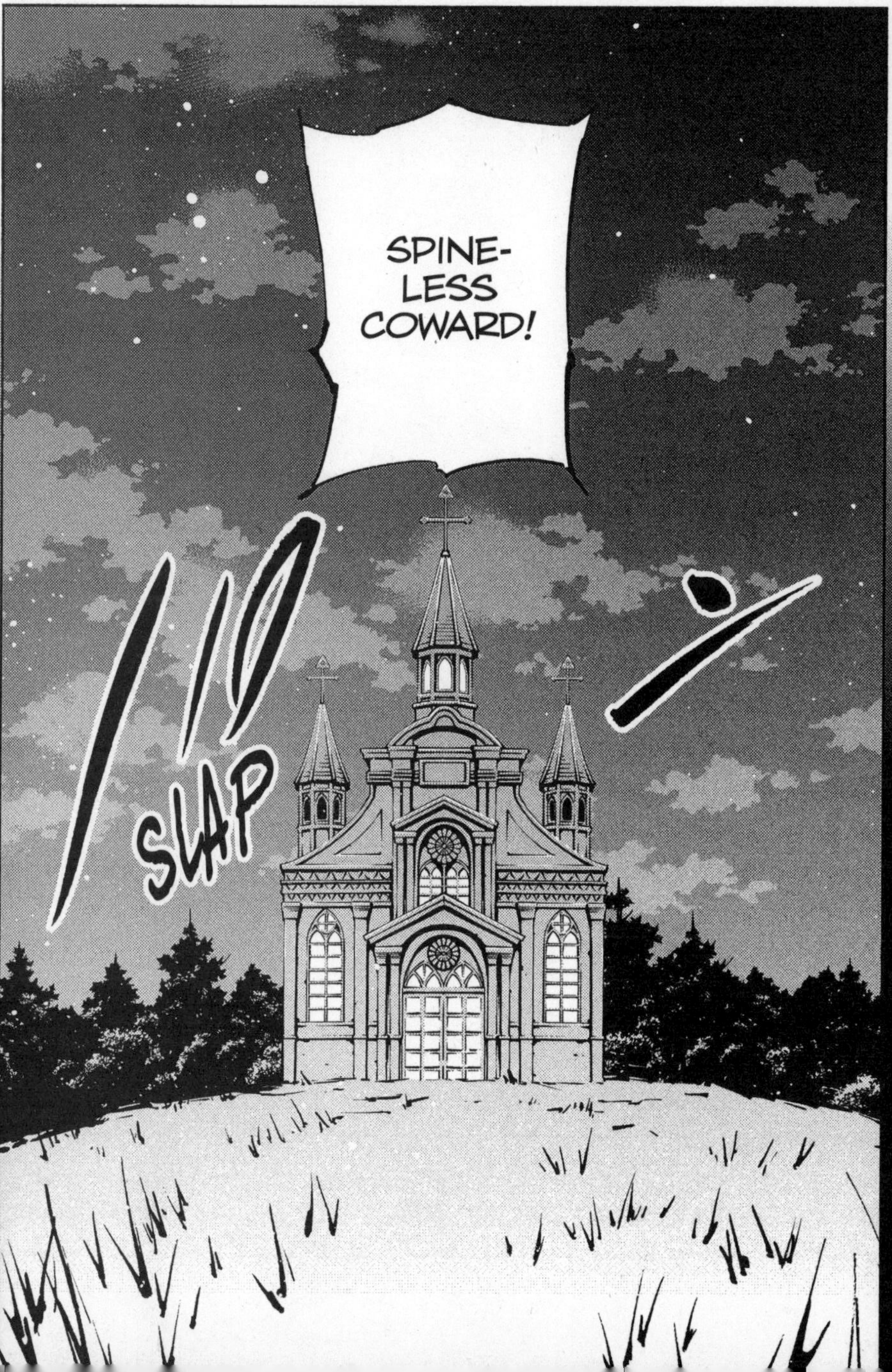
SPINE-LESS COWARD!
SLAP

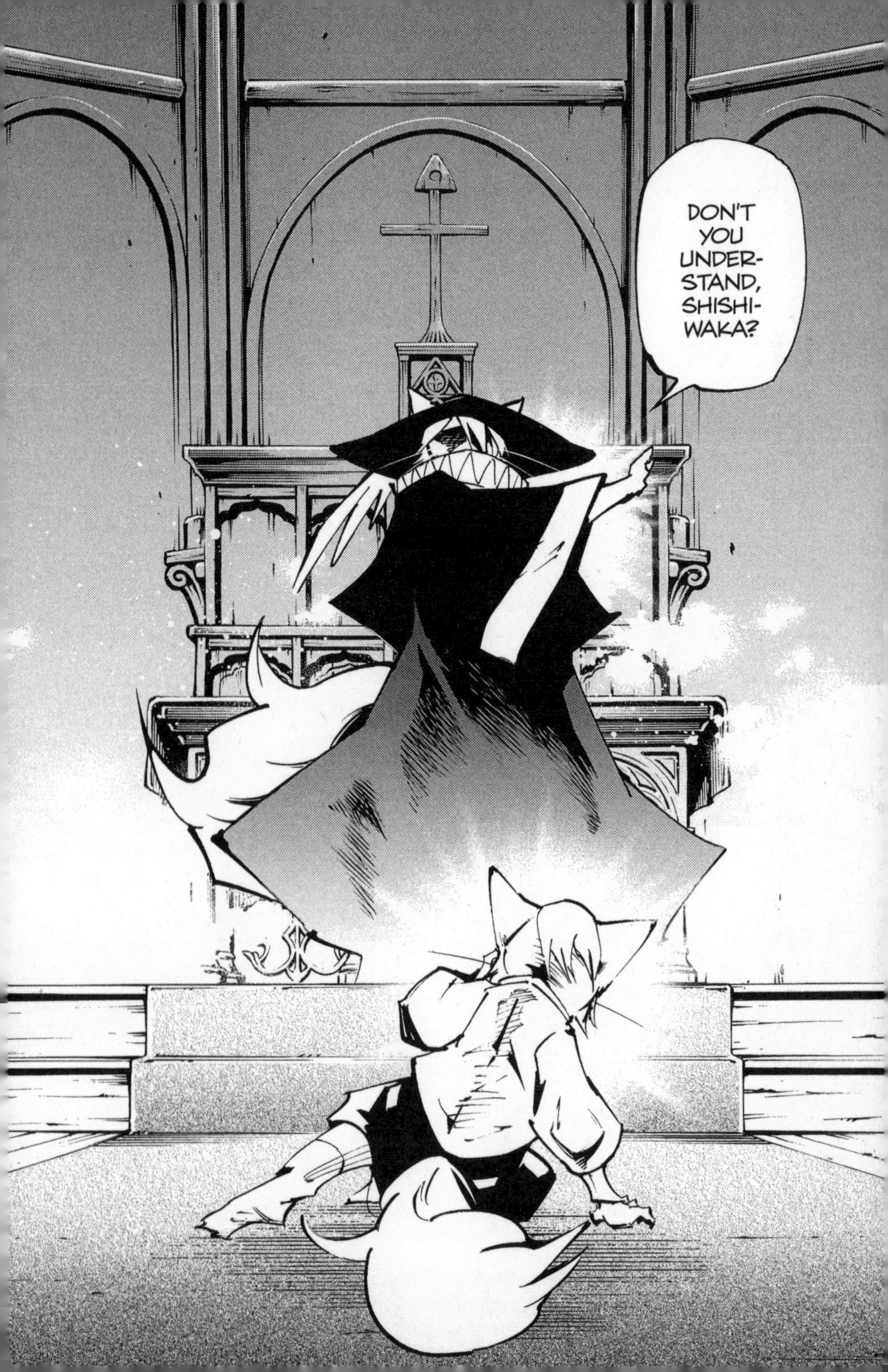
DON'T YOU UNDER-STAND, SHISHI-WAKA?

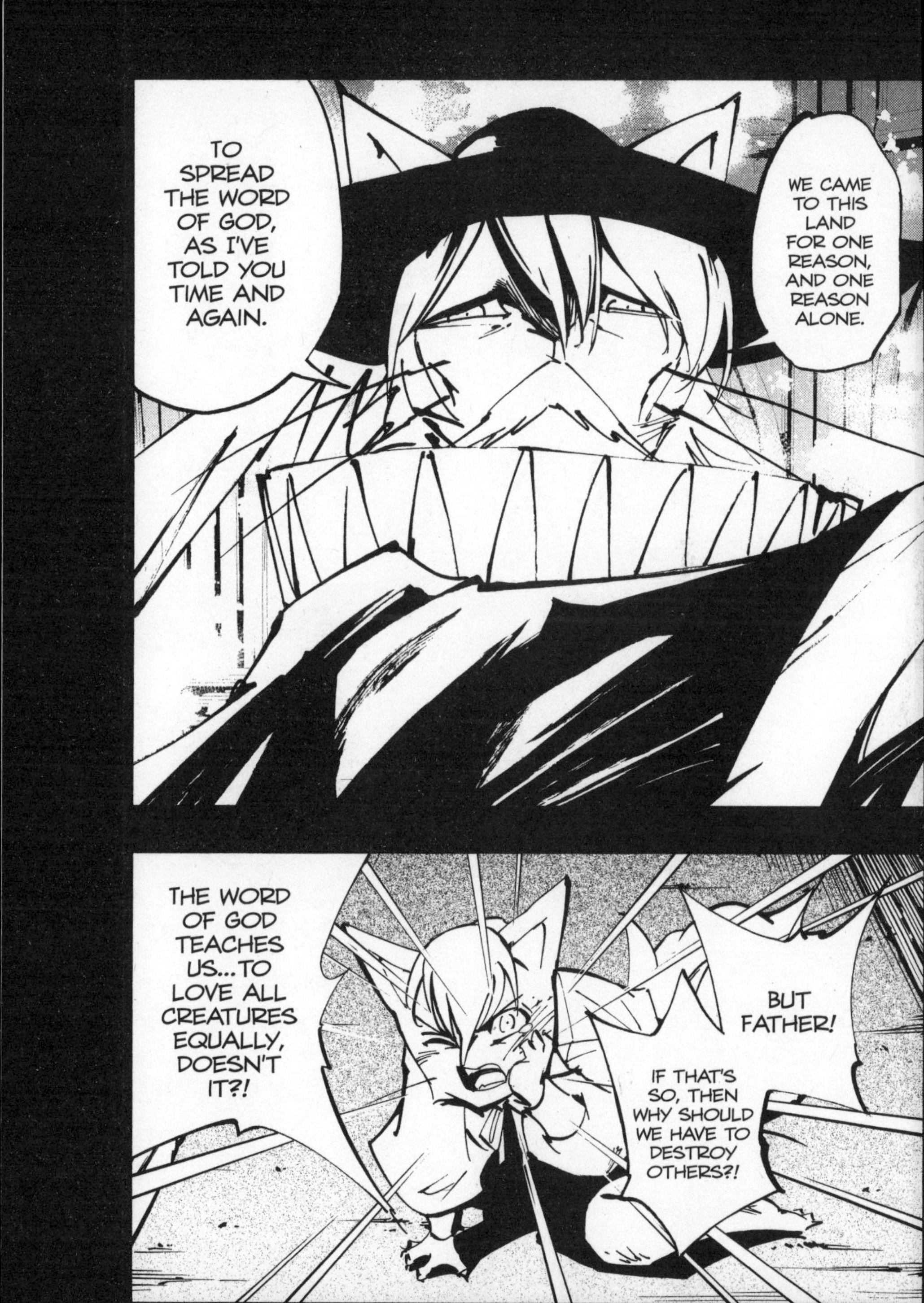
WE CAME TO THIS LAND FOR ONE REASON, AND ONE REASON ALONE.
TO SPREAD THE WORD OF GOD, AS I'VE TOLD YOU TIME AND AGAIN.
BUT FATHER!
IF THAT'S SO, THEN WHY SHOULD WE HAVE TO DESTROY OTHERS?!
THE WORD OF GOD TEACHES US...TO LOVE ALL CREATURES EQUALLY, DOESN'T IT?!

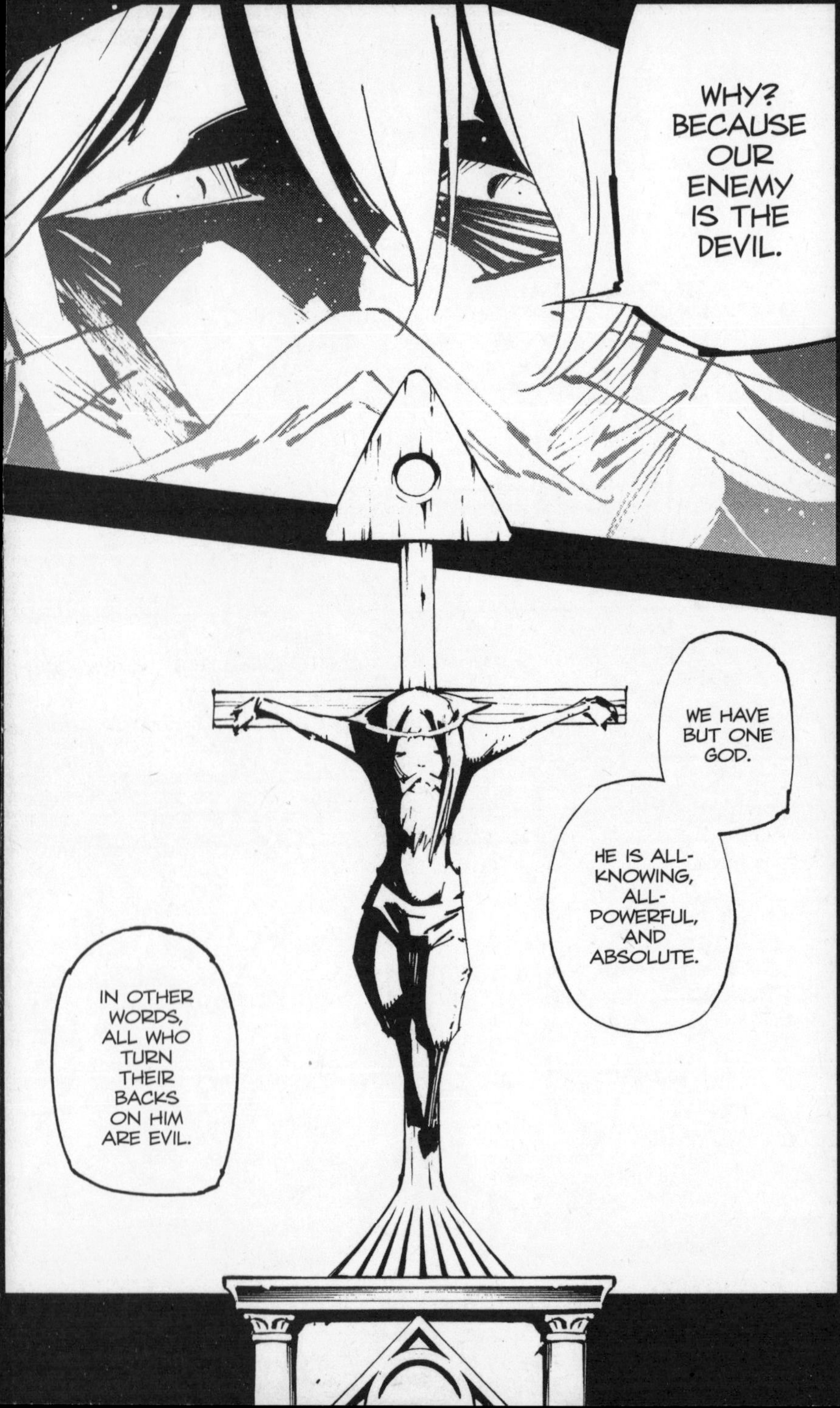
WHY? BECAUSE OUR ENEMY IS THE DEVIL.
WE HAVE BUT ONE GOD.
HE IS ALL-KNOWING, ALL-POWERFUL, AND ABSOLUTE.
IN OTHER WORDS, ALL WHO TURN THEIR BACKS ON HIM ARE EVIL.

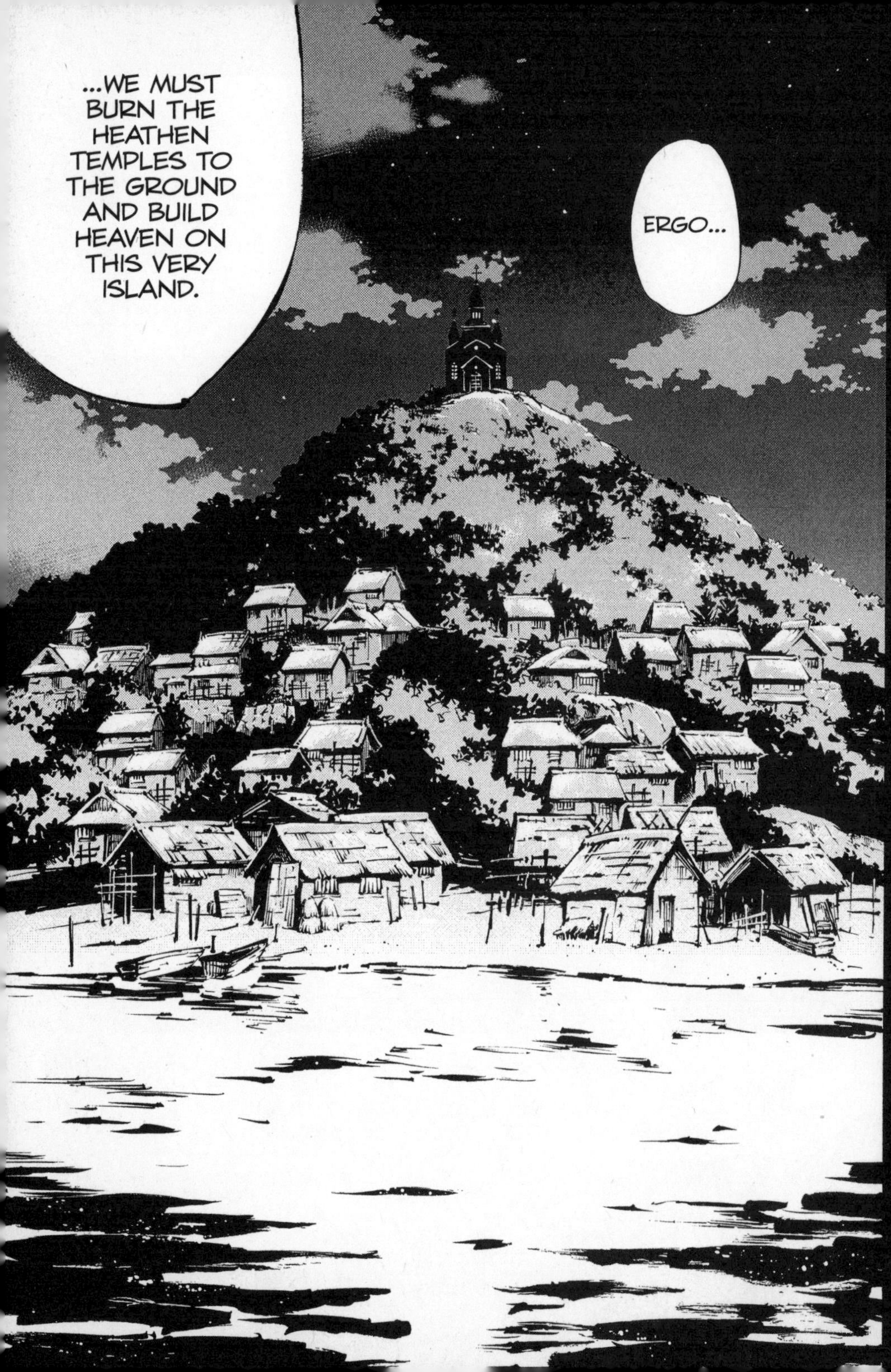
ERGO...
...WE MUST BURN THE HEATHEN TEMPLES TO THE GROUND AND BUILD HEAVEN ON THIS VERY ISLAND.

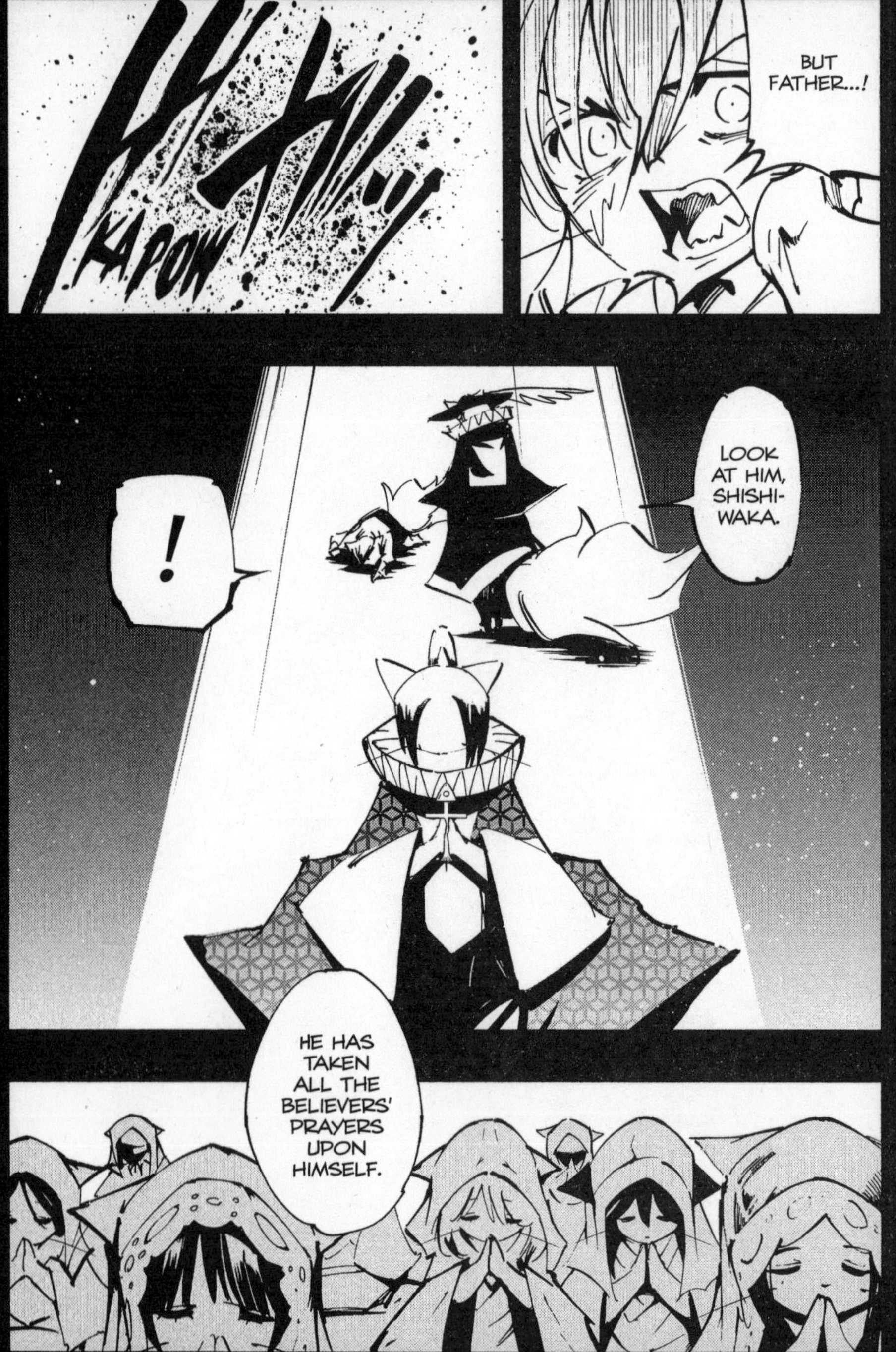
BUT FATHER...!
KA POW
LOOK AT HIM, SHISHI-WAKA.
!
HE HAS TAKEN ALL THE BELIEVERS' PRAYERS UPON HIMSELF.

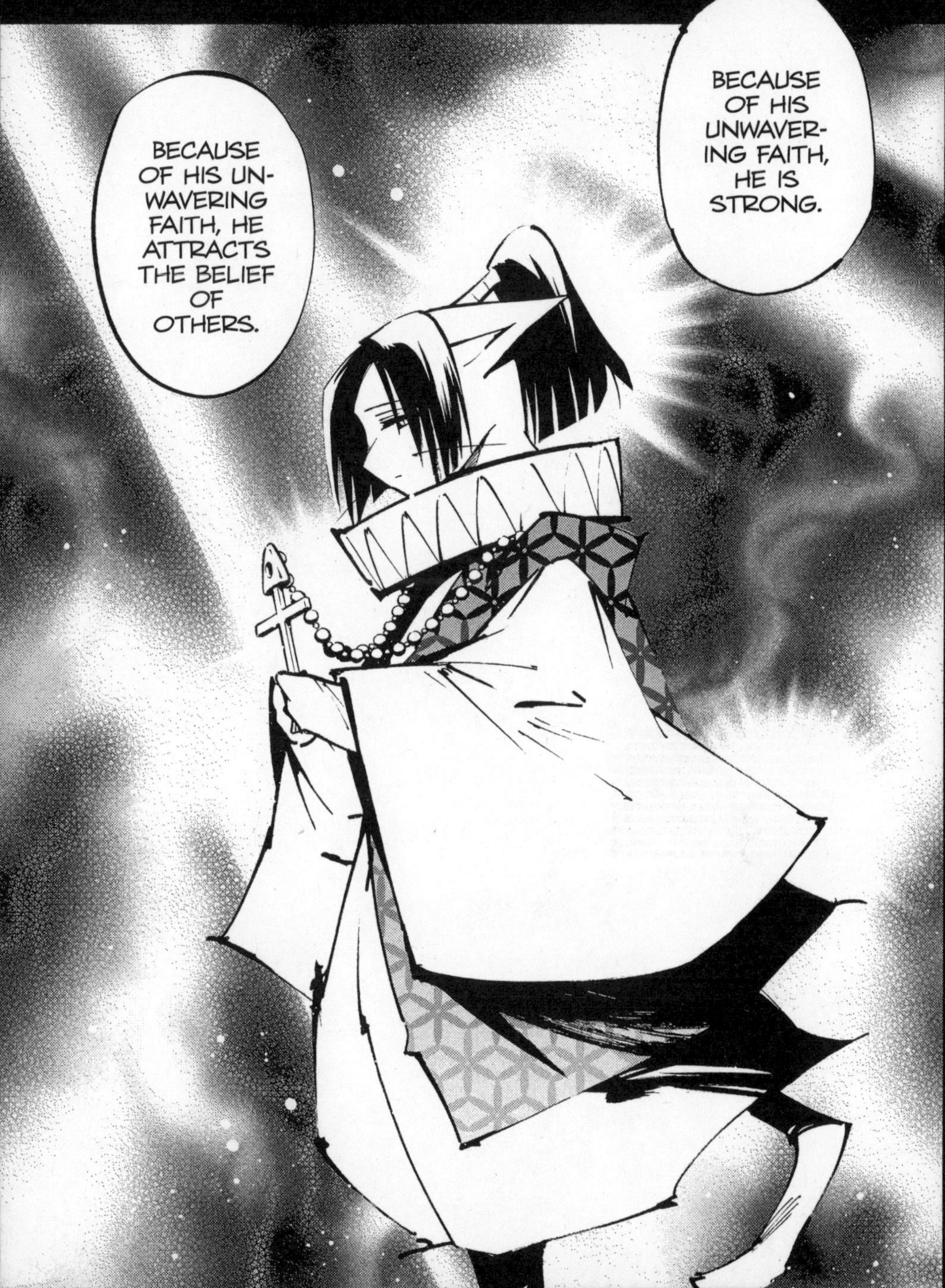
BECAUSE OF HIS UNWAVER-ING FAITH, HE IS STRONG.
BECAUSE OF HIS UN-WAVERING FAITH, HE ATTRACTS THE BELIEF OF OTHERS.

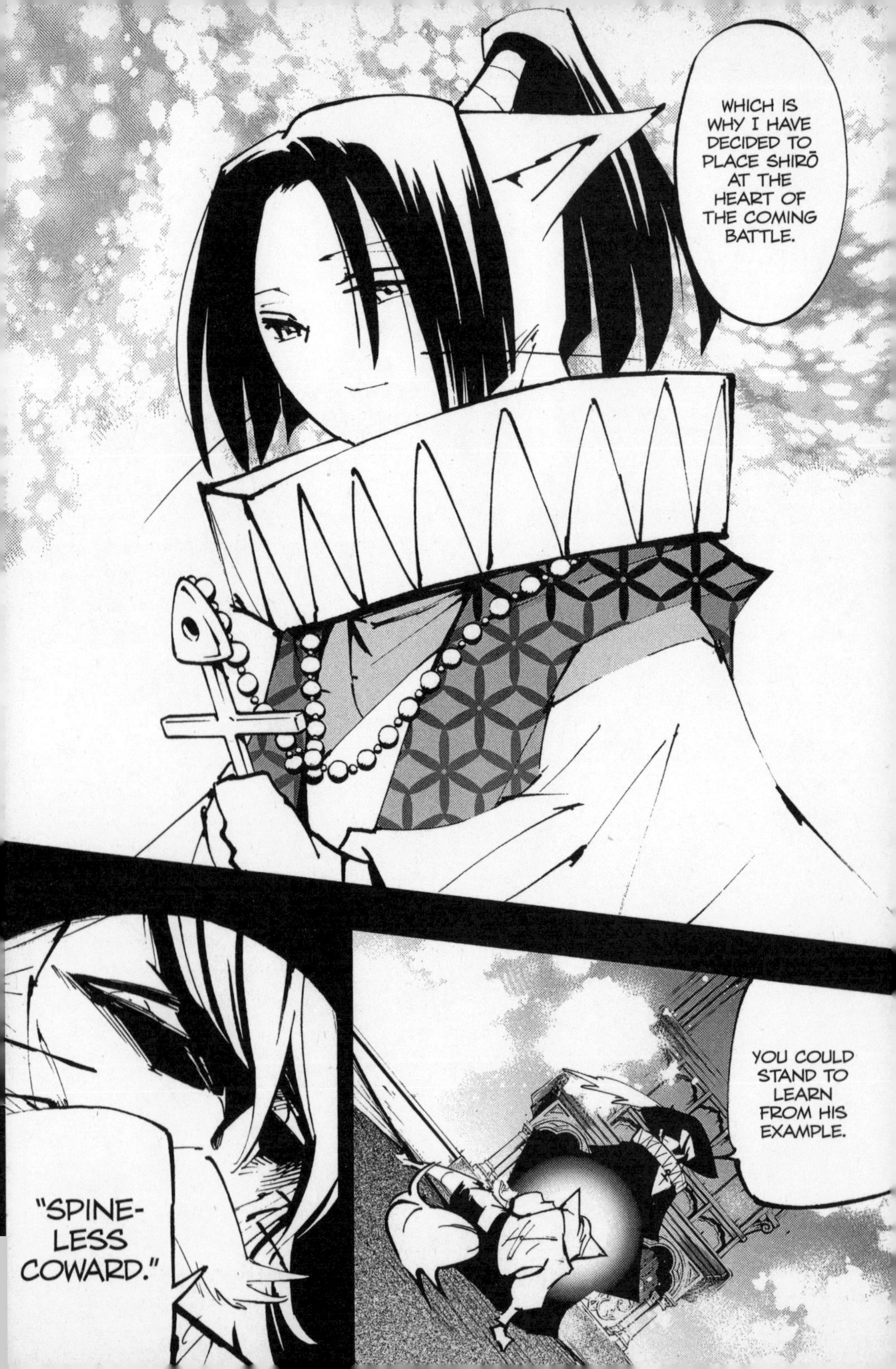
WHICH IS WHY I HAVE DECIDED TO PLACE SHIRŌ AT THE HEART OF THE COMING BATTLE.
YOU COULD STAND TO LEARN FROM HIS EXAMPLE.
"SPINE-LESS COWARD."

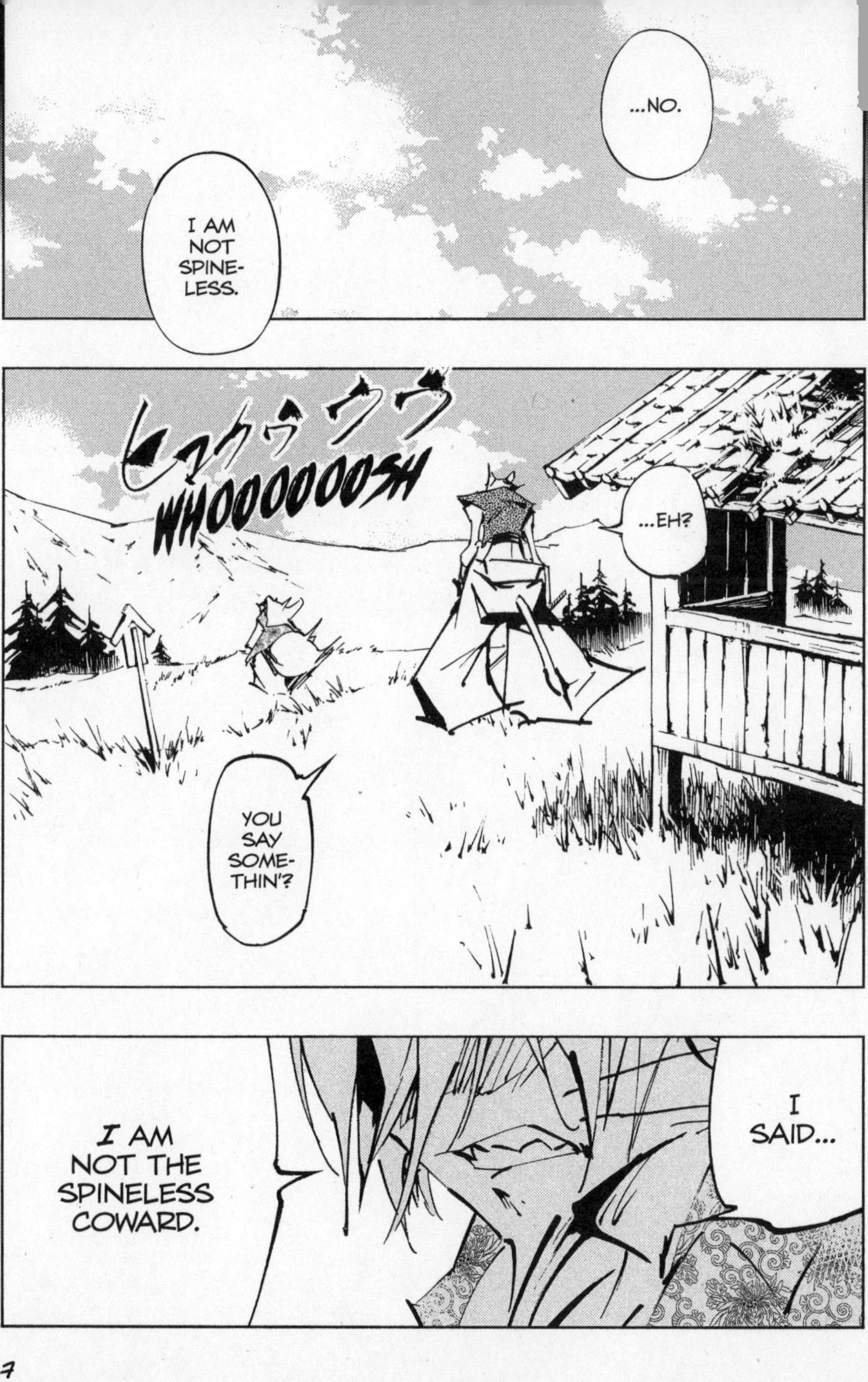
...NO.
I AM NOT SPINE-LESS.
...EH?
WHOOOOOOSH
YOU SAY SOME-THIN'?
I SAID...
I AM NOT THE SPINELESS COWARD.

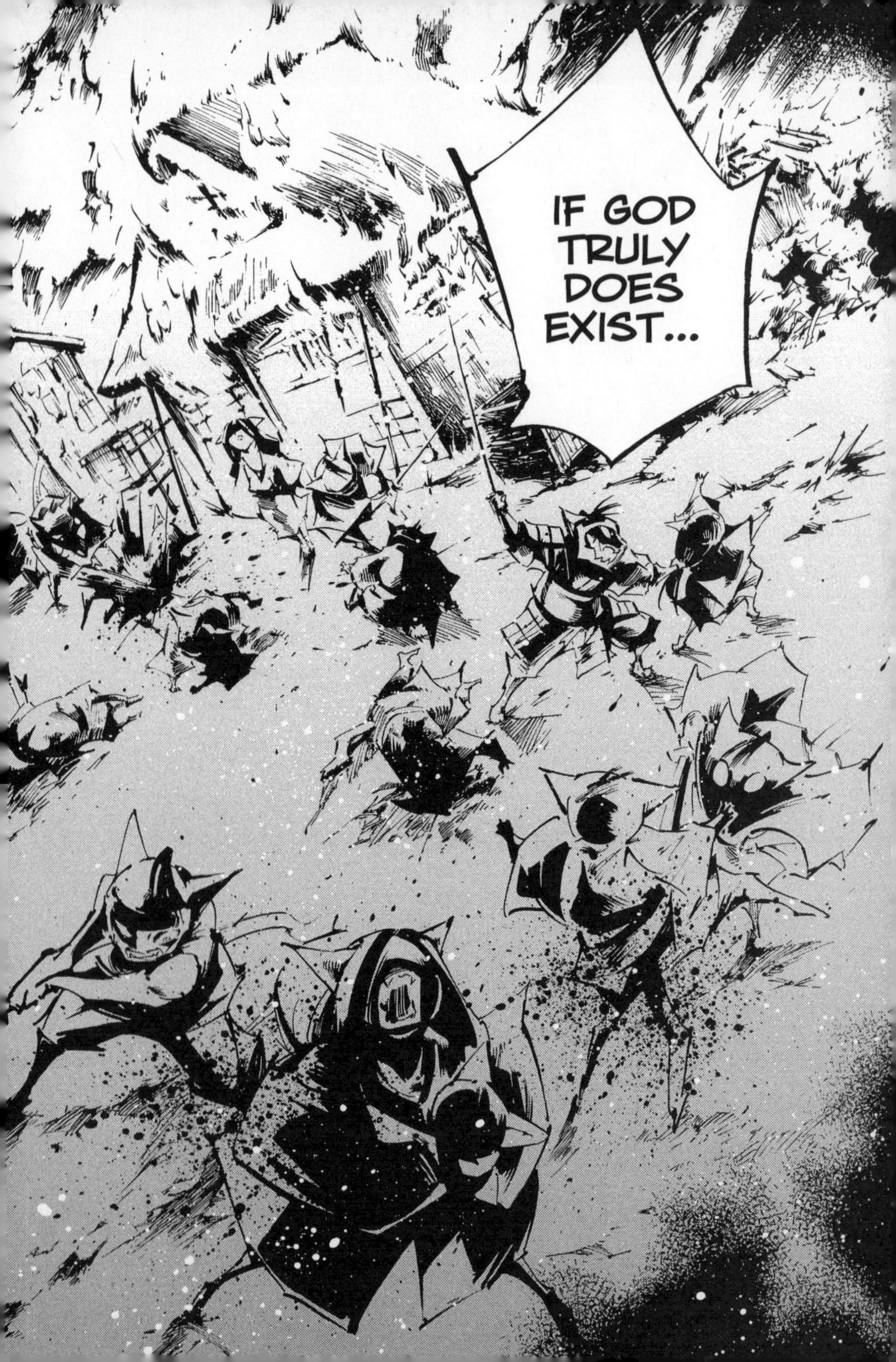
IF GOD TRULY DOES EXIST...

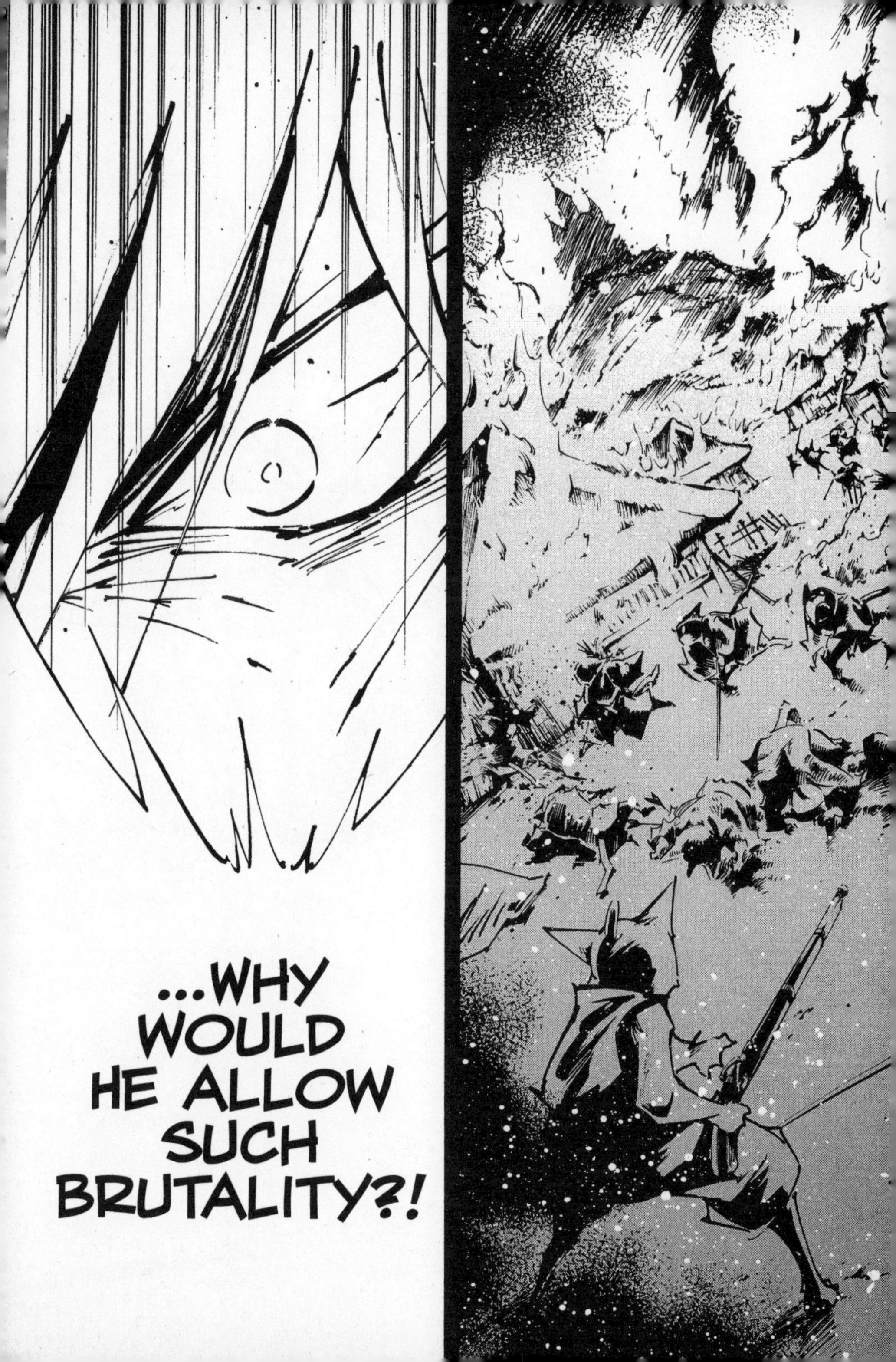
...WHY WOULD HE ALLOW SUCH BRUTALITY?!

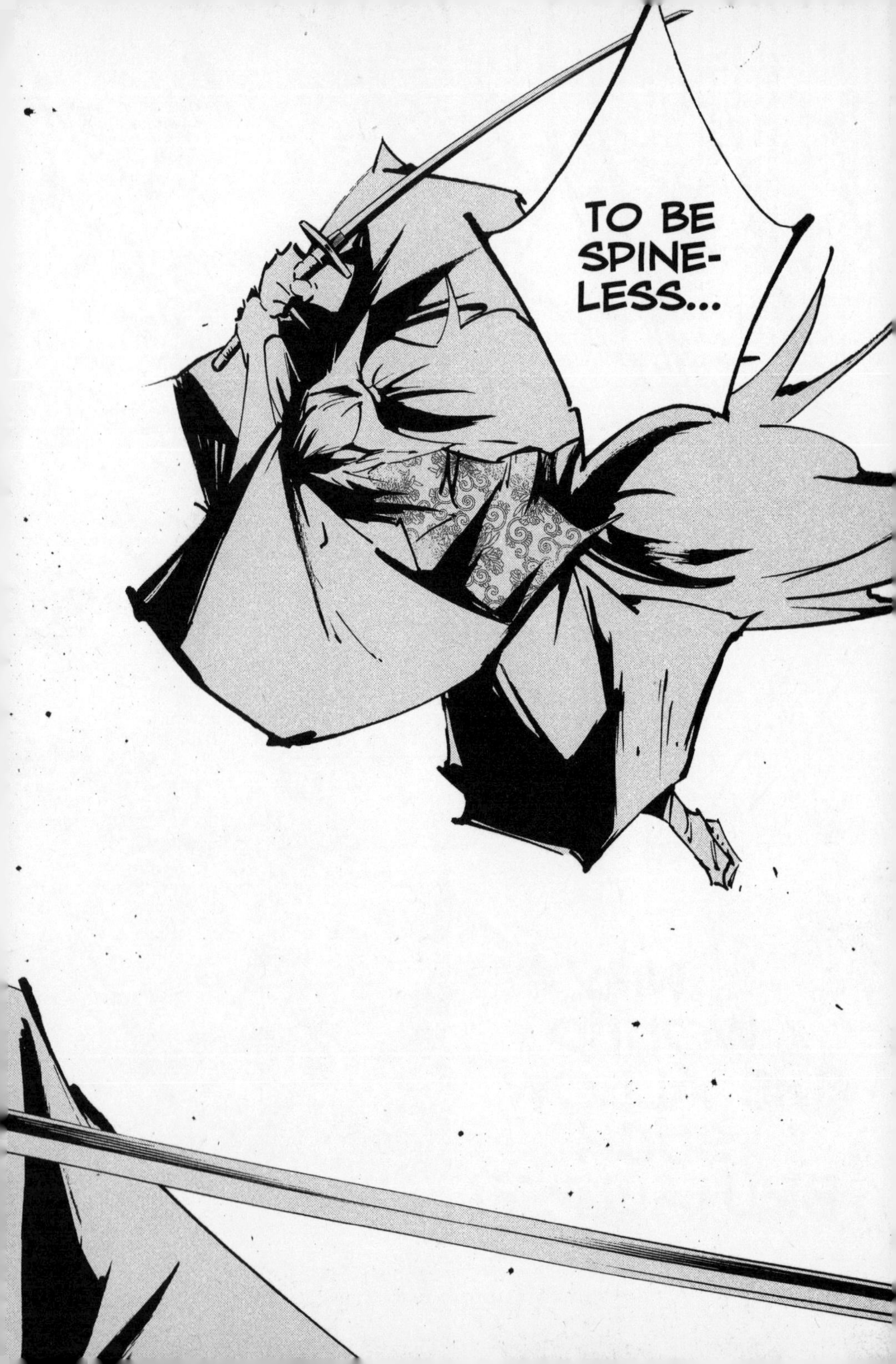
TO BE SPINE-LESS...

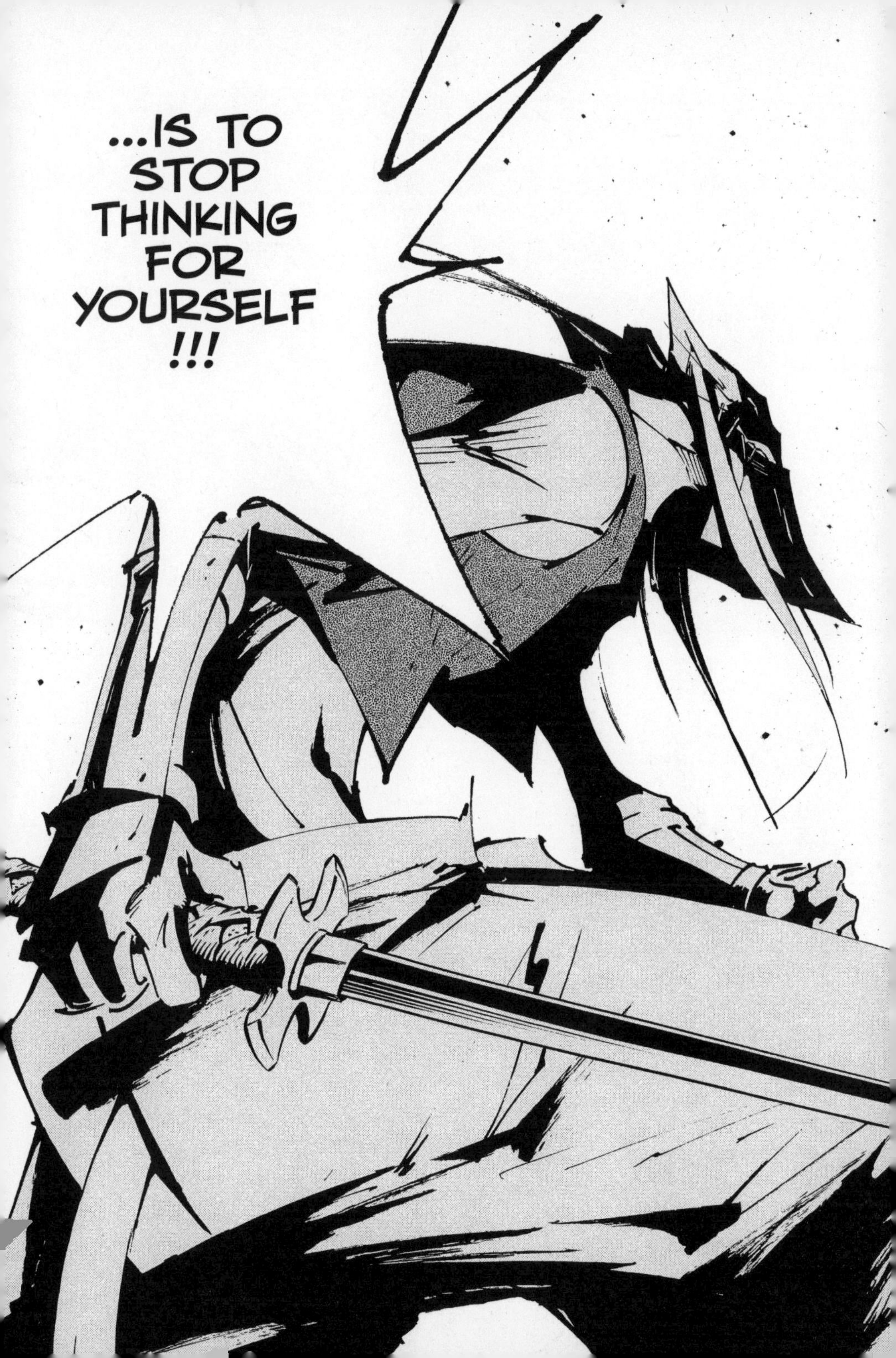
...IS TO STOP THINKING FOR YOURSELF !!!

猫ヶ原

NekoGaHara

ネコガハラ

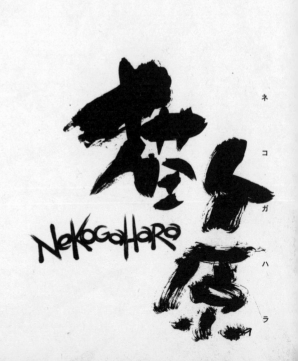

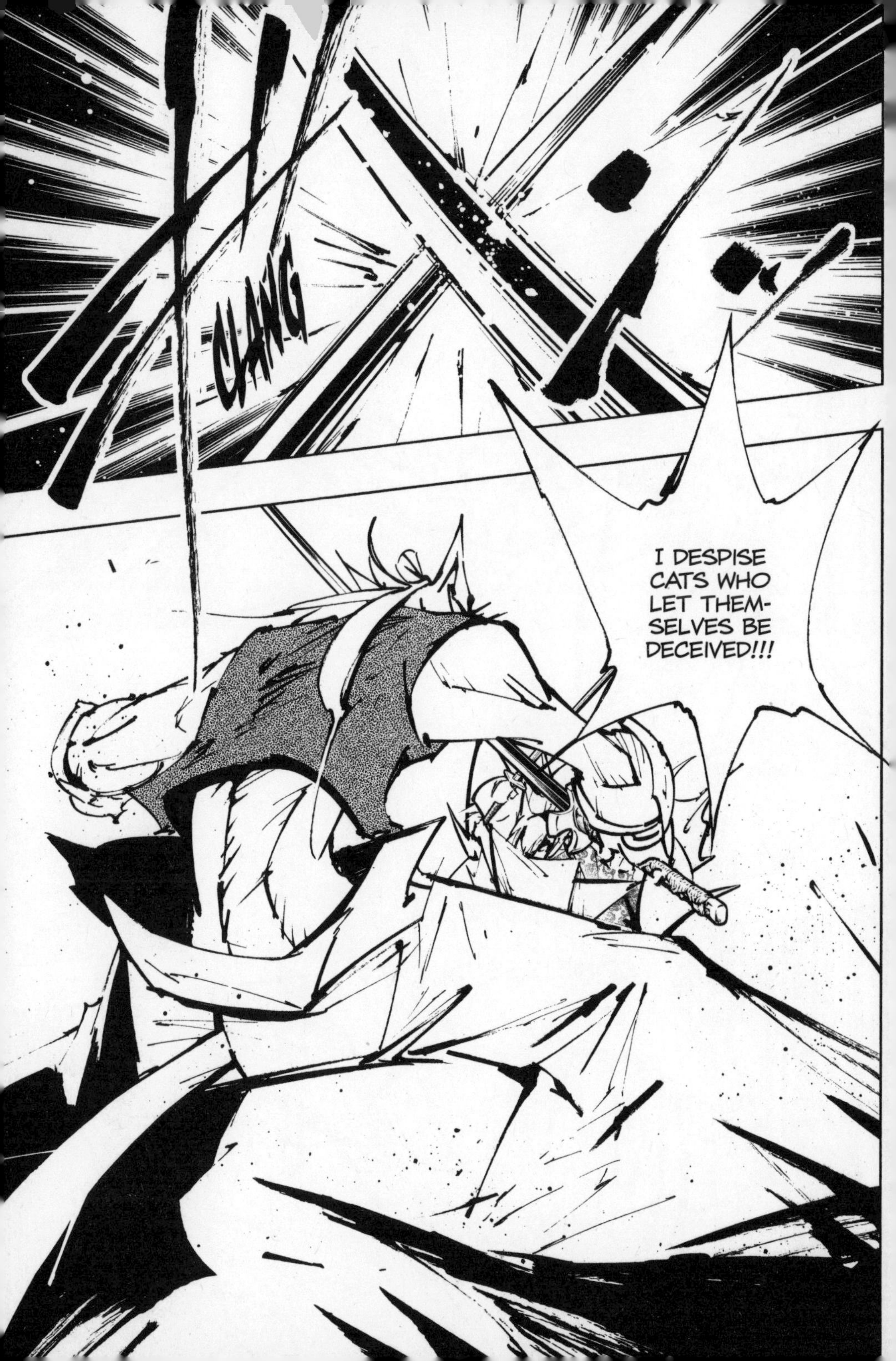
CLANG
I DESPISE CATS WHO LET THEM-SELVES BE DECEIVED!!!

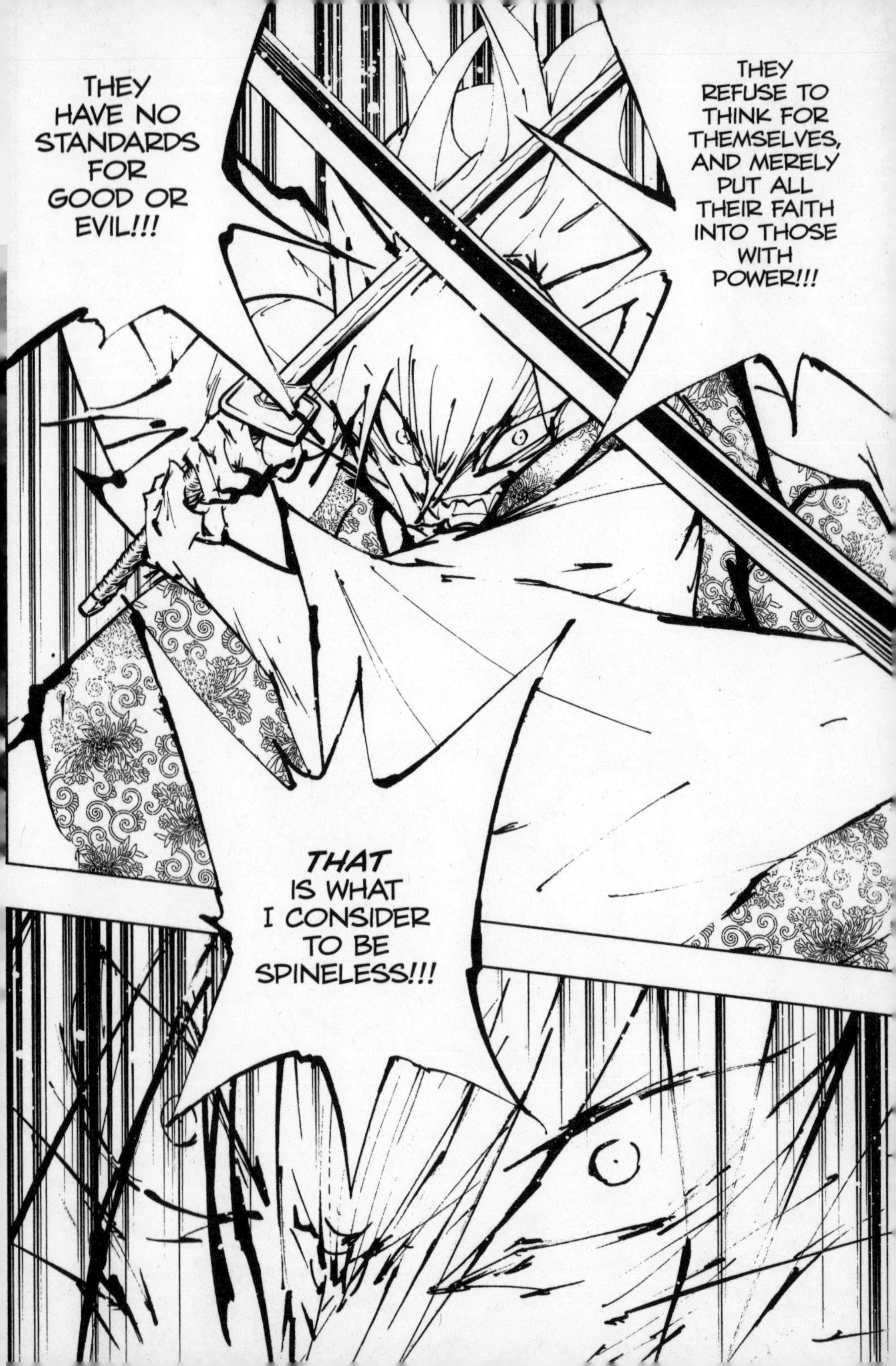

THEY REFUSE TO THINK FOR THEMSELVES, AND MERELY PUT ALL THEIR FAITH INTO THOSE WITH POWER!!!
THEY HAVE NO STANDARDS FOR GOOD OR EVIL!!!
THAT IS WHAT I CONSIDER TO BE SPINELESS!!!

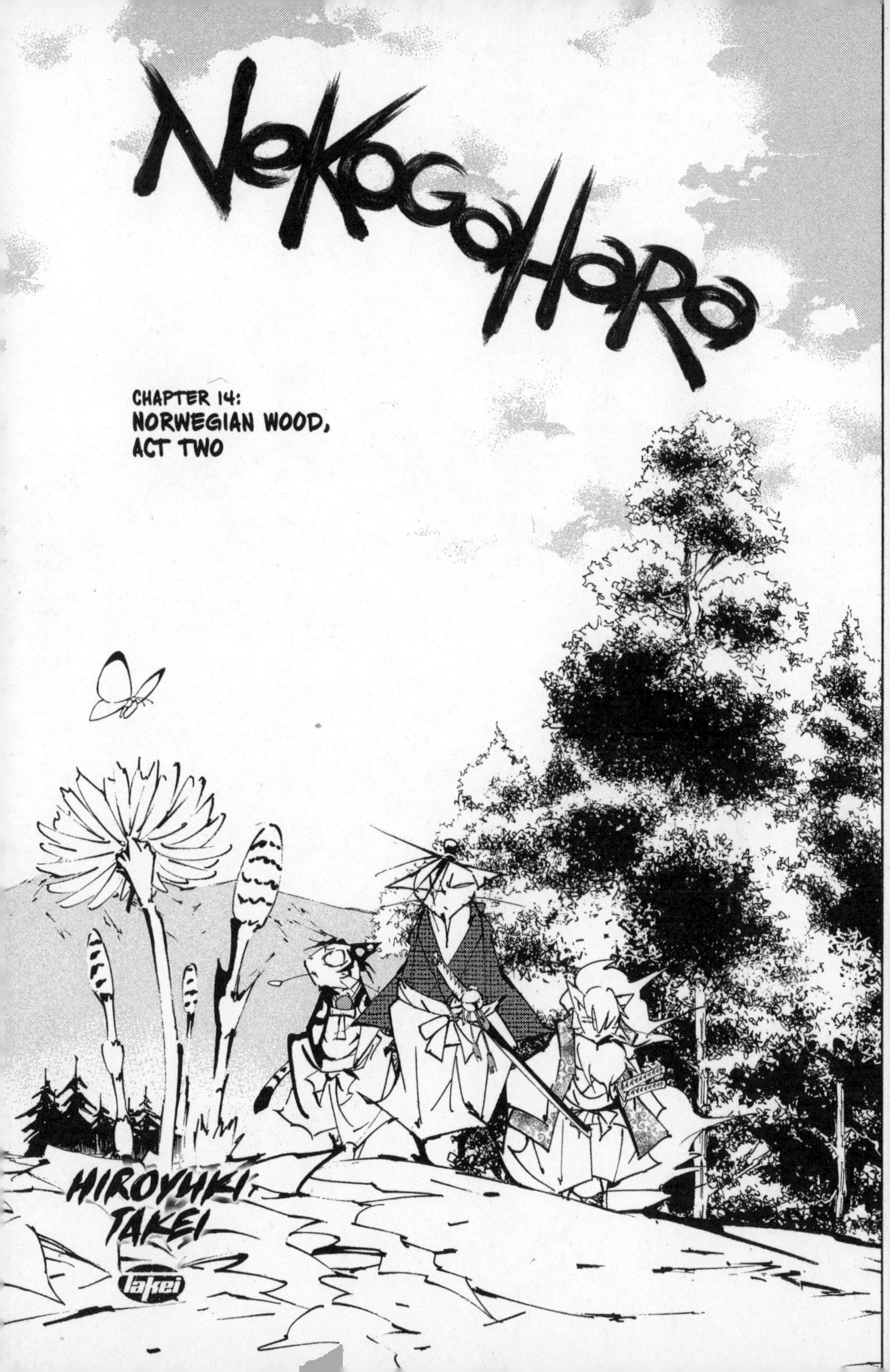
NekoGaHara
CHAPTER 14:
NORWEGIAN WOOD,
ACT TWO
HIROYUKI TAKEI
Takei

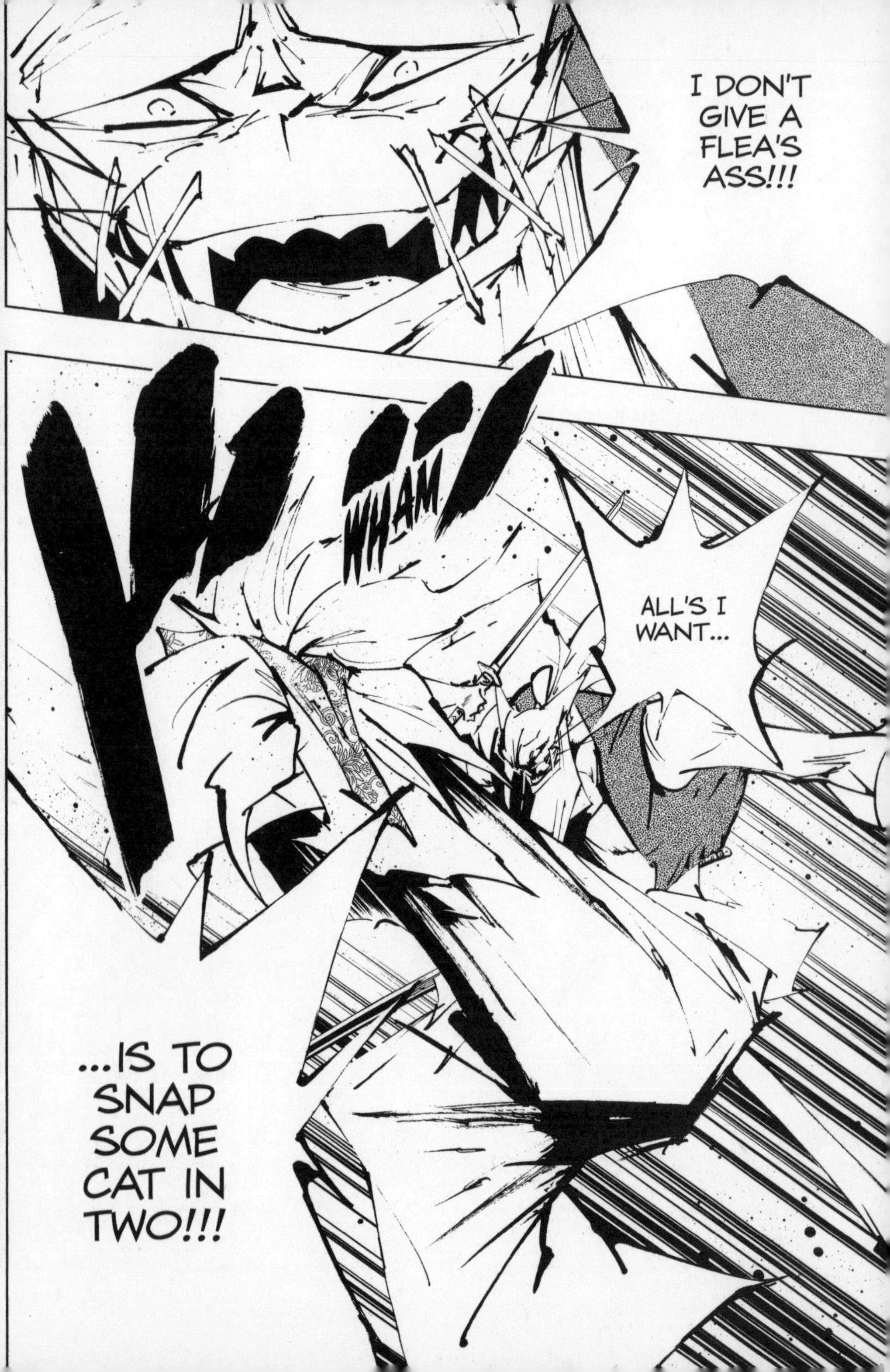
I DON'T GIVE A FLEA'S ASS!!!
WHAM
ALL'S I WANT...
...IS TO SNAP SOME CAT IN TWO!!!

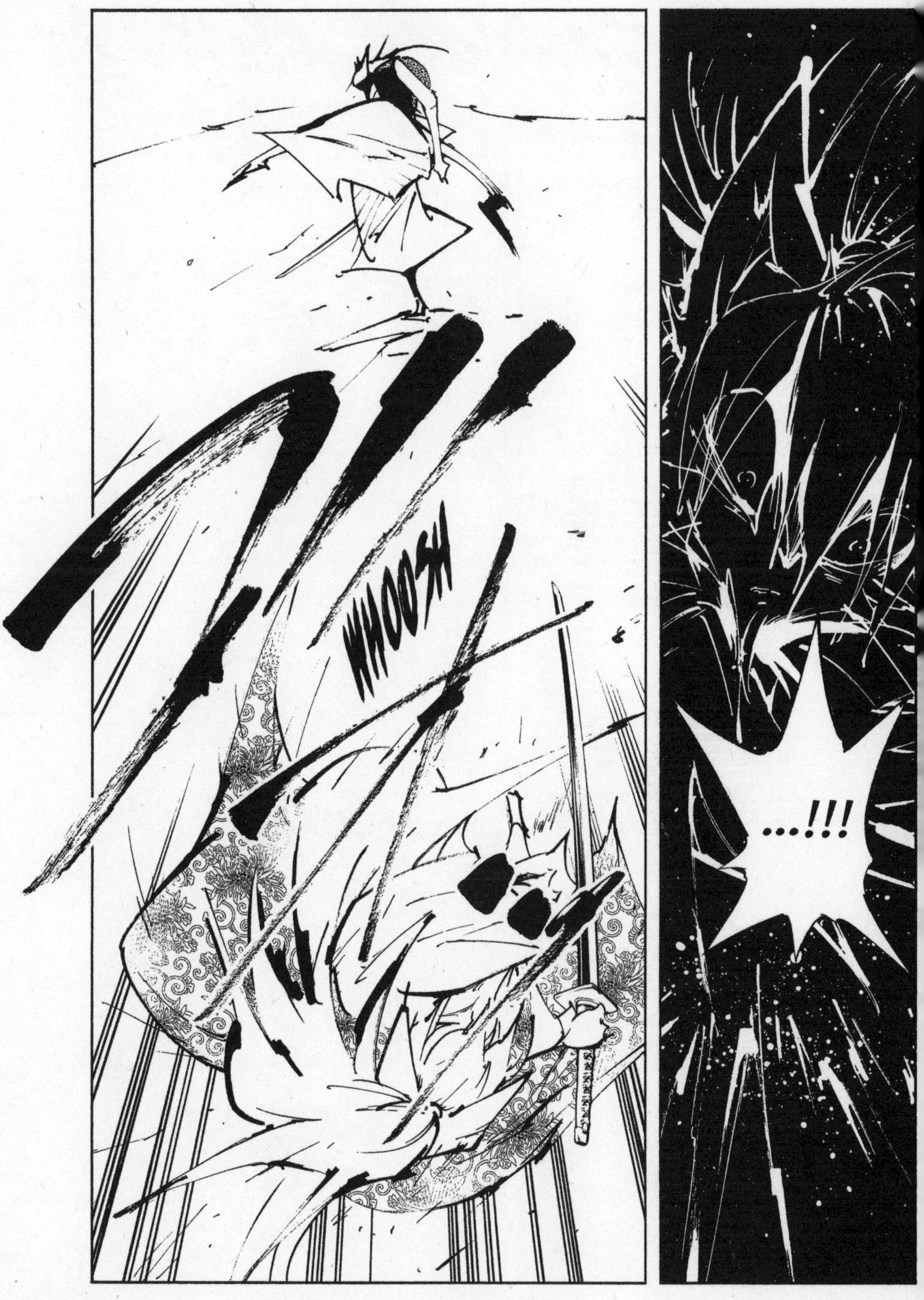
...!!!
WHOOSH

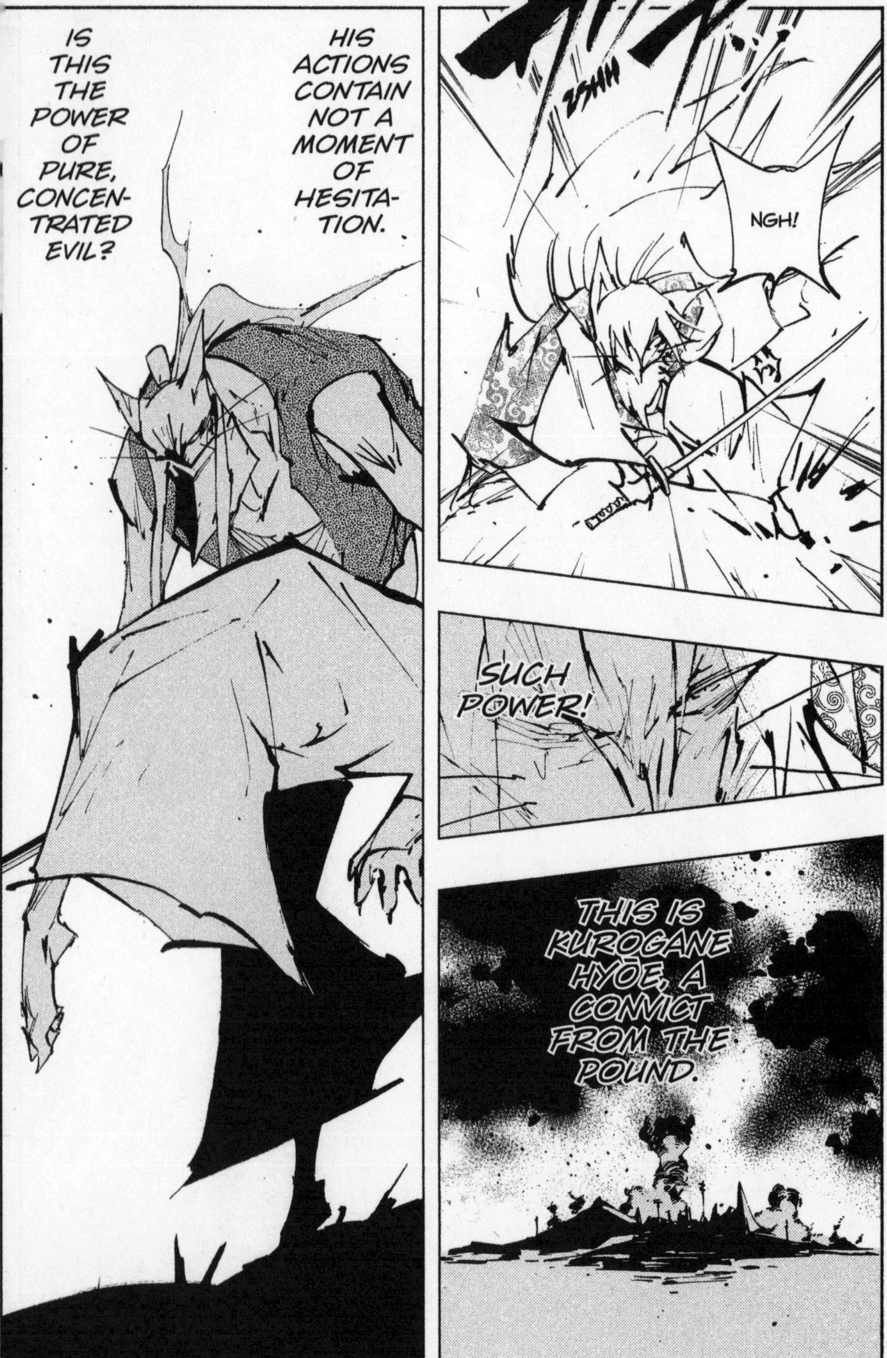
ZSHH
NGH!
SUCH POWER!
THIS IS KUROGANE HYOE, A CONVICT FROM THE POUND.
HIS ACTIONS CONTAIN NOT A MOMENT OF HESITATION.
IS THIS THE POWER OF PURE, CONCENTRATED EVIL?

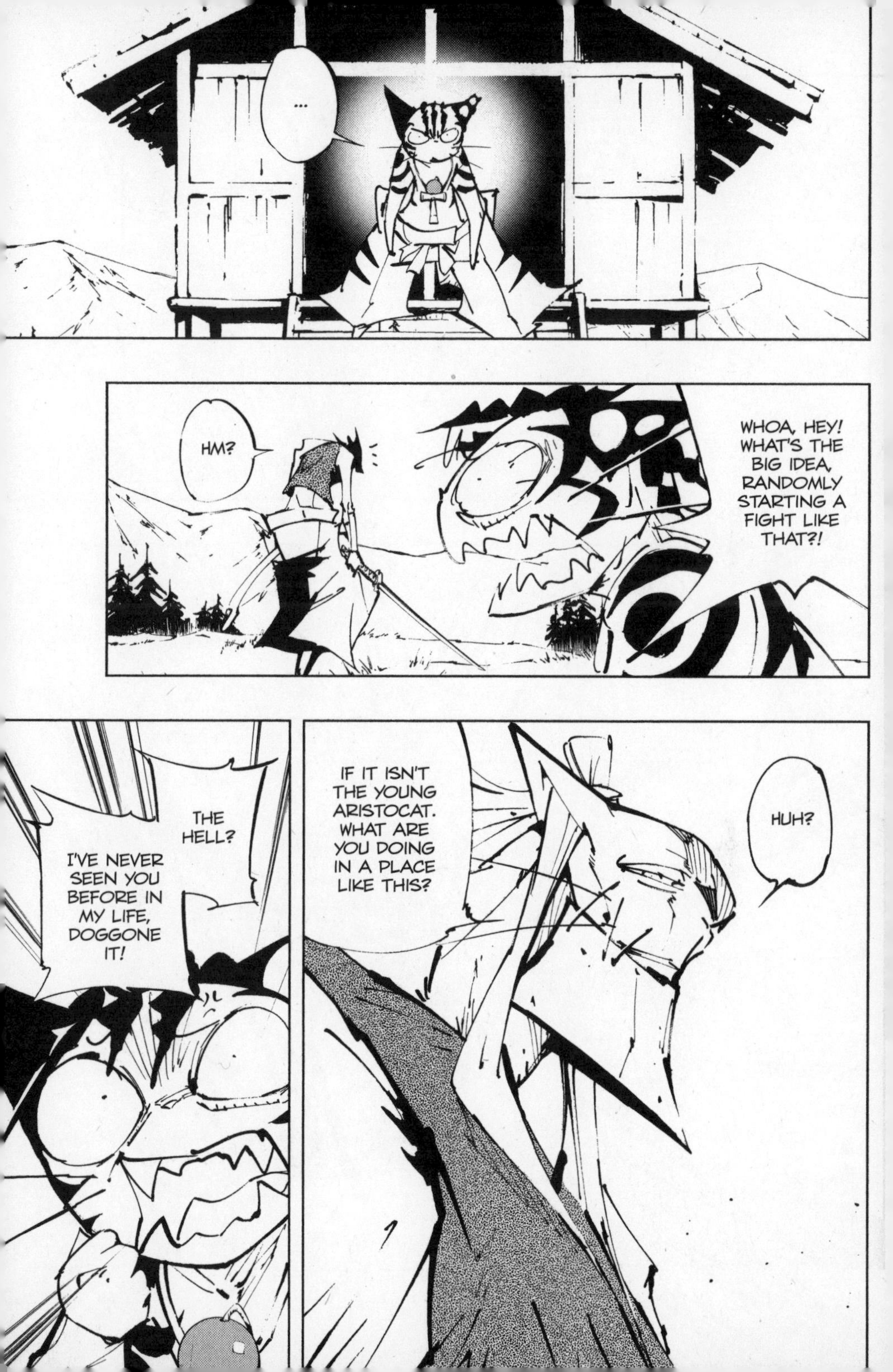
...
WHOA, HEY! WHAT'S THE BIG IDEA, RANDOMLY STARTING A FIGHT LIKE THAT?!
HM?
HUH?
IF IT ISN'T THE YOUNG ARISTOCAT. WHAT ARE YOU DOING IN A PLACE LIKE THIS?
THE HELL?
I'VE NEVER SEEN YOU BEFORE IN MY LIFE, DOGGONE IT!

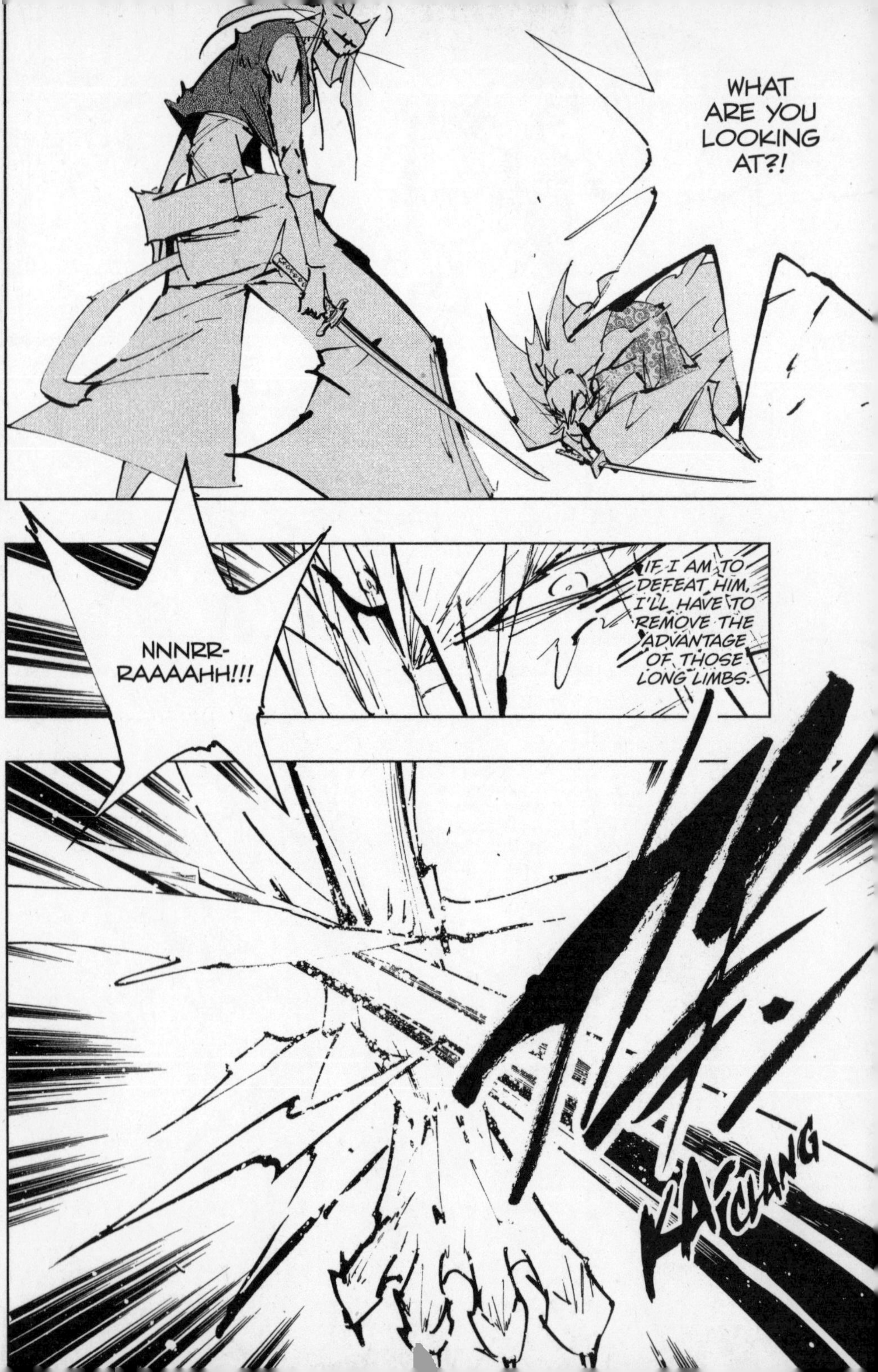
WHAT ARE YOU LOOKING AT?!
IF I AM TO DEFEAT HIM, I'LL HAVE TO REMOVE THE ADVANTAGE OF THOSE LONG LIMBS.
NNNRR-RAAAAHH!!!
KA CLANG

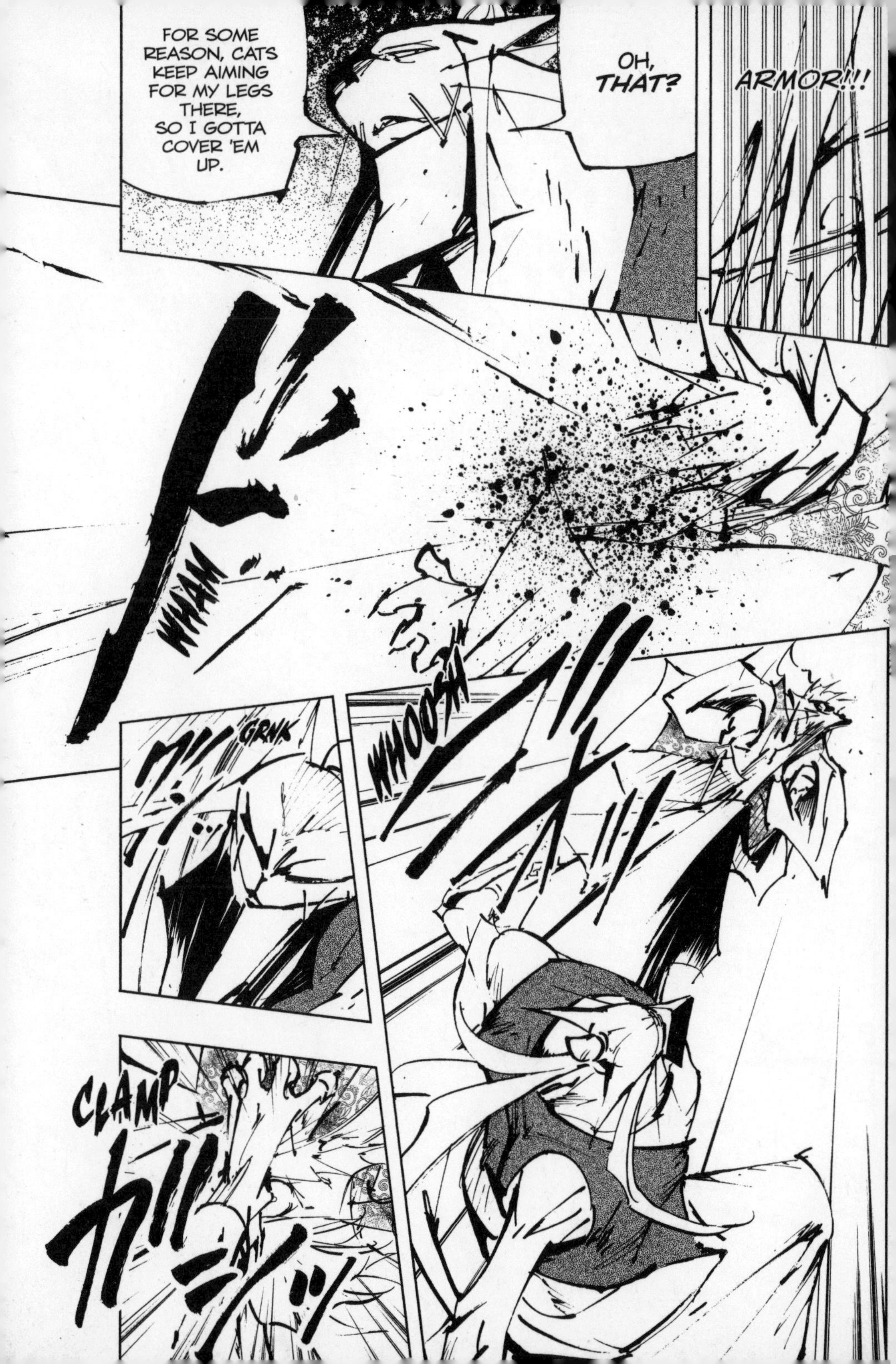
ARMOR!!!
OH, THAT?
FOR SOME REASON, CATS KEEP AIMING FOR MY LEGS THERE, SO I GOTTA COVER 'EM UP.
WHAM
WHOOSH
GRNK
CLAMP

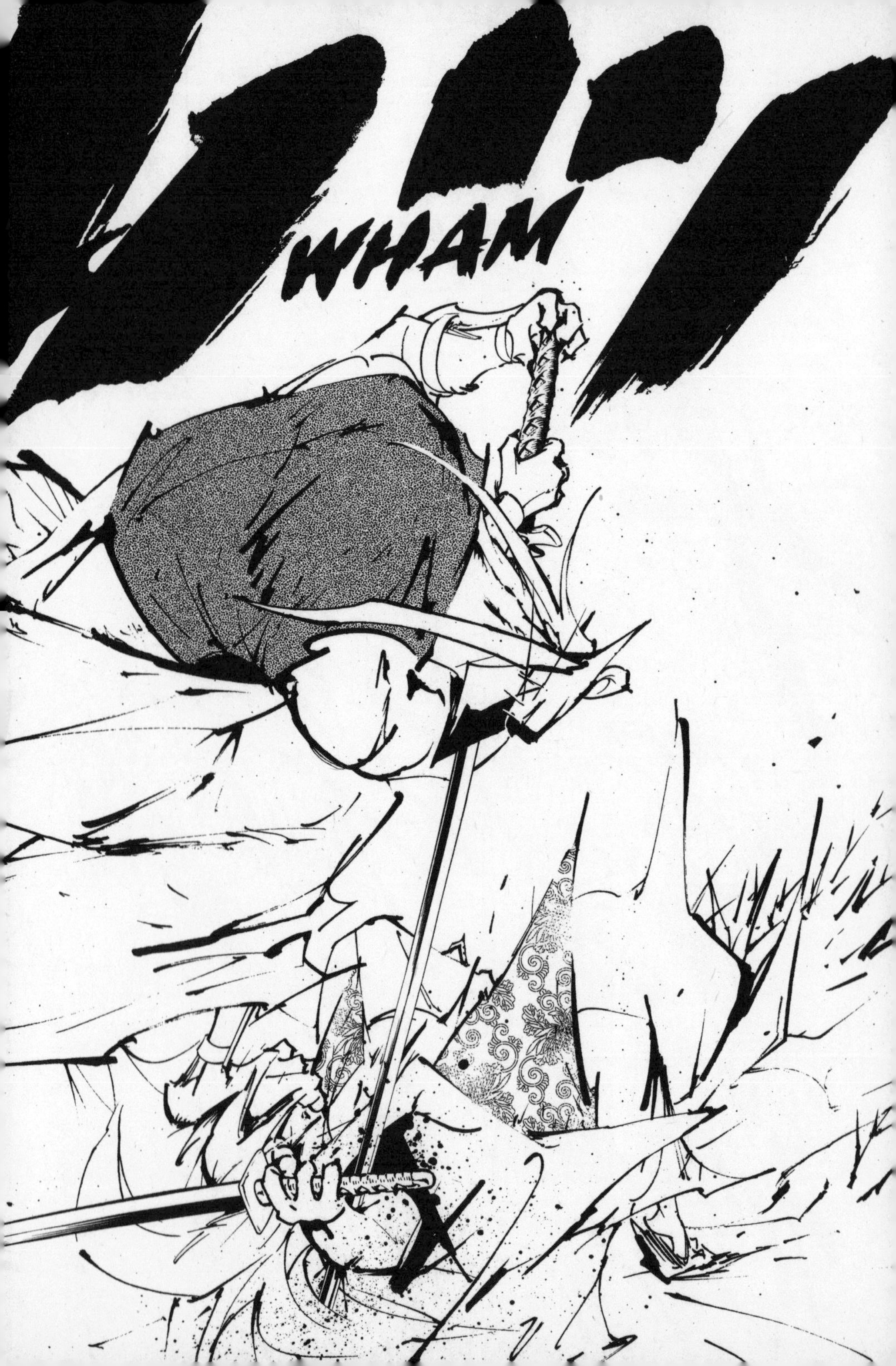
WHAM

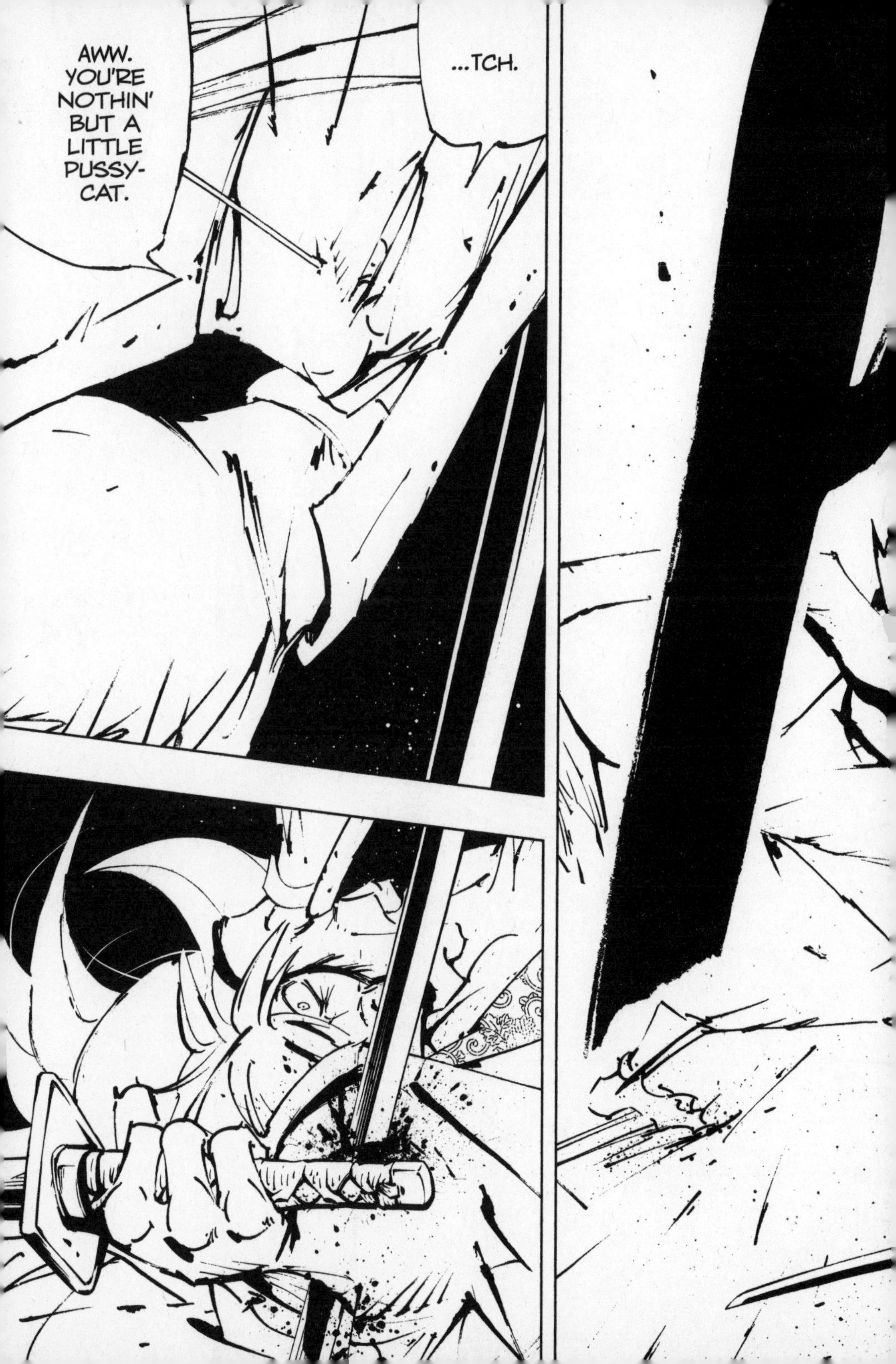
...TCH.
AWW. YOU'RE NOTHIN' BUT A LITTLE PUSSY-CAT.

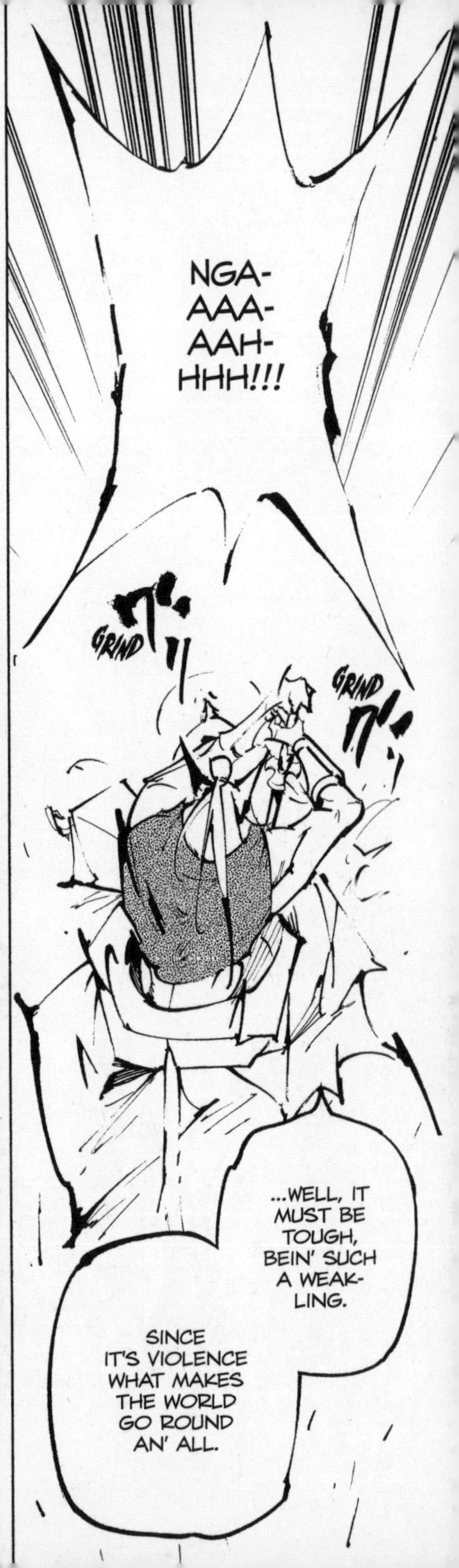
NGA-AAA-AAH-HHH!!!
GRIND
GRIND
...WELL, IT MUST BE TOUGH, BEIN' SUCH A WEAK-LING.
SINCE IT'S VIOLENCE WHAT MAKES THE WORLD GO ROUND AN' ALL.
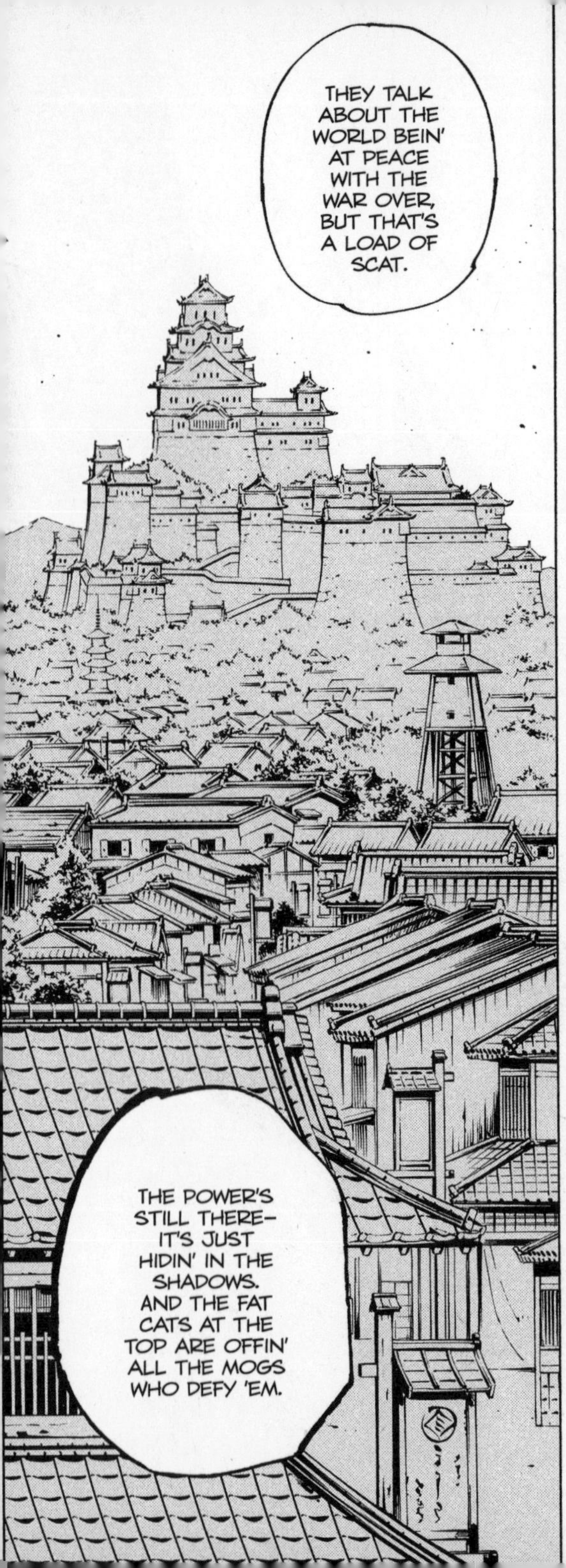
THEY TALK ABOUT THE WORLD BEIN' AT PEACE WITH THE WAR OVER, BUT THAT'S A LOAD OF SCAT.
THE POWER'S STILL THERE– IT'S JUST HIDIN' IN THE SHADOWS. AND THE FAT CATS AT THE TOP ARE OFFIN' ALL THE MOGS WHO DEFY 'EM.

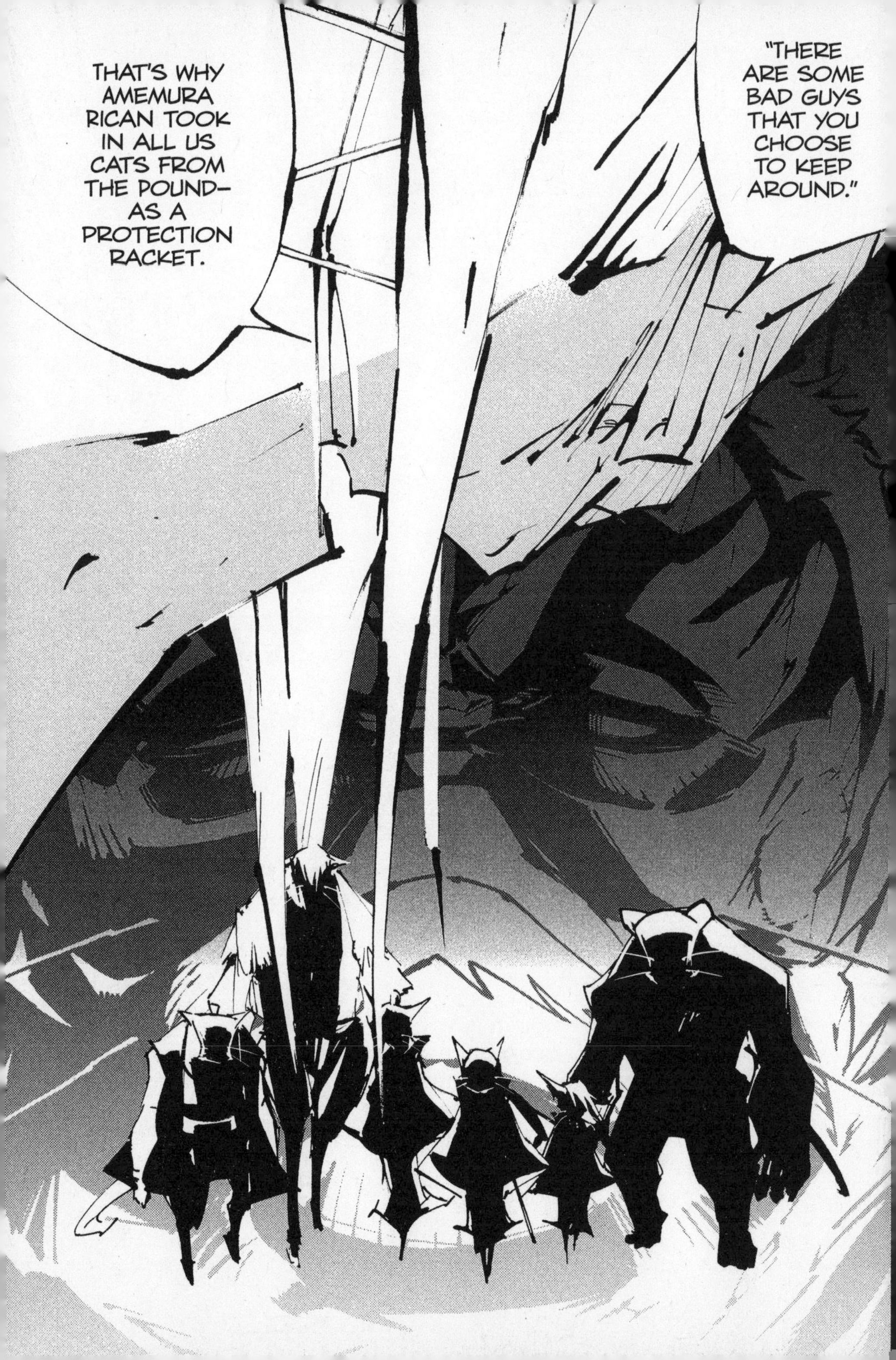
"THERE ARE SOME BAD GUYS THAT YOU CHOOSE TO KEEP AROUND."
THAT'S WHY AMEMURA RICAN TOOK IN ALL US CATS FROM THE POUND— AS A PROTECTION RACKET.

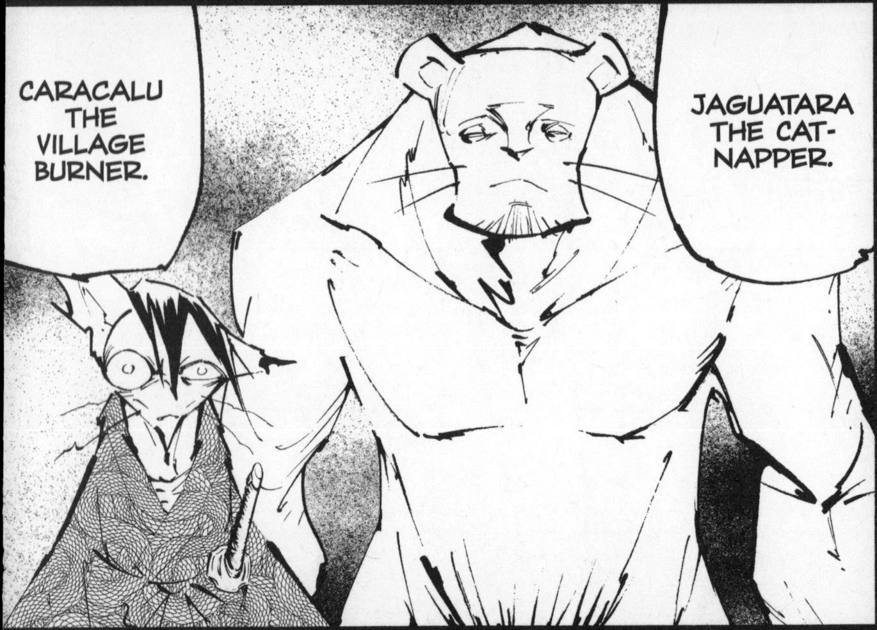
JAGUATARA THE CAT-NAPPER.
CARACALU THE VILLAGE BURNER.

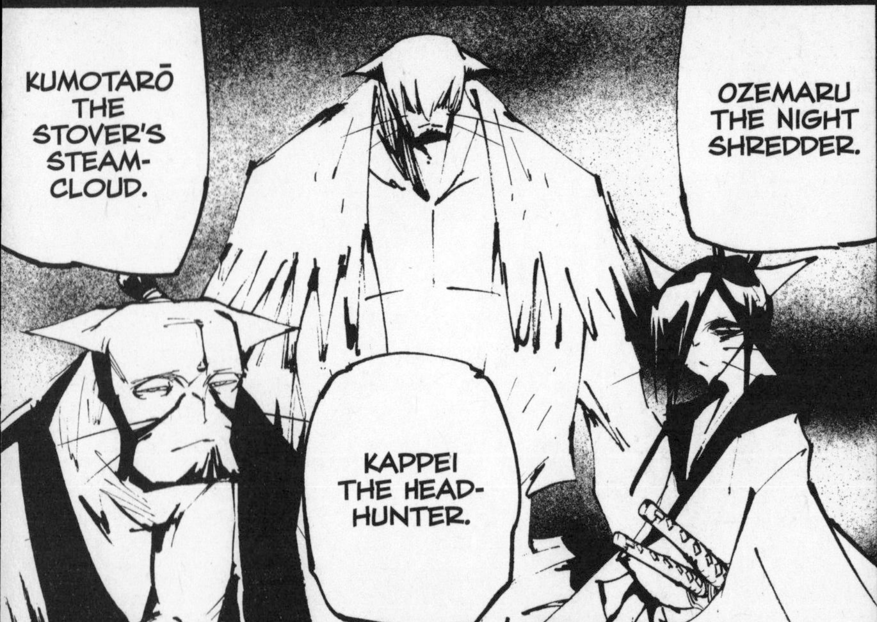
OZEMARU THE NIGHT SHREDDER.
KUMOTARŌ THE STOVER'S STEAM-CLOUD.
KAPPEI THE HEAD-HUNTER.

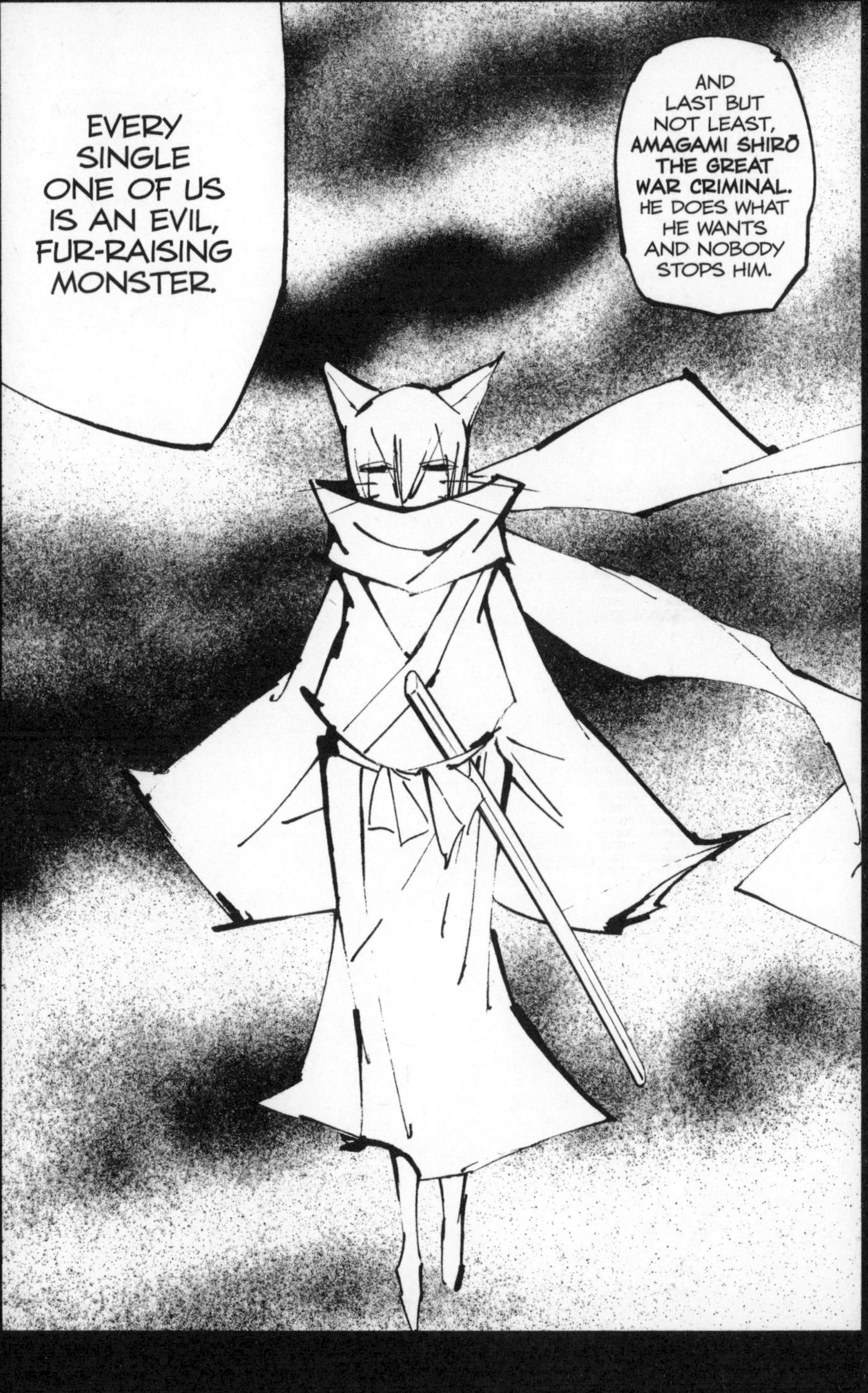
AND LAST BUT NOT LEAST, AMAGAMI SHIRŌ THE GREAT WAR CRIMINAL. HE DOES WHAT HE WANTS AND NOBODY STOPS HIM.
EVERY SINGLE ONE OF US IS AN EVIL, FUR-RAISING MONSTER.

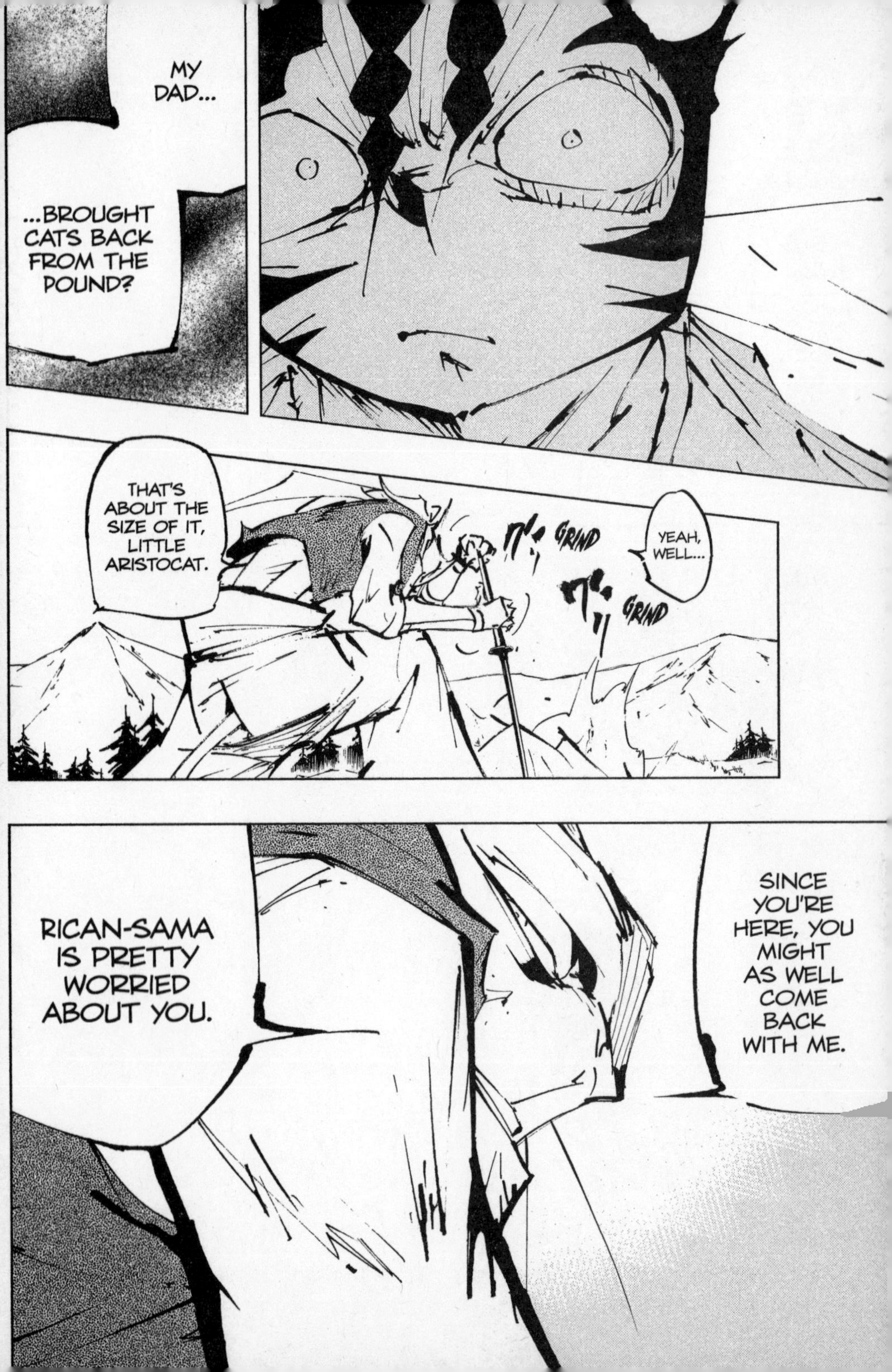
MY DAD...
...BROUGHT CATS BACK FROM THE POUND?
YEAH, WELL...
GRIND
GRIND
THAT'S ABOUT THE SIZE OF IT, LITTLE ARISTOCAT.
SINCE YOU'RE HERE, YOU MIGHT AS WELL COME BACK WITH ME.
RICAN-SAMA IS PRETTY WORRIED ABOUT YOU.

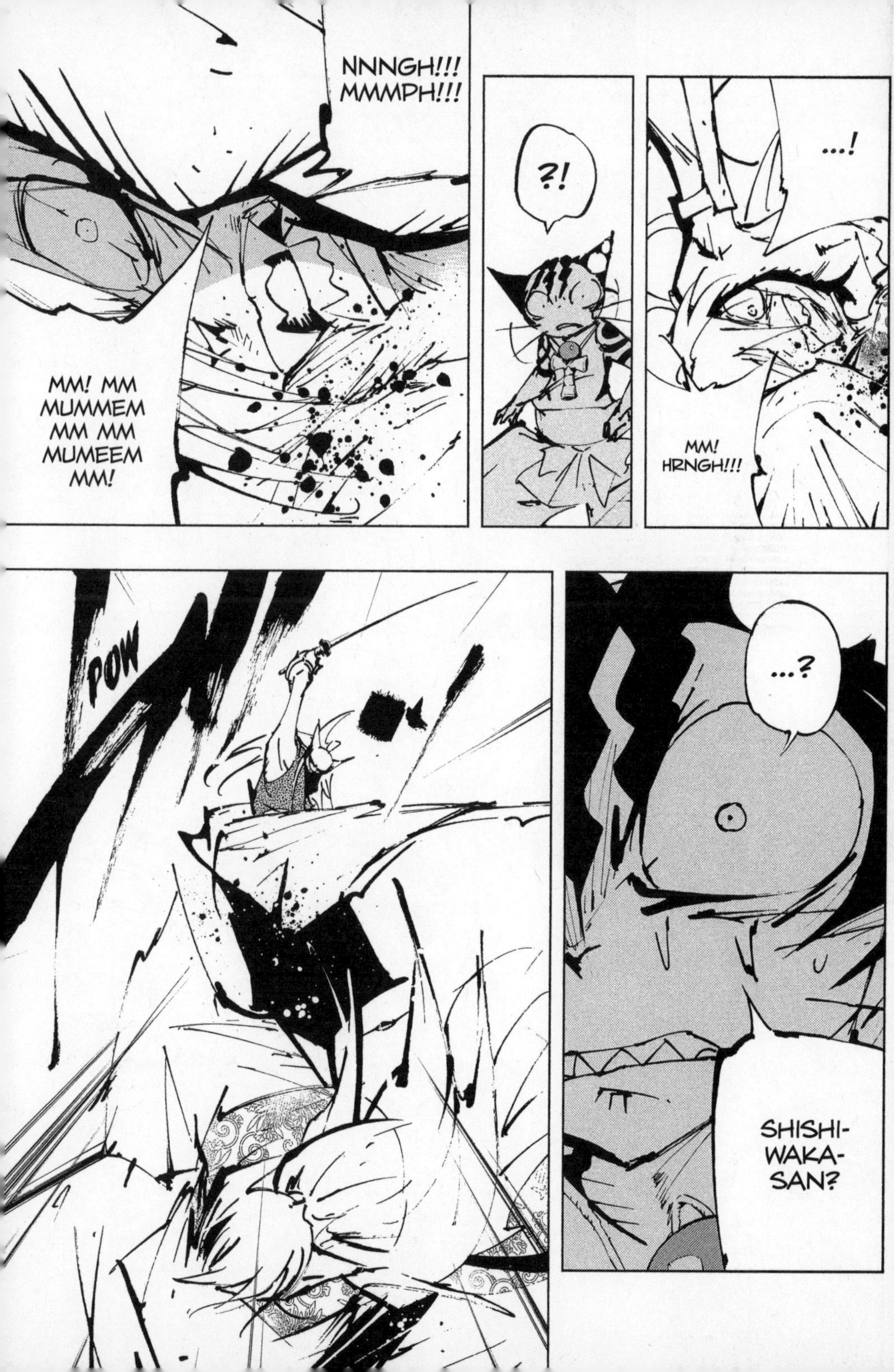
...!
MM! HRNGH!!!
?!
NNNGH!!! MMMPH!!!
MM! MM MUMMEM MM MM MUMEEM MM!
...?
SHISHI-WAKA-SAN?
POW

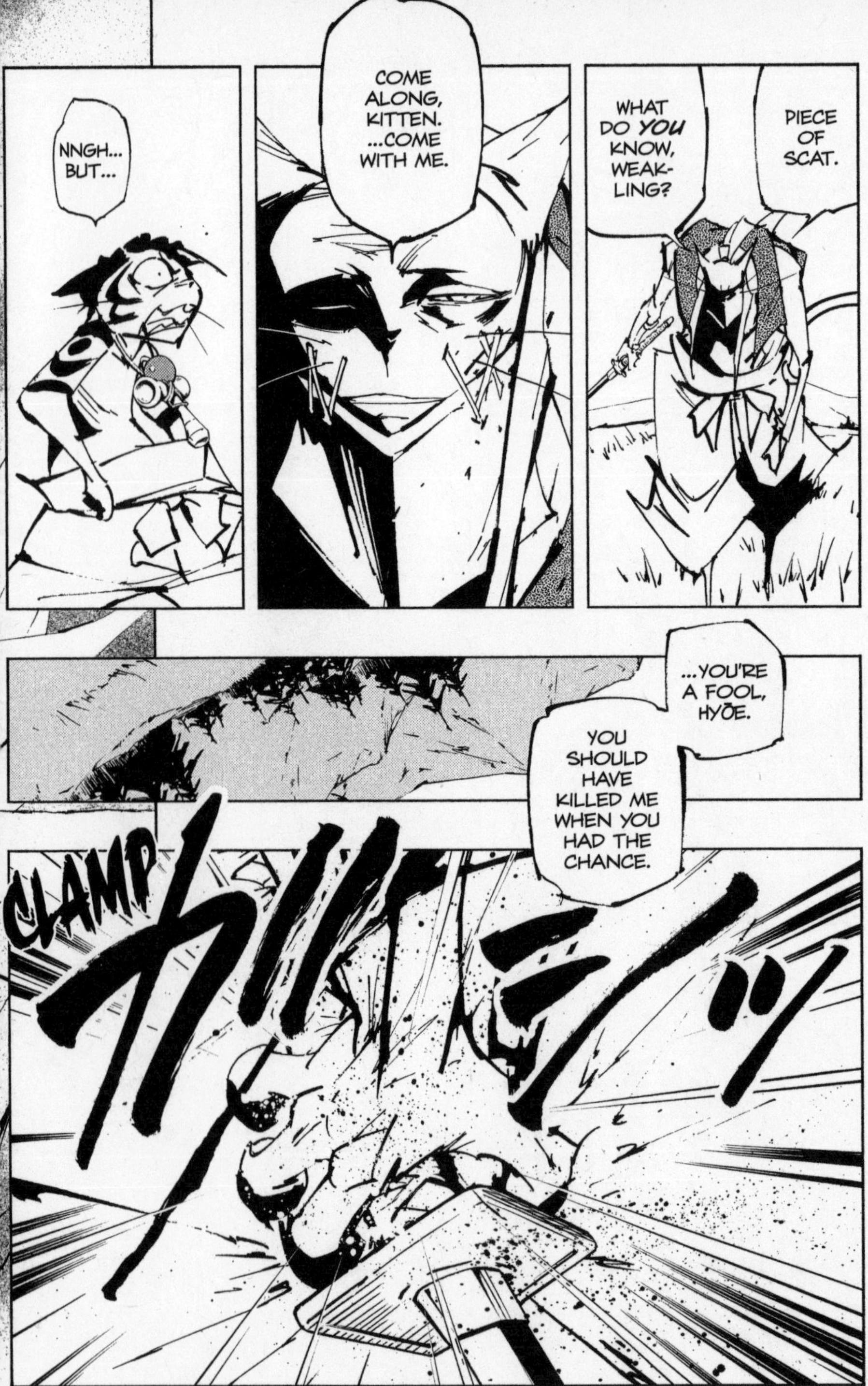
PIECE OF SCAT.
WHAT DO *YOU* KNOW, WEAK-LING?
COME ALONG, KITTEN. ...COME WITH ME.
NNGH... BUT...
...YOU'RE A FOOL, HYŌE.
YOU SHOULD HAVE KILLED ME WHEN YOU HAD THE CHANCE.
CLAMP

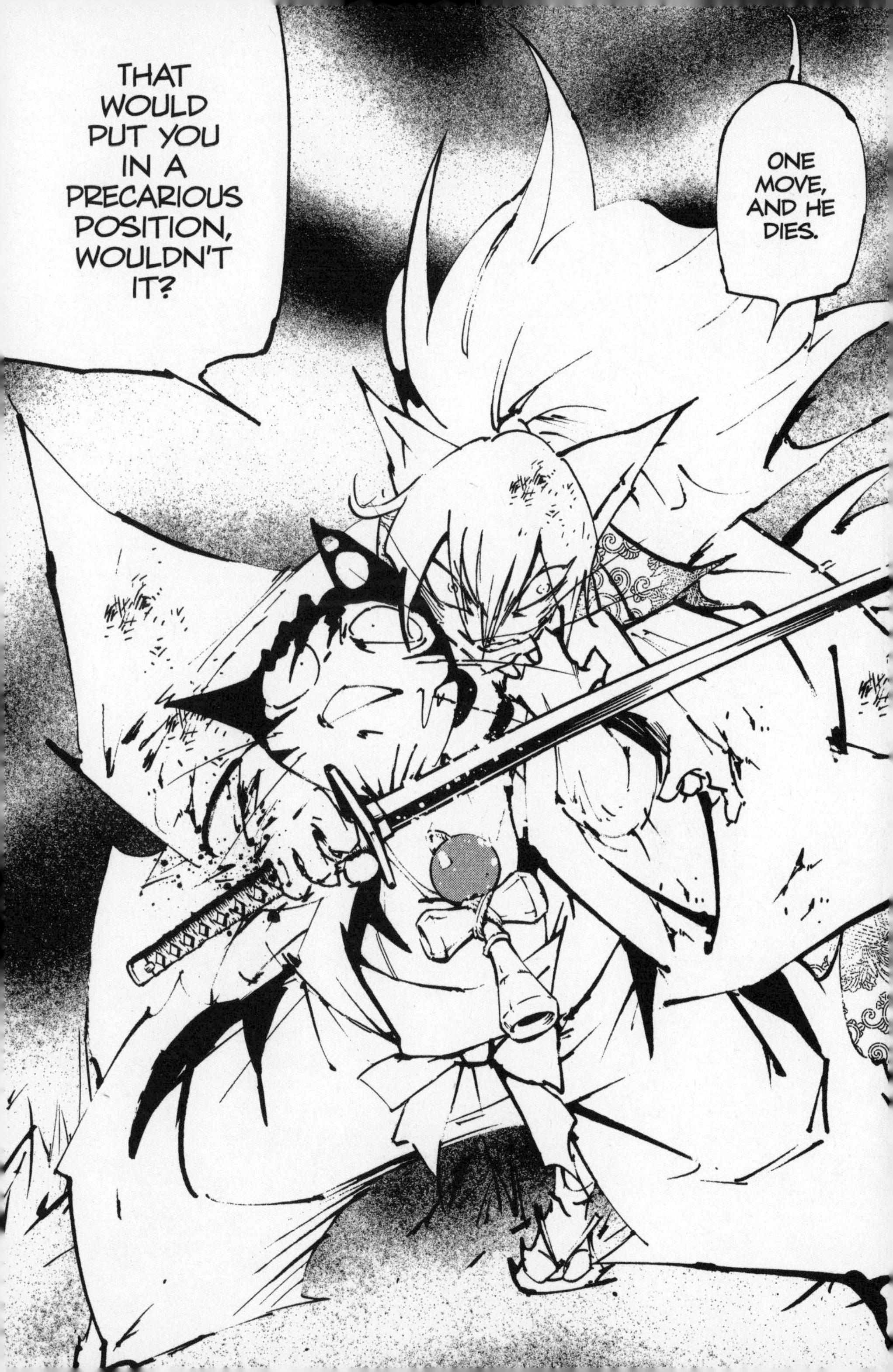
ONE MOVE, AND HE DIES.
THAT WOULD PUT YOU IN A PRECARIOUS POSITION, WOULDN'T IT?

猫ヶ原

ネコガハラ

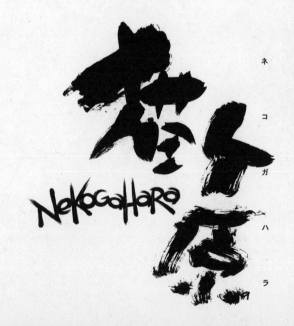

NeKoGaHaRa

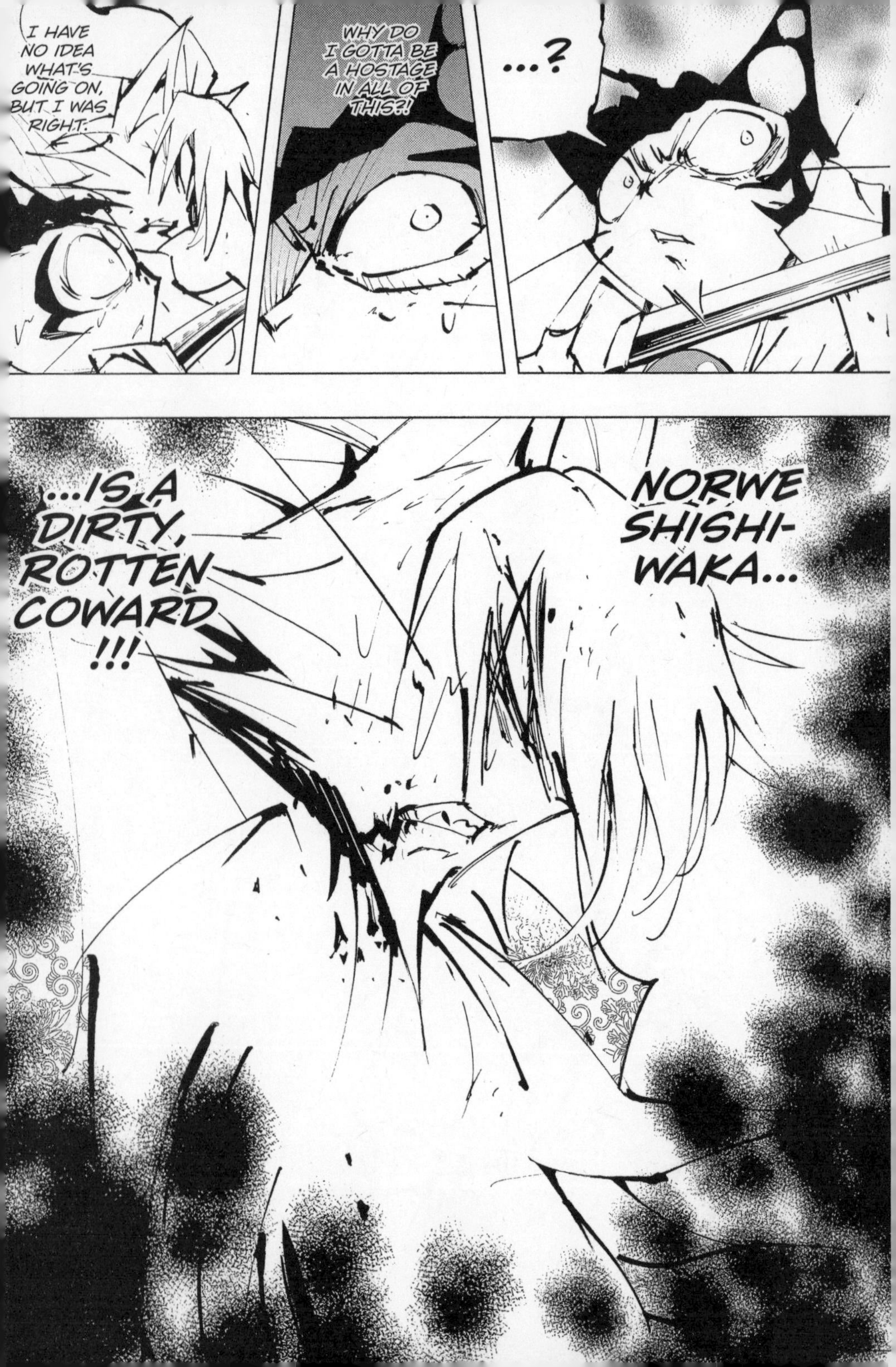
...?
WHY DO I GOTTA BE A HOSTAGE IN ALL OF THIS?!
I HAVE NO IDEA WHAT'S GOING ON, BUT I WAS RIGHT.
NORWE SHISHIWAKA...
...IS A DIRTY, ROTTEN COWARD!!!

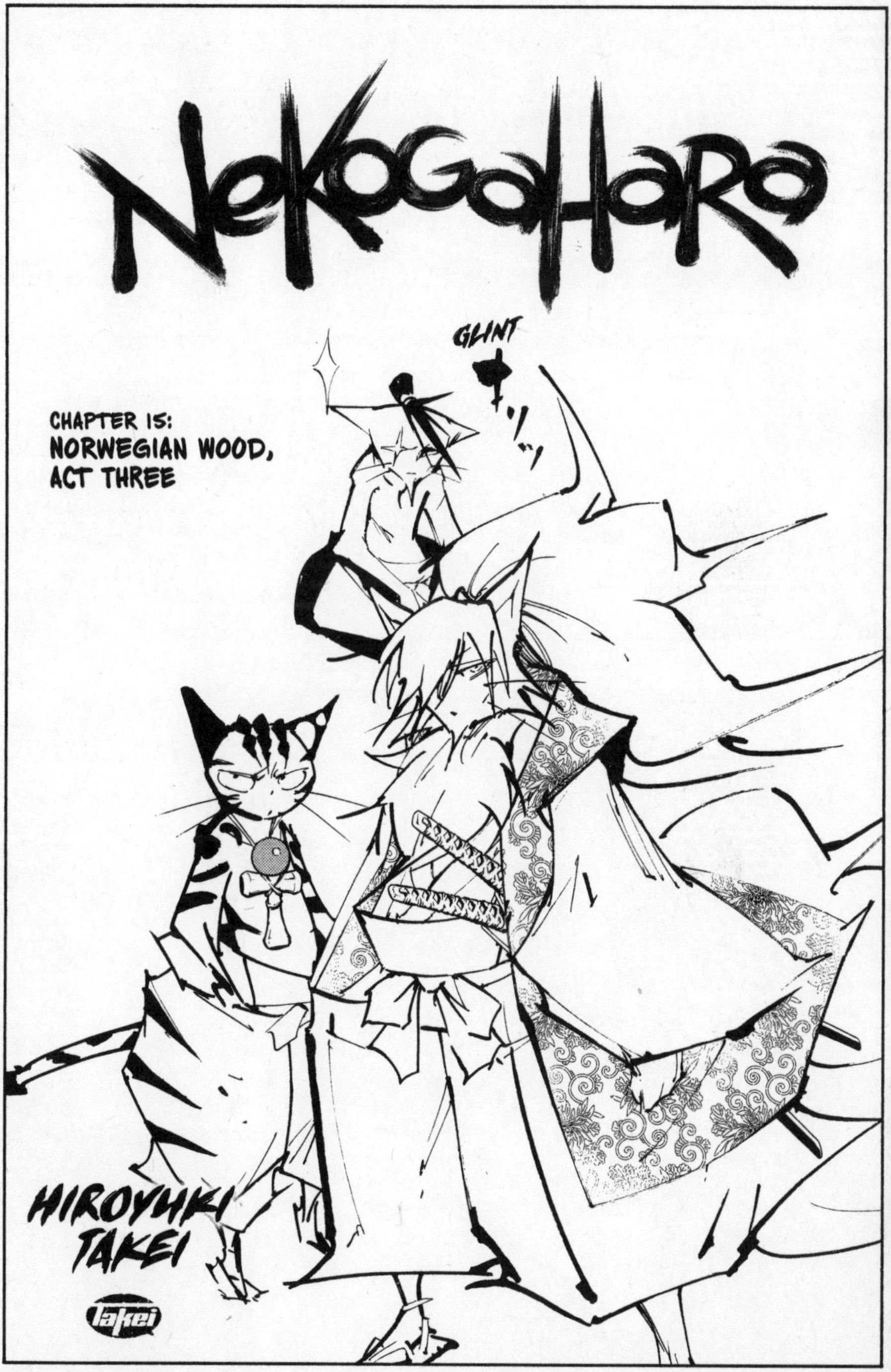
NEKOGAHARA
GLINT
CHAPTER 15:
NORWEGIAN WOOD,
ACT THREE
HIROYUKI
TAKEI
Takei

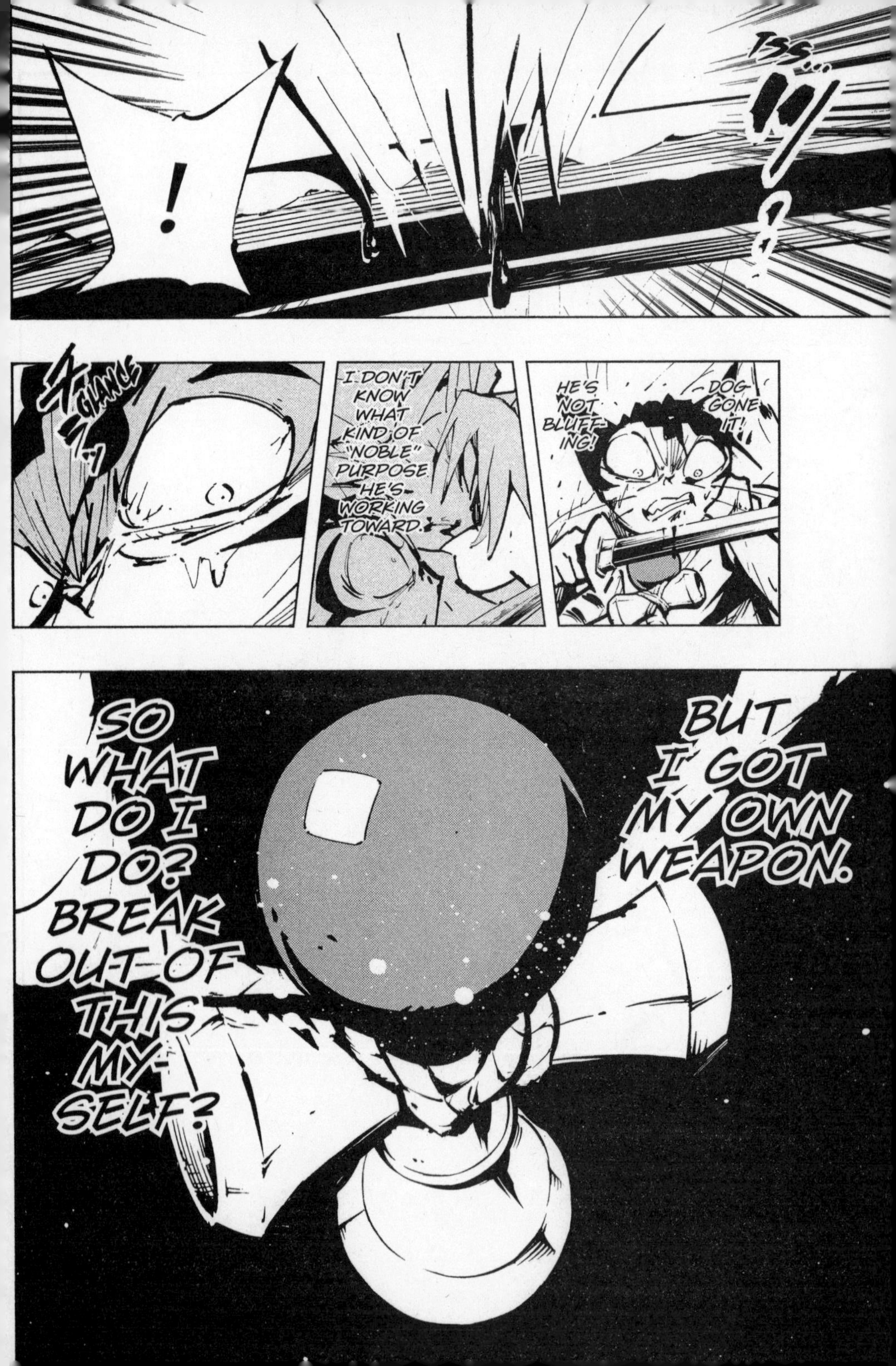
TSS...
!
DOG GONE IT!
HE'S NOT BLUFF-ING!
I DON'T KNOW WHAT KIND OF "NOBLE" PURPOSE HE'S WORKING TOWARD.
GLANCE
BUT I GOT MY OWN WEAPON.
SO WHAT DO I DO? BREAK OUT OF THIS MY-SELF?

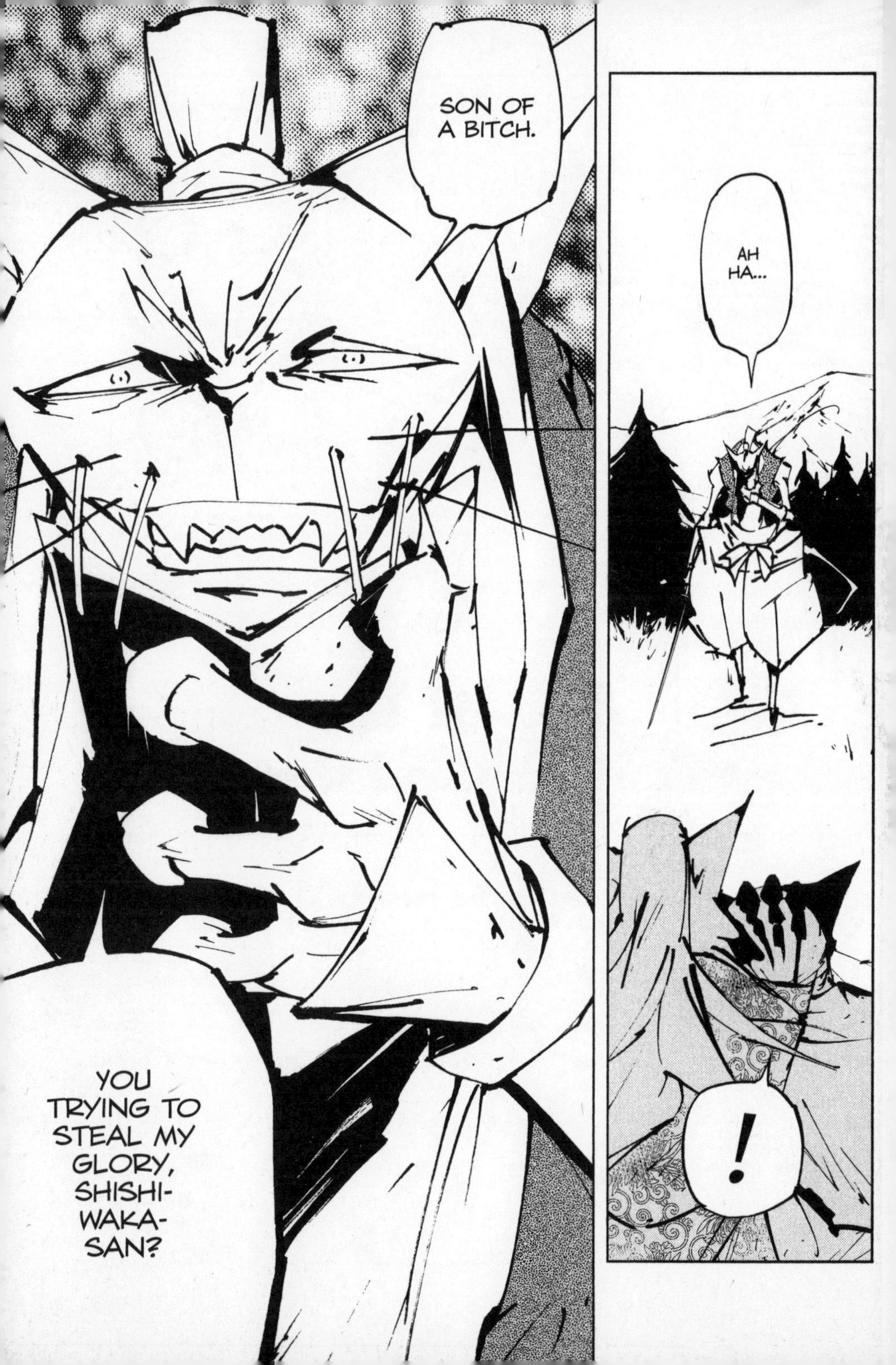
AH HA...
!
SON OF A BITCH.
YOU TRYING TO STEAL MY GLORY, SHISHIWAKA-SAN?

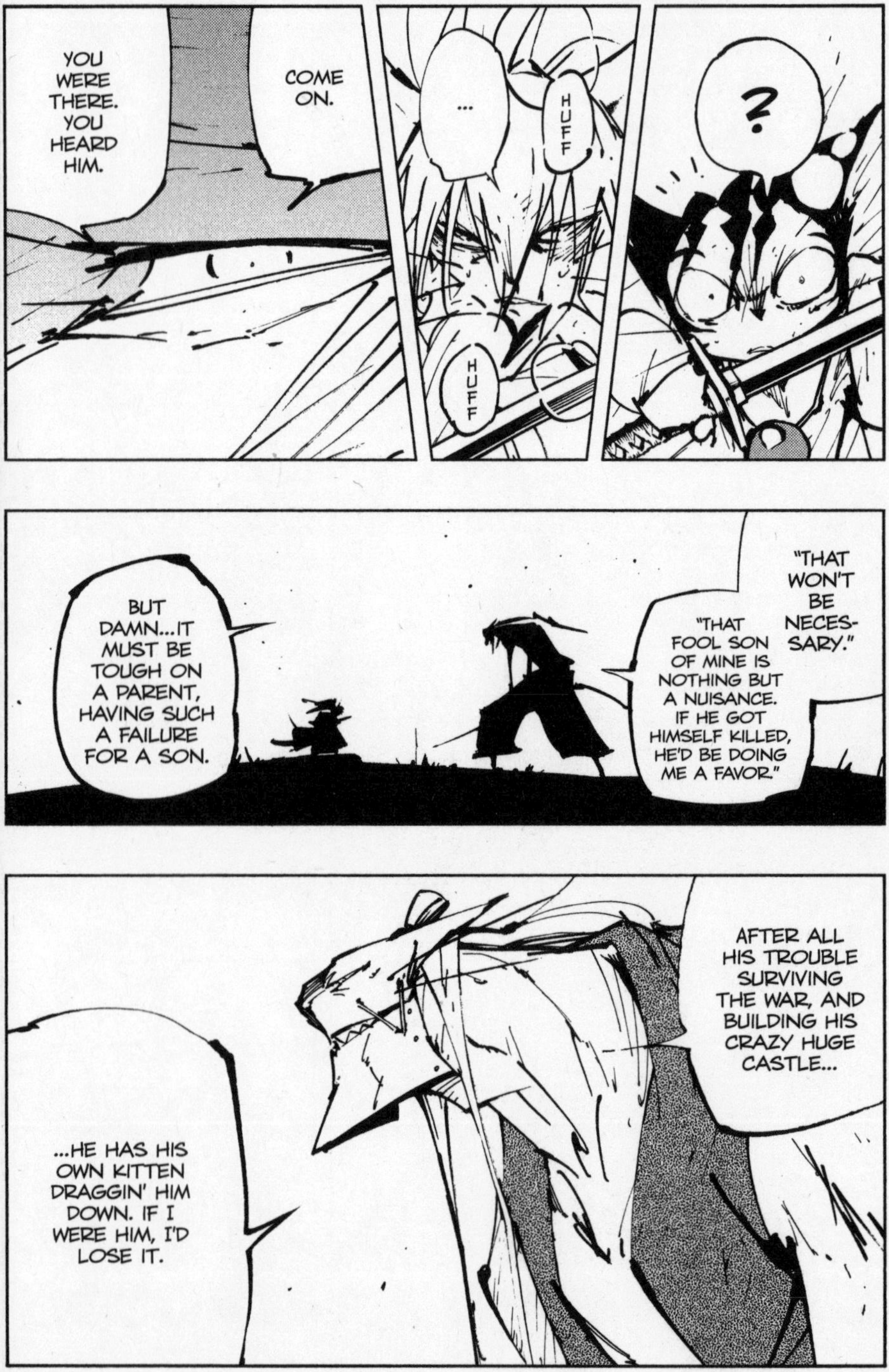
?
HUFF
...
HUFF
COME ON.
YOU WERE THERE. YOU HEARD HIM.
"THAT WON'T BE NECES-SARY."
"THAT FOOL SON OF MINE IS NOTHING BUT A NUISANCE. IF HE GOT HIMSELF KILLED, HE'D BE DOING ME A FAVOR."
BUT DAMN...IT MUST BE TOUGH ON A PARENT, HAVING SUCH A FAILURE FOR A SON.
AFTER ALL HIS TROUBLE SURVIVING THE WAR, AND BUILDING HIS CRAZY HUGE CASTLE...
...HE HAS HIS OWN KITTEN DRAGGIN' HIM DOWN. IF I WERE HIM, I'D LOSE IT.

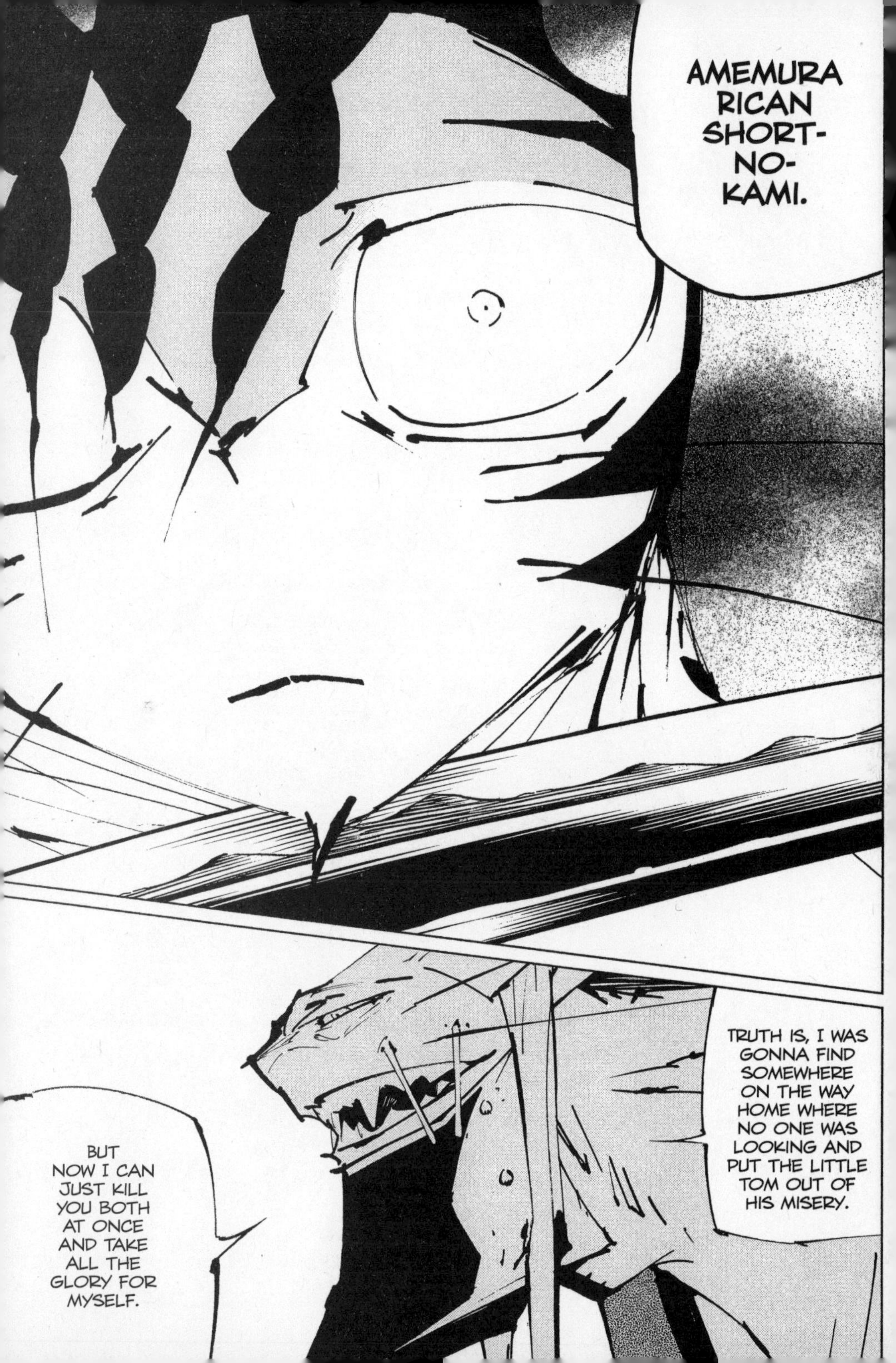
AMEMURA RICAN SHORT-NO-KAMI.
TRUTH IS, I WAS GONNA FIND SOMEWHERE ON THE WAY HOME WHERE NO ONE WAS LOOKING AND PUT THE LITTLE TOM OUT OF HIS MISERY.
BUT NOW I CAN JUST KILL YOU BOTH AT ONCE AND TAKE ALL THE GLORY FOR MYSELF.

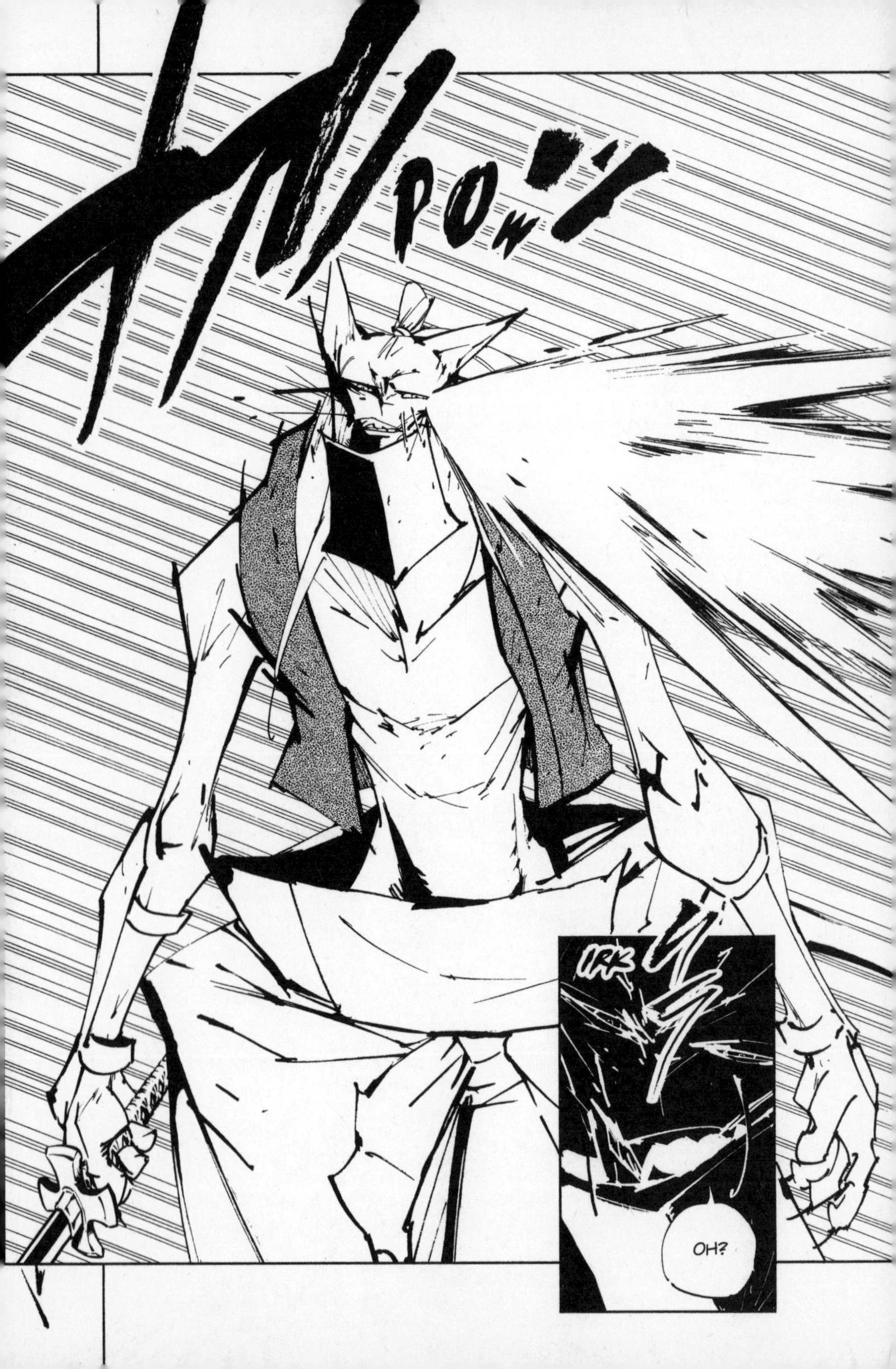
POW!
IRK
OH?

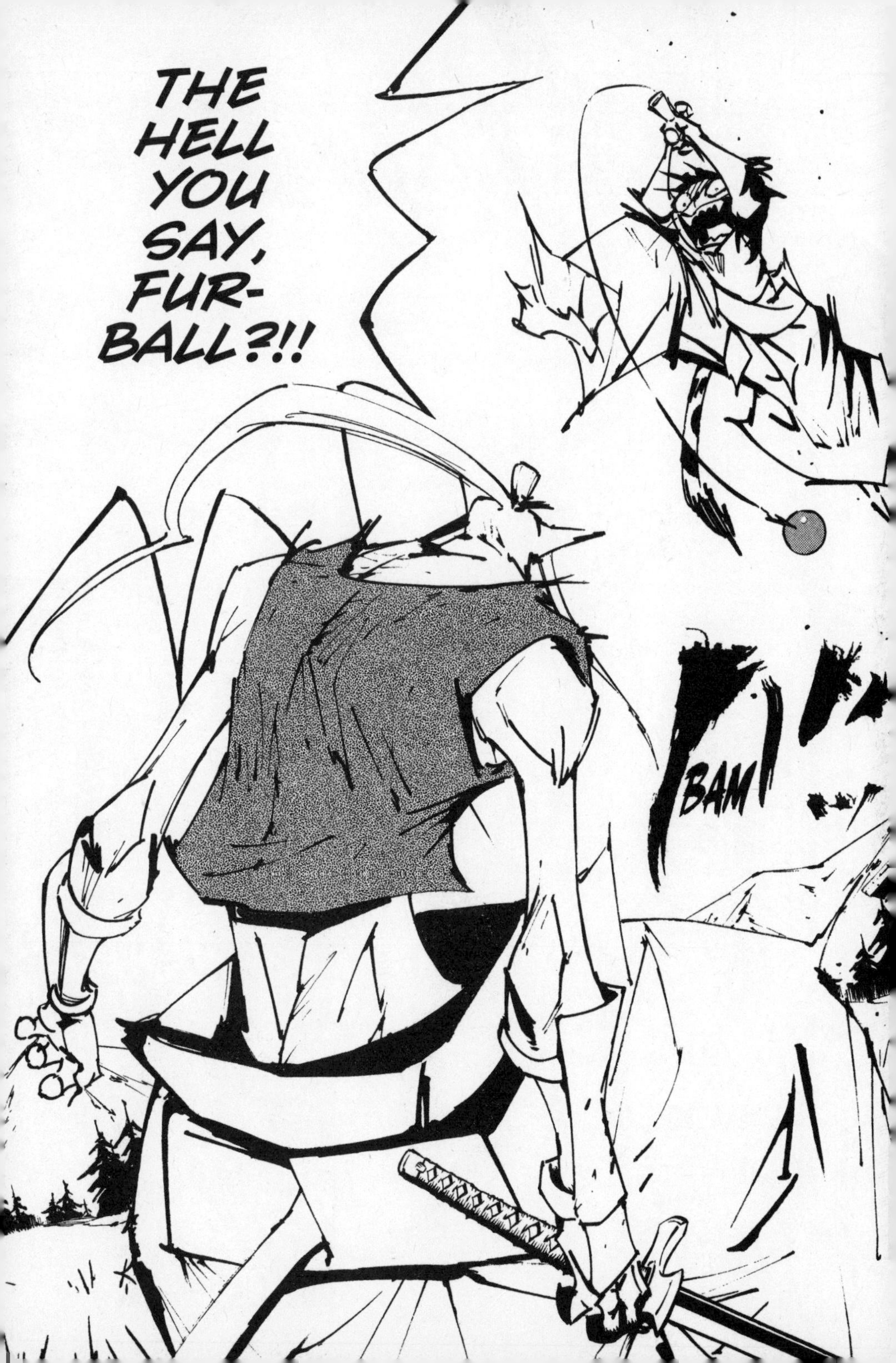
THE HELL YOU SAY, FUR-BALL?!!
BAM

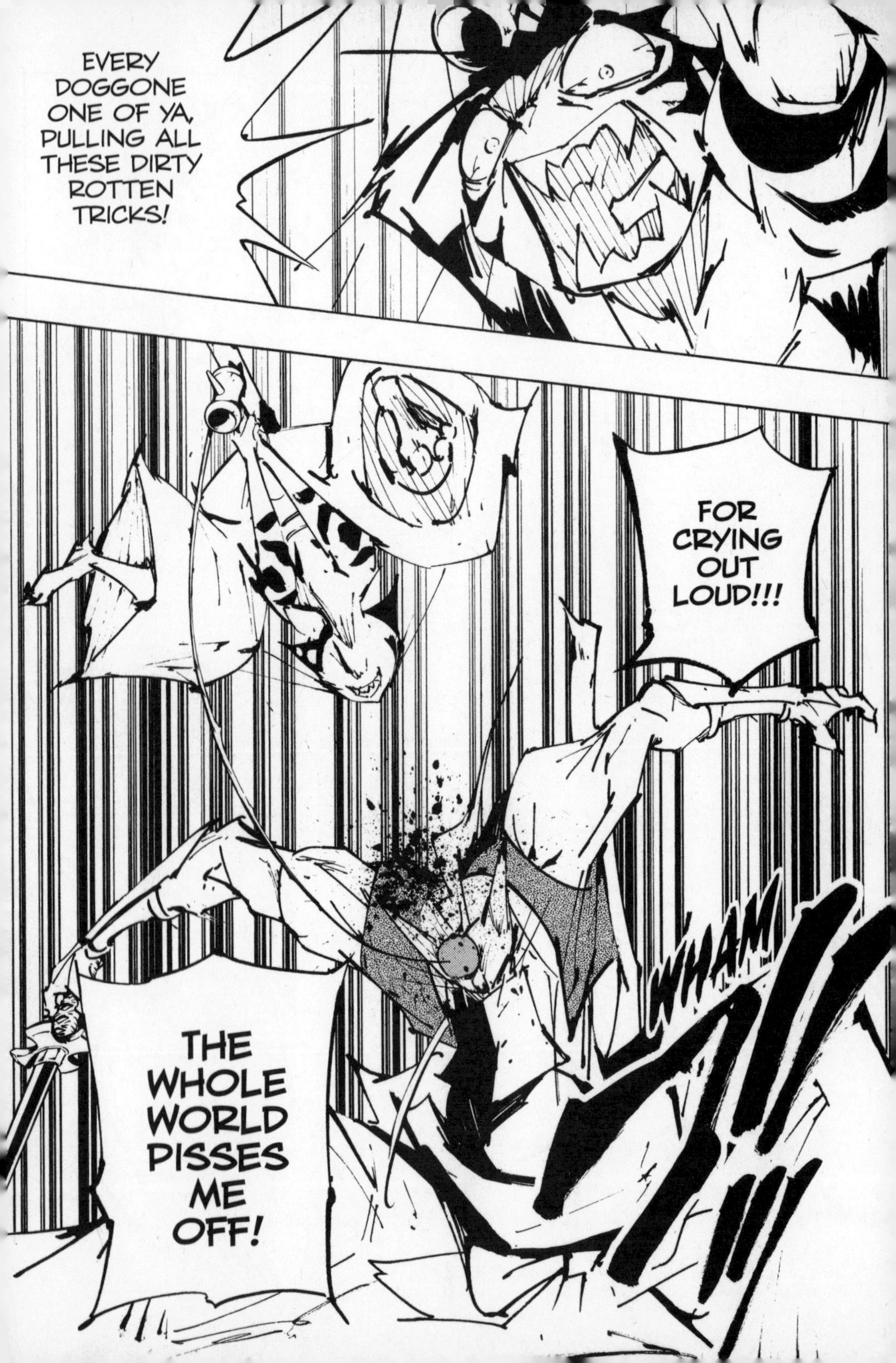
EVERY DOGGONE ONE OF YA, PULLING ALL THESE DIRTY ROTTEN TRICKS!
FOR CRYING OUT LOUD!!!
WHAM
THE WHOLE WORLD PISSES ME OFF!

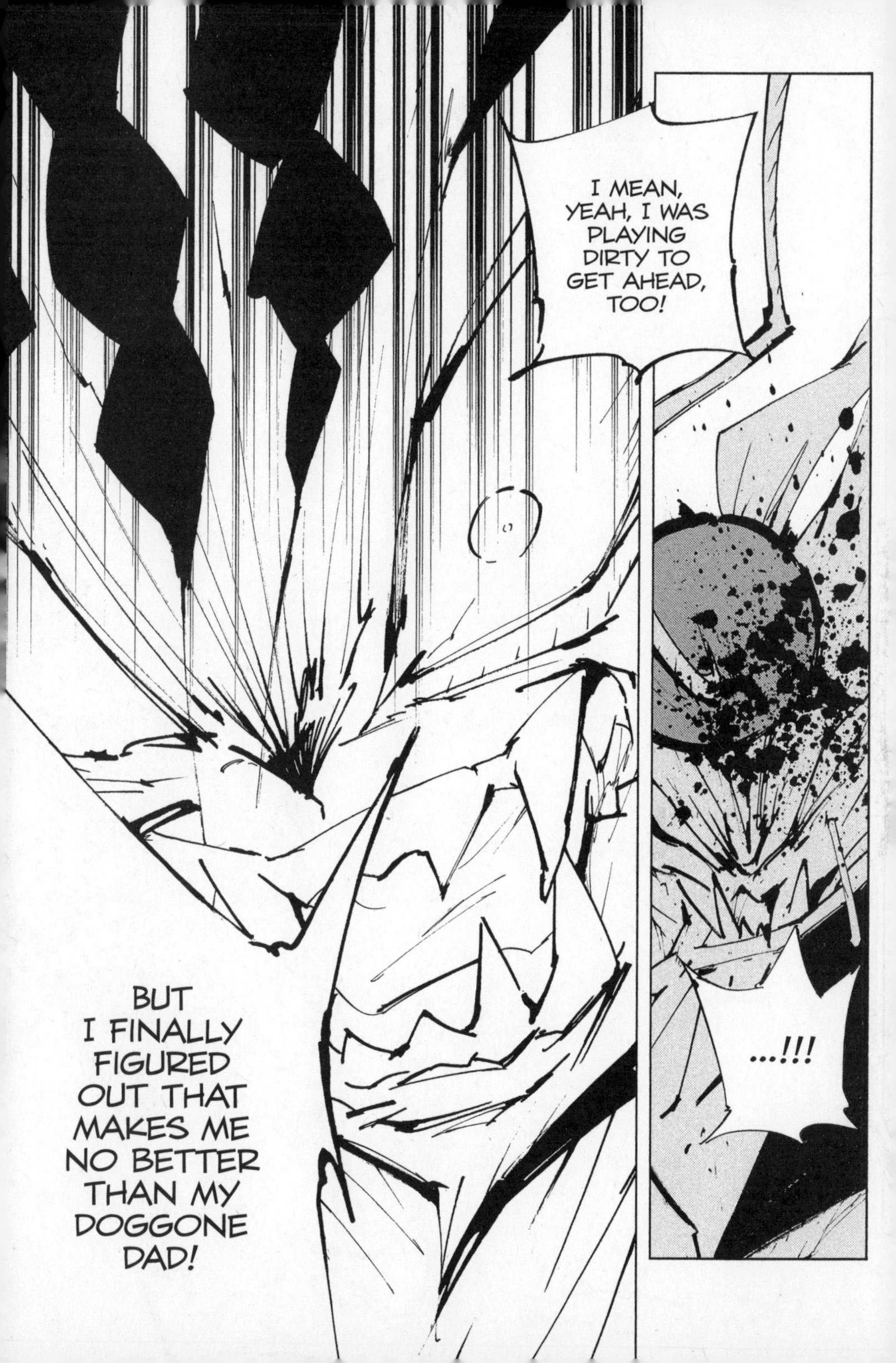
I MEAN, YEAH, I WAS PLAYING DIRTY TO GET AHEAD, TOO!
...!!!
BUT I FINALLY FIGURED OUT THAT MAKES ME NO BETTER THAN MY DOGGONE DAD!

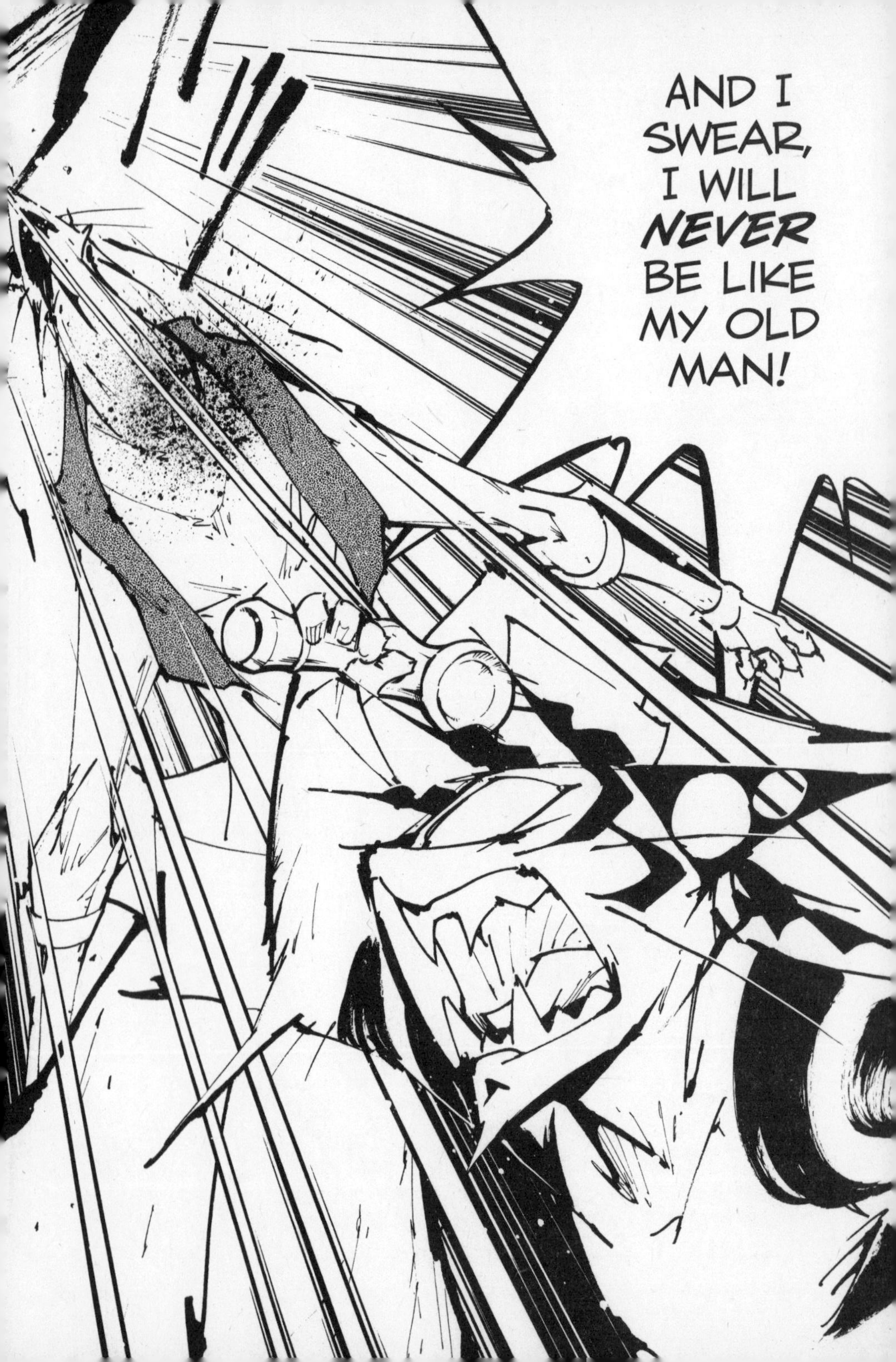
AND I SWEAR, I WILL NEVER BE LIKE MY OLD MAN!

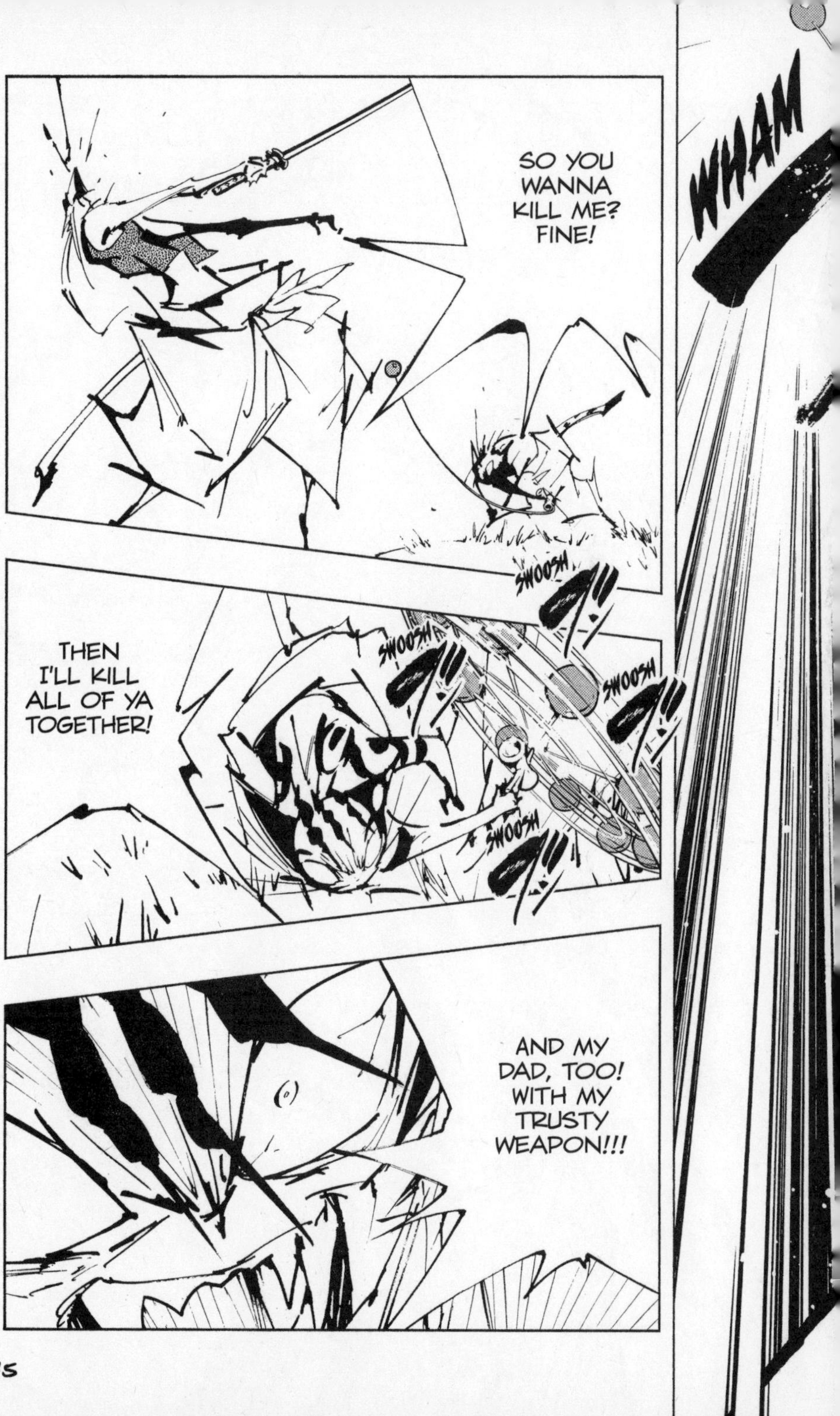
WHAM
SO YOU WANNA KILL ME? FINE!
SWOOSH
SWOOSH
SWOOSH
THEN I'LL KILL ALL OF YA TOGETHER!
SWOOSH
AND MY DAD, TOO! WITH MY TRUSTY WEAPON!!!

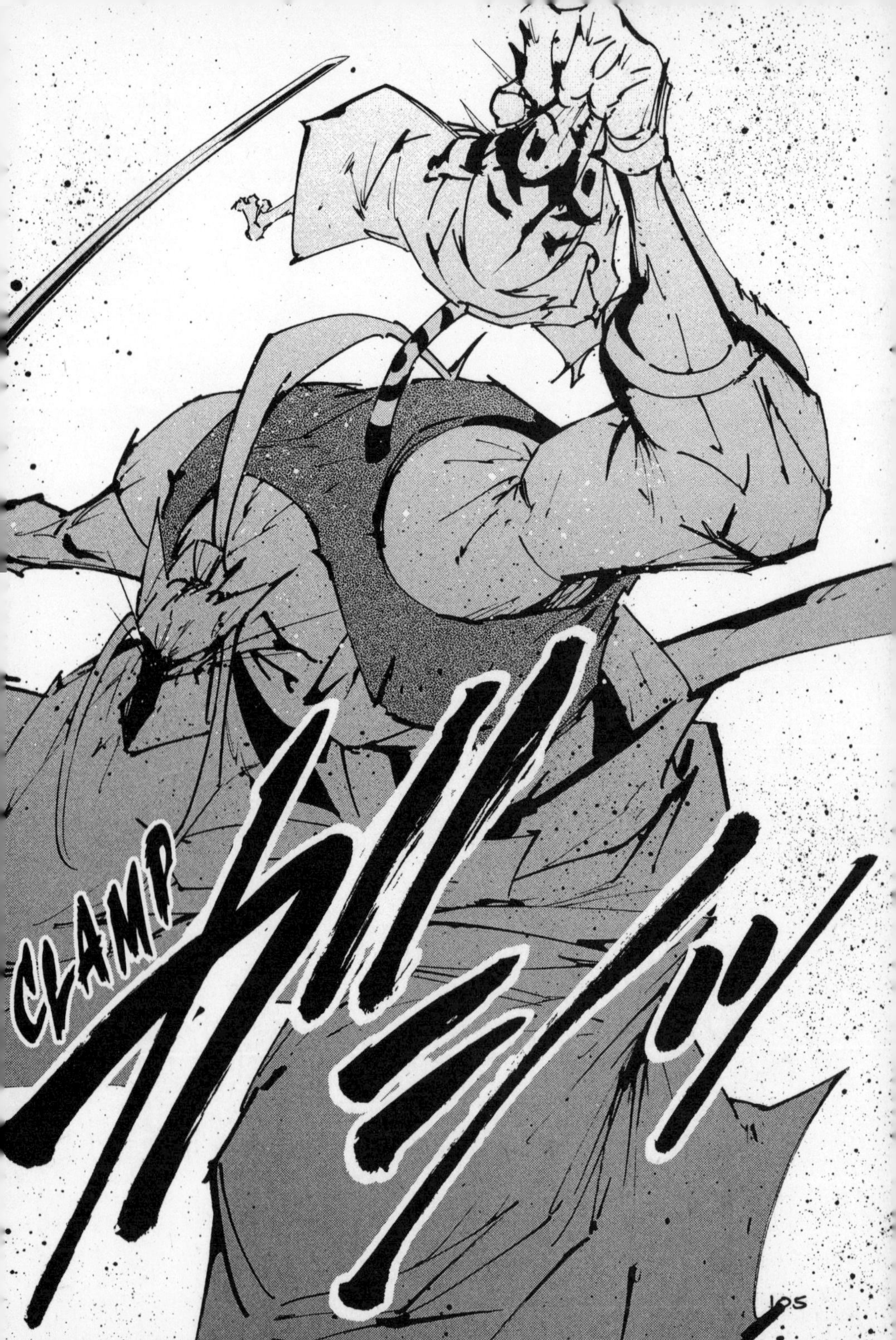
CLAMP

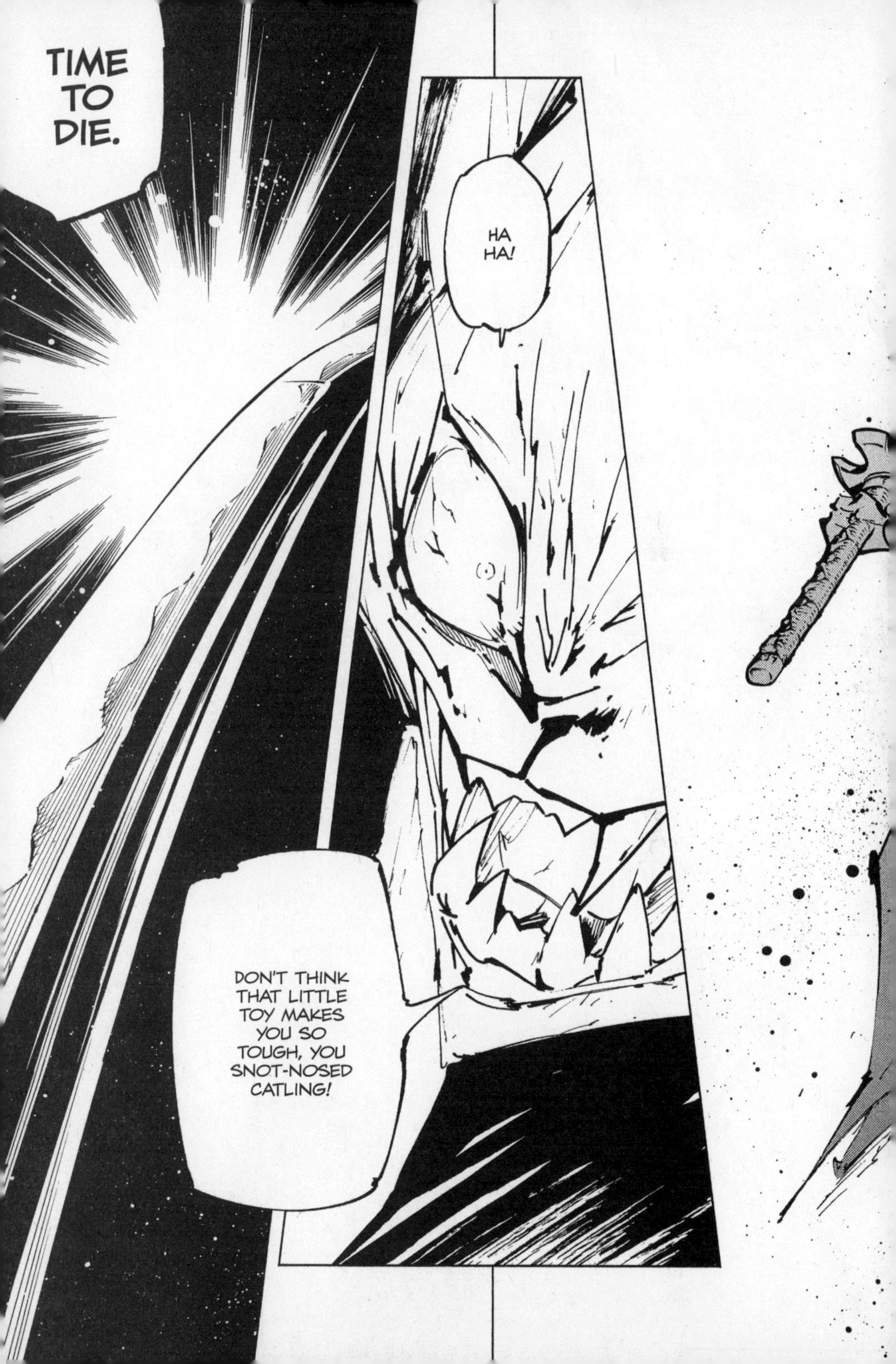
HA HA!
DON'T THINK THAT LITTLE TOY MAKES YOU SO TOUGH, YOU SNOT-NOSED CATLING!
TIME TO DIE.

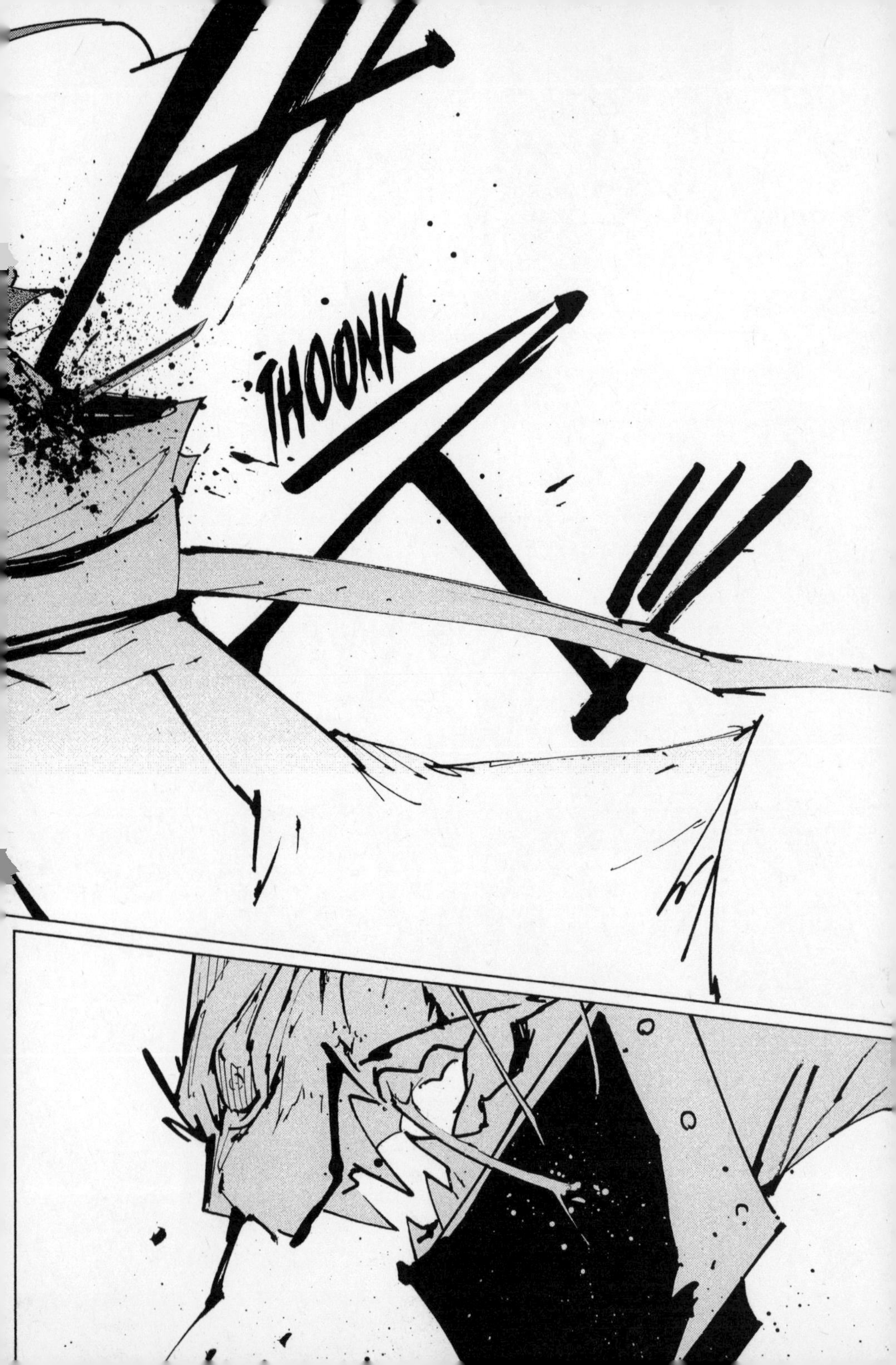
THOONK

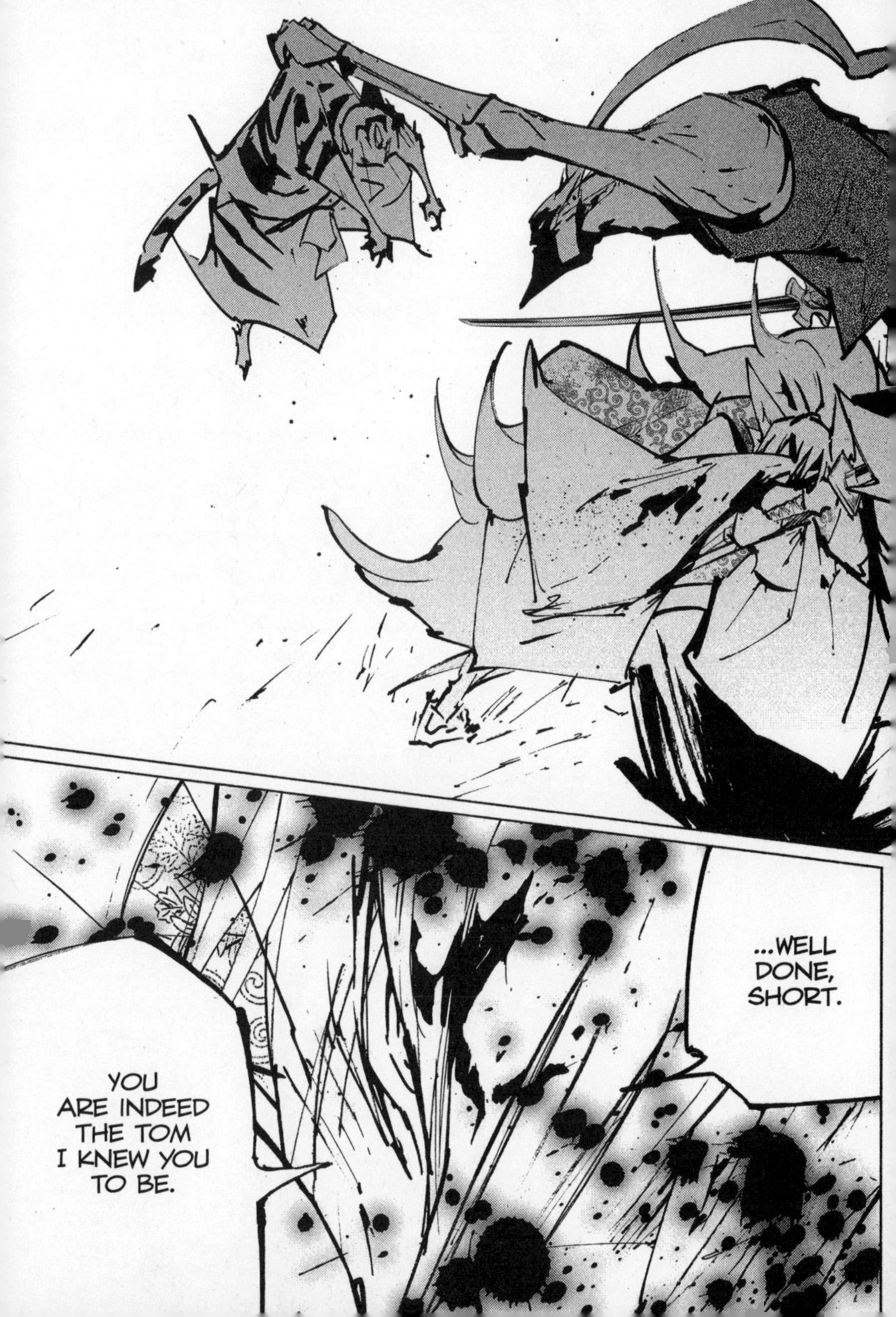
...WELL DONE, SHORT.
YOU ARE INDEED THE TOM I KNEW YOU TO BE.

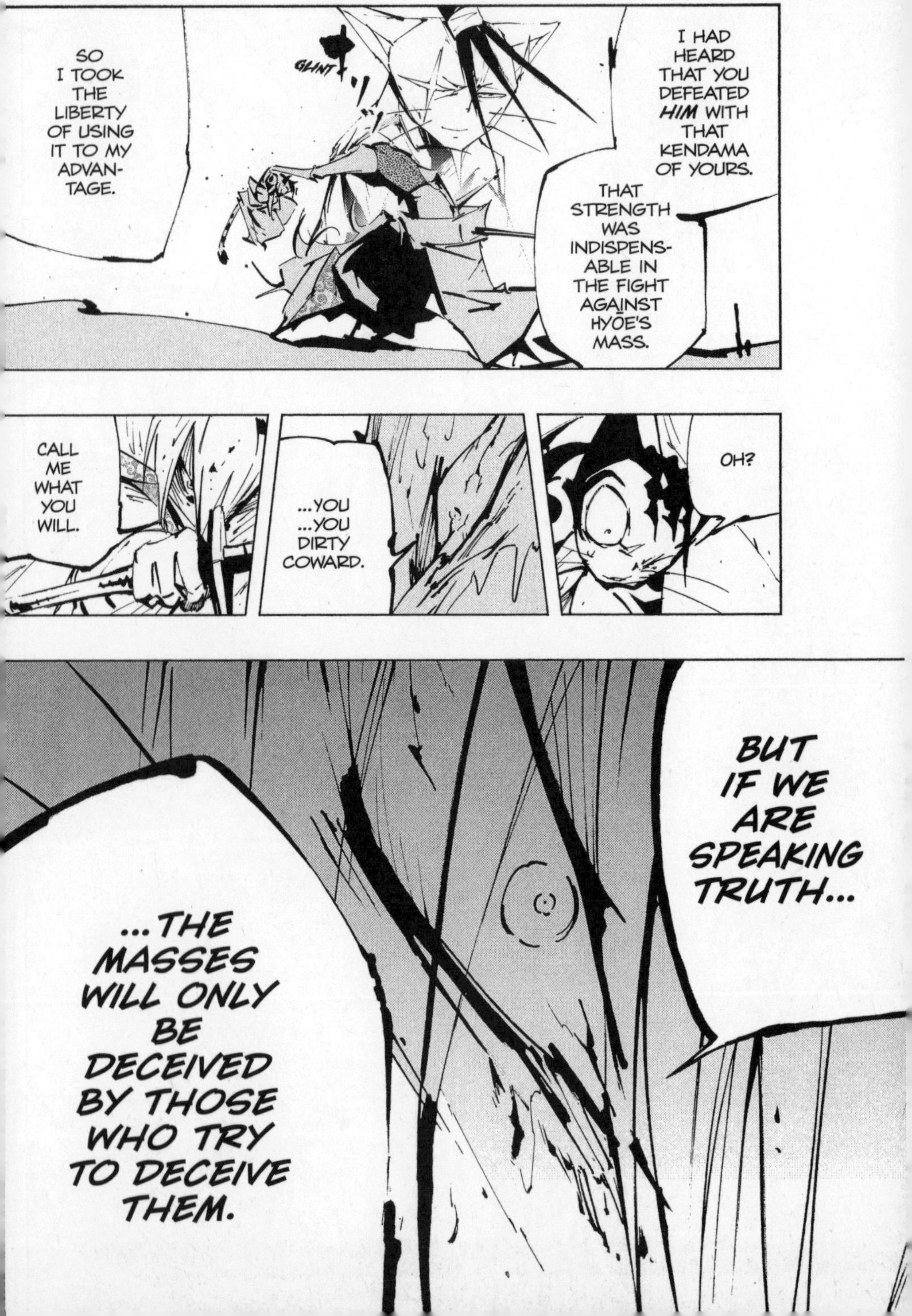
I HAD HEARD THAT YOU DEFEATED *HIM* WITH THAT KENDAMA OF YOURS.
THAT STRENGTH WAS INDISPENSABLE IN THE FIGHT AGAINST HYŌE'S MASS.
GLINT
SO I TOOK THE LIBERTY OF USING IT TO MY ADVANTAGE.
OH?
...YOU ...YOU DIRTY COWARD.
CALL ME WHAT YOU WILL.
BUT IF WE ARE SPEAKING TRUTH...
...THE MASSES WILL ONLY BE DECEIVED BY THOSE WHO TRY TO DECEIVE THEM.

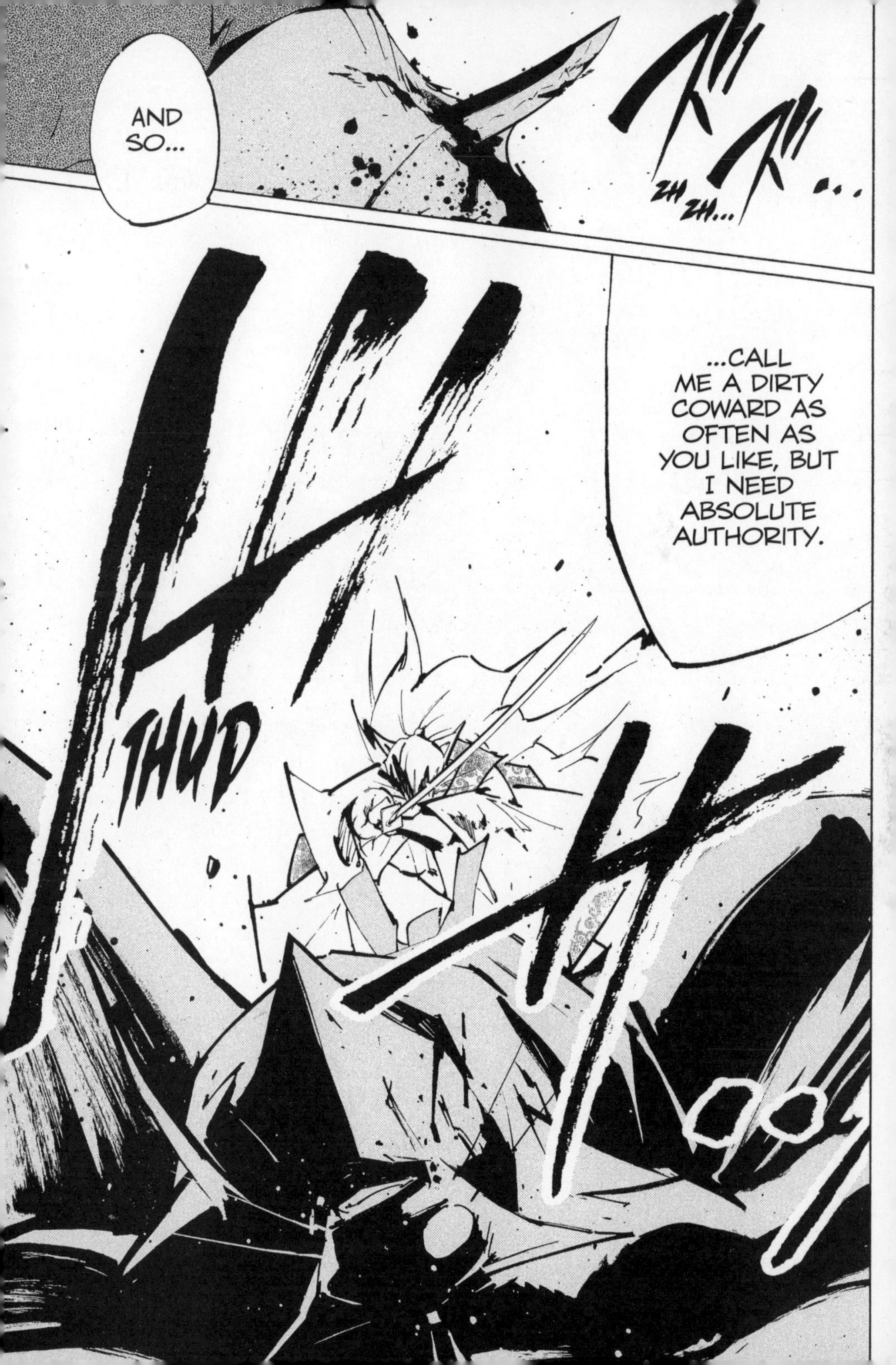
ZH ZH...
AND SO...
...CALL ME A DIRTY COWARD AS OFTEN AS YOU LIKE, BUT I NEED ABSOLUTE AUTHORITY.
THUD

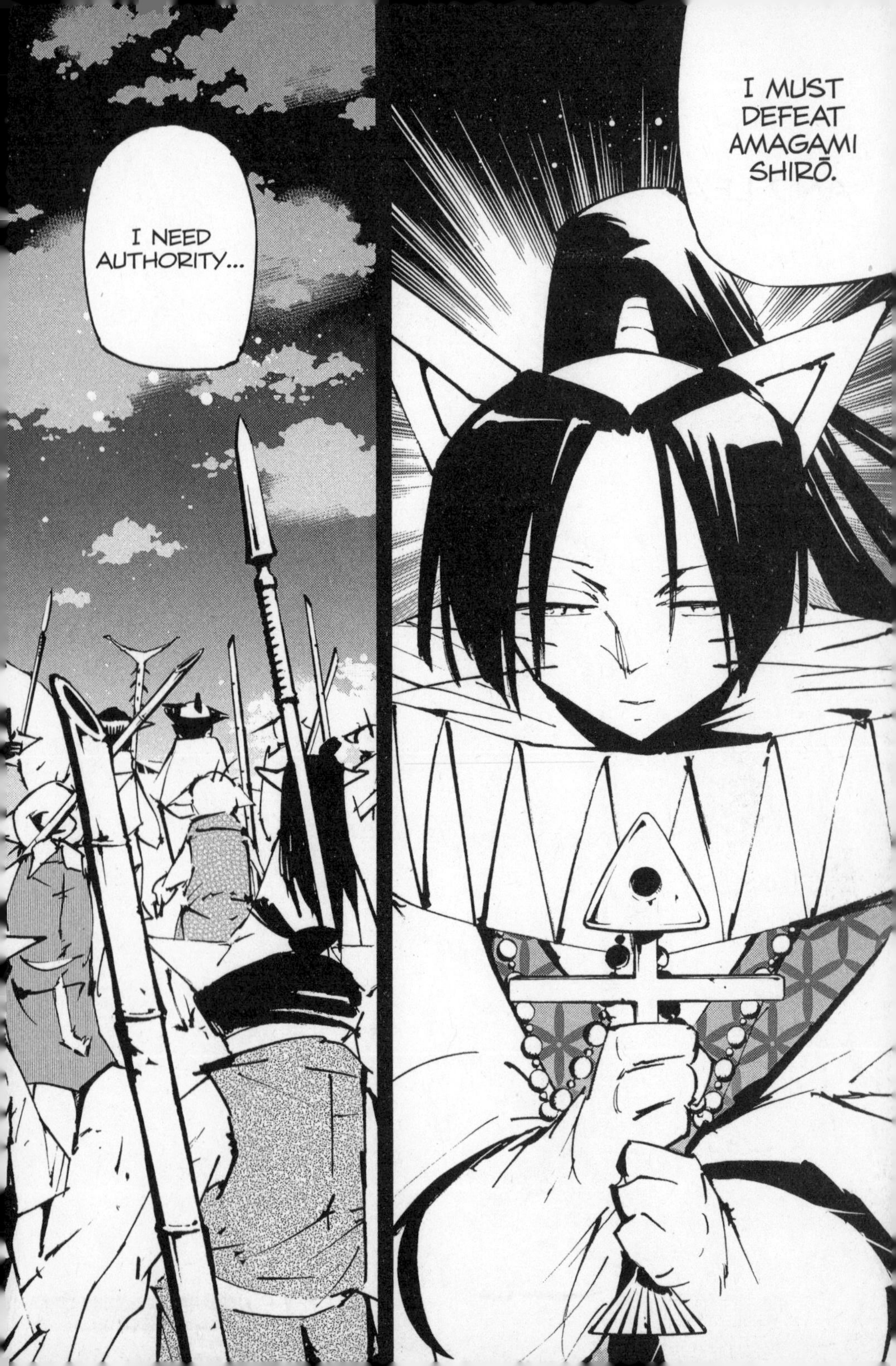
I MUST DEFEAT AMAGAMI SHIRŌ.
I NEED AUTHORITY...

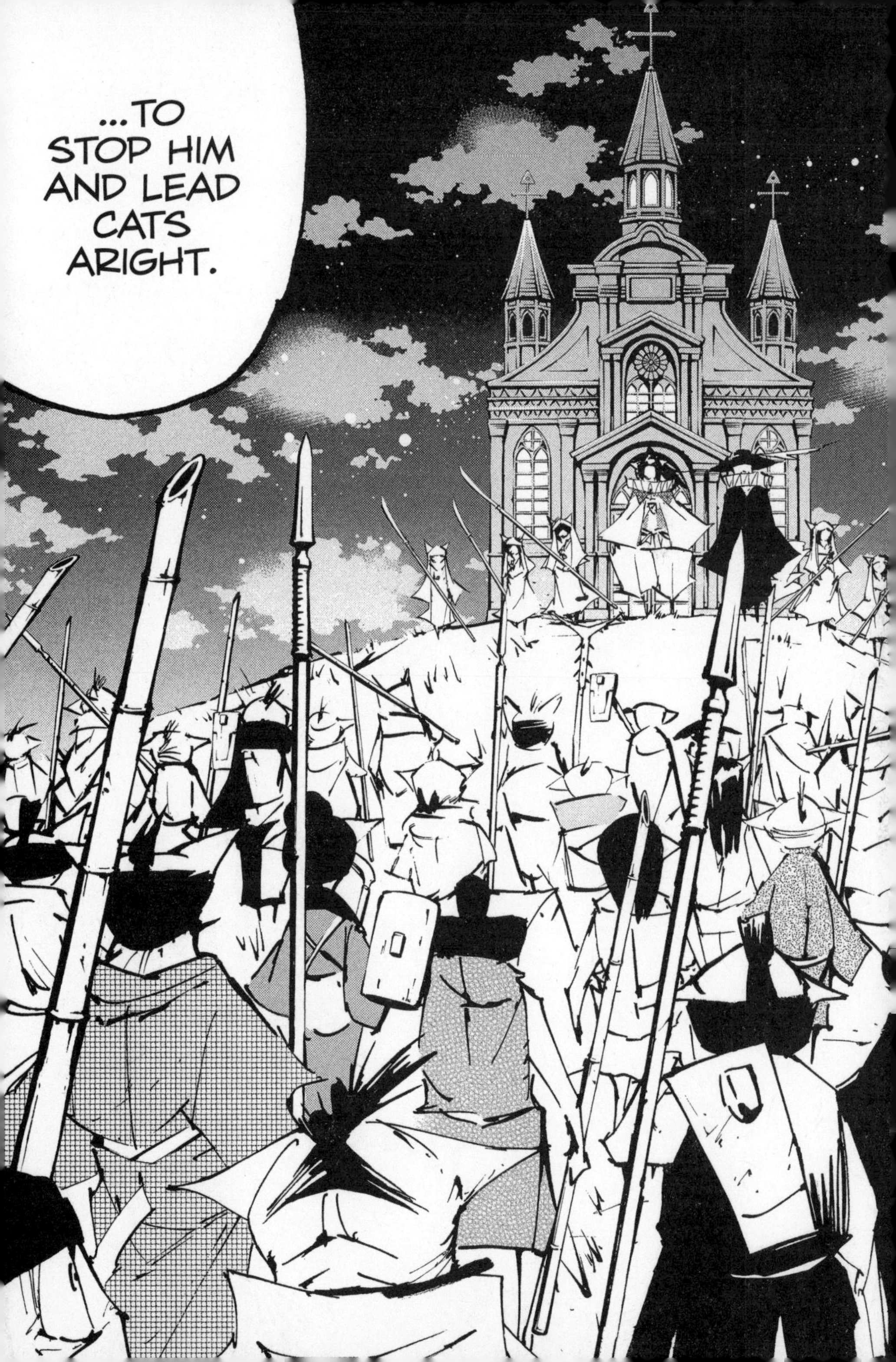
...TO STOP HIM AND LEAD CATS ARIGHT.

NeKoGaHaRa

ネコガハラ

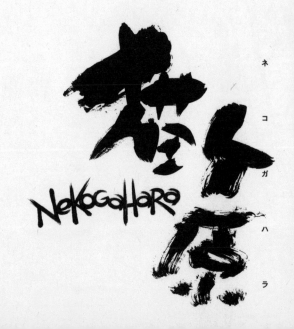

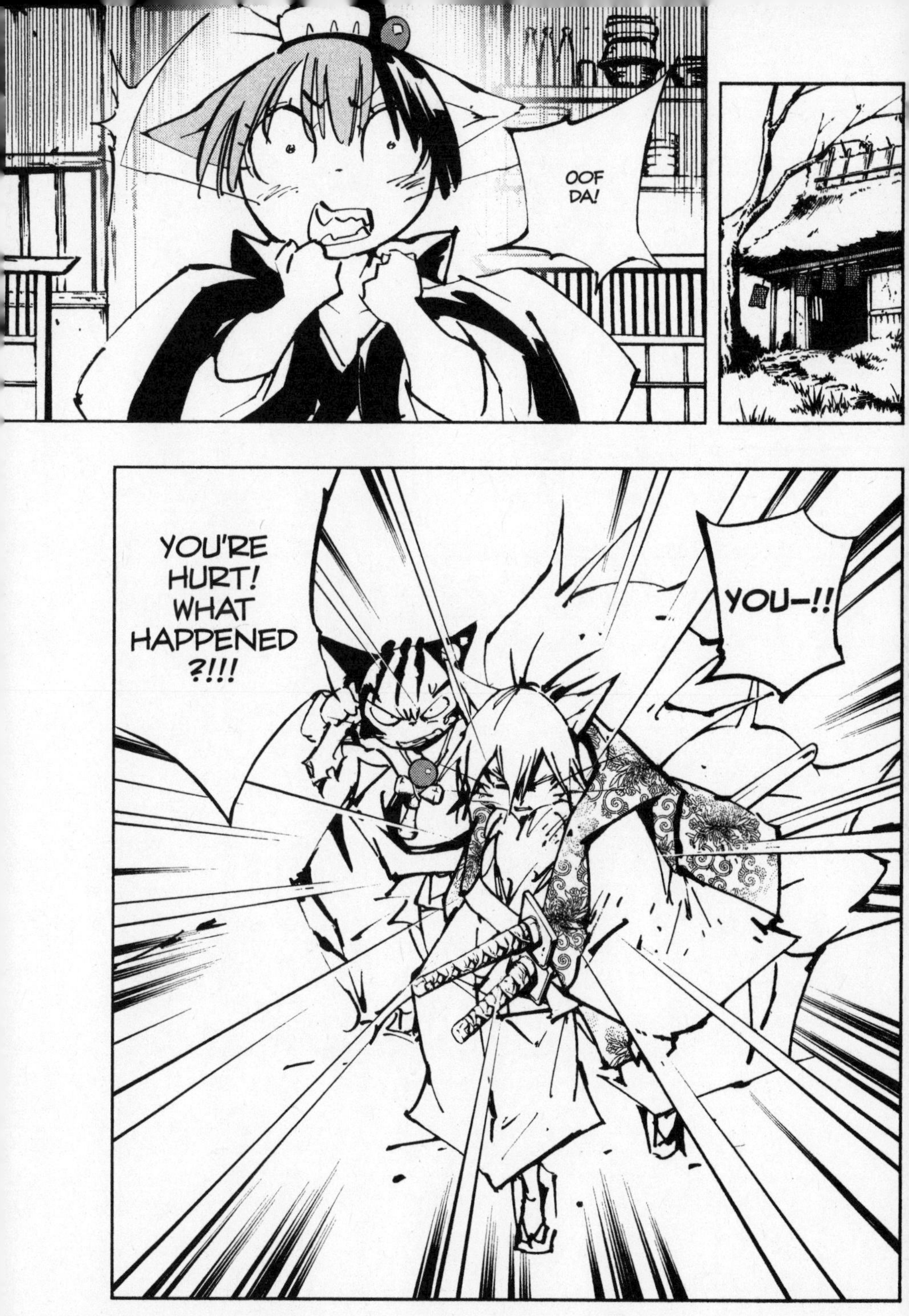
OOF DA!
YOU–!!
YOU'RE HURT! WHAT HAPPENED ?!!!

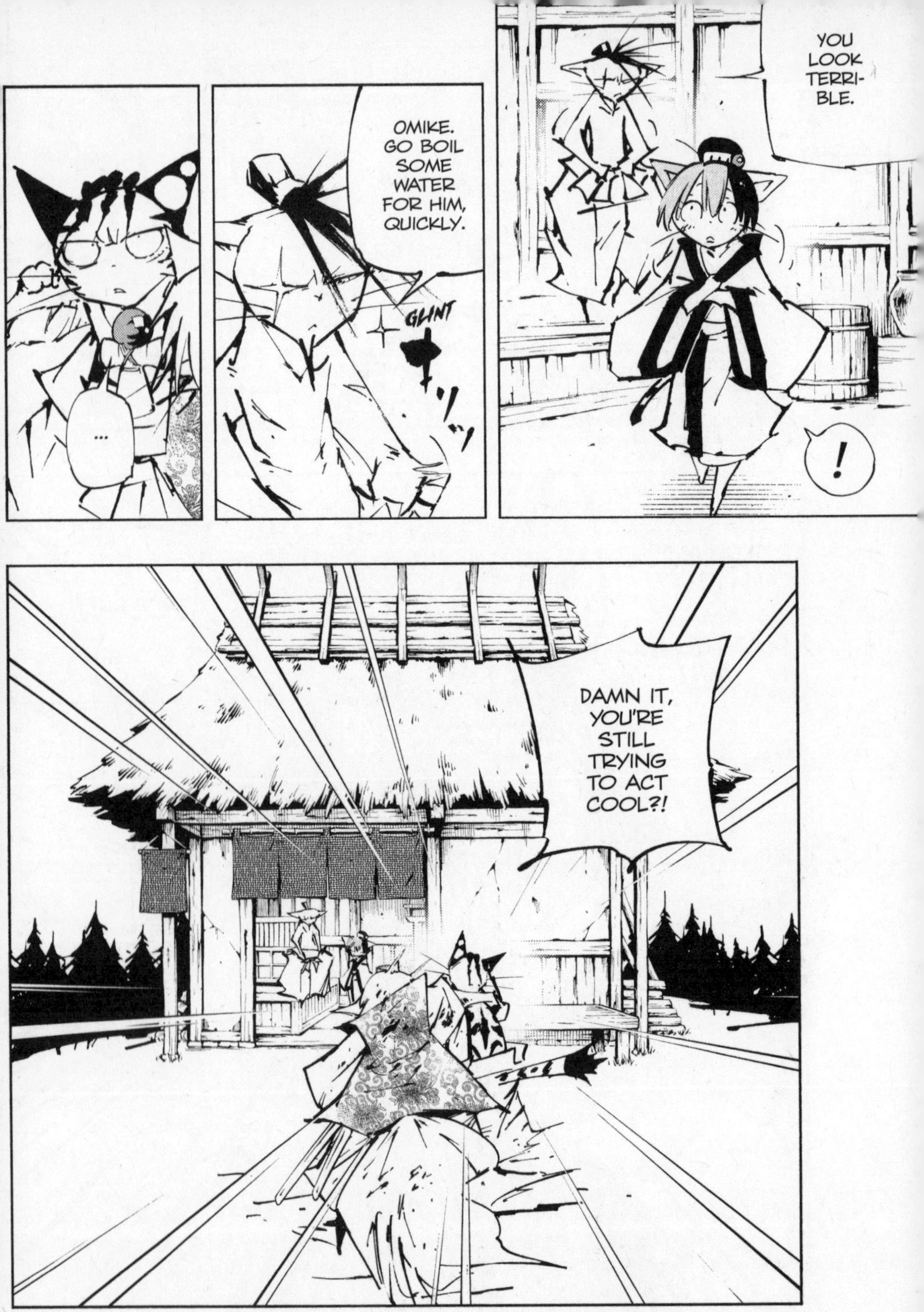
YOU LOOK TERRI- BLE.
!
OMIKE. GO BOIL SOME WATER FOR HIM, QUICKLY.
GLINT
...
DAMN IT, YOU'RE STILL TRYING TO ACT COOL?!

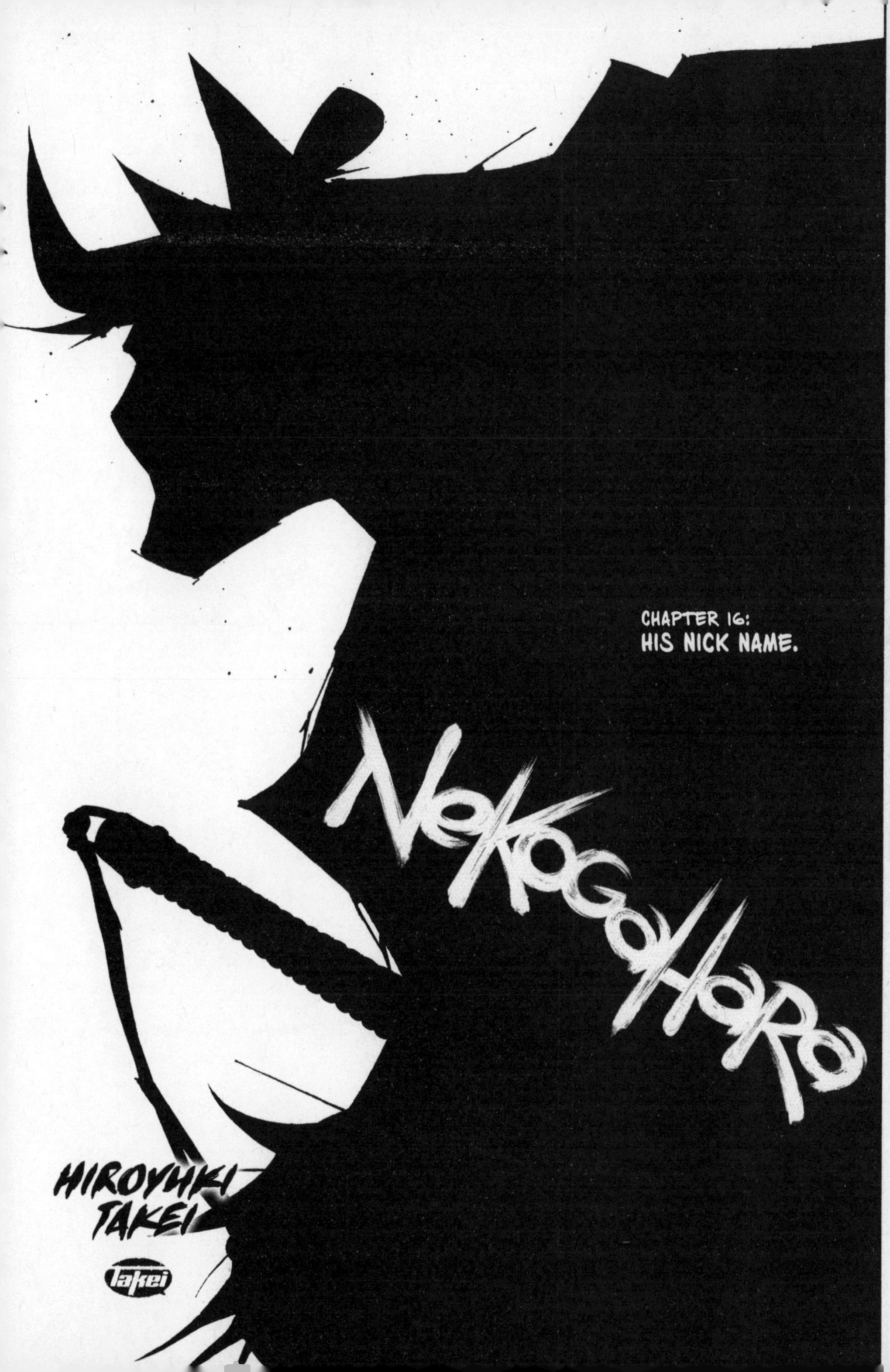
CHAPTER 16:
HIS NICK NAME.
NekoGaHara
HIROYUKI TAKEI
Takei

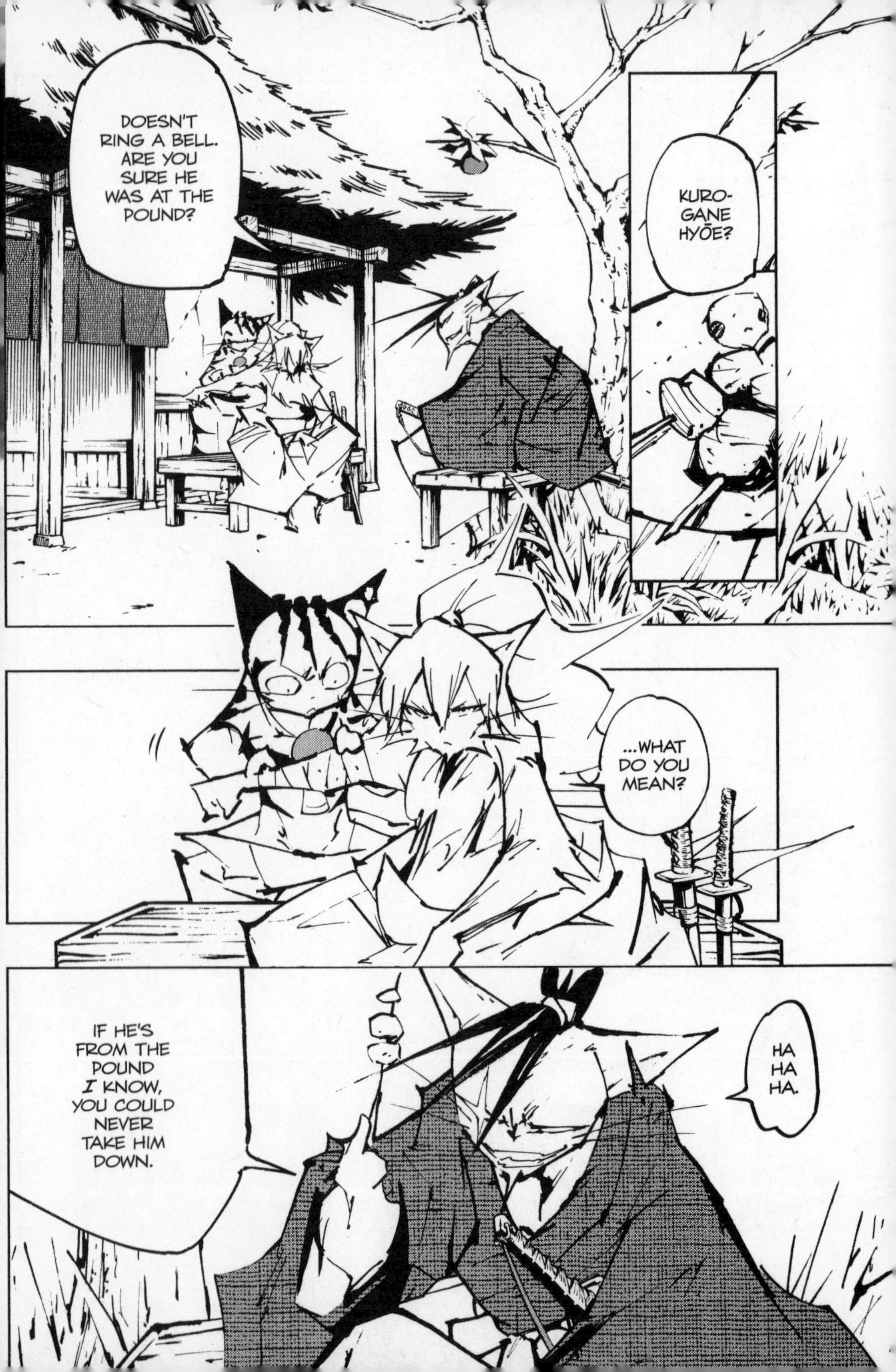
KURO-GANE HYŌE?
DOESN'T RING A BELL. ARE YOU SURE HE WAS AT THE POUND?
...WHAT DO YOU MEAN?
HA HA HA.
IF HE'S FROM THE POUND *I* KNOW, YOU COULD NEVER TAKE HIM DOWN.

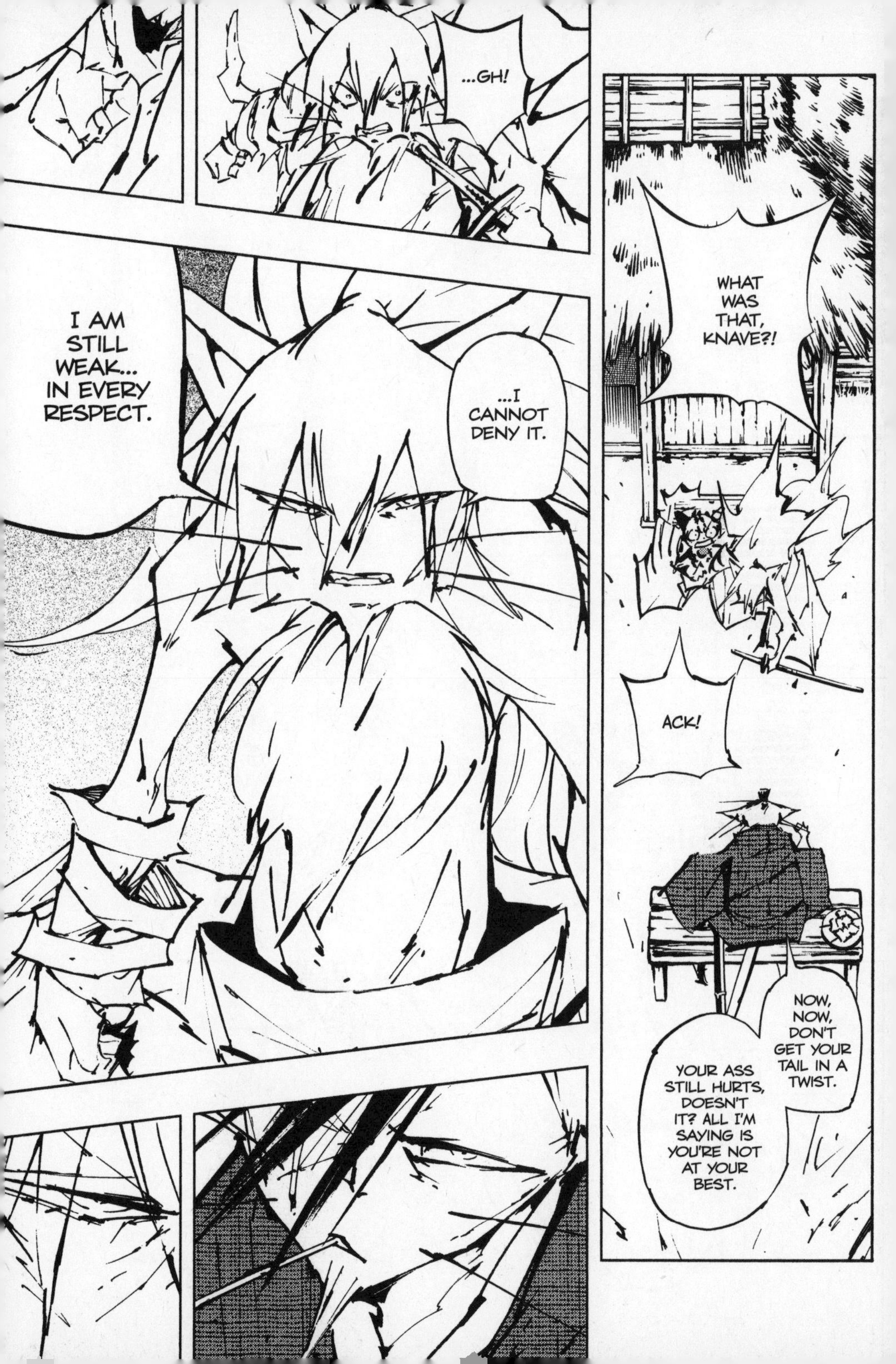
WHAT WAS THAT, KNAVE?!
ACK!
NOW, NOW, DON'T GET YOUR TAIL IN A TWIST.
YOUR ASS STILL HURTS, DOESN'T IT? ALL I'M SAYING IS YOU'RE NOT AT YOUR BEST.
...GH!
...I CANNOT DENY IT.
I AM STILL WEAK... IN EVERY RESPECT.

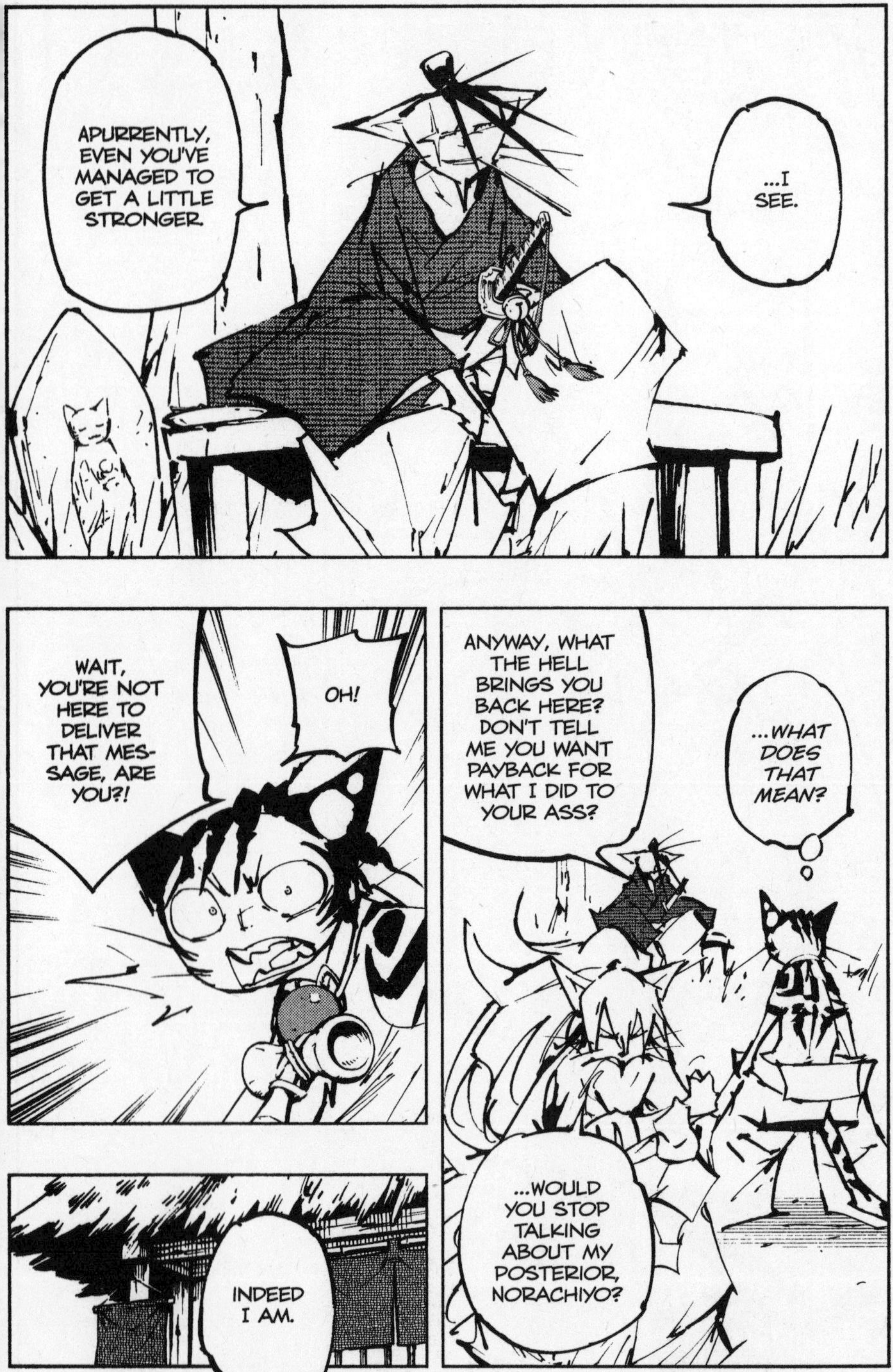
...I SEE.
APURRENTLY, EVEN YOU'VE MANAGED TO GET A LITTLE STRONGER.
ANYWAY, WHAT THE HELL BRINGS YOU BACK HERE? DON'T TELL ME YOU WANT PAYBACK FOR WHAT I DID TO YOUR ASS?
...WHAT DOES THAT MEAN?
...WOULD YOU STOP TALKING ABOUT MY POSTERIOR, NORACHIYO?
OH!
WAIT, YOU'RE NOT HERE TO DELIVER THAT MES-SAGE, ARE YOU?!
INDEED I AM.

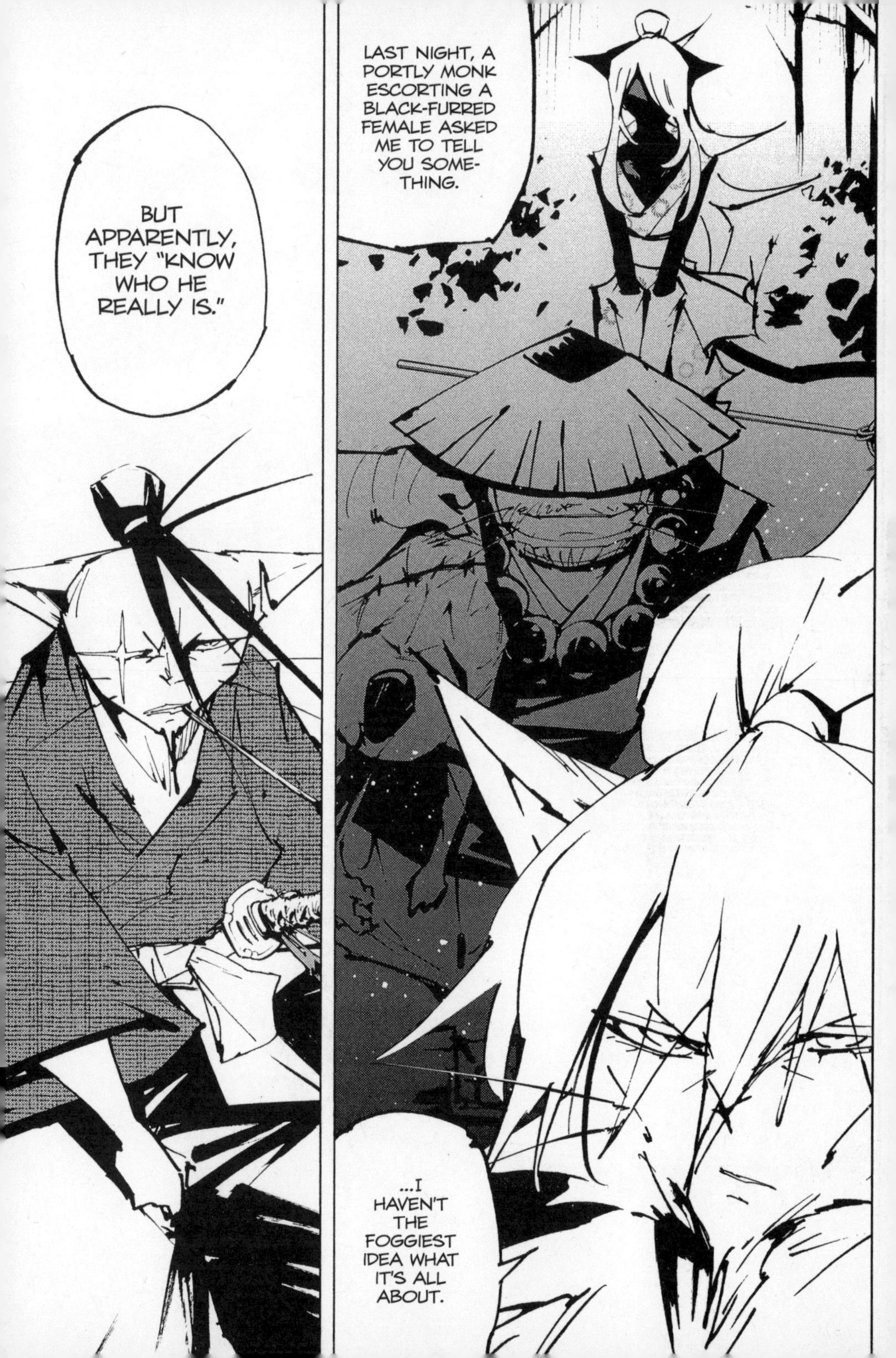
LAST NIGHT, A PORTLY MONK ESCORTING A BLACK-FURRED FEMALE ASKED ME TO TELL YOU SOME-THING.
...I HAVEN'T THE FOGGIEST IDEA WHAT IT'S ALL ABOUT.
BUT APPARENTLY, THEY "KNOW WHO HE REALLY IS."

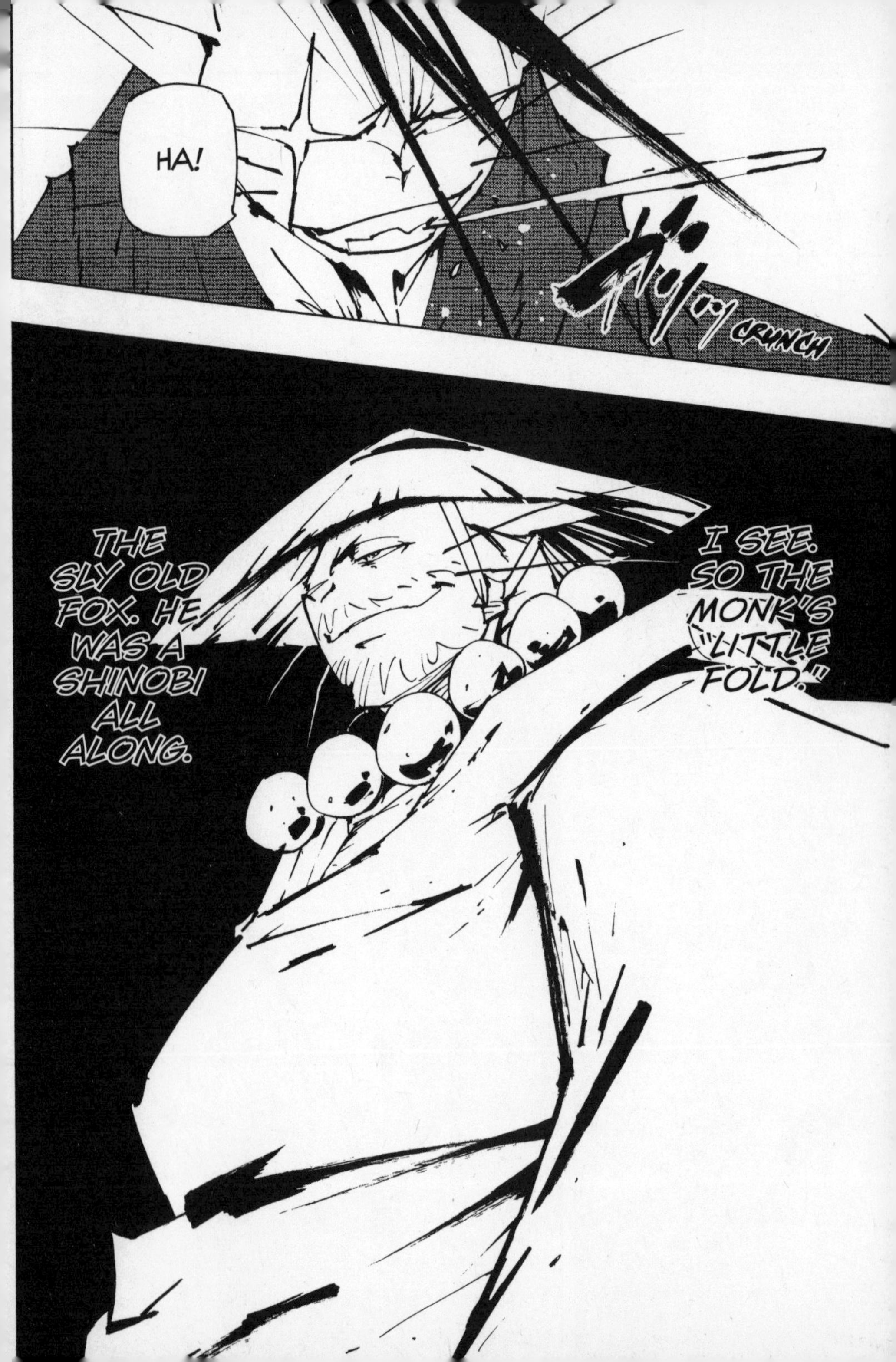
HA!
CRUNCH
I SEE. SO THE MONK'S "LITTLE FOLD."
THE SLY OLD FOX. HE WAS A SHINOBI ALL ALONG.

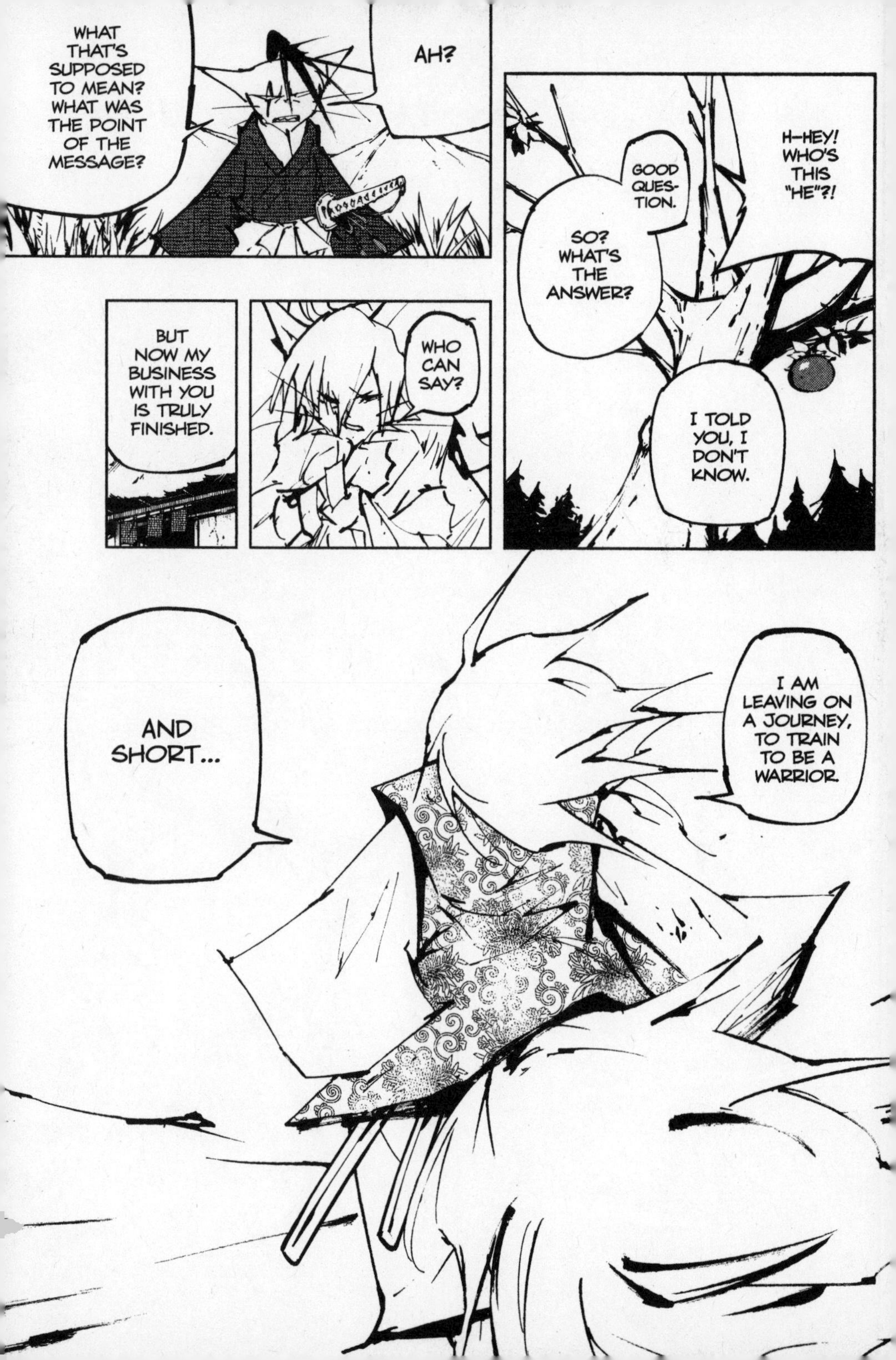
AH?
WHAT THAT'S SUPPOSED TO MEAN? WHAT WAS THE POINT OF THE MESSAGE?
H-HEY! WHO'S THIS "HE"?!
GOOD QUES-TION.
SO? WHAT'S THE ANSWER?
I TOLD YOU, I DON'T KNOW.
WHO CAN SAY?
BUT NOW MY BUSINESS WITH YOU IS TRULY FINISHED.
I AM LEAVING ON A JOURNEY, TO TRAIN TO BE A WARRIOR.
AND SHORT...

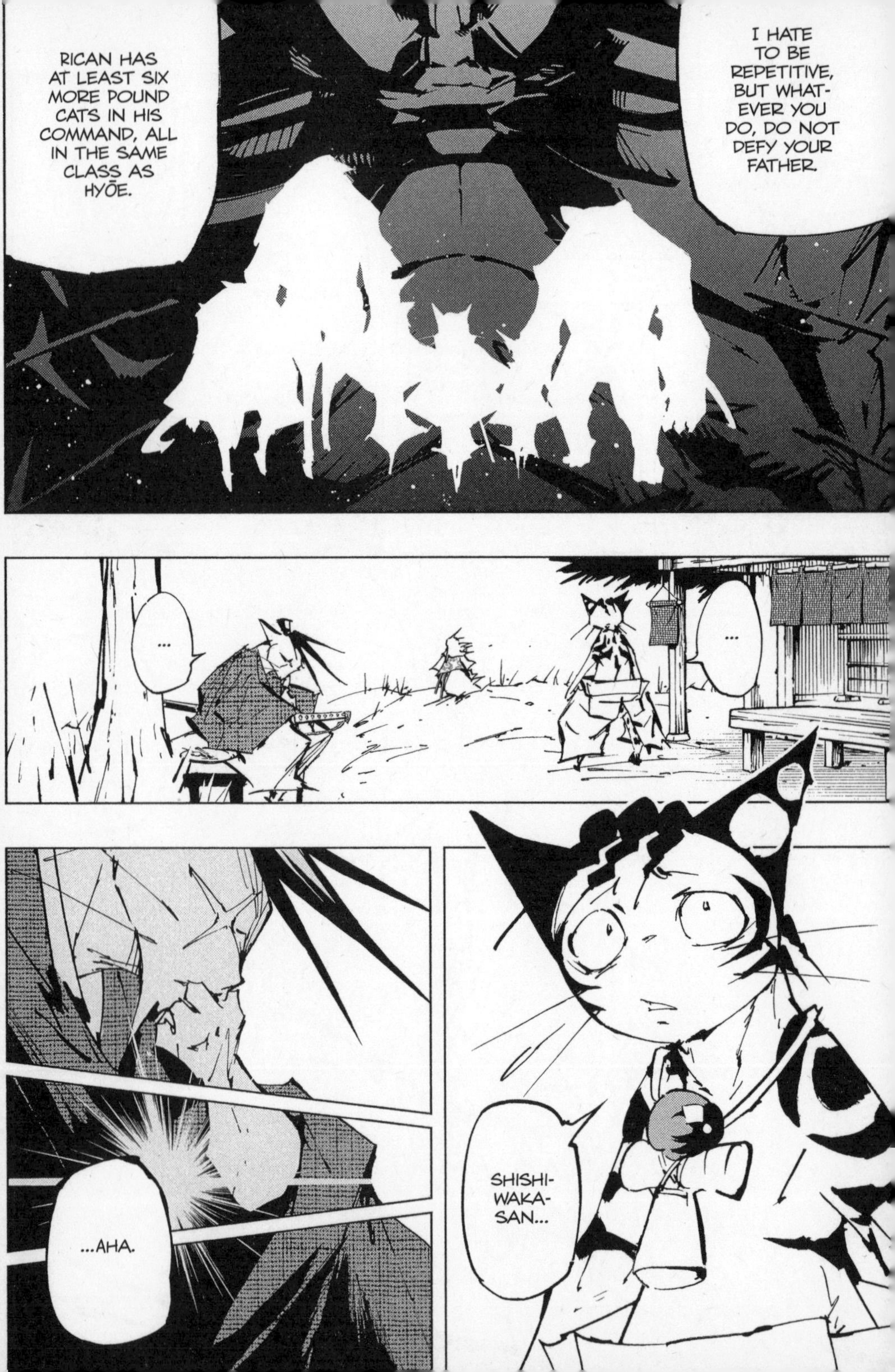
I HATE TO BE REPETITIVE, BUT WHAT-EVER YOU DO, DO NOT DEFY YOUR FATHER.
RICAN HAS AT LEAST SIX MORE POUND CATS IN HIS COMMAND, ALL IN THE SAME CLASS AS HYŌE.
...
...
SHISHI-WAKA-SAN...
...AHA.

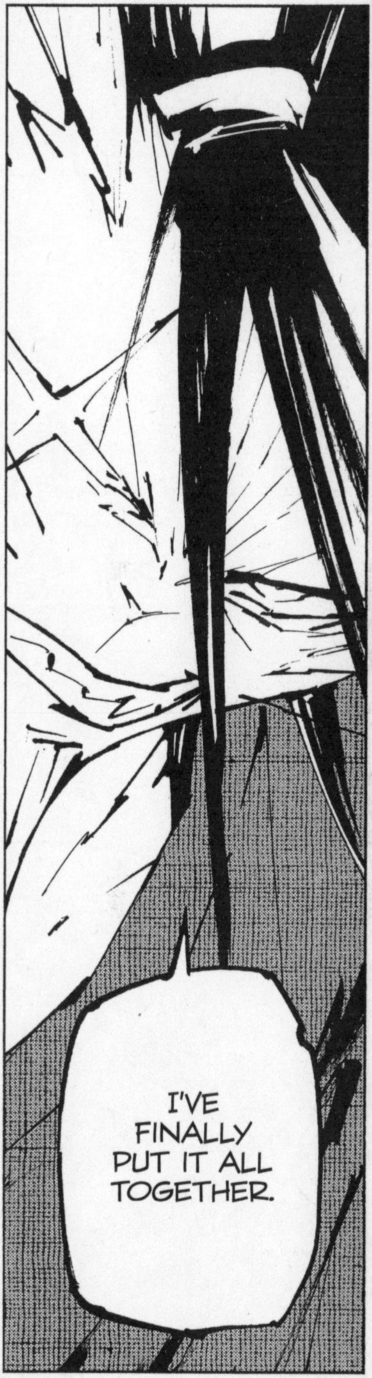
I'VE FINALLY PUT IT ALL TOGETHER.

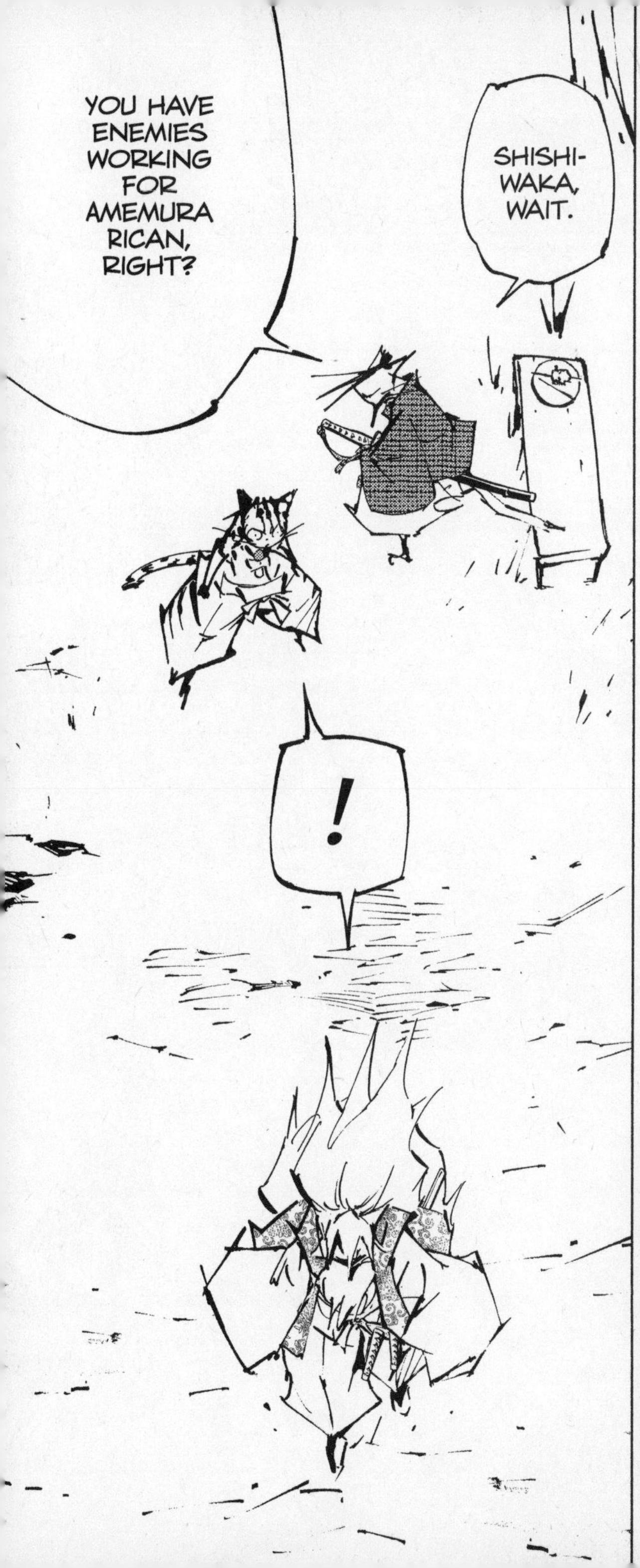
SHISHI-WAKA, WAIT.
YOU HAVE ENEMIES WORKING FOR AMEMURA RICAN, RIGHT?
!

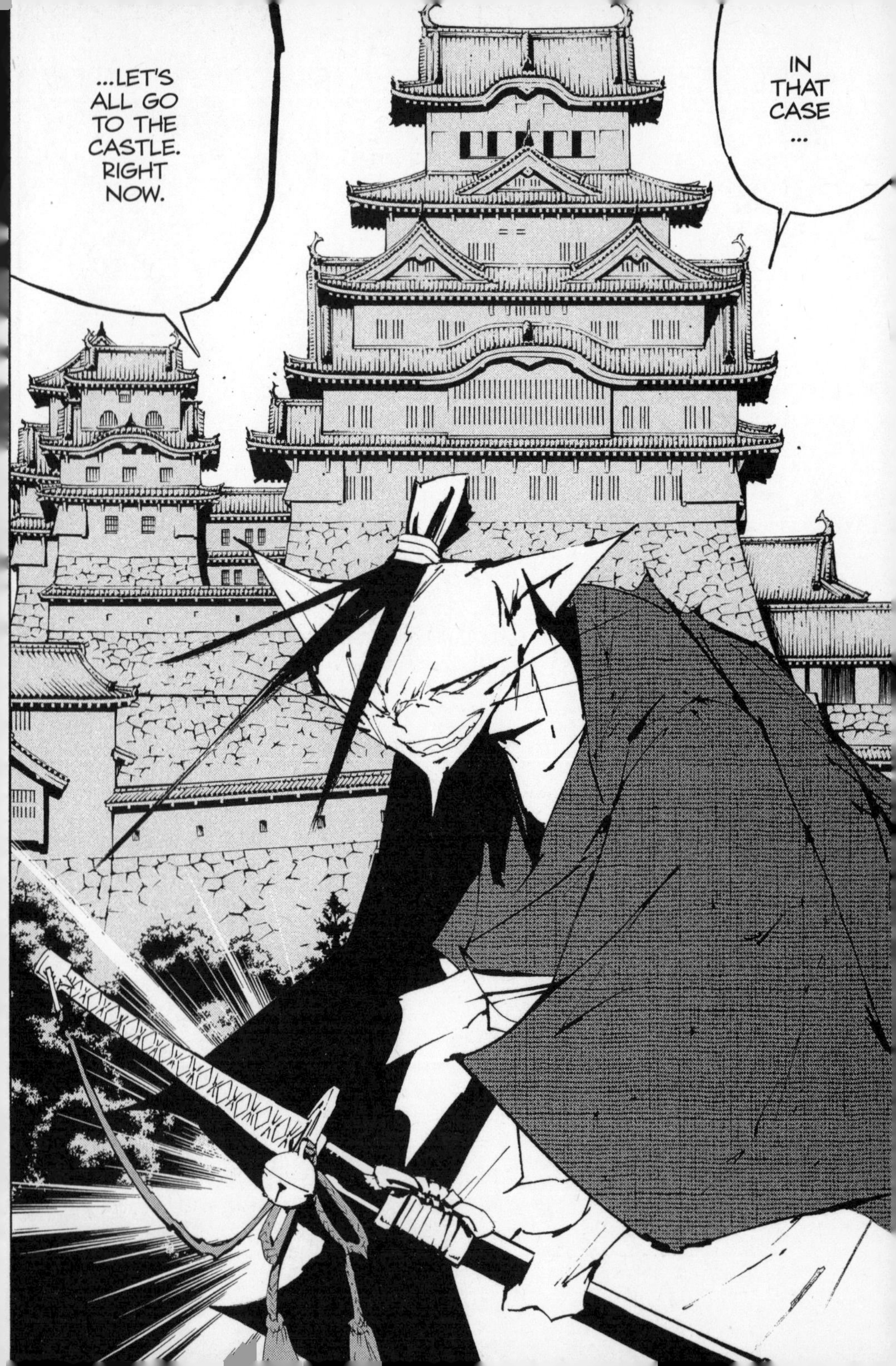
IN THAT CASE ...
...LET'S ALL GO TO THE CASTLE. RIGHT NOW.

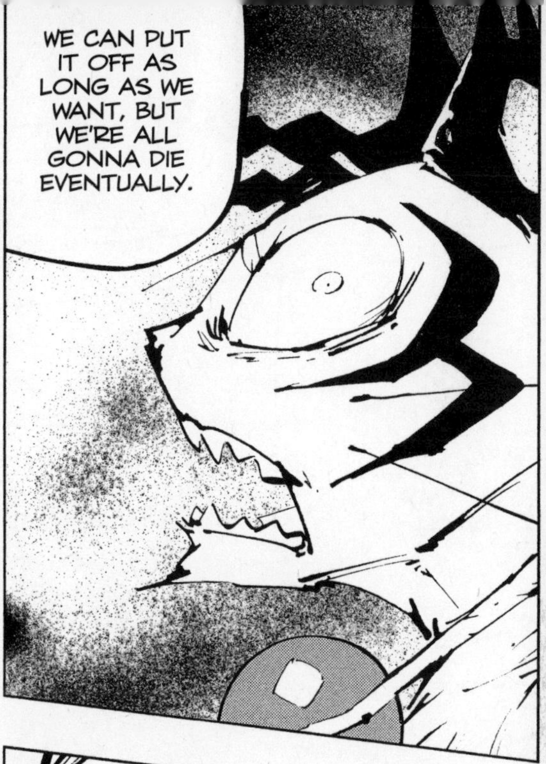
WE CAN PUT IT OFF AS LONG AS WE WANT, BUT WE'RE ALL GONNA DIE EVENTUALLY.
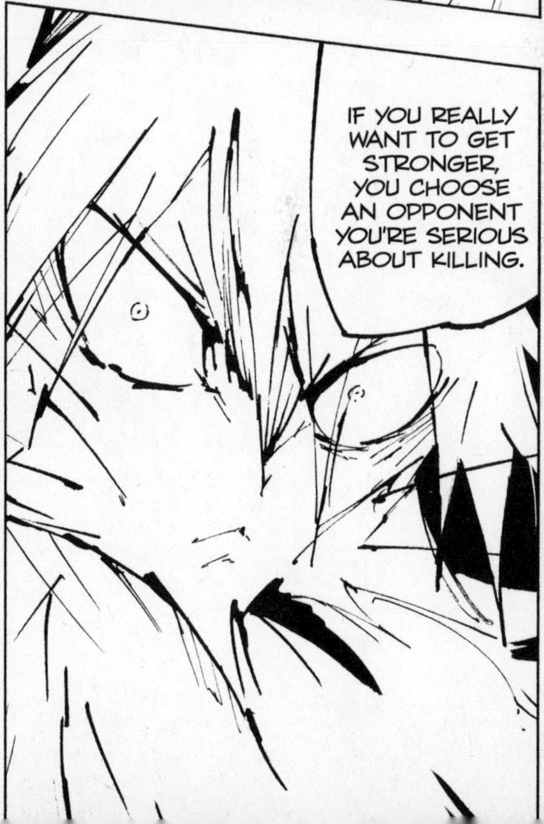
IF YOU REALLY WANT TO GET STRONGER, YOU CHOOSE AN OPPONENT YOU'RE SERIOUS ABOUT KILLING.
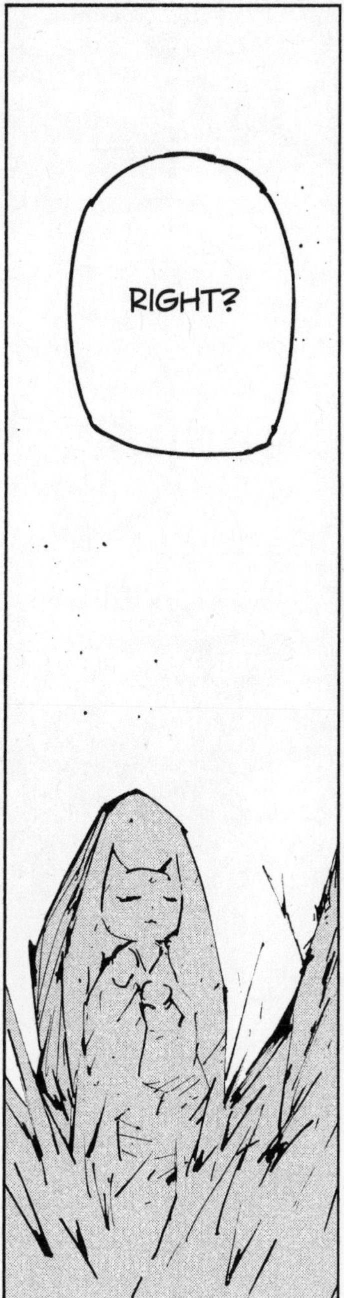
RIGHT?

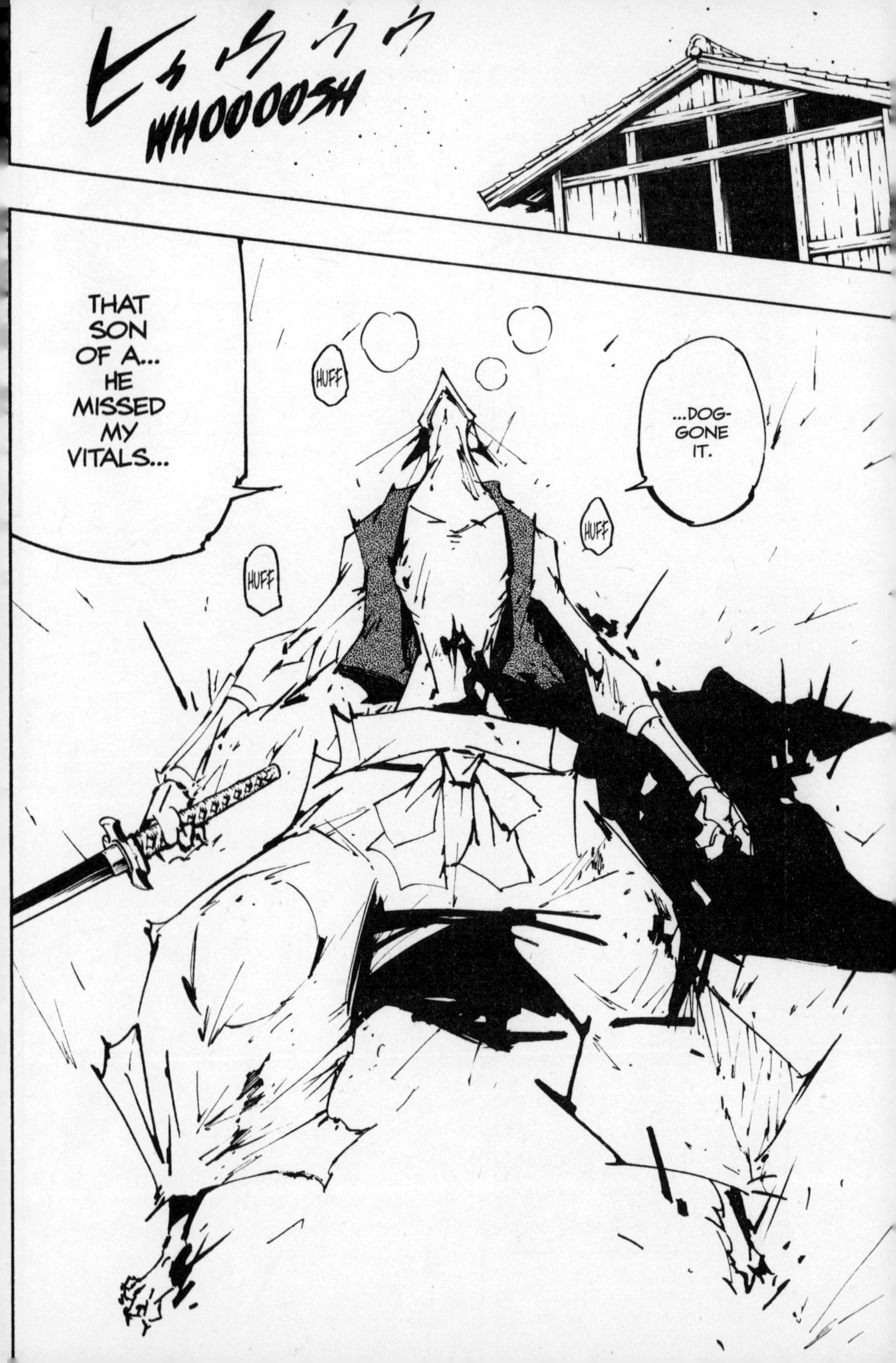

WHOOOOSH
THAT SON OF A... HE MISSED MY VITALS...
HUFF
HUFF
HUFF
...DOG-GONE IT.

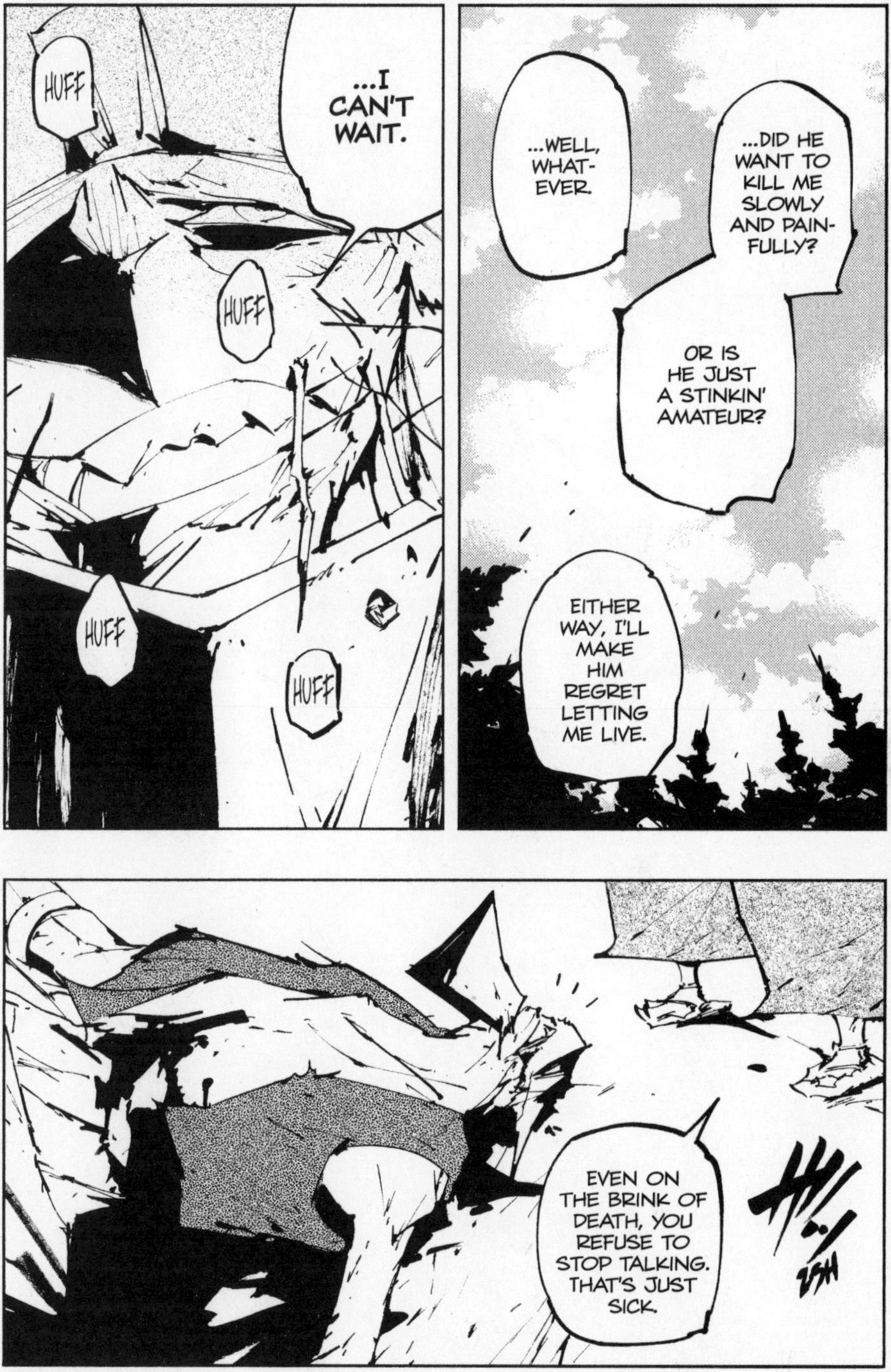
...DID HE WANT TO KILL ME SLOWLY AND PAIN-FULLY?
OR IS HE JUST A STINKIN' AMATEUR?
...WELL, WHAT-EVER.
EITHER WAY, I'LL MAKE HIM REGRET LETTING ME LIVE.
...I CAN'T WAIT.
HUFF
HUFF
HUFF
HUFF
EVEN ON THE BRINK OF DEATH, YOU REFUSE TO STOP TALKING. THAT'S JUST SICK.

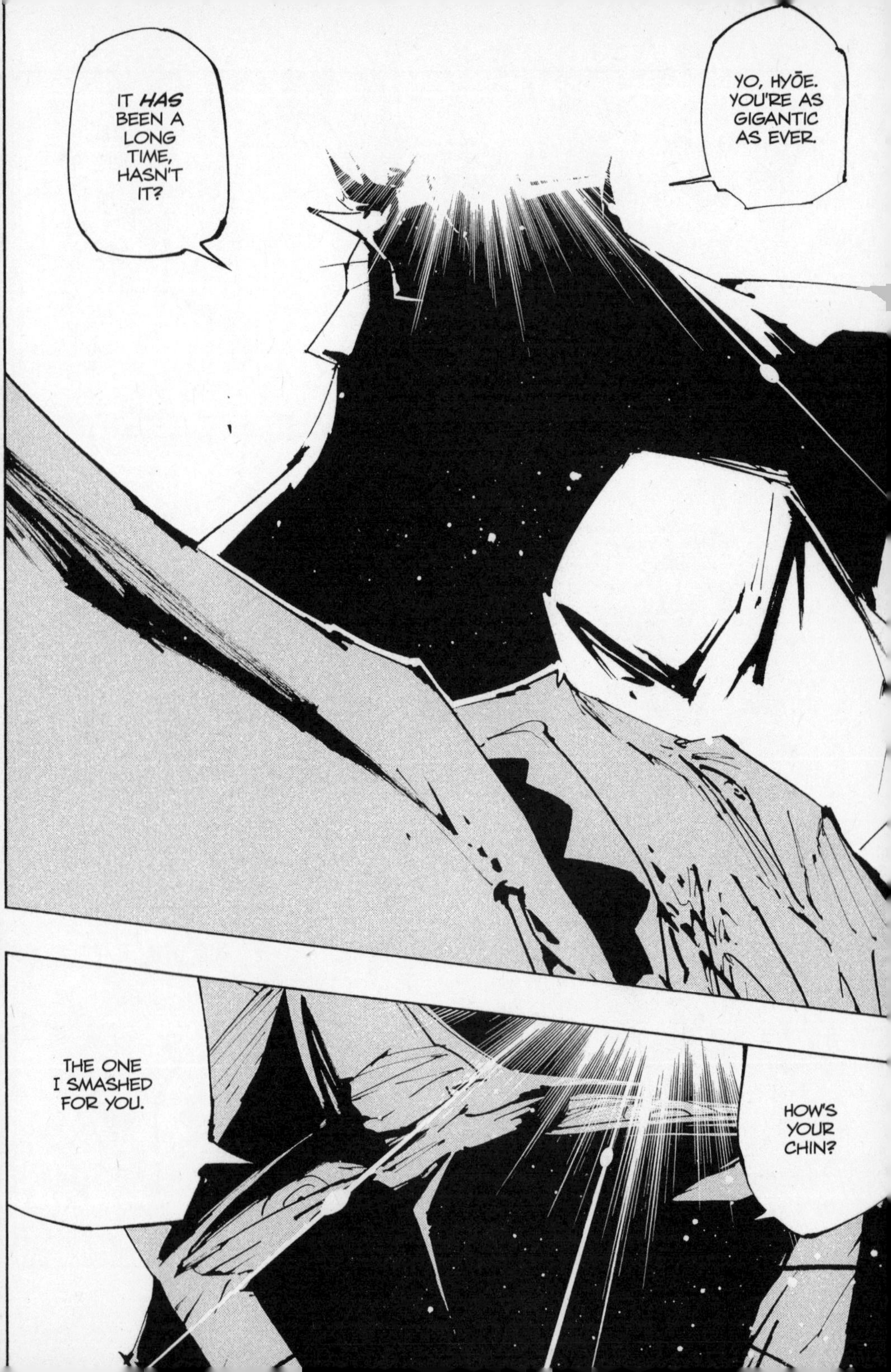
YO, HYŌE. YOU'RE AS GIGANTIC AS EVER.
IT *HAS* BEEN A LONG TIME, HASN'T IT?
HOW'S YOUR CHIN?
THE ONE I SMASHED FOR YOU.

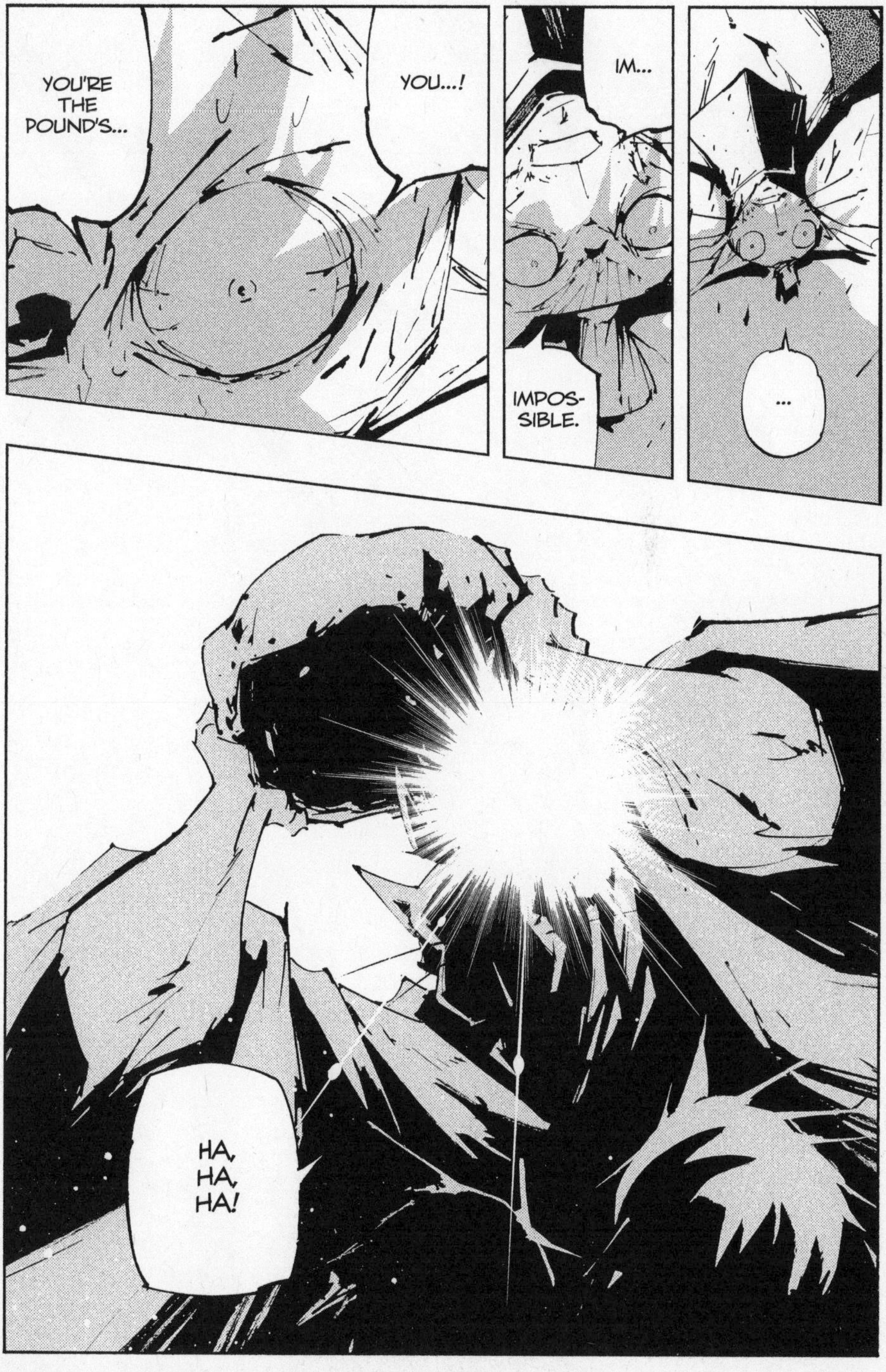
...
IM...
IMPOS-SIBLE.
YOU...!
YOU'RE THE POUND'S...
HA, HA, HA!

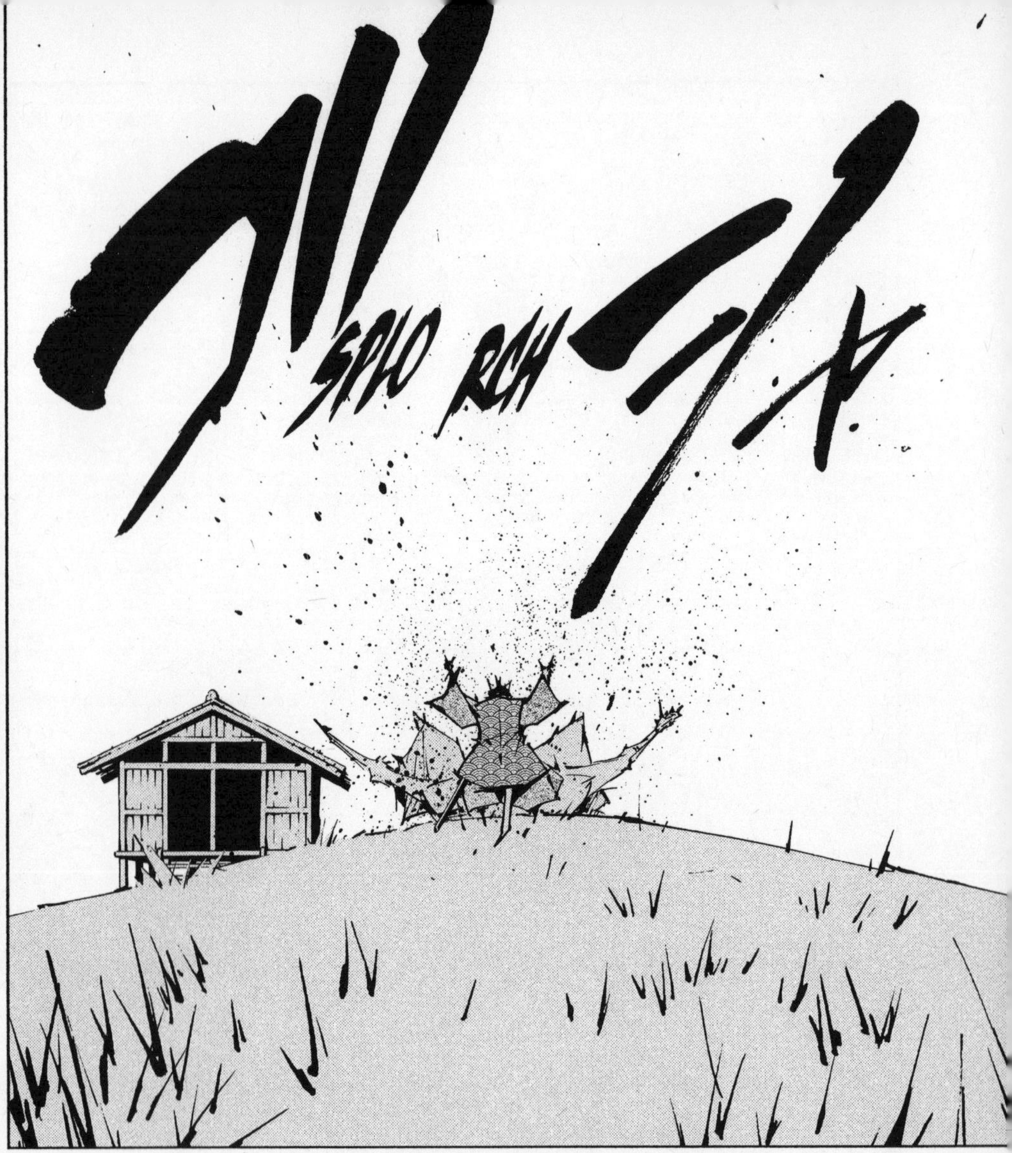
SPLORCH

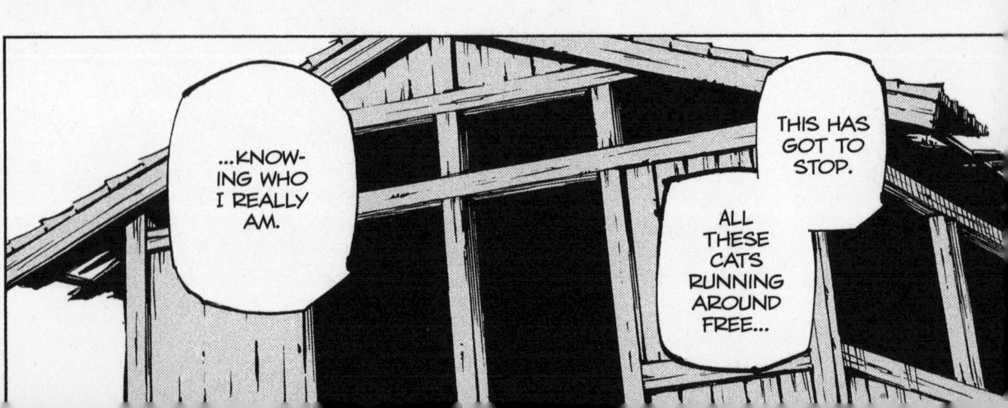
THIS HAS GOT TO STOP.
ALL THESE CATS RUNNING AROUND FREE...
...KNOWING WHO I REALLY AM.

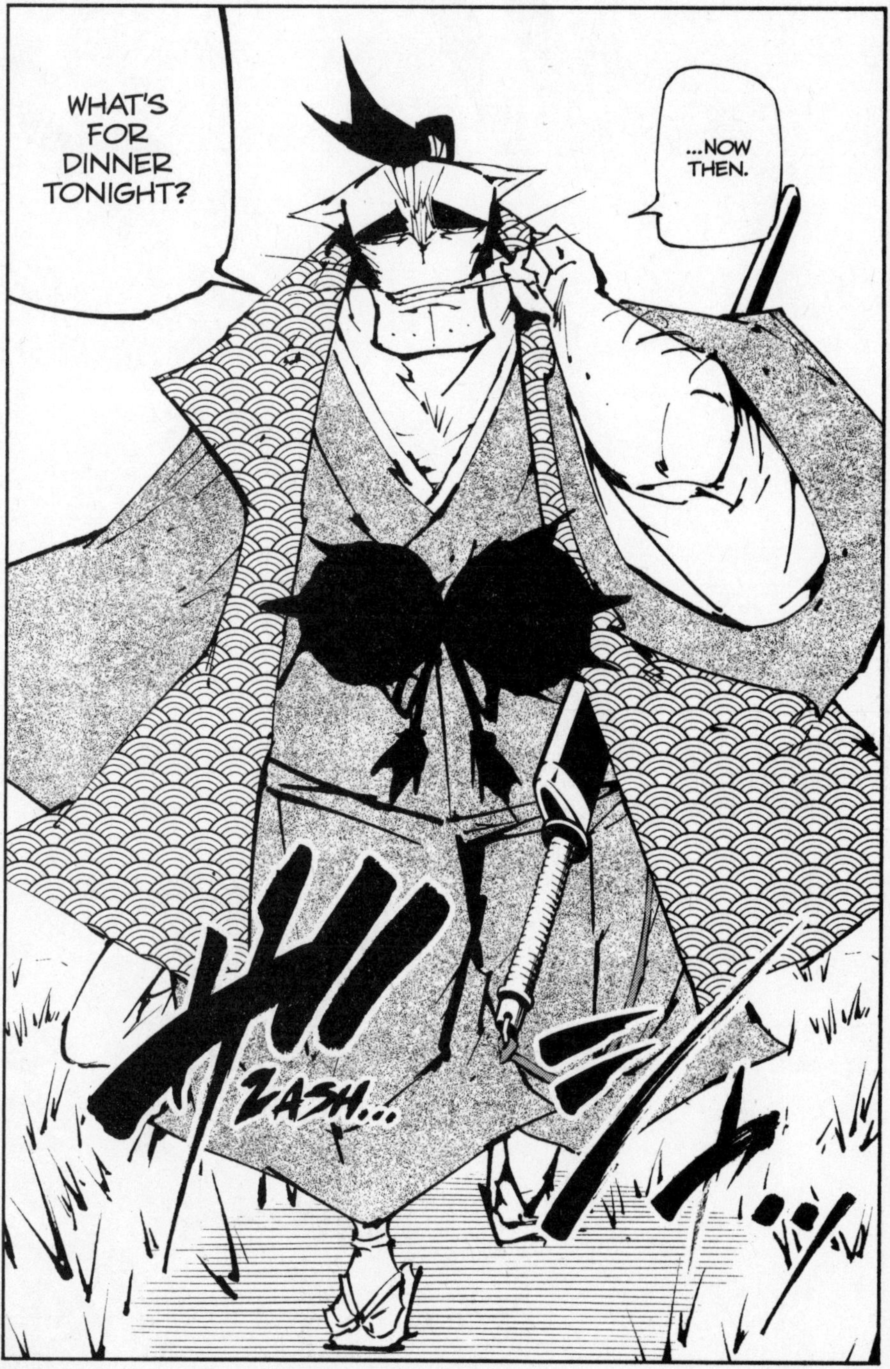
...NOW THEN.
WHAT'S FOR DINNER TONIGHT?
ZASH...

猫ヶ原

NEKOGAHARA

ネコガハラ

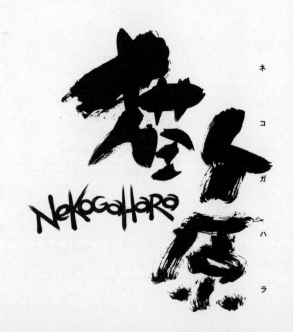

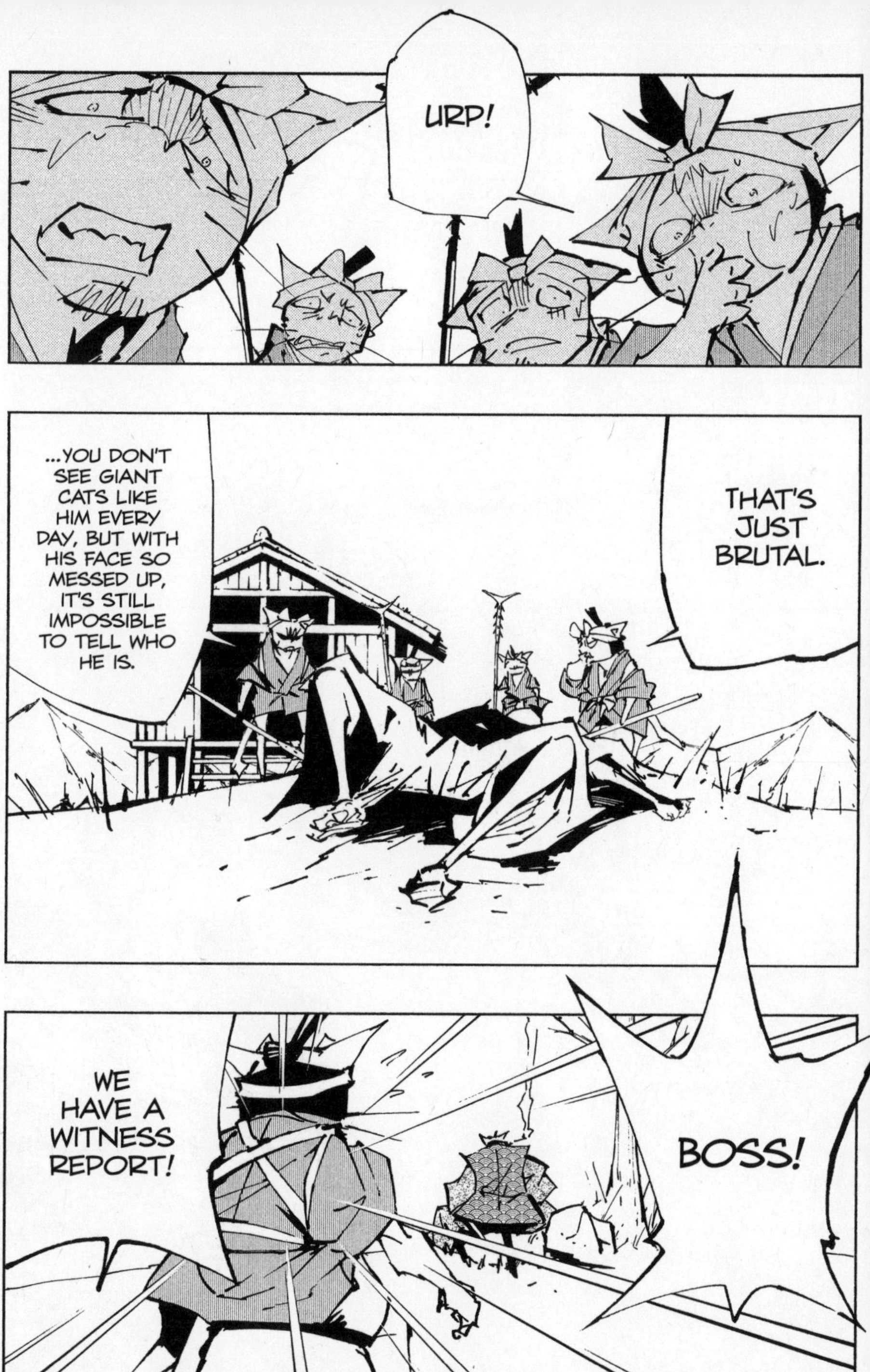
URP!
THAT'S JUST BRUTAL.
...YOU DON'T SEE GIANT CATS LIKE HIM EVERY DAY, BUT WITH HIS FACE SO MESSED UP, IT'S STILL IMPOSSIBLE TO TELL WHO HE IS.
BOSS!
WE HAVE A WITNESS REPORT!

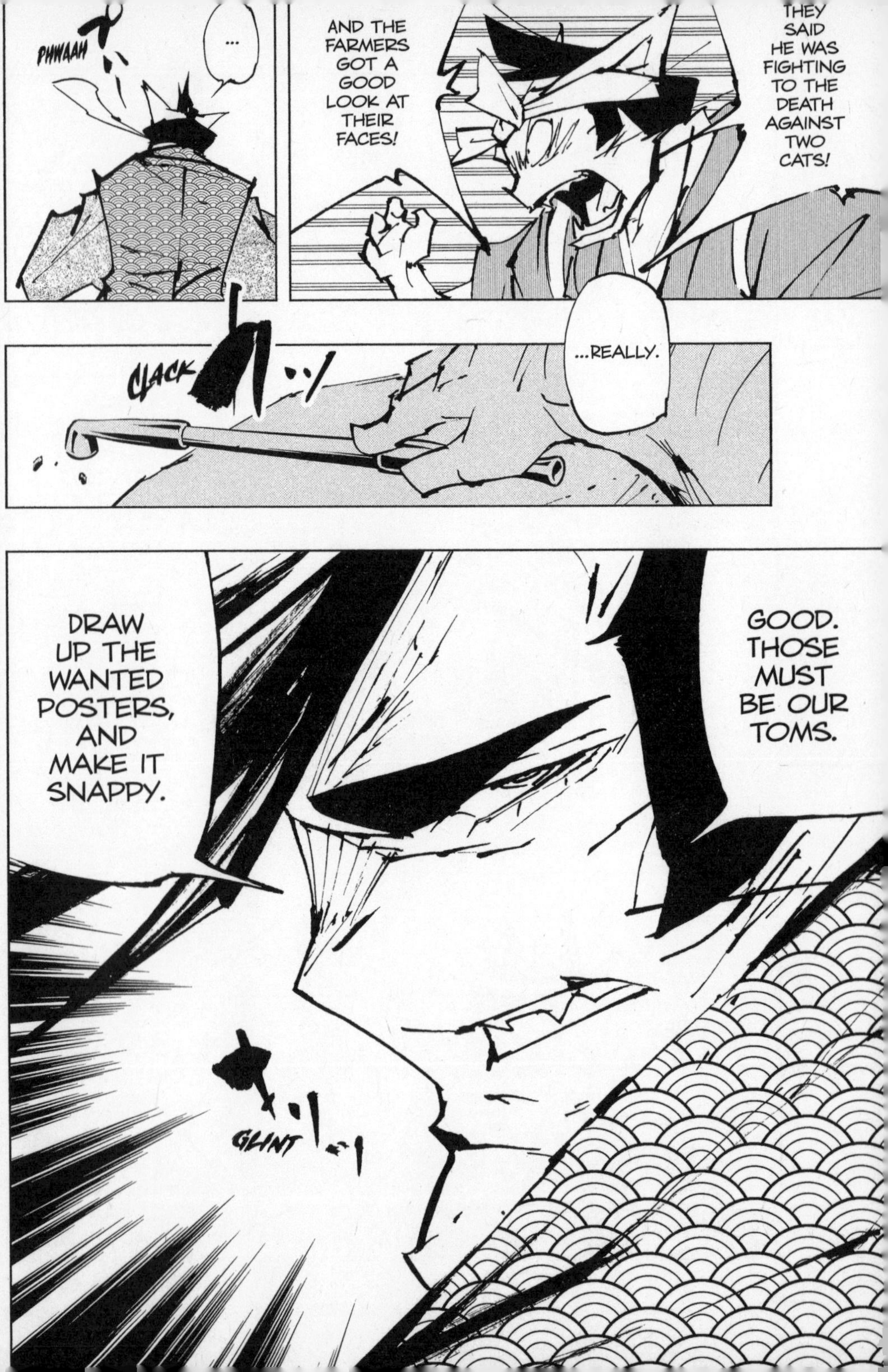
THEY SAID HE WAS FIGHTING TO THE DEATH AGAINST TWO CATS!
AND THE FARMERS GOT A GOOD LOOK AT THEIR FACES!
...
PHWAAH
...REALLY.
CLACK
GOOD. THOSE MUST BE OUR TOMS.
DRAW UP THE WANTED POSTERS, AND MAKE IT SNAPPY.
GLINT

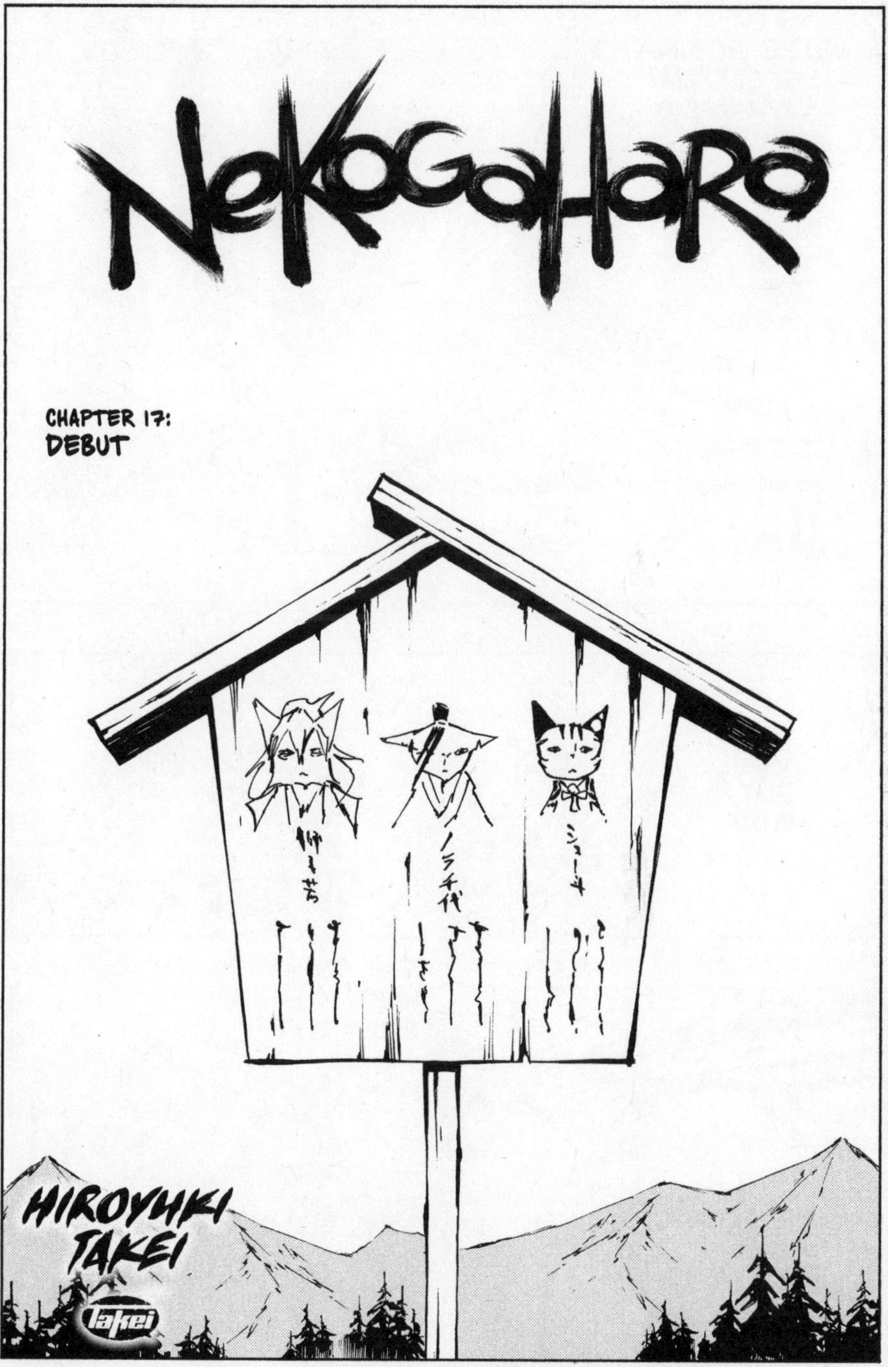
NeKoGaHara
CHAPTER 17:
DEBUT
HIROYUKI TAKEI
Takei

POSTER: [RIGHT] SHORT
POSTER: [MIDDLE] NORACHIYO
POSTER: [LEFT] SHISHIWAKA

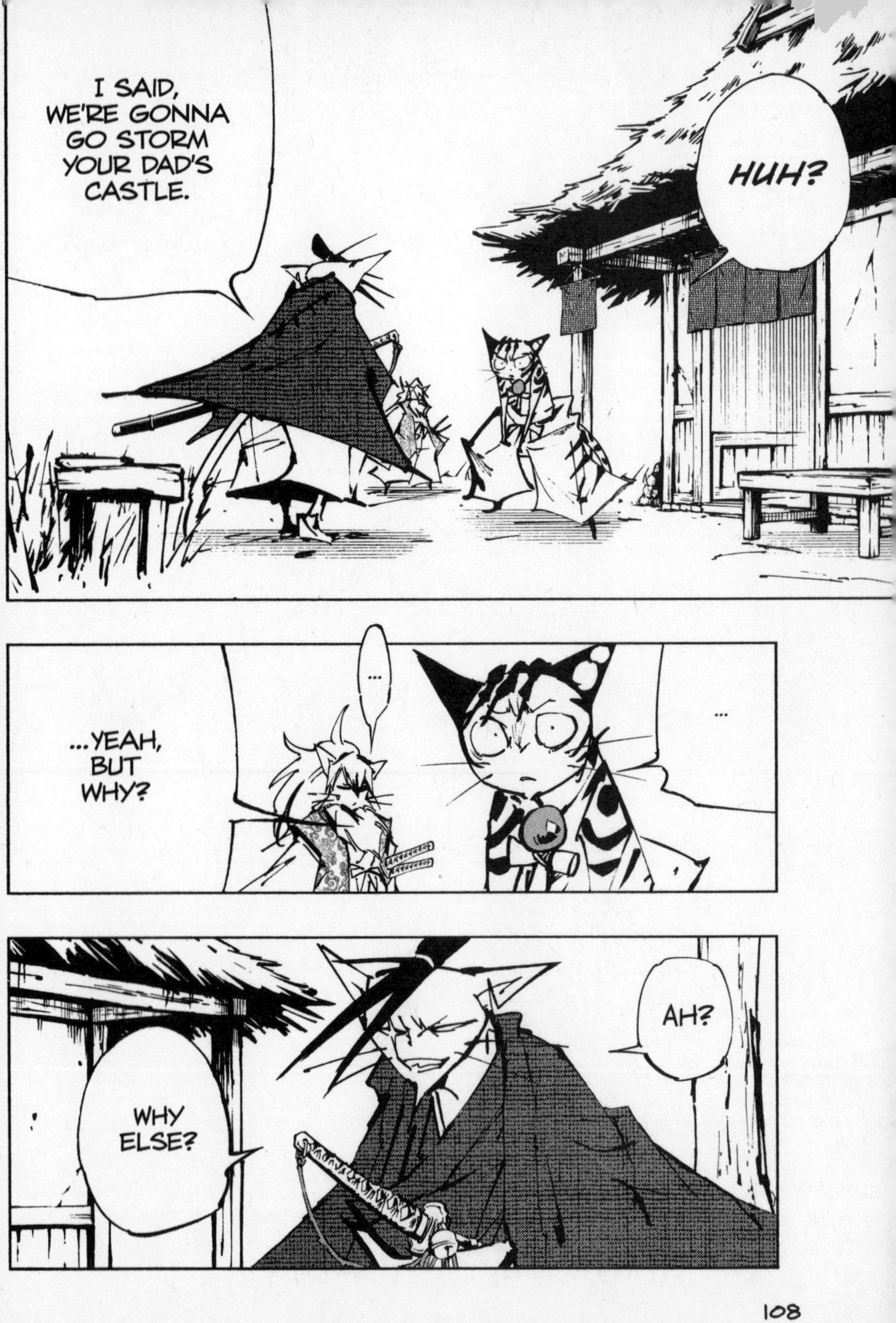
HUH?
I SAID, WE'RE GONNA GO STORM YOUR DAD'S CASTLE.
...
...
...YEAH, BUT WHY?
AH?
WHY ELSE?

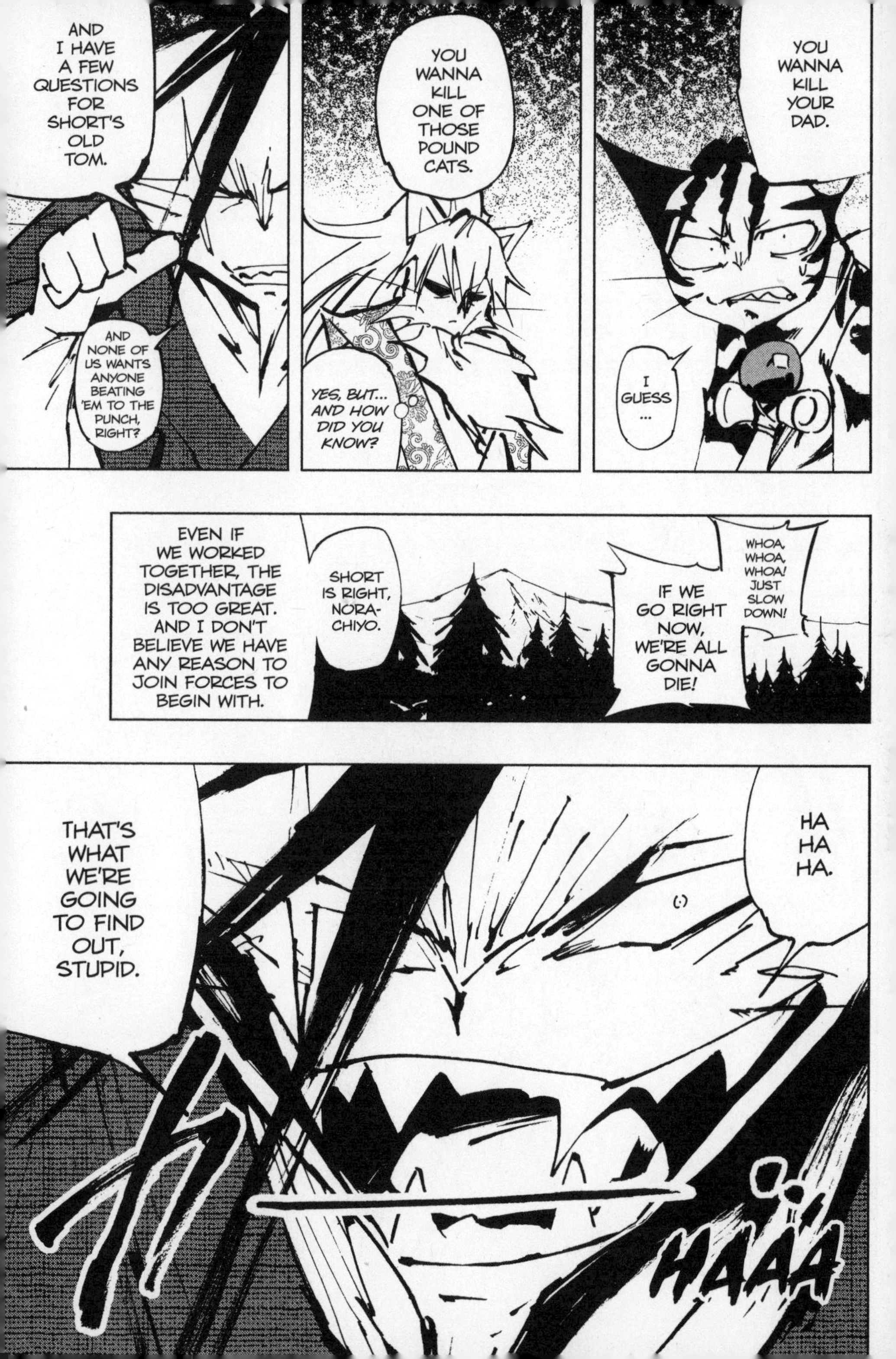
YOU WANNA KILL YOUR DAD.
I GUESS ...
YOU WANNA KILL ONE OF THOSE POUND CATS.
YES, BUT... AND HOW DID YOU KNOW?
AND I HAVE A FEW QUESTIONS FOR SHORT'S OLD TOM.
AND NONE OF US WANTS ANYONE BEATING 'EM TO THE PUNCH, RIGHT?
WHOA, WHOA, WHOA! JUST SLOW DOWN!
IF WE GO RIGHT NOW, WE'RE ALL GONNA DIE!
SHORT IS RIGHT, NORA-CHIYO.
EVEN IF WE WORKED TOGETHER, THE DISADVANTAGE IS TOO GREAT. AND I DON'T BELIEVE WE HAVE ANY REASON TO JOIN FORCES TO BEGIN WITH.
HA HA HA.
THAT'S WHAT WE'RE GOING TO FIND OUT, STUPID.
HAAA

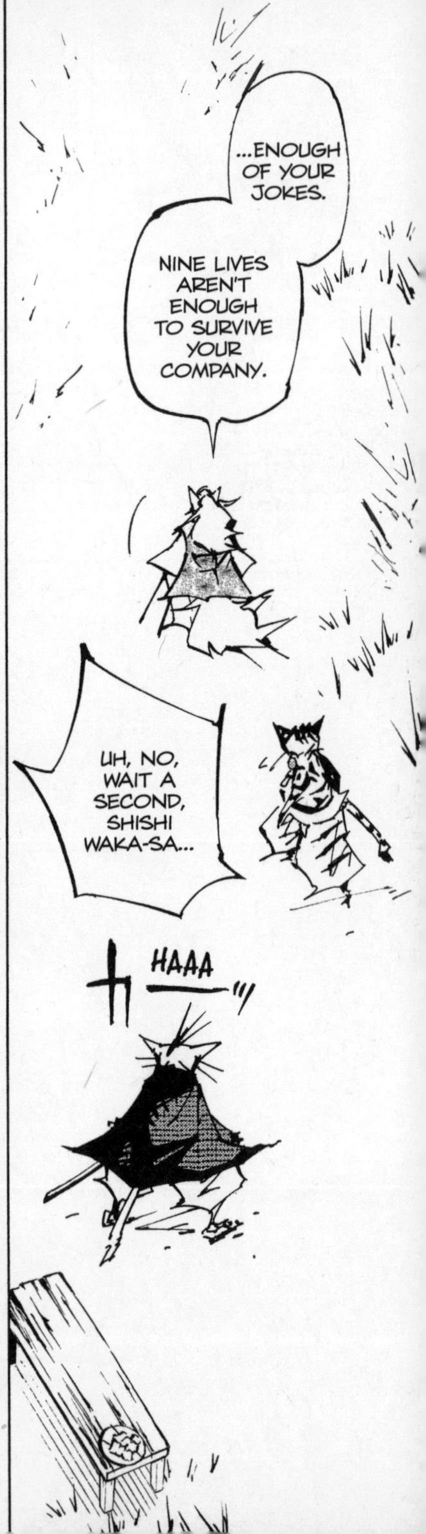
...ENOUGH OF YOUR JOKES.
NINE LIVES AREN'T ENOUGH TO SURVIVE YOUR COMPANY.
UH, NO, WAIT A SECOND, SHISHI WAKA-SA...
HAAA

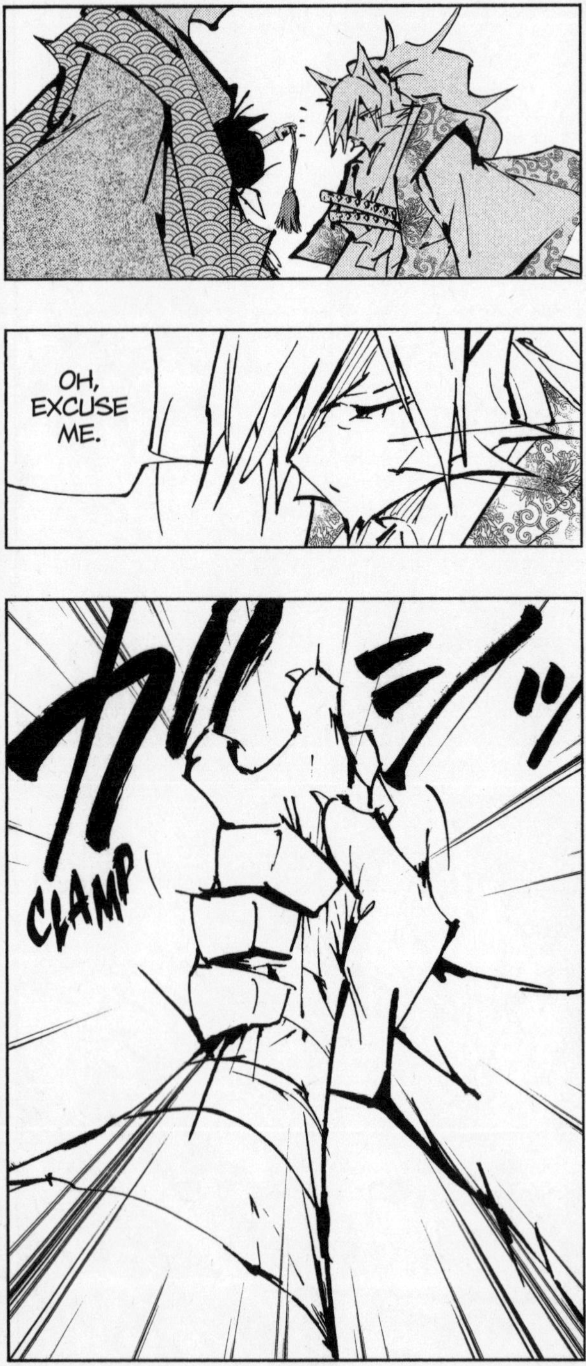
OH, EXCUSE ME.
CLAMP

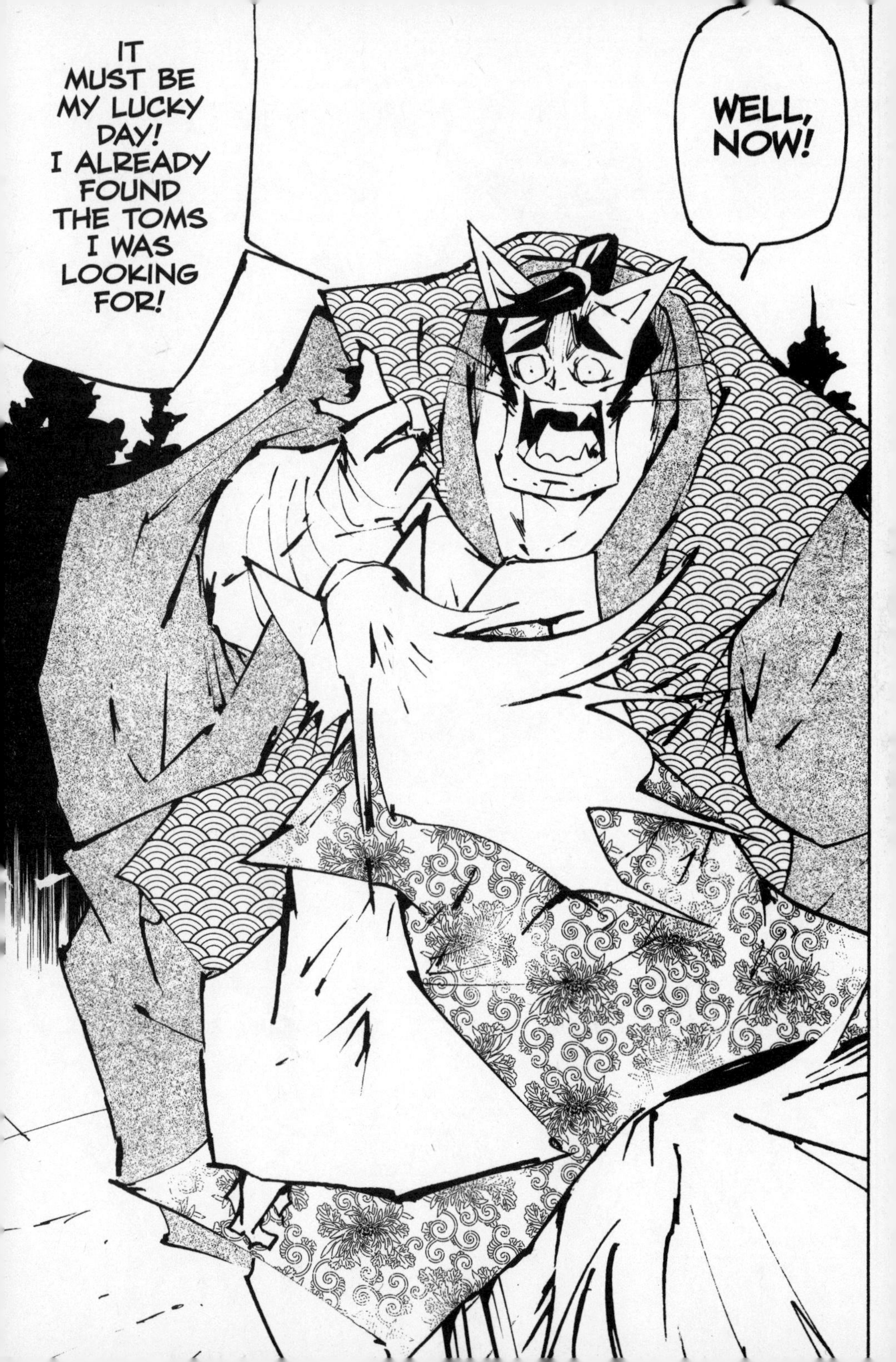
WELL, NOW!
IT MUST BE MY LUCKY DAY! I ALREADY FOUND THE TOMS I WAS LOOKING FOR!

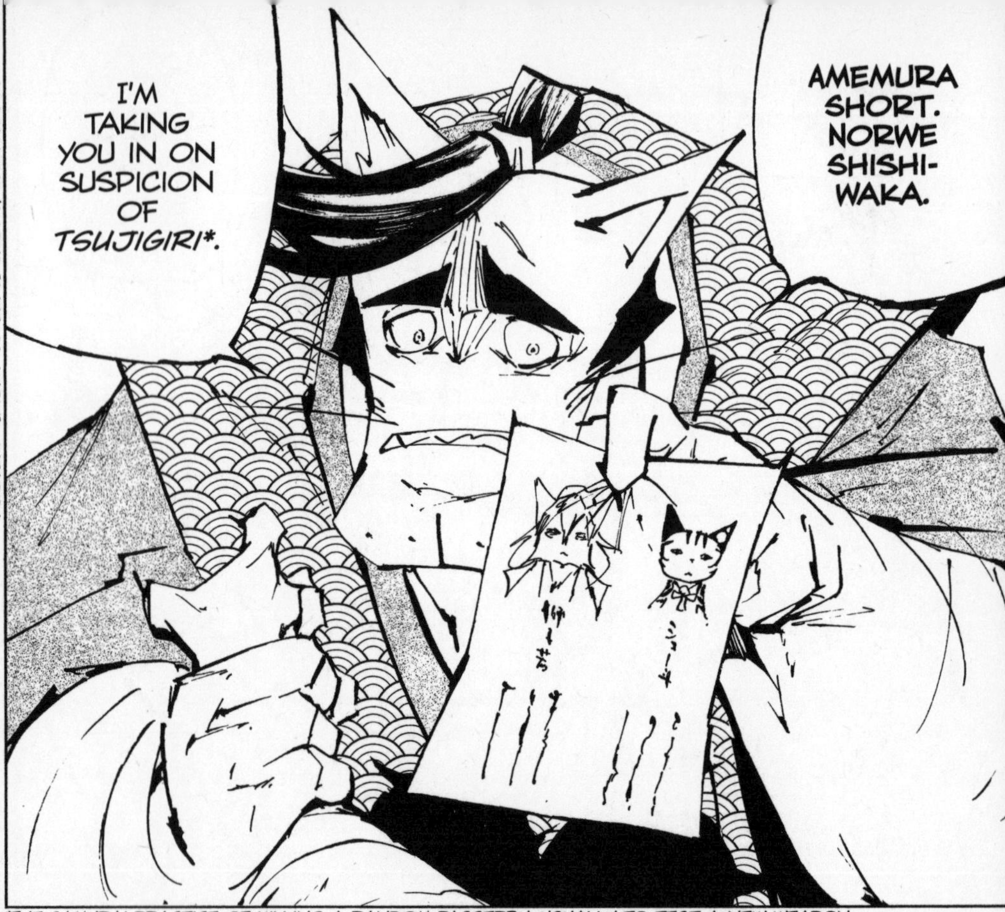
AMEMURA SHORT. NORWE SHISHIWAKA.
I'M TAKING YOU IN ON SUSPICION OF TSUJIGIRI*.
POSTER: (RIGHT TO LEFT) SHORT, SHISHIWAKA

*THE SAMURAI PRACTICE OF KILLING A RANDOM PASSERBY, USUALLY TO TEST A NEW WEAPON.

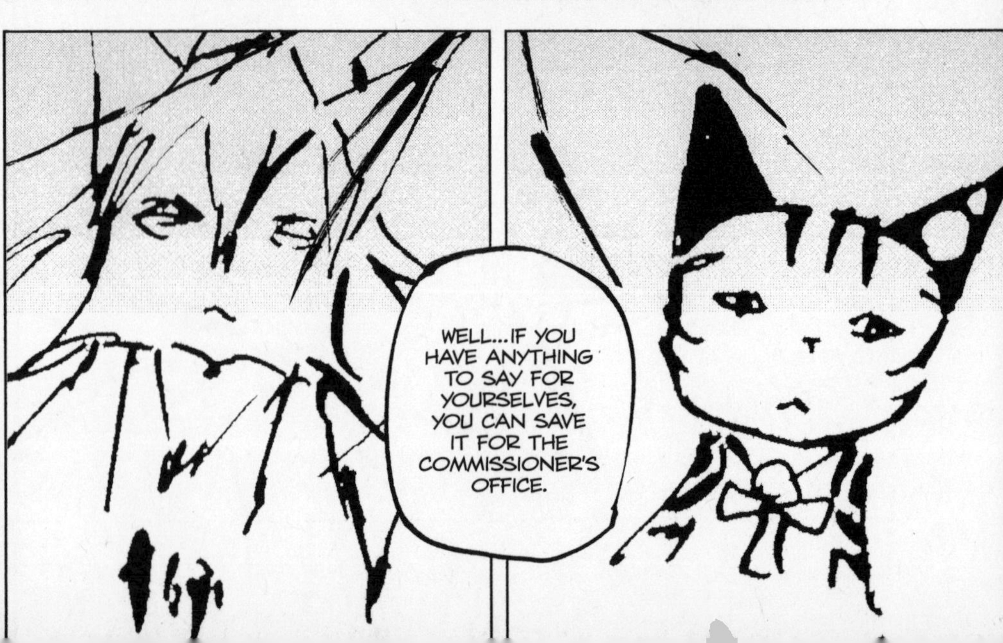
WELL...IF YOU HAVE ANYTHING TO SAY FOR YOURSELVES, YOU CAN SAVE IT FOR THE COMMISSIONER'S OFFICE.

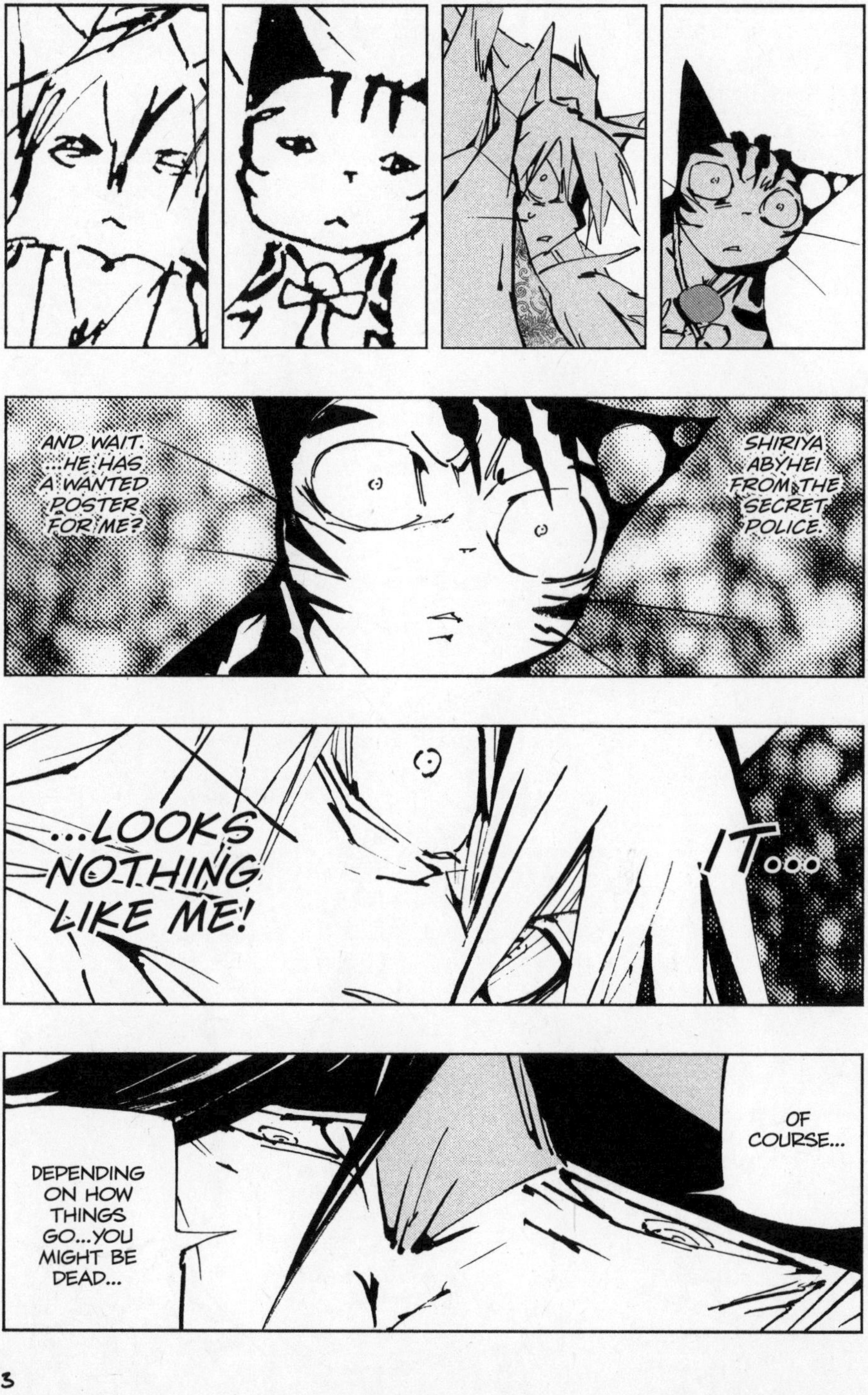
SHIRIYA ABYHEI FROM THE SECRET POLICE.
AND WAIT. ...HE HAS A WANTED POSTER FOR ME?
IT...
...LOOKS NOTHING LIKE ME!
OF COURSE...
DEPENDING ON HOW THINGS GO...YOU MIGHT BE DEAD...

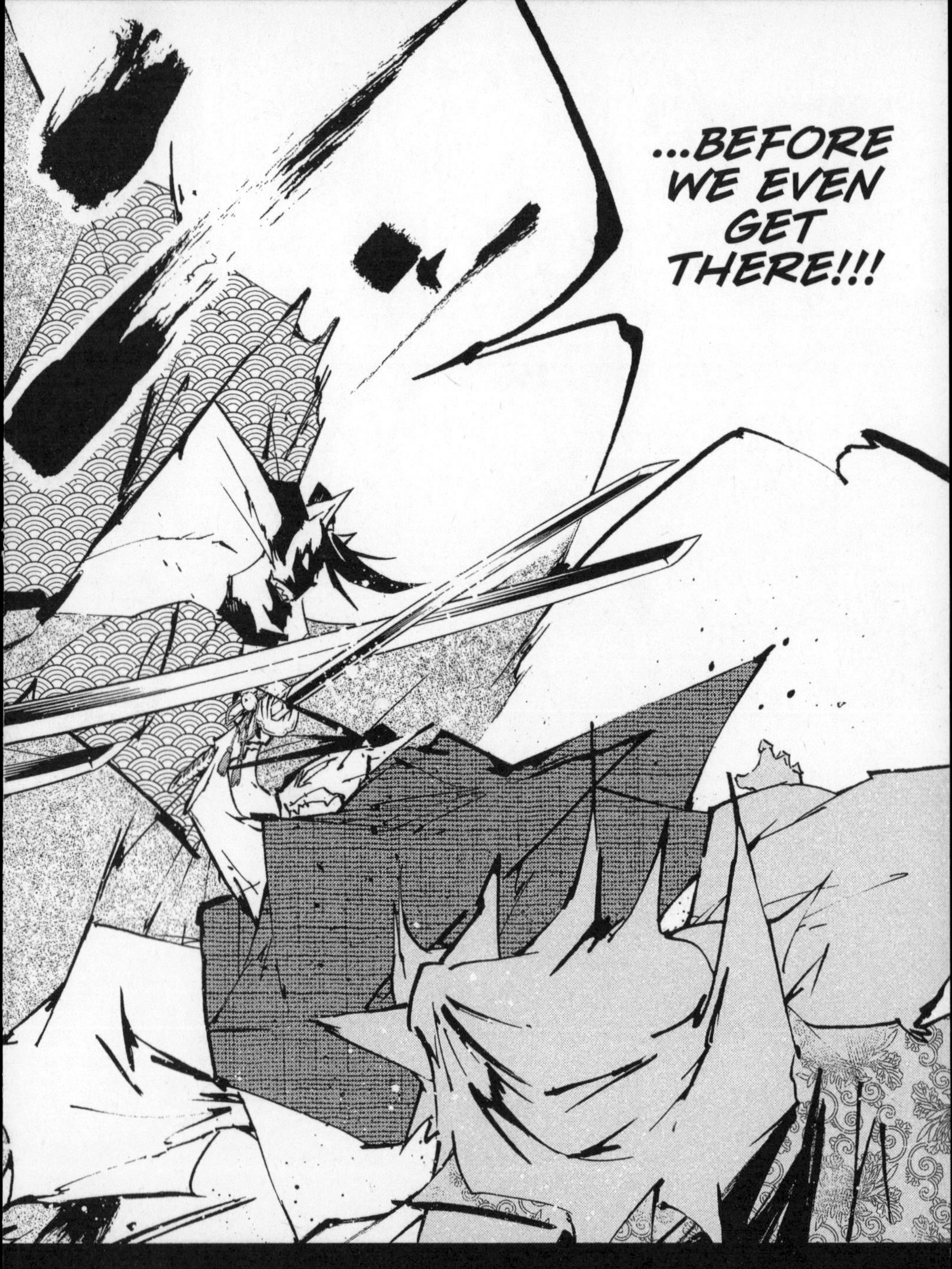
...BEFORE WE EVEN GET THERE!!!

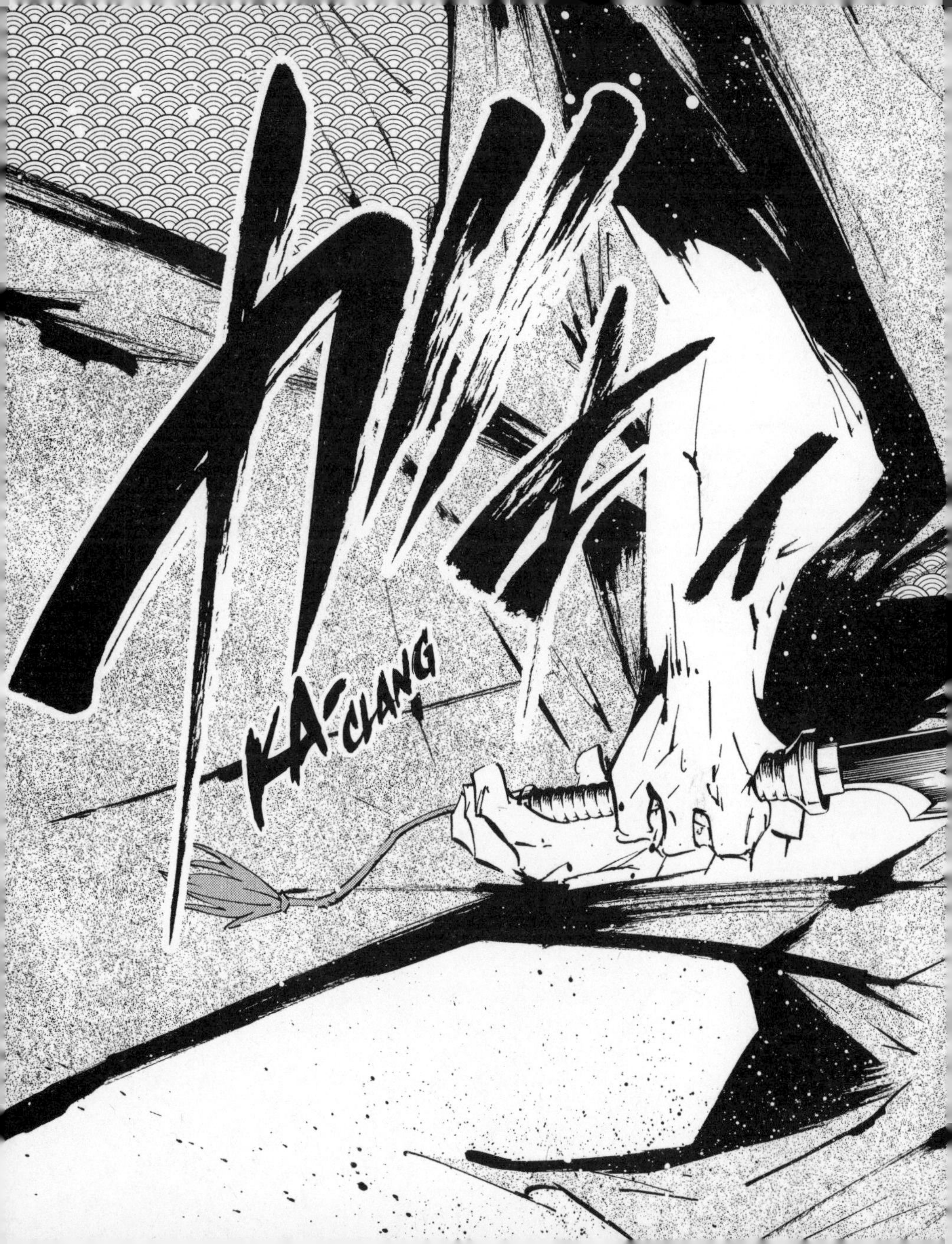

KA-CLANG

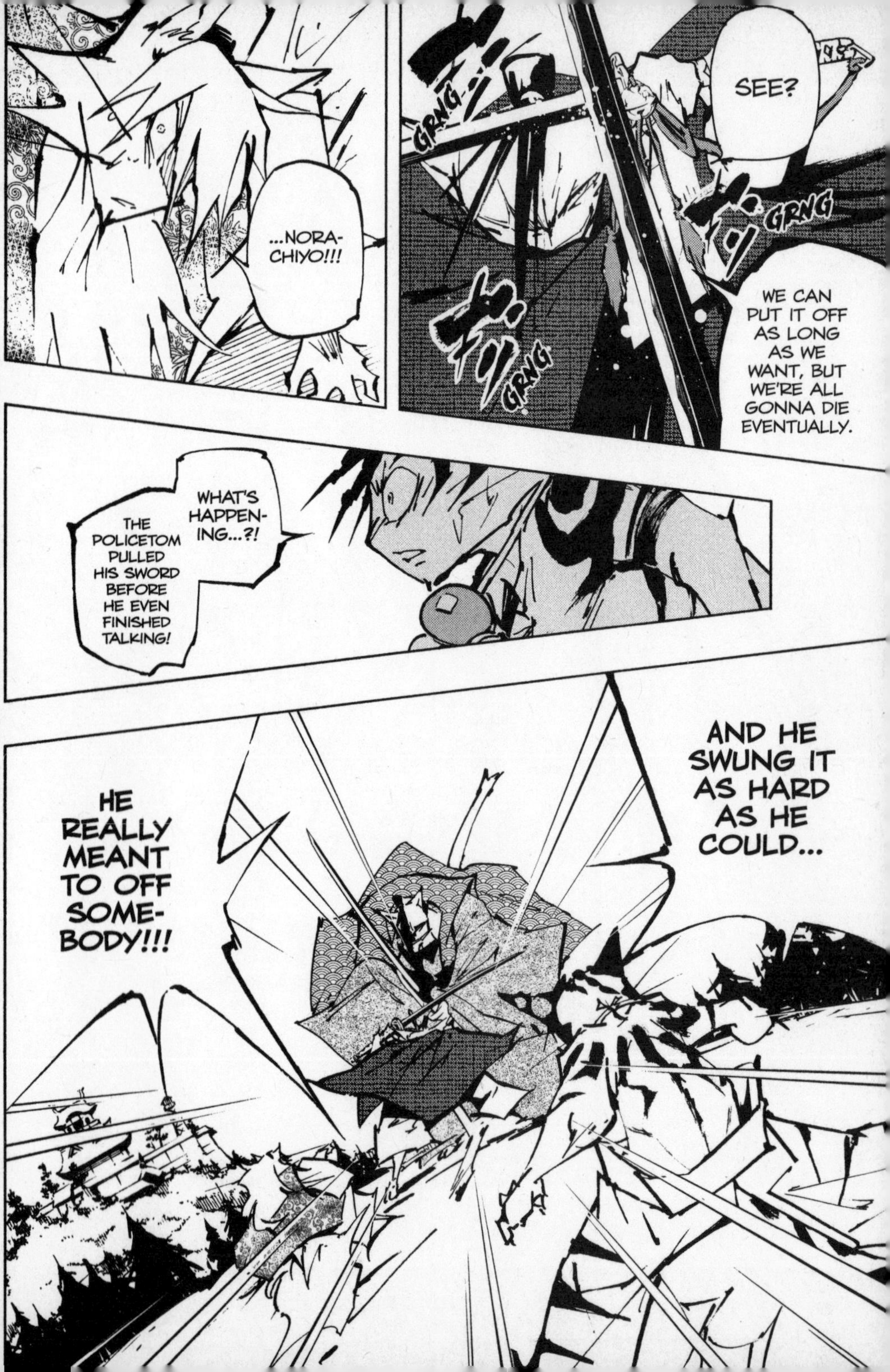
SEE?
GRNG
GRNG
GRNG
GRNG
WE CAN PUT IT OFF AS LONG AS WE WANT, BUT WE'RE ALL GONNA DIE EVENTUALLY.
...NORA-CHIYO!!!
WHAT'S HAPPEN-ING...?!
THE POLICETOM PULLED HIS SWORD BEFORE HE EVEN FINISHED TALKING!
AND HE SWUNG IT AS HARD AS HE COULD...
HE REALLY MEANT TO OFF SOME-BODY!!!

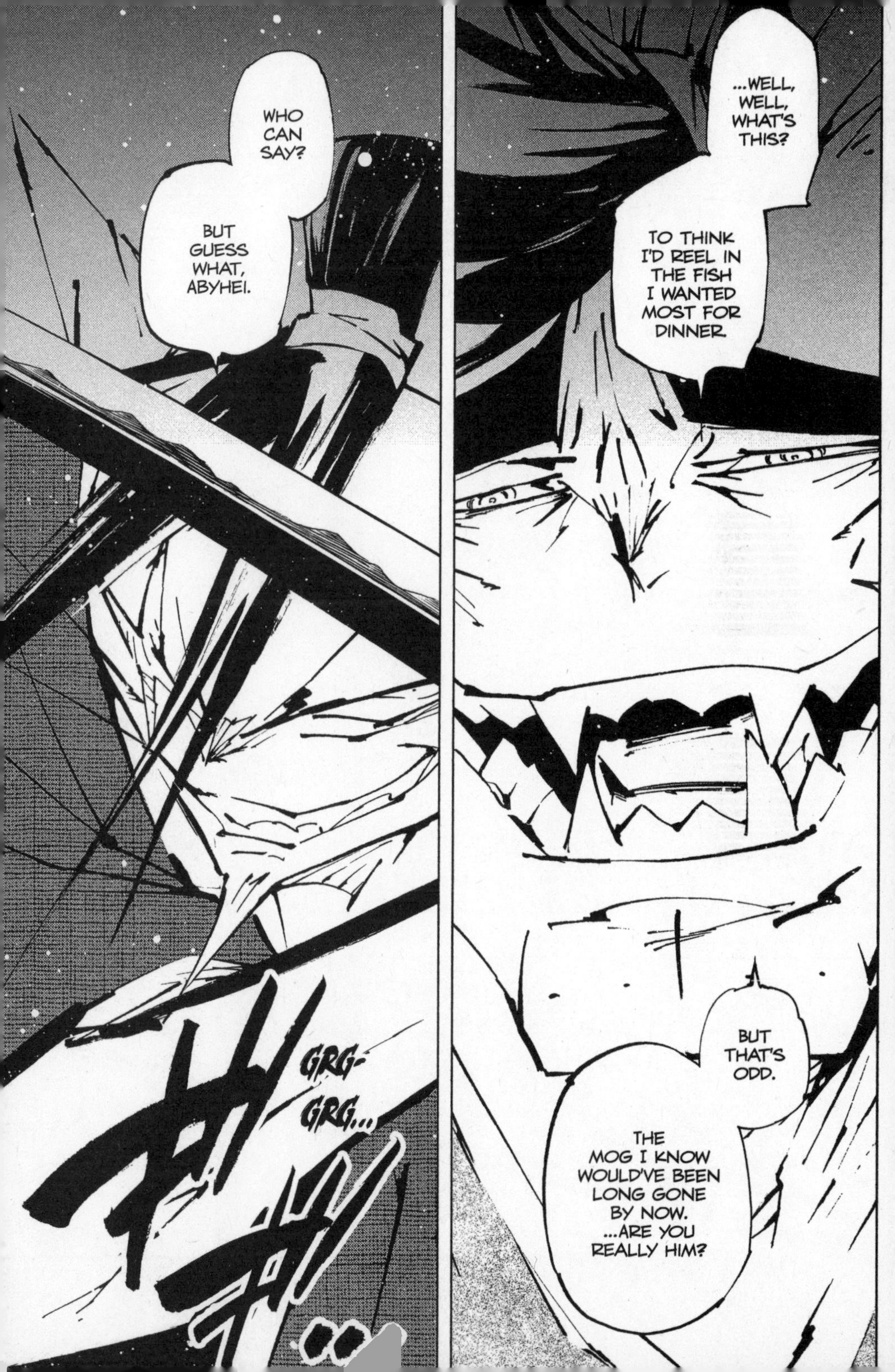
...WELL, WELL, WHAT'S THIS?
TO THINK I'D REEL IN THE FISH I WANTED MOST FOR DINNER.
BUT THAT'S ODD.
THE MOG I KNOW WOULD'VE BEEN LONG GONE BY NOW. ...ARE YOU REALLY HIM?
WHO CAN SAY?
BUT GUESS WHAT, ABYHEI.
GRG-GRG...

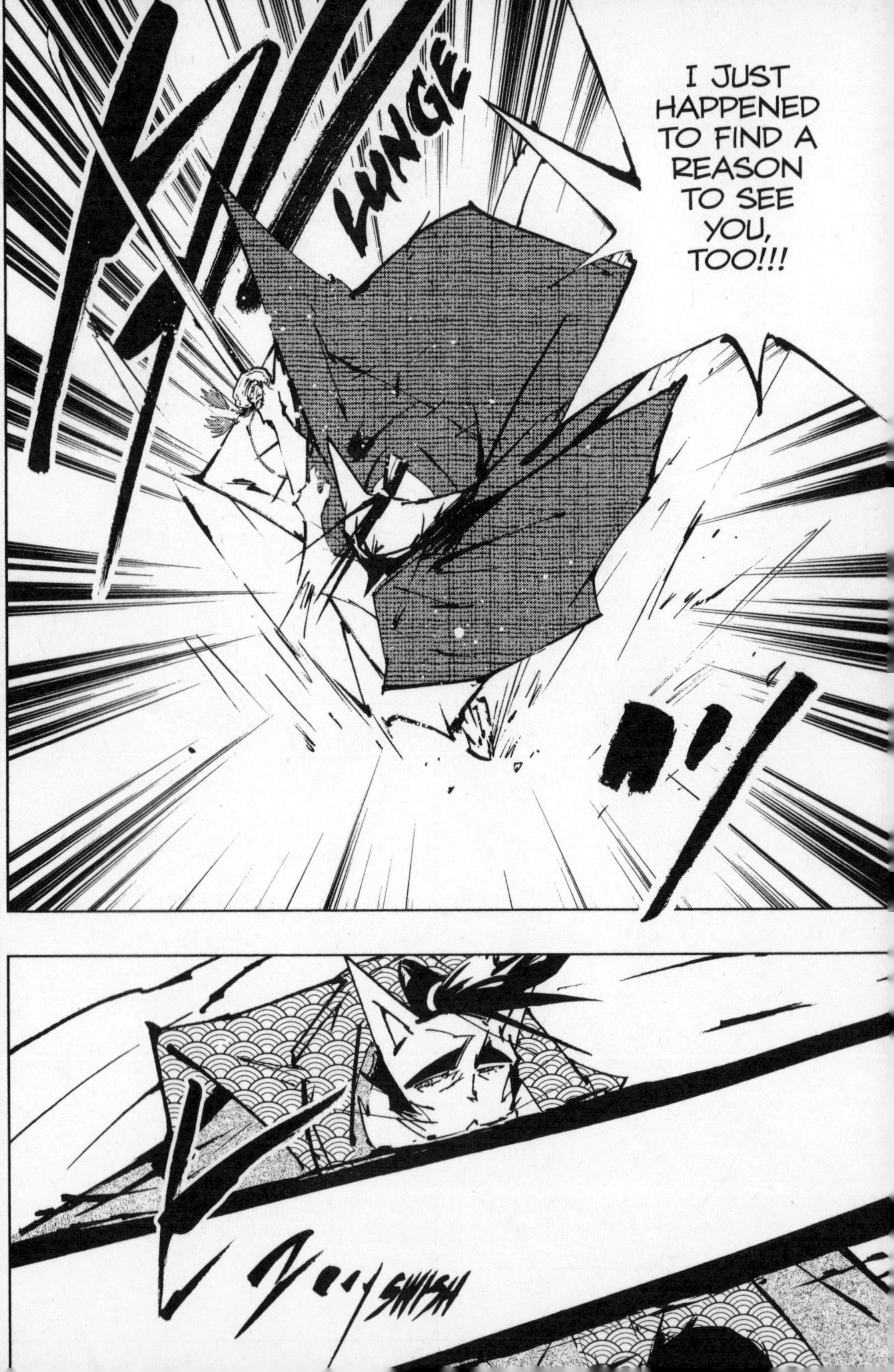
I JUST HAPPENED TO FIND A REASON TO SEE YOU, TOO!!!
LUNGE
SWISH

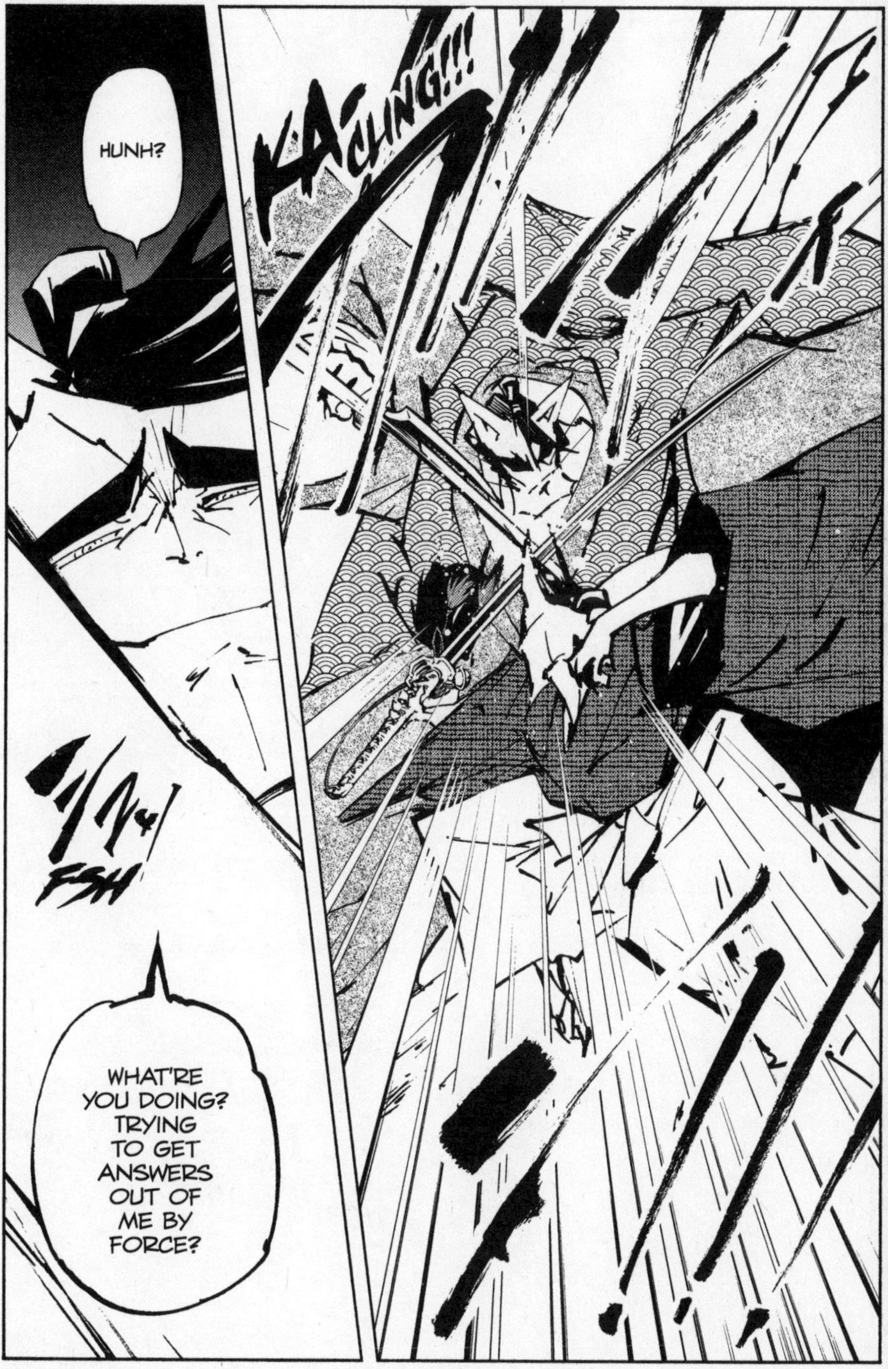
KA-CHING!!!
HUNH?
FSH
WHAT'RE YOU DOING? TRYING TO GET ANSWERS OUT OF ME BY FORCE?

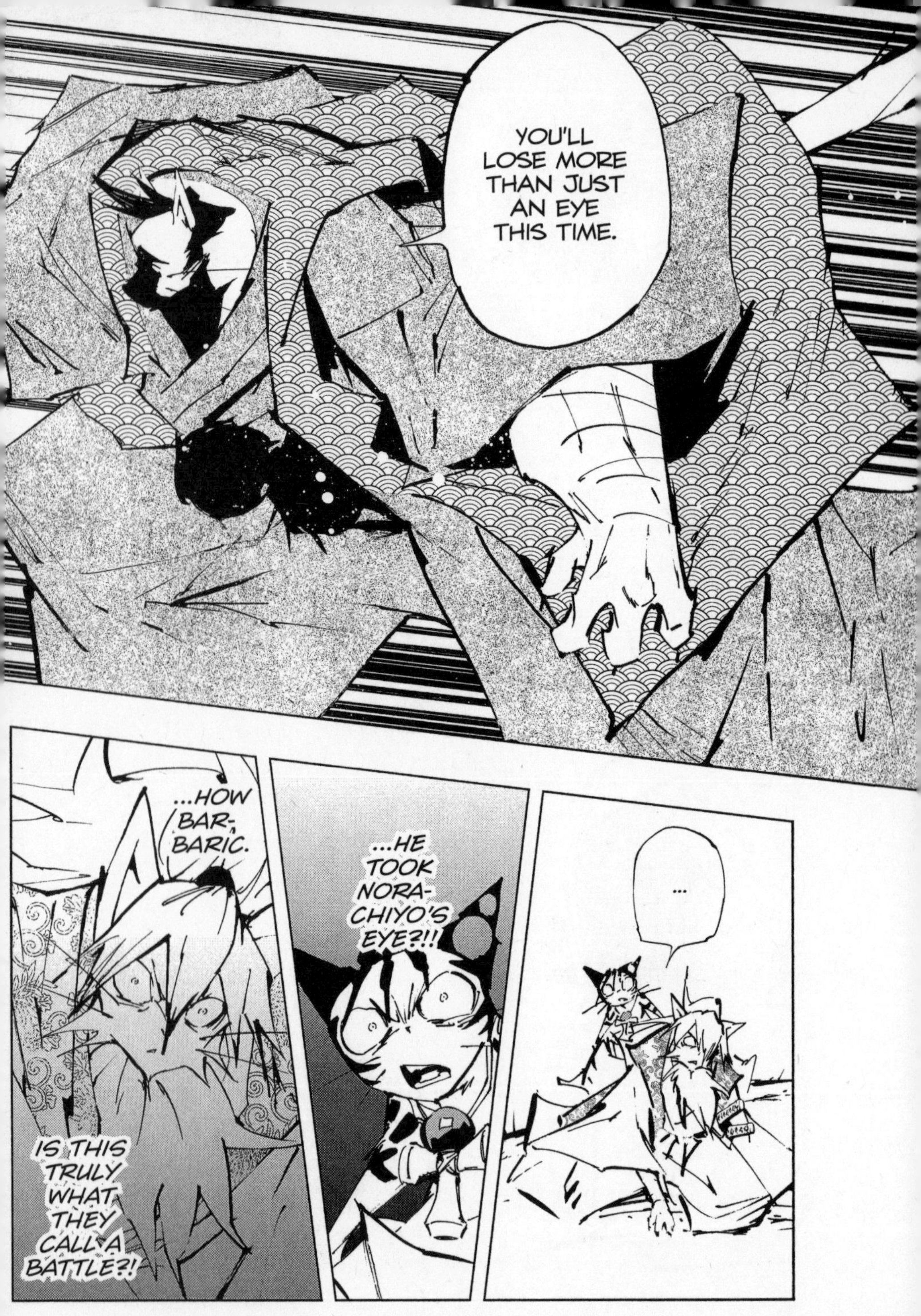
YOU'LL LOSE MORE THAN JUST AN EYE THIS TIME.
...
...HE TOOK NORA-CHIYO'S EYE?!!
...HOW BAR-BARIC.
IS THIS TRULY WHAT THEY CALL A BATTLE?!

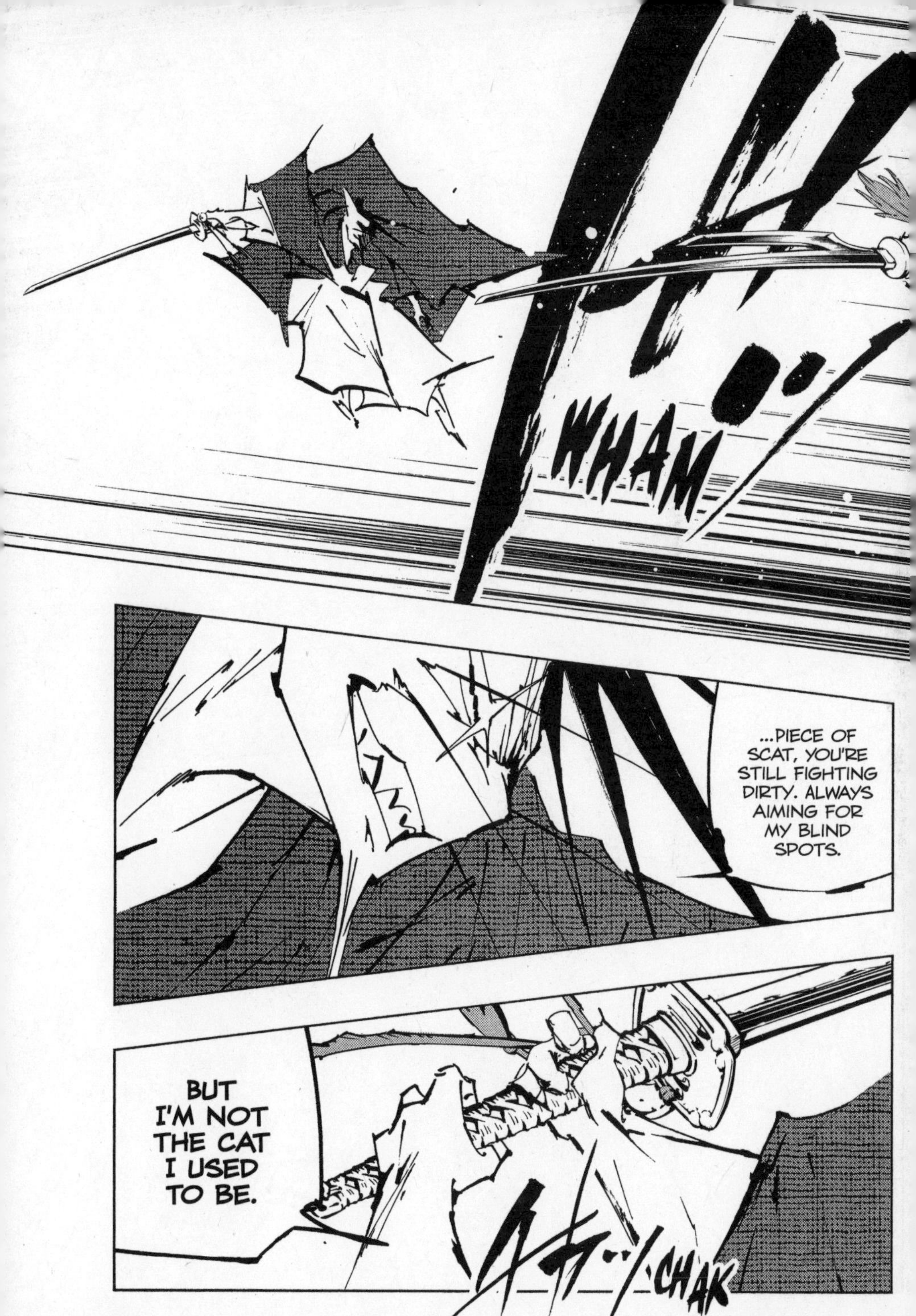
WHAM
...PIECE OF SCAT, YOU'RE STILL FIGHTING DIRTY. ALWAYS AIMING FOR MY BLIND SPOTS.
BUT I'M NOT THE CAT I USED TO BE.
CHAK

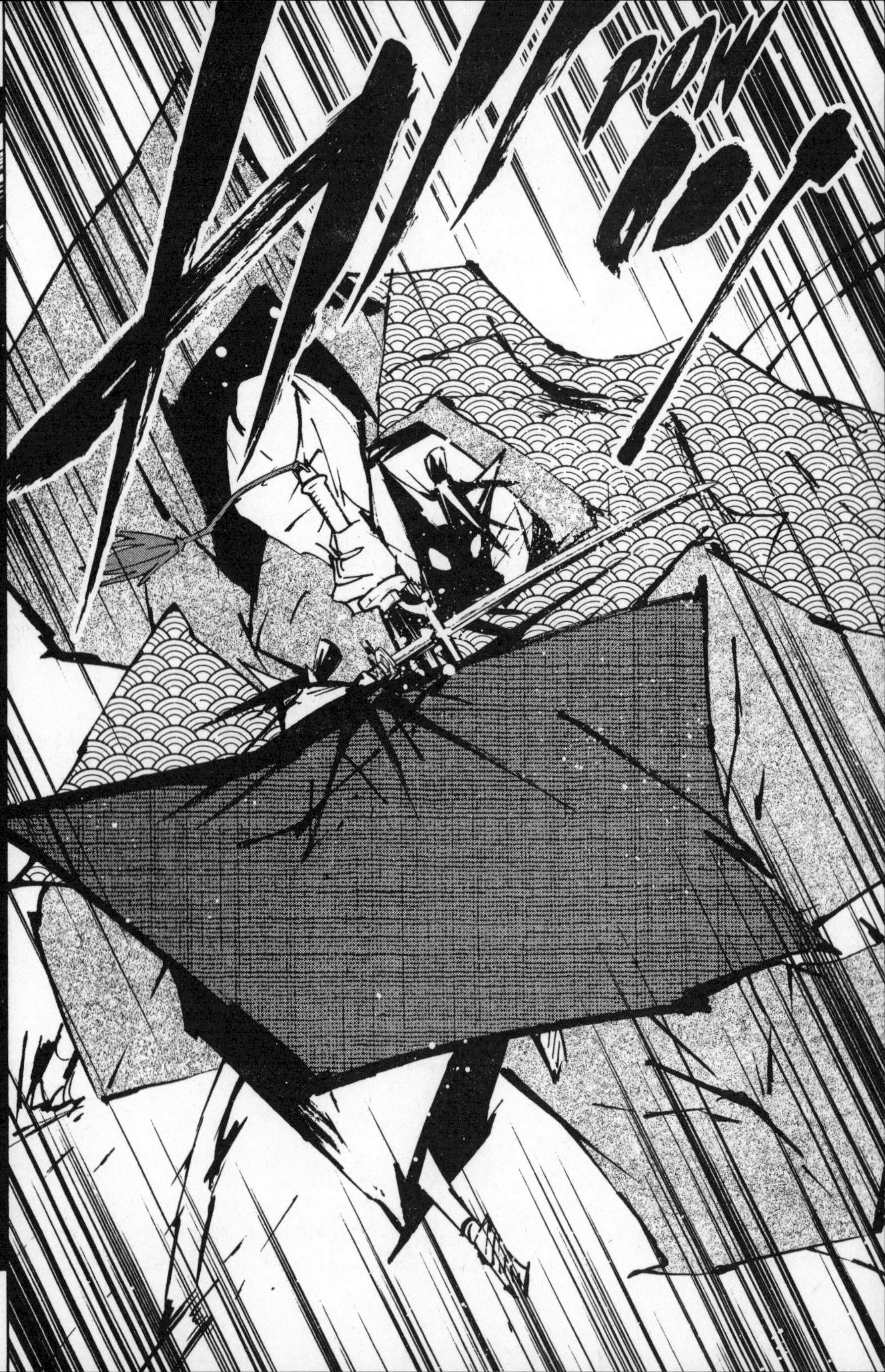

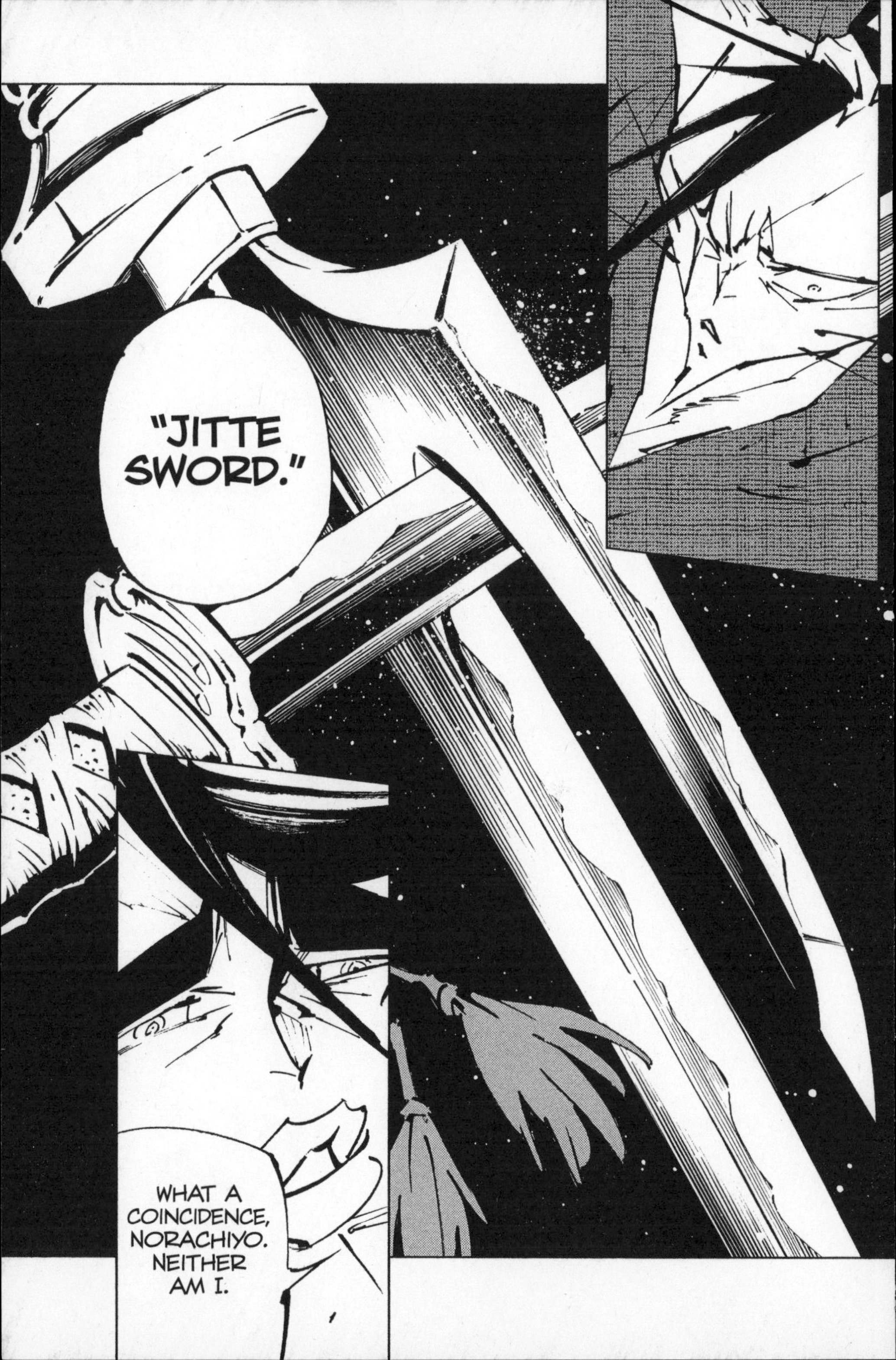
"JITTE SWORD."
WHAT A COINCIDENCE, NORACHIYO. NEITHER AM I.

猫ヶ原

NeKoGaHaRa

ネコガハラ

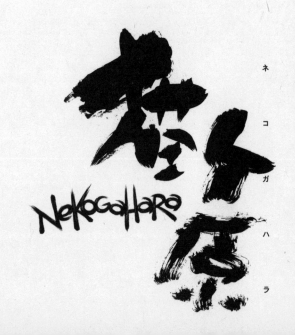

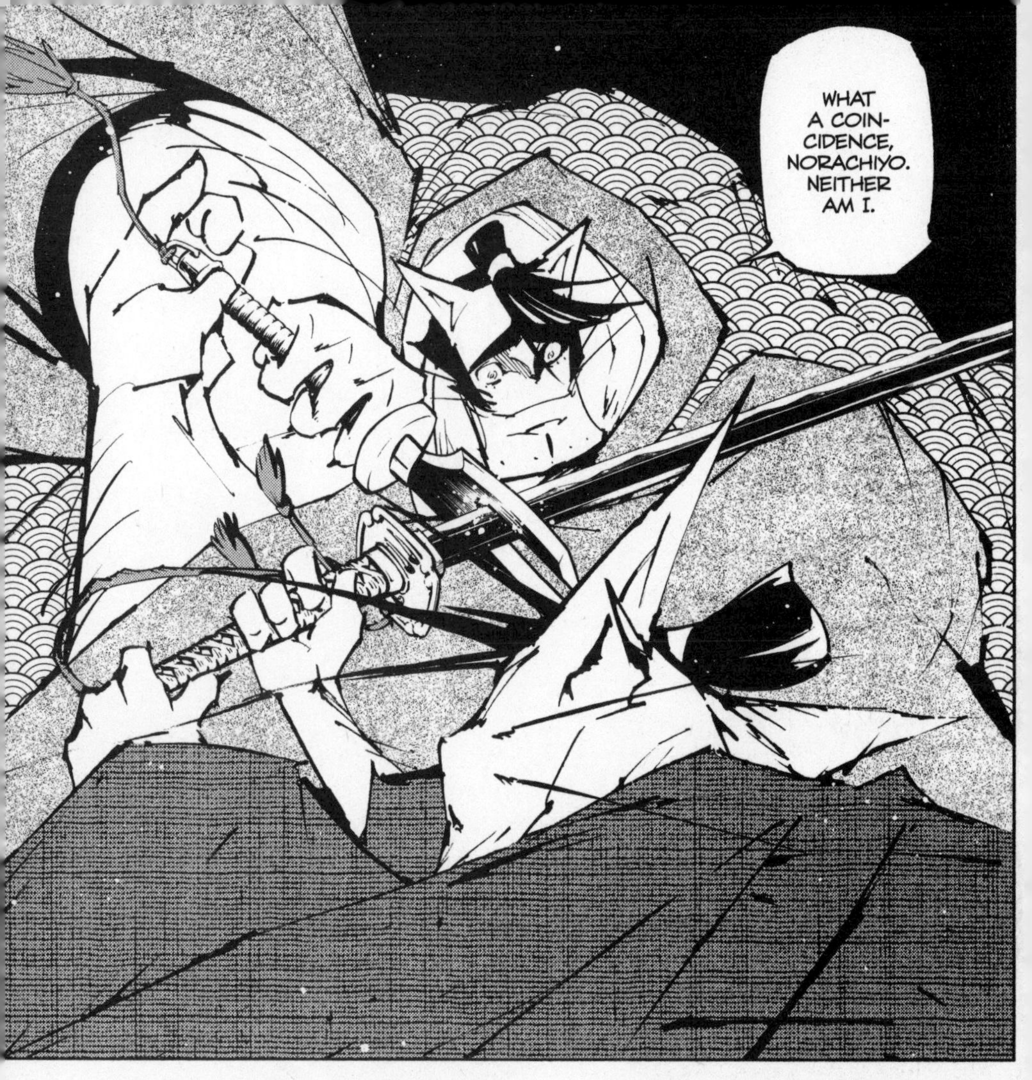
WHAT A COIN-CIDENCE, NORACHIYO. NEITHER AM I.

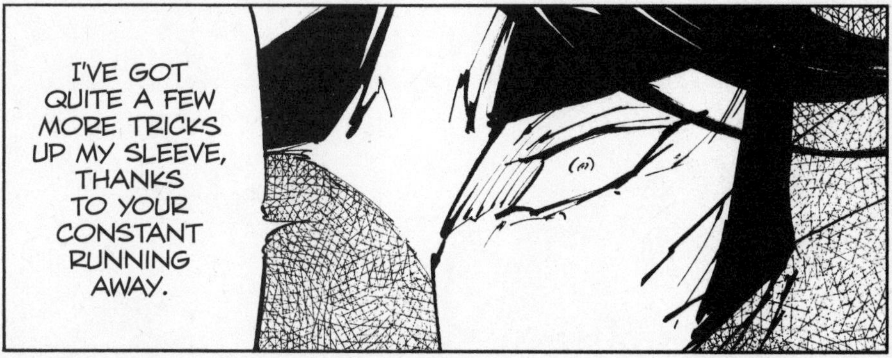
I'VE GOT QUITE A FEW MORE TRICKS UP MY SLEEVE, THANKS TO YOUR CONSTANT RUNNING AWAY.

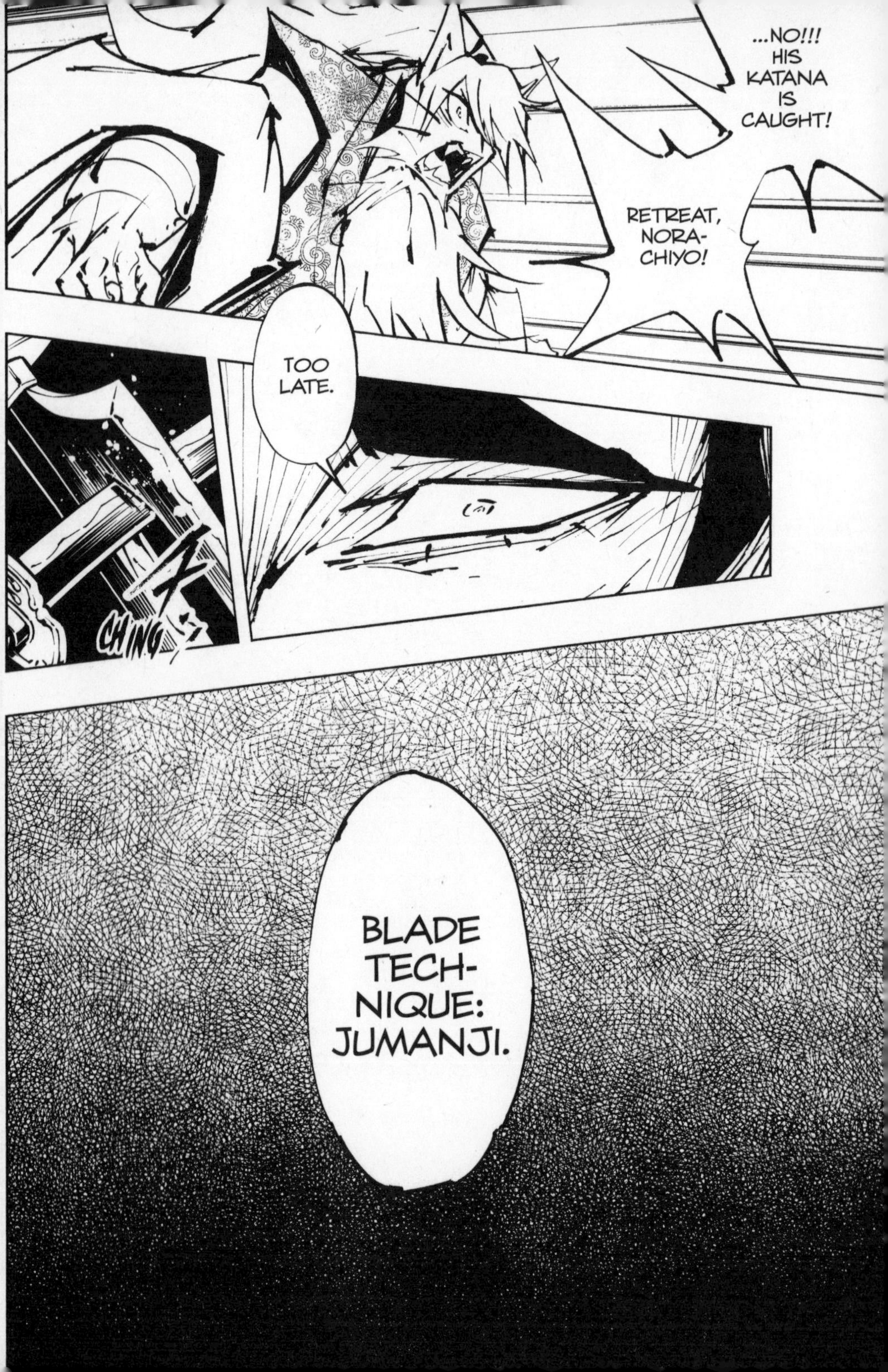
...NO!!! HIS KATANA IS CAUGHT!
RETREAT, NORA-CHIYO!
TOO LATE.
CHING
BLADE TECH-NIQUE: JUMANJI.

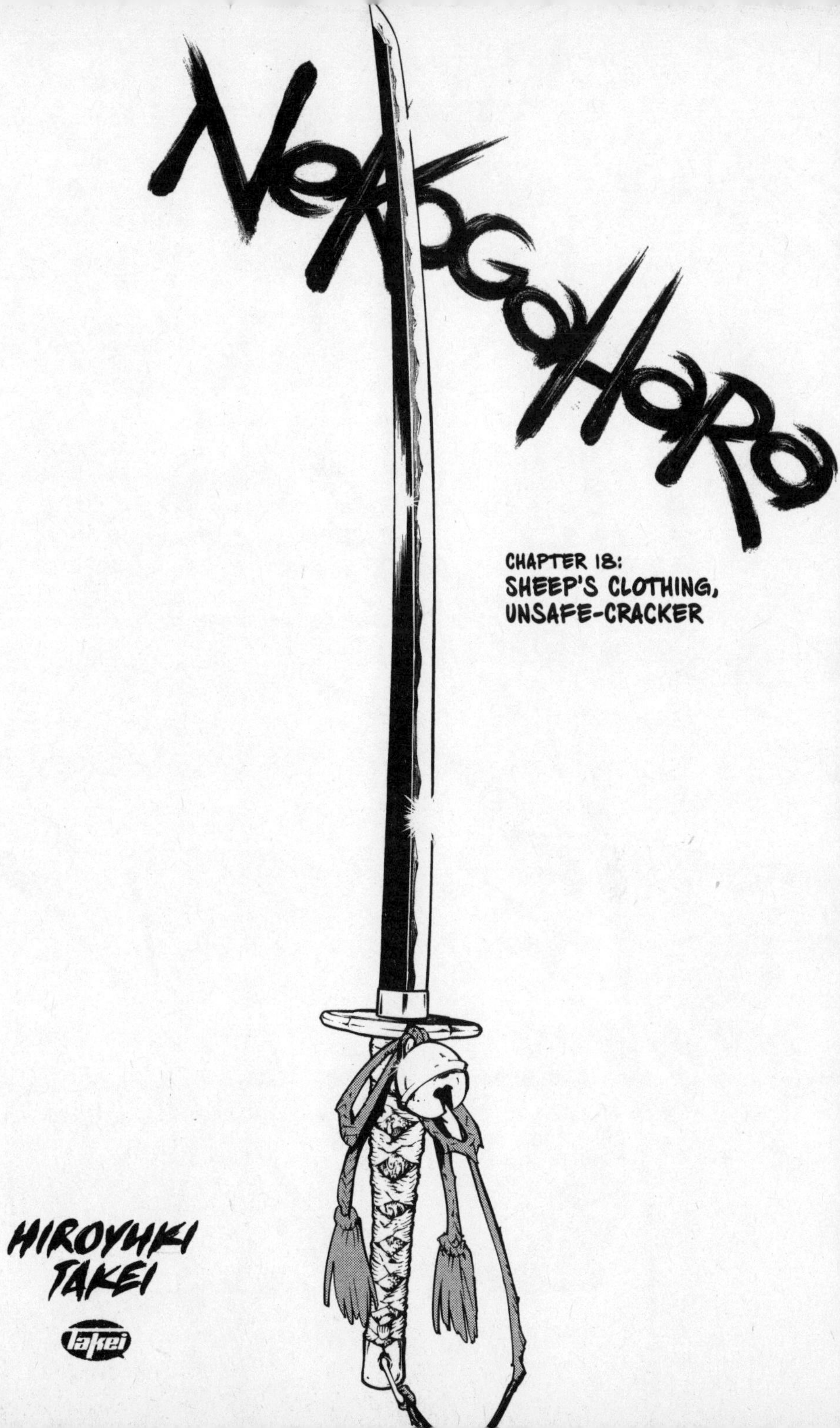
NEKOGAHARA
CHAPTER 18:
SHEEP'S CLOTHING,
UNSAFE-CRACKER
HIROYUKI
TAKEI
Takei

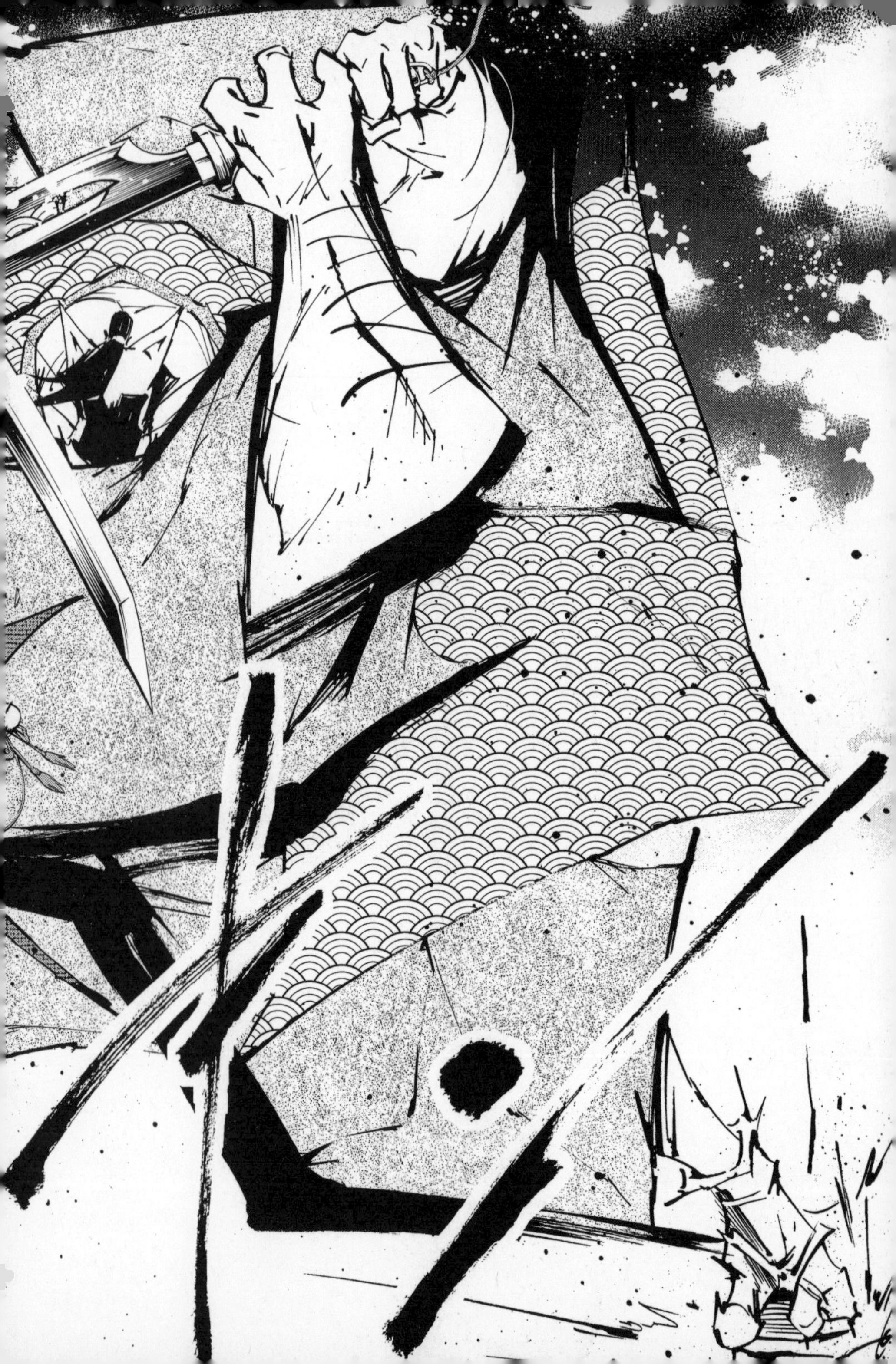

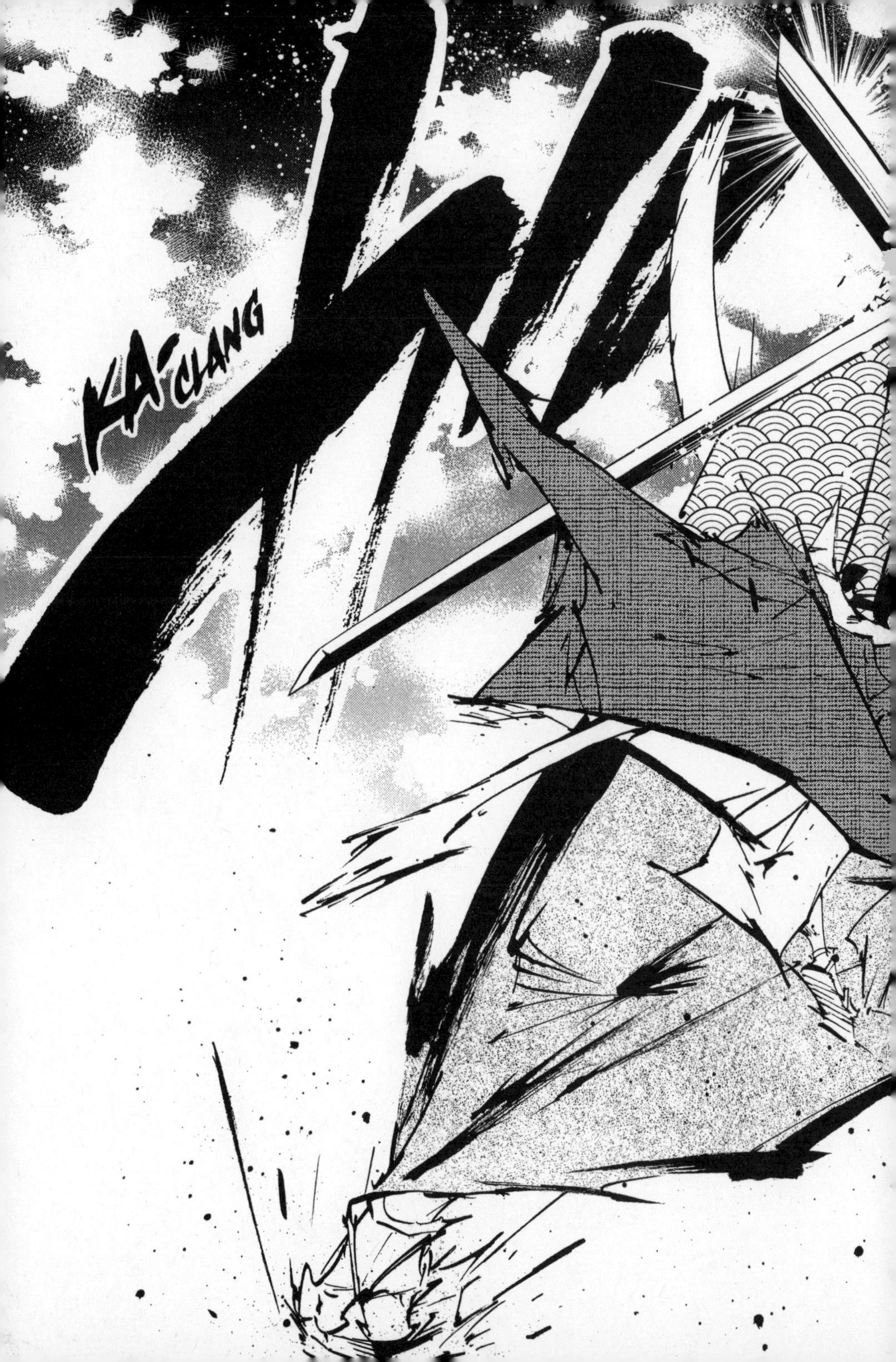
KA-CLANG

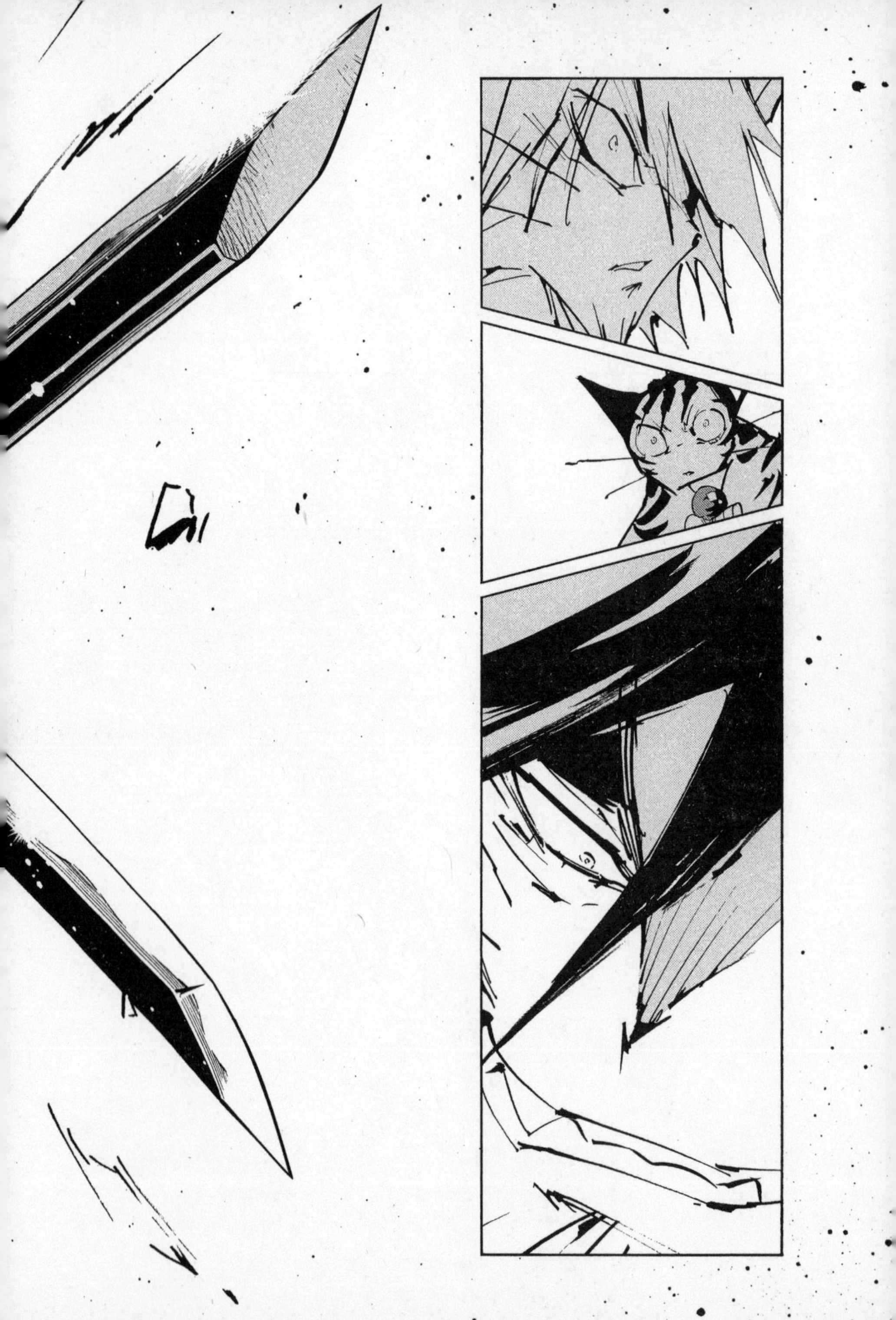

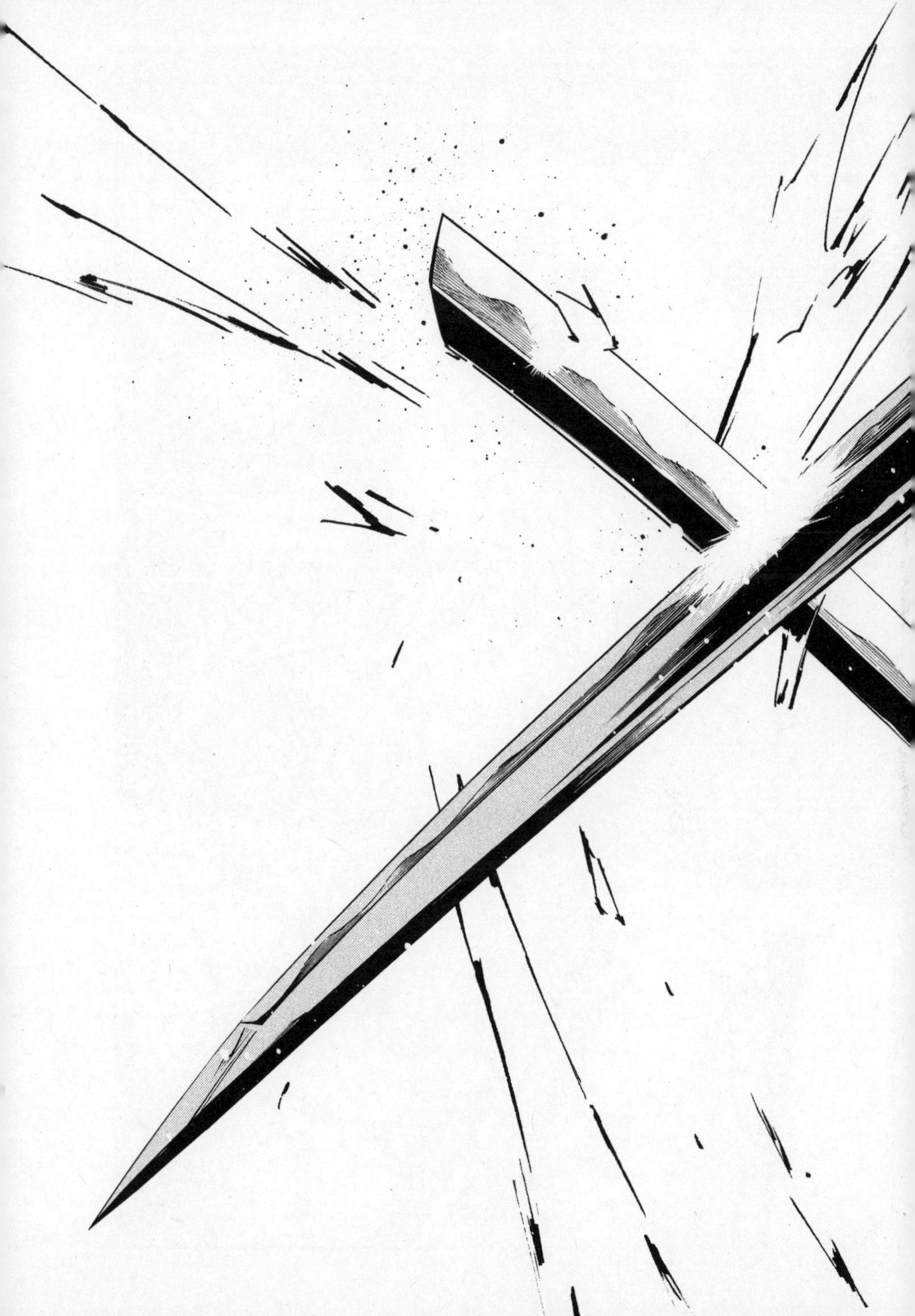

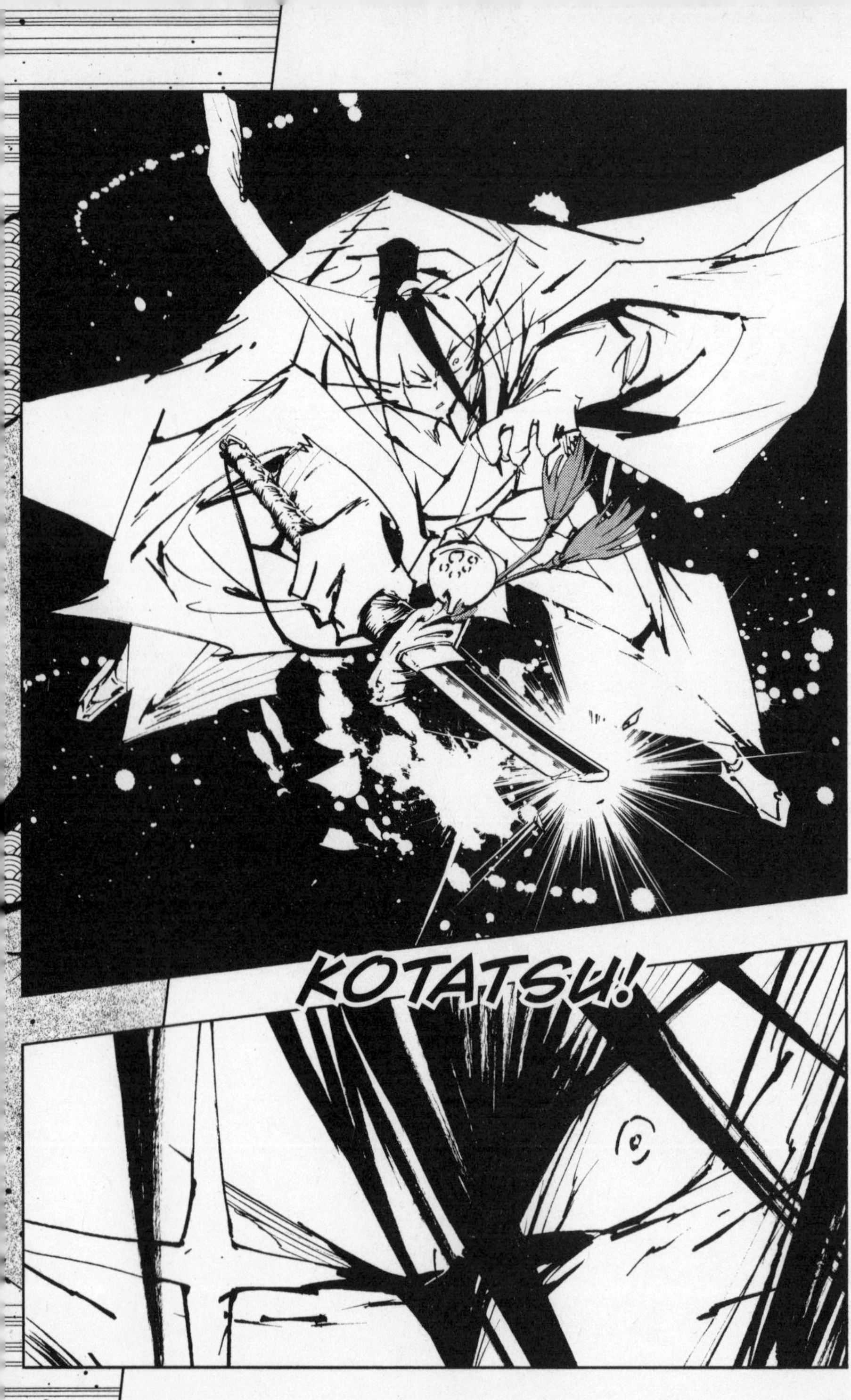
KOTATSU!

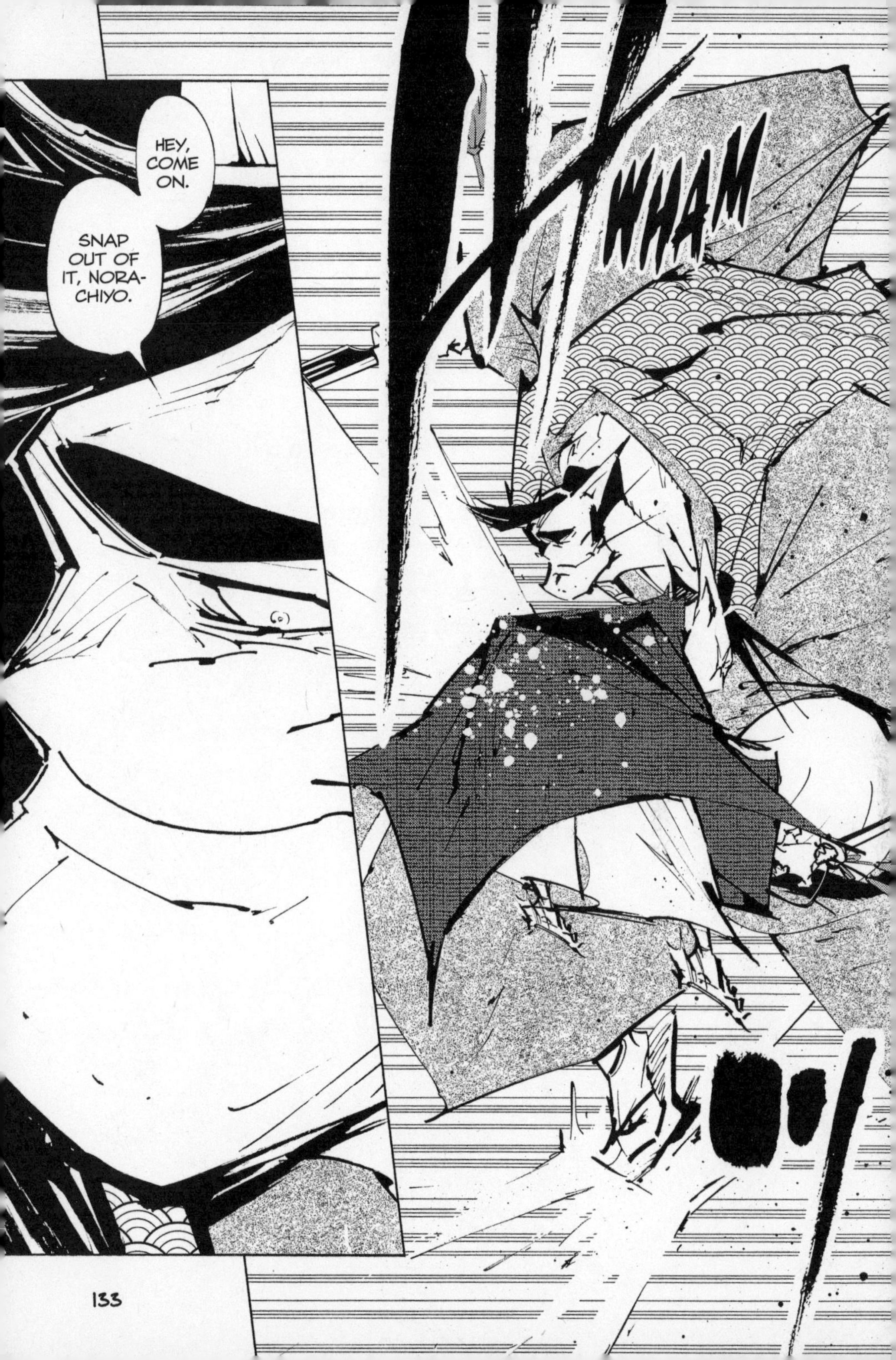
WHAM
HEY, COME ON.
SNAP OUT OF IT, NORA-CHIYO.

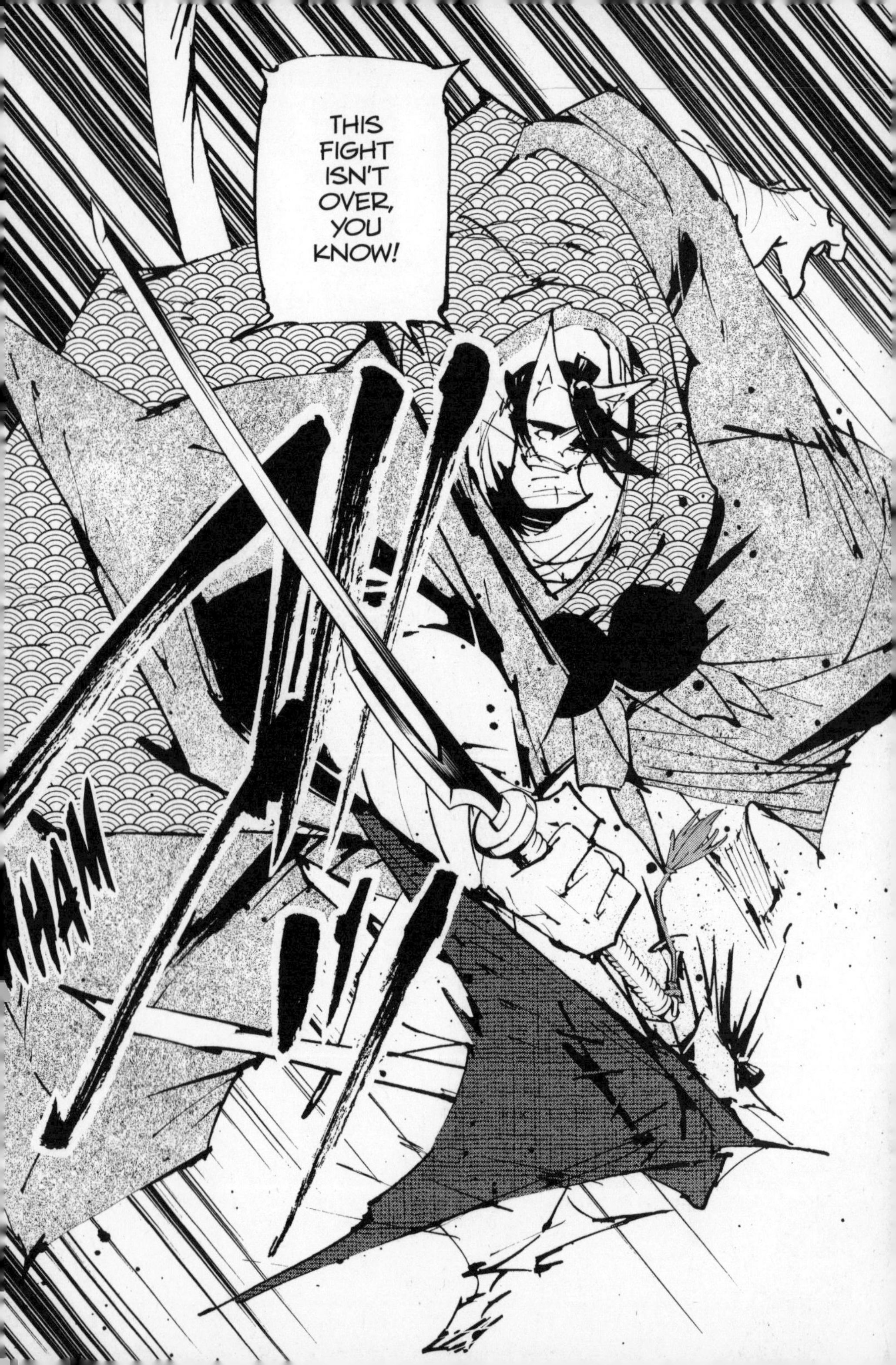
THIS FIGHT ISN'T OVER, YOU KNOW!
WHAM

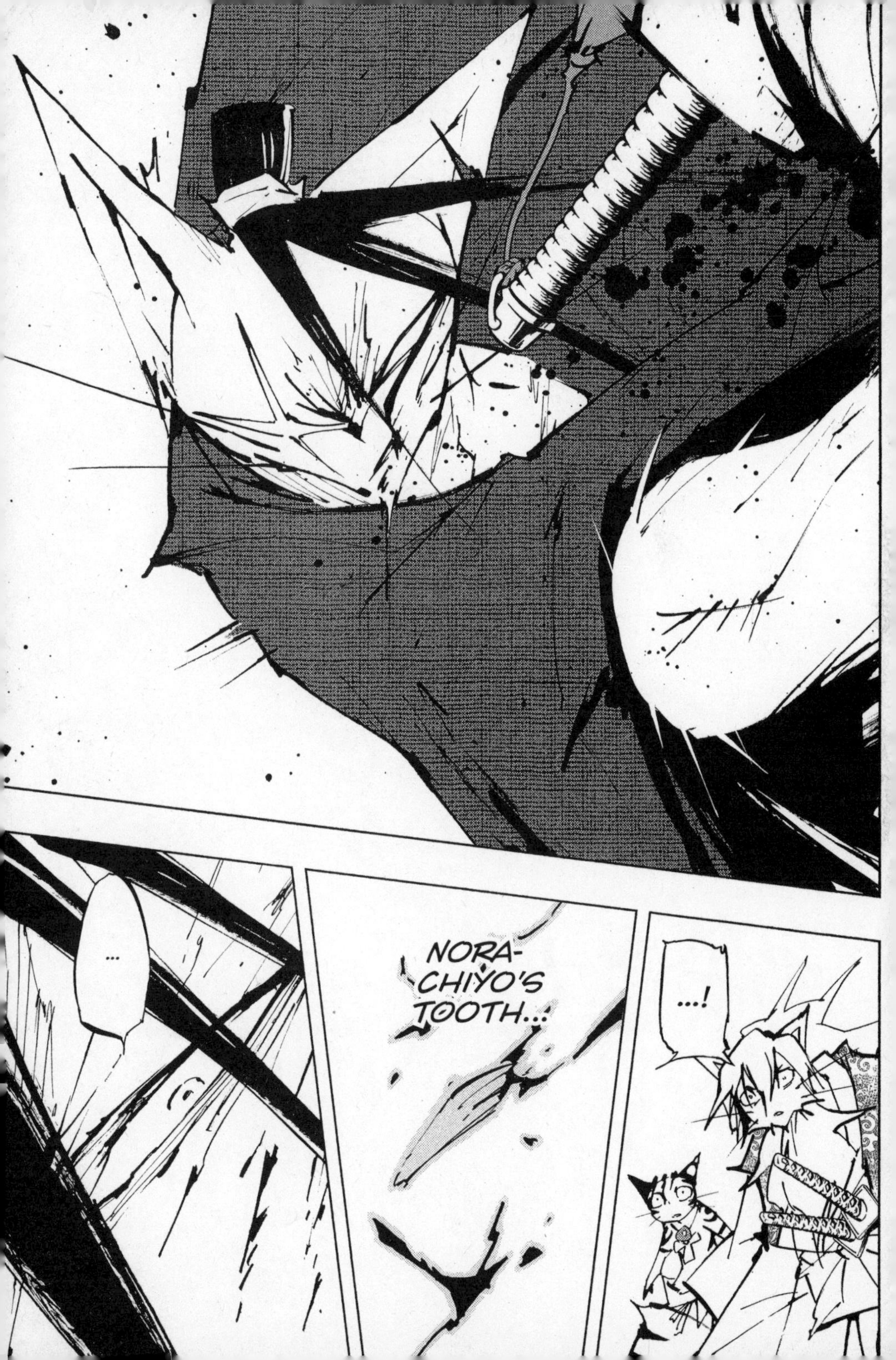
...!
NORA-CHIYO'S TOOTH...
...

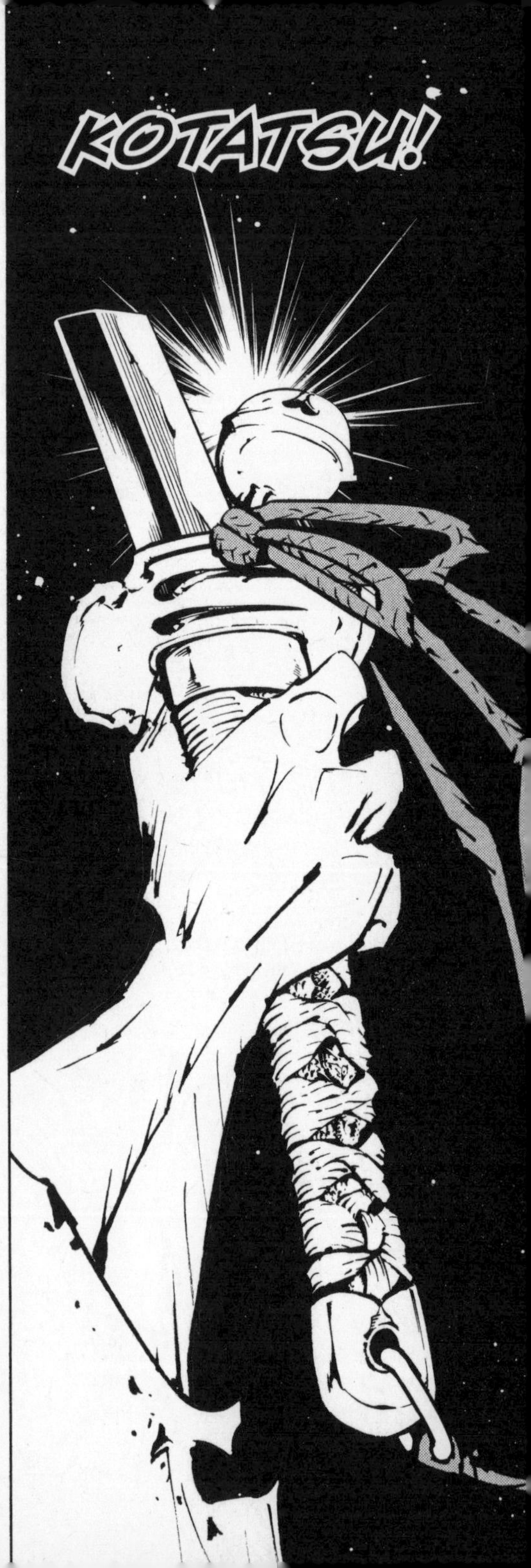
KOTATSU!

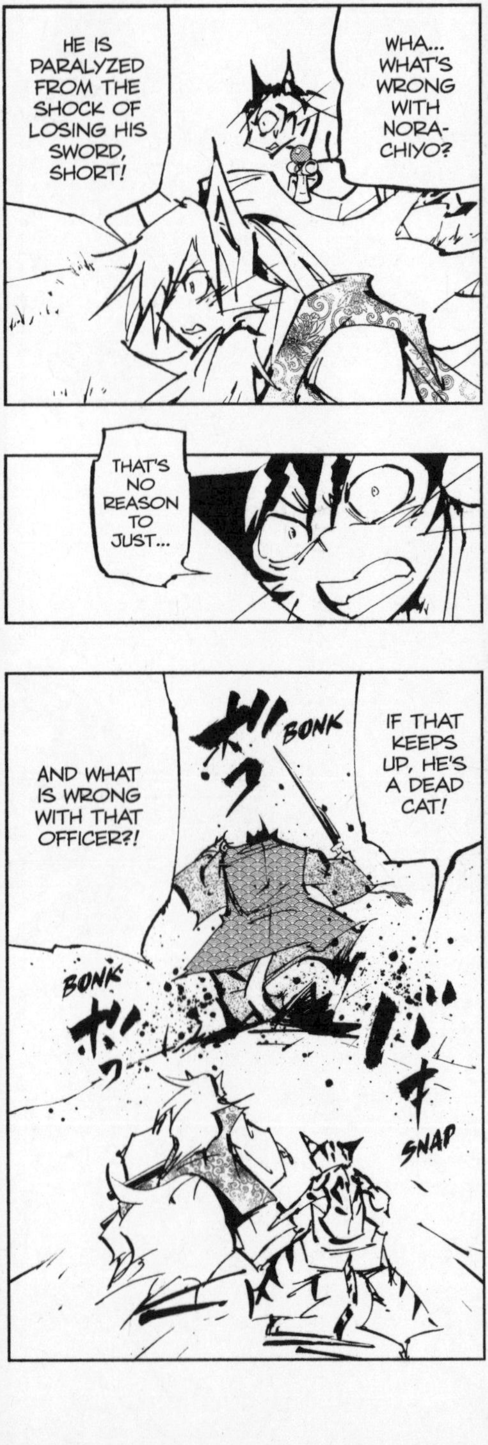
WHA... WHAT'S WRONG WITH NORA-CHIYO?
HE IS PARALYZED FROM THE SHOCK OF LOSING HIS SWORD, SHORT!
THAT'S NO REASON TO JUST...
IF THAT KEEPS UP, HE'S A DEAD CAT!
BONK
AND WHAT IS WRONG WITH THAT OFFICER?!
BONK
SNAP

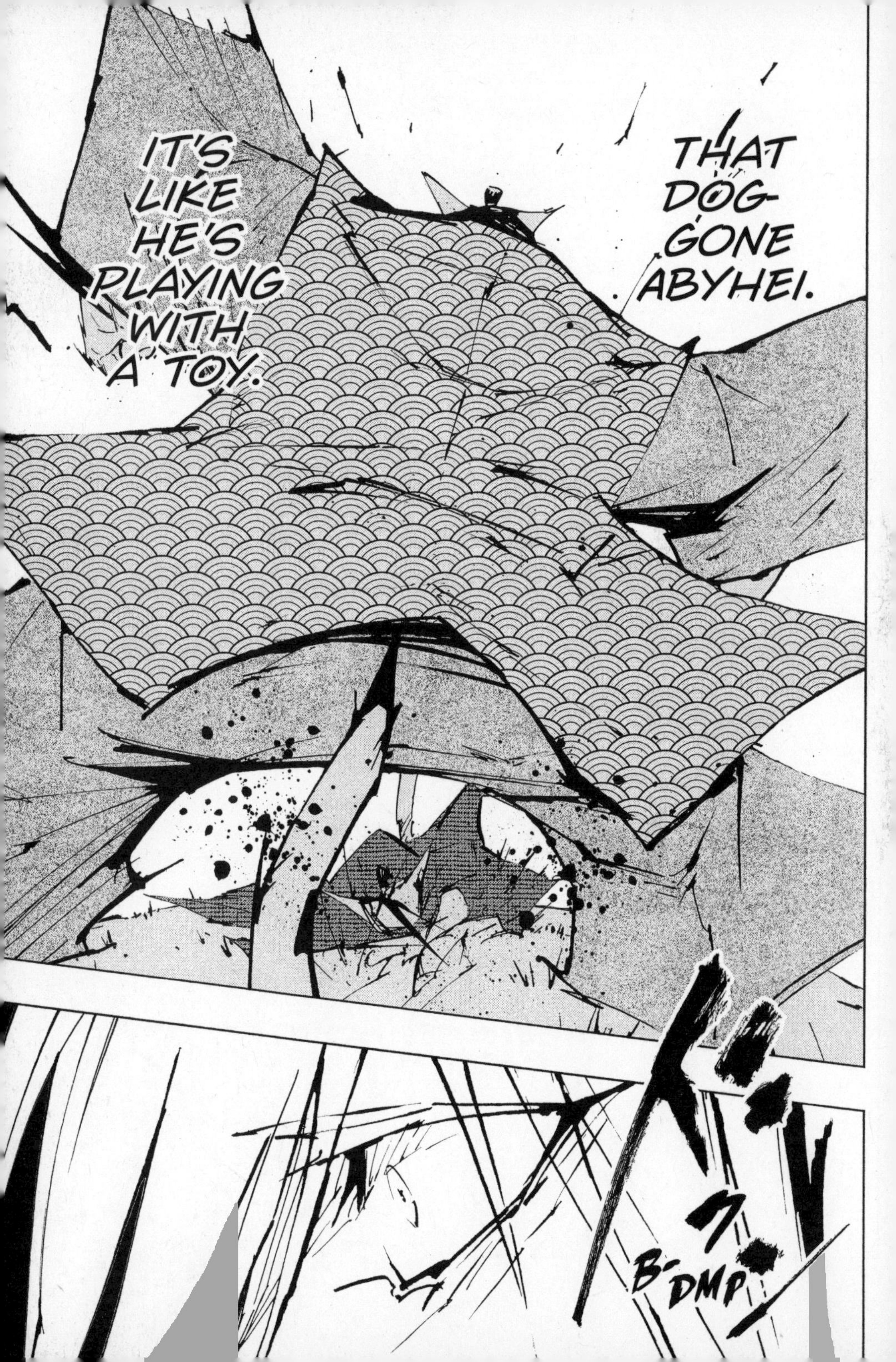
THAT DOG-GONE ABYHEI.
IT'S LIKE HE'S PLAYING WITH A TOY.
B-DMP

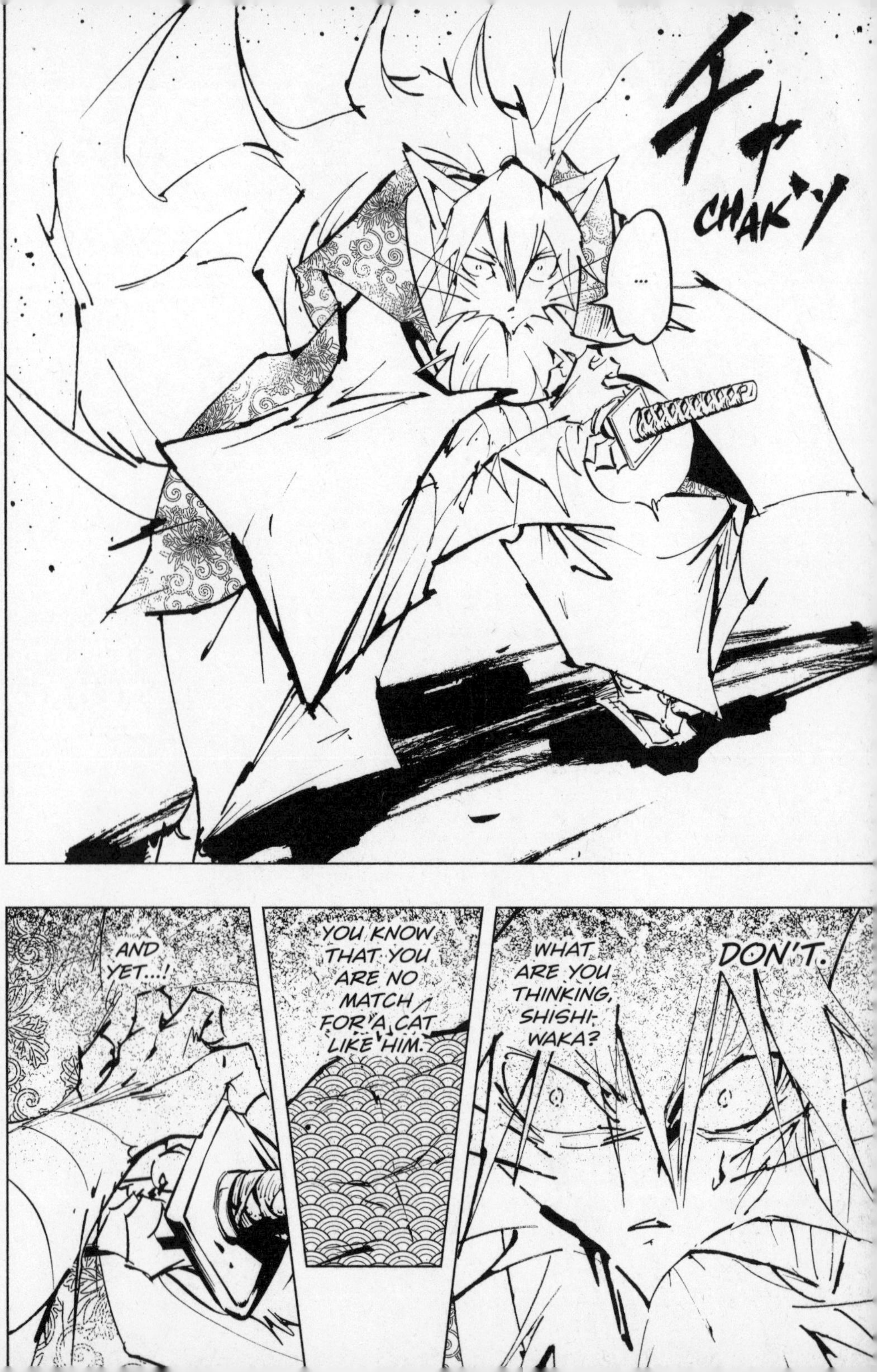
CHAK
...
DON'T.
WHAT ARE YOU THINKING, SHISHI-WAKA?
YOU KNOW THAT YOU ARE NO MATCH FOR A CAT LIKE HIM.
AND YET...!

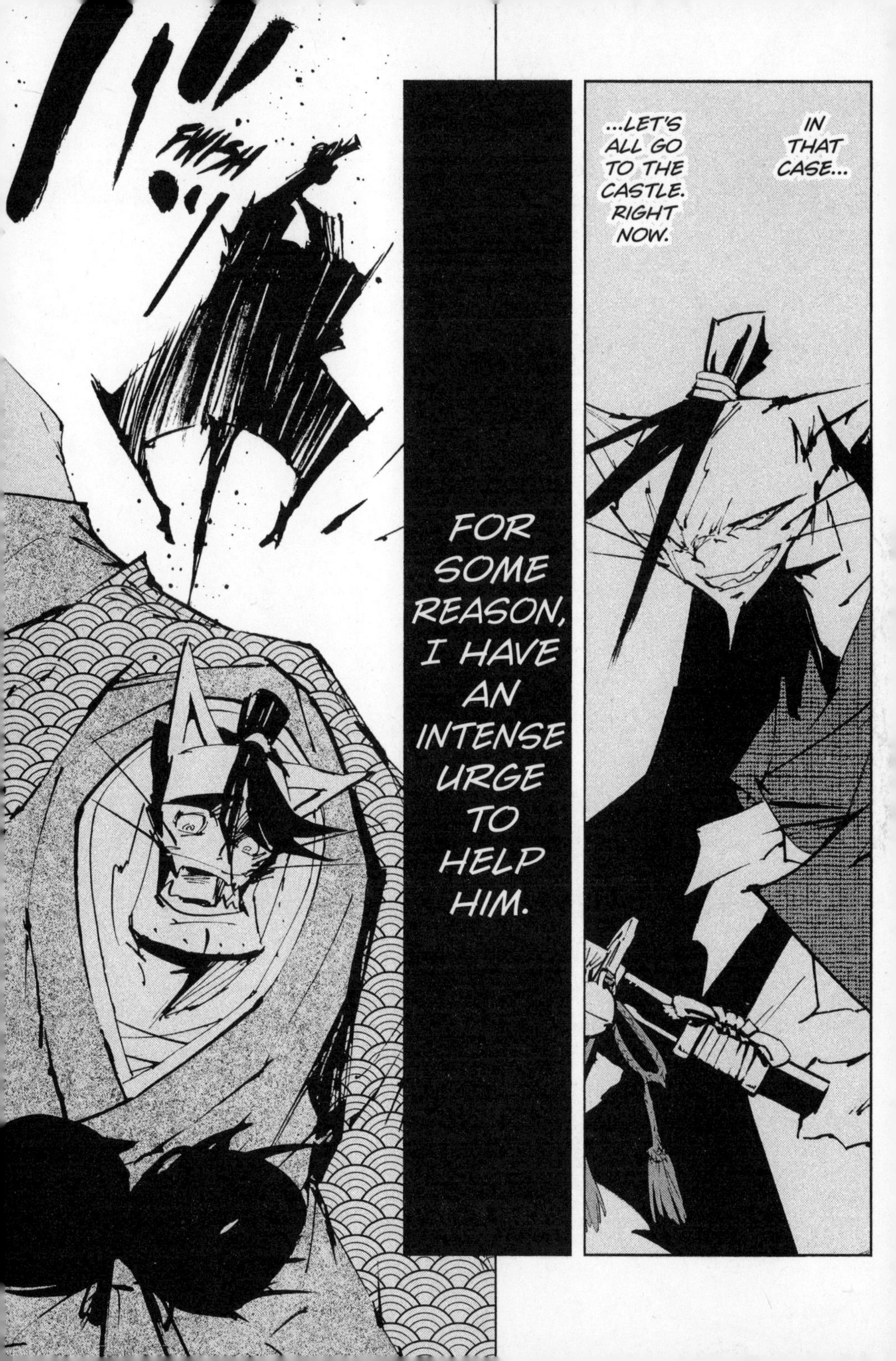
IN THAT CASE...
...LET'S ALL GO TO THE CASTLE. RIGHT NOW.
FOR SOME REASON, I HAVE AN INTENSE URGE TO HELP HIM.
FWISH

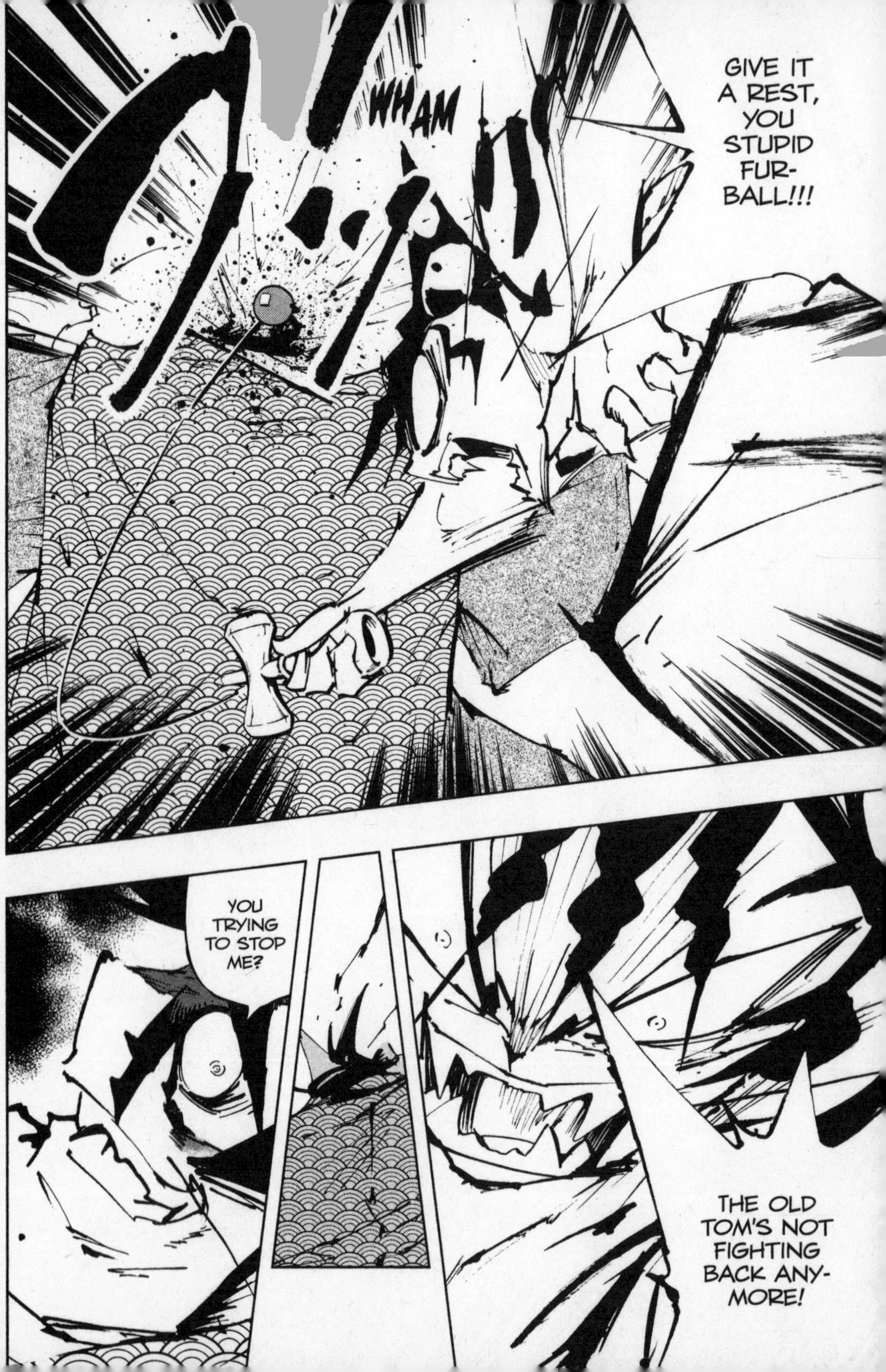
GIVE IT A REST, YOU STUPID FUR-BALL!!!
WHAM
THE OLD TOM'S NOT FIGHTING BACK ANY-MORE!
YOU TRYING TO STOP ME?

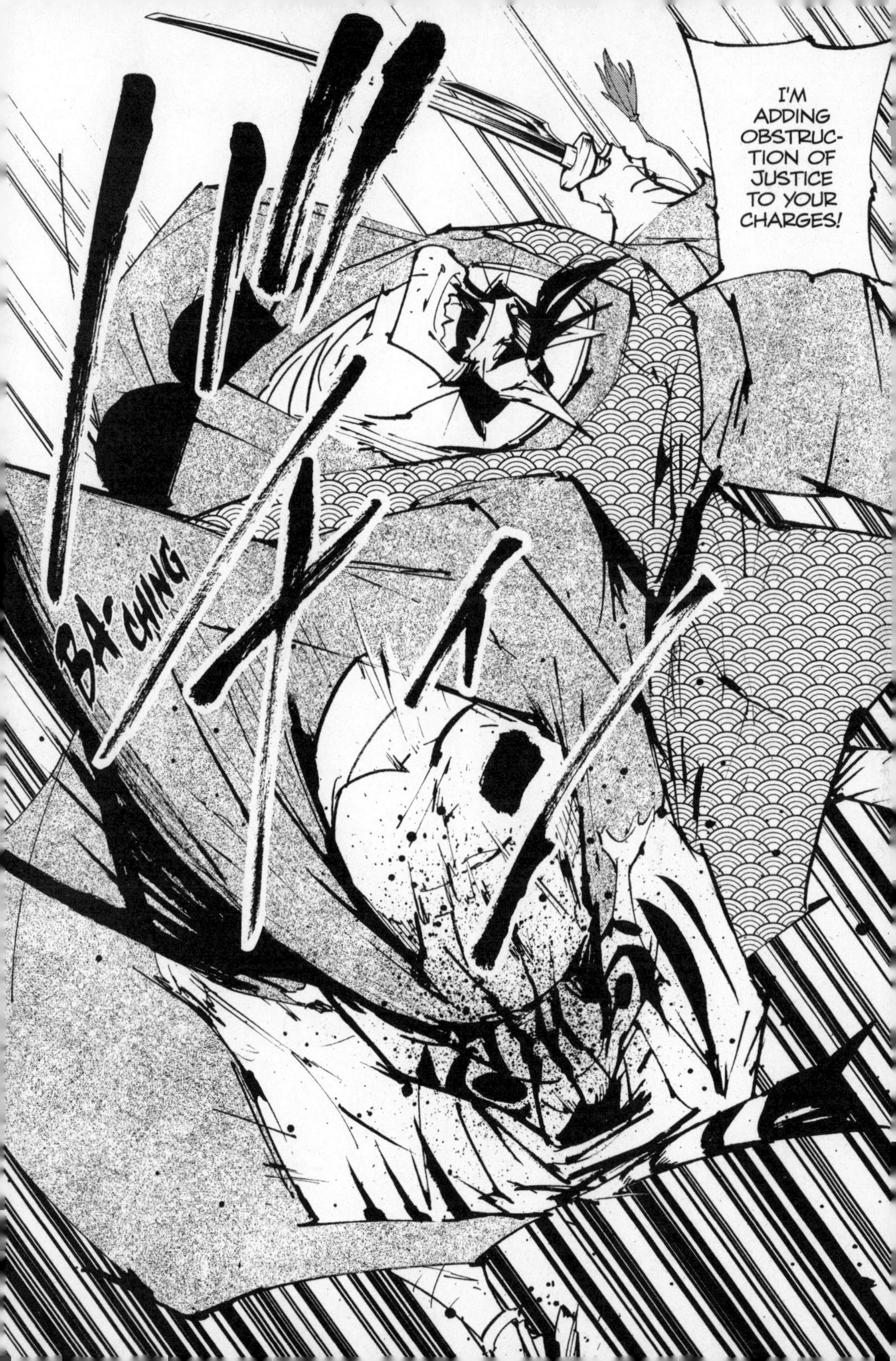
I'M ADDING OBSTRUCTION OF JUSTICE TO YOUR CHARGES!
BA-CHING

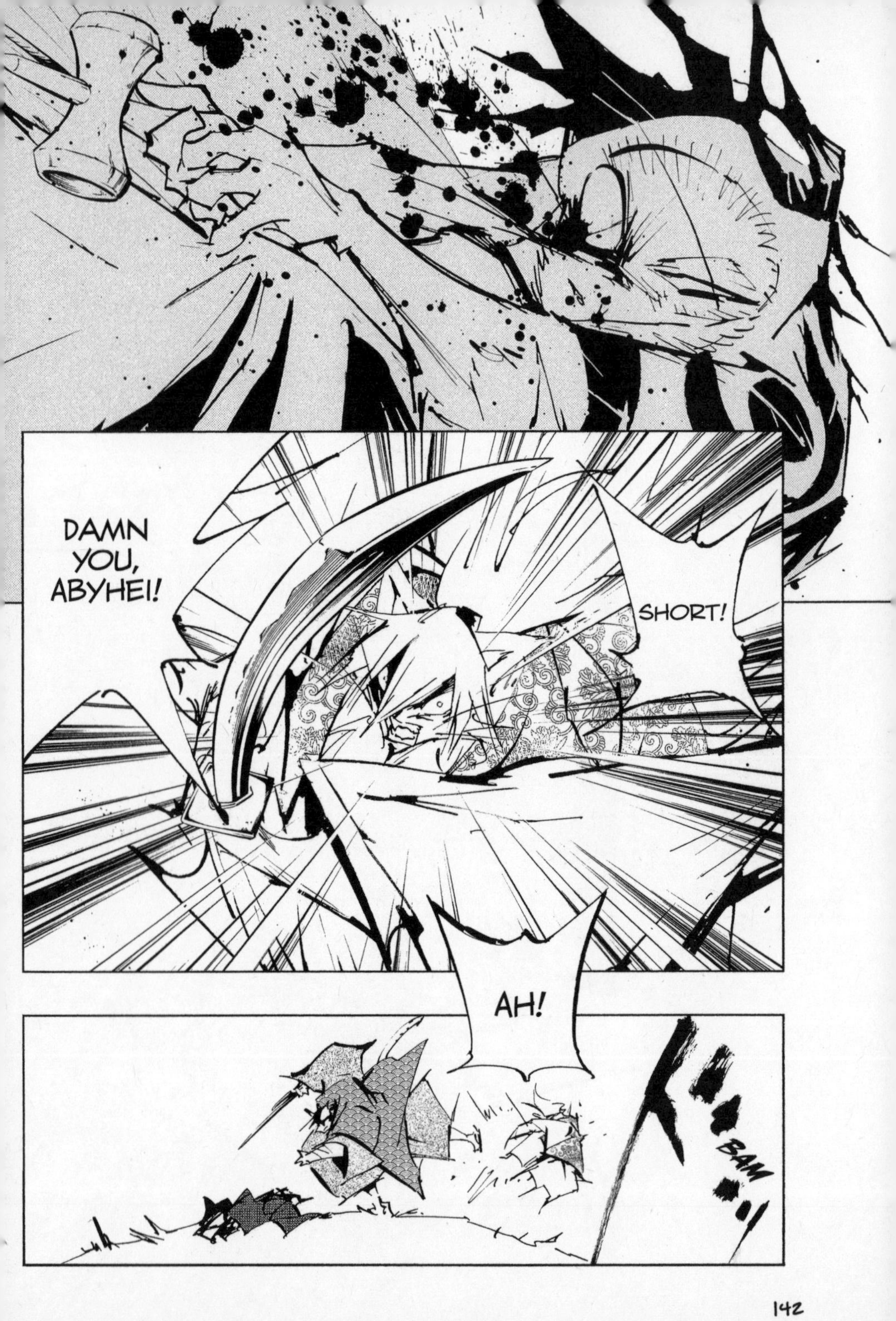
SHORT!
DAMN YOU, ABYHEI!
AH!
BAM

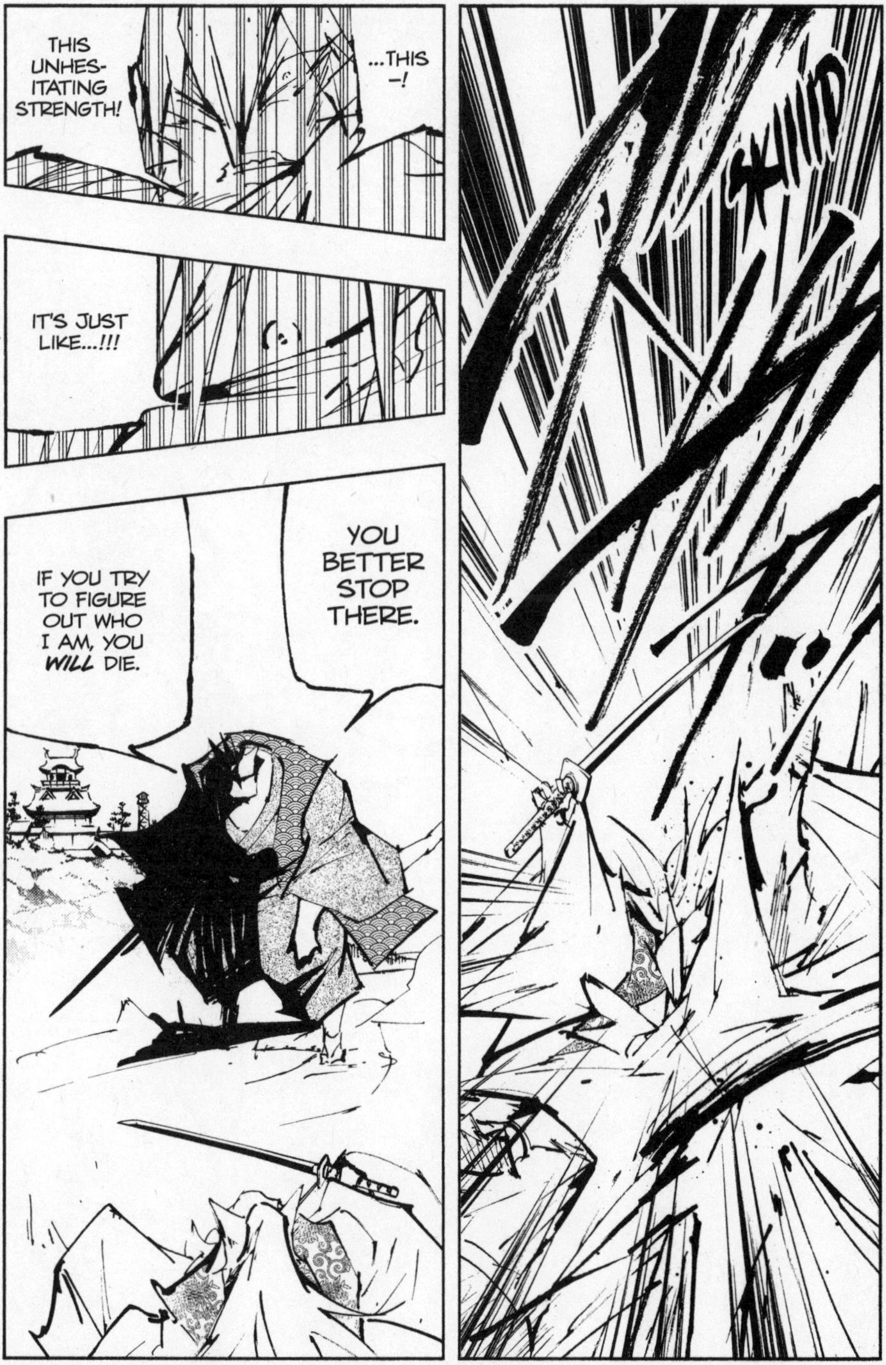
SKIIID
THIS UNHES-ITATING STRENGTH!
...THIS —!
IT'S JUST LIKE...!!!
YOU BETTER STOP THERE.
IF YOU TRY TO FIGURE OUT WHO I AM, YOU *WILL* DIE.

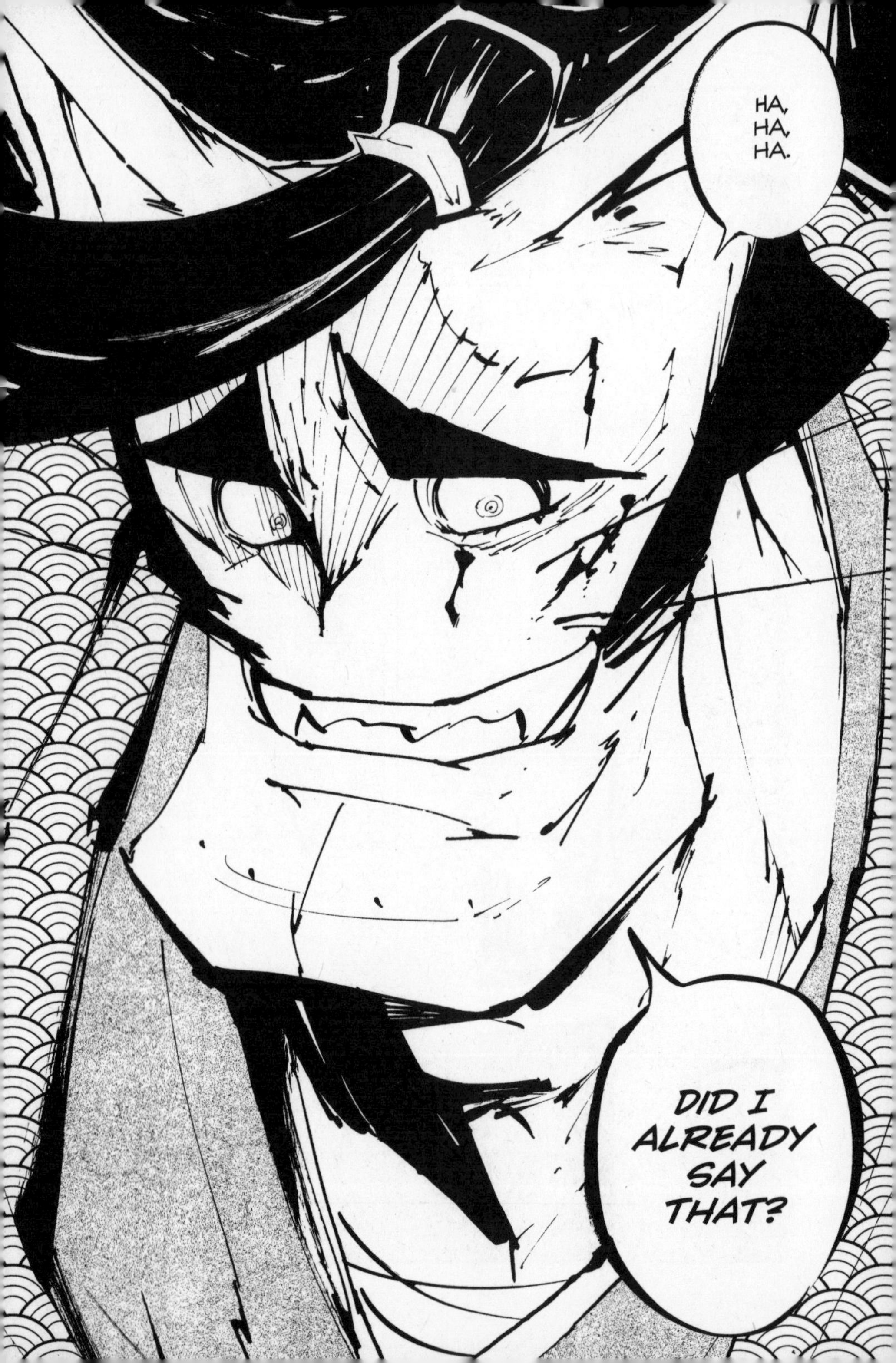
HA, HA, HA.
DID I ALREADY SAY THAT?

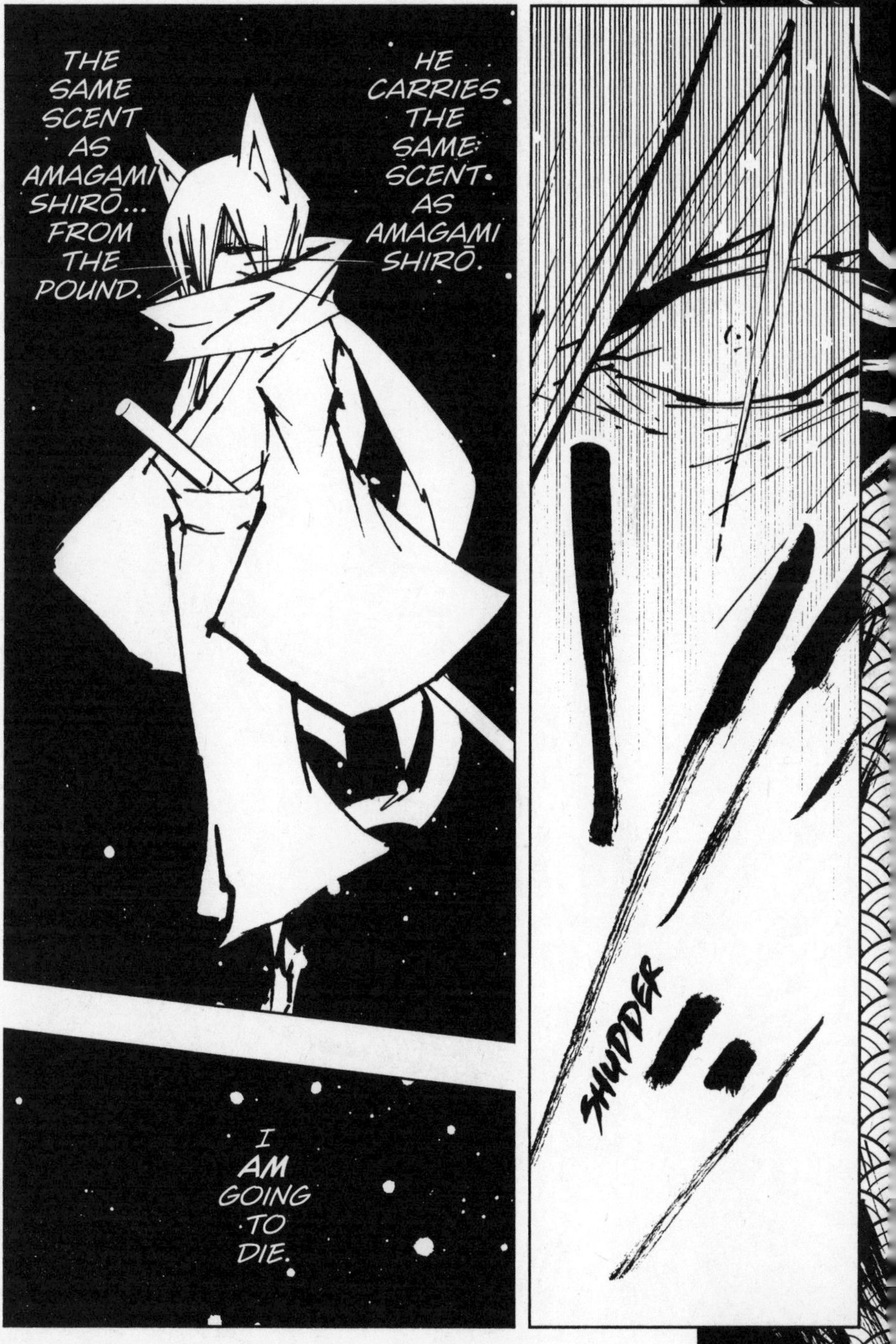
SHUDDER
HE CARRIES THE SAME SCENT AS AMAGAMI SHIRŌ.
THE SAME SCENT AS AMAGAMI SHIRŌ... FROM THE POUND.
I **AM** GOING TO DIE.

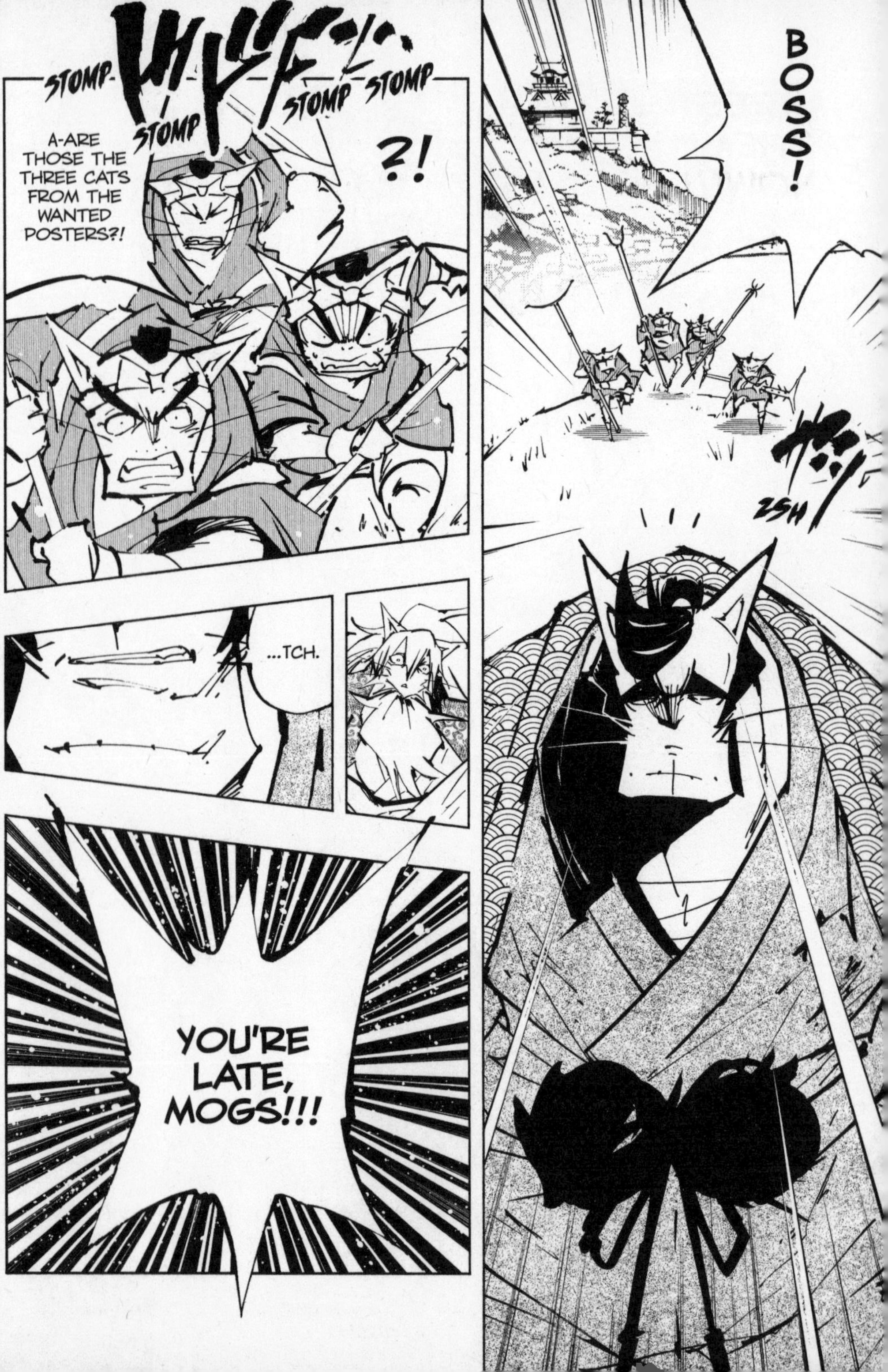
BOSS!
ZSH
STOMP
STOMP
STOMP
STOMP
STOMP
A-ARE THOSE THE THREE CATS FROM THE WANTED POSTERS?!
?!
...TCH.
YOU'RE LATE, MOGS!!!

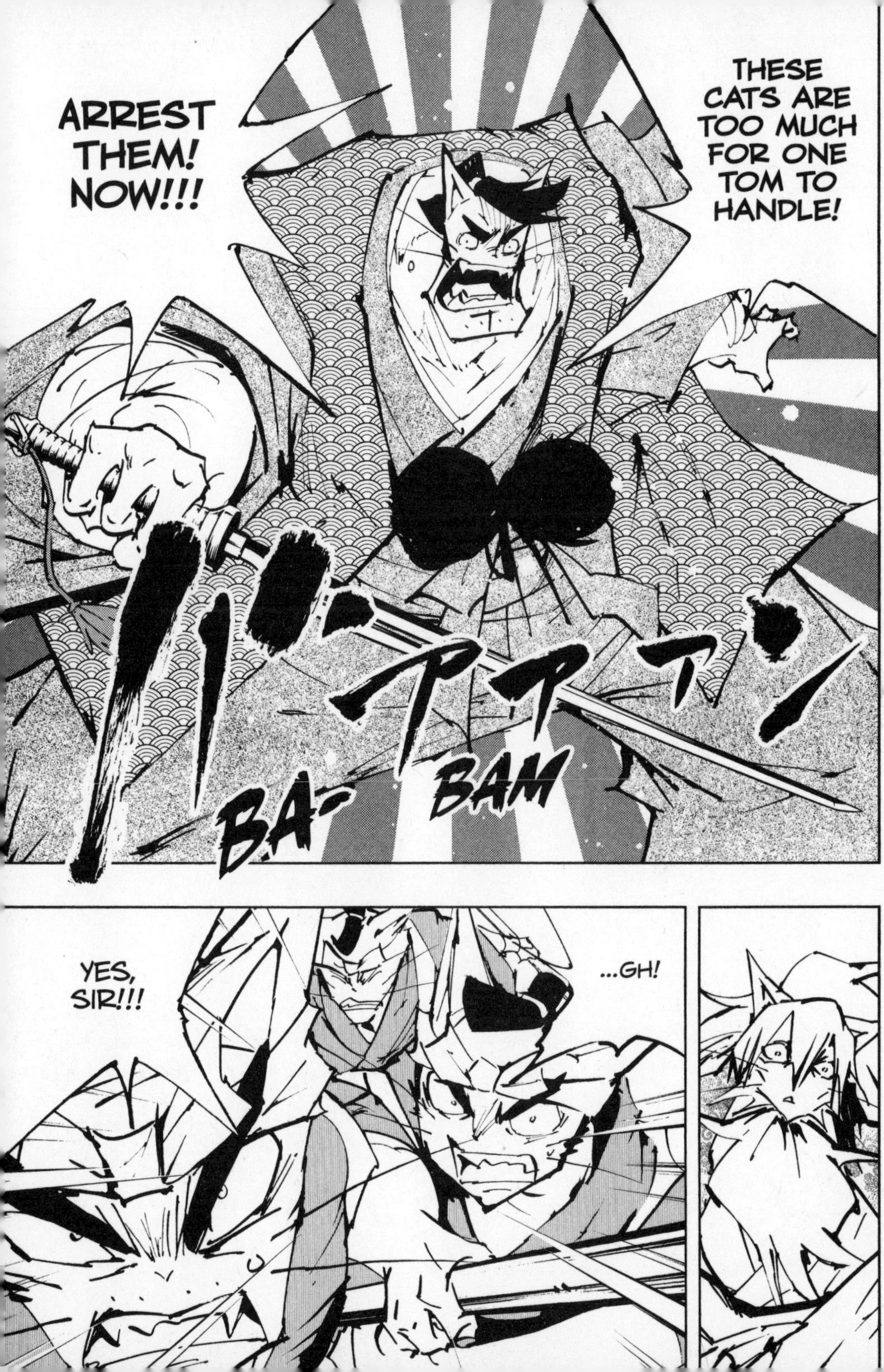
THESE CATS ARE TOO MUCH FOR ONE TOM TO HANDLE!
ARREST THEM! NOW!!!
BA- BAM
...GH!
YES, SIR!!!

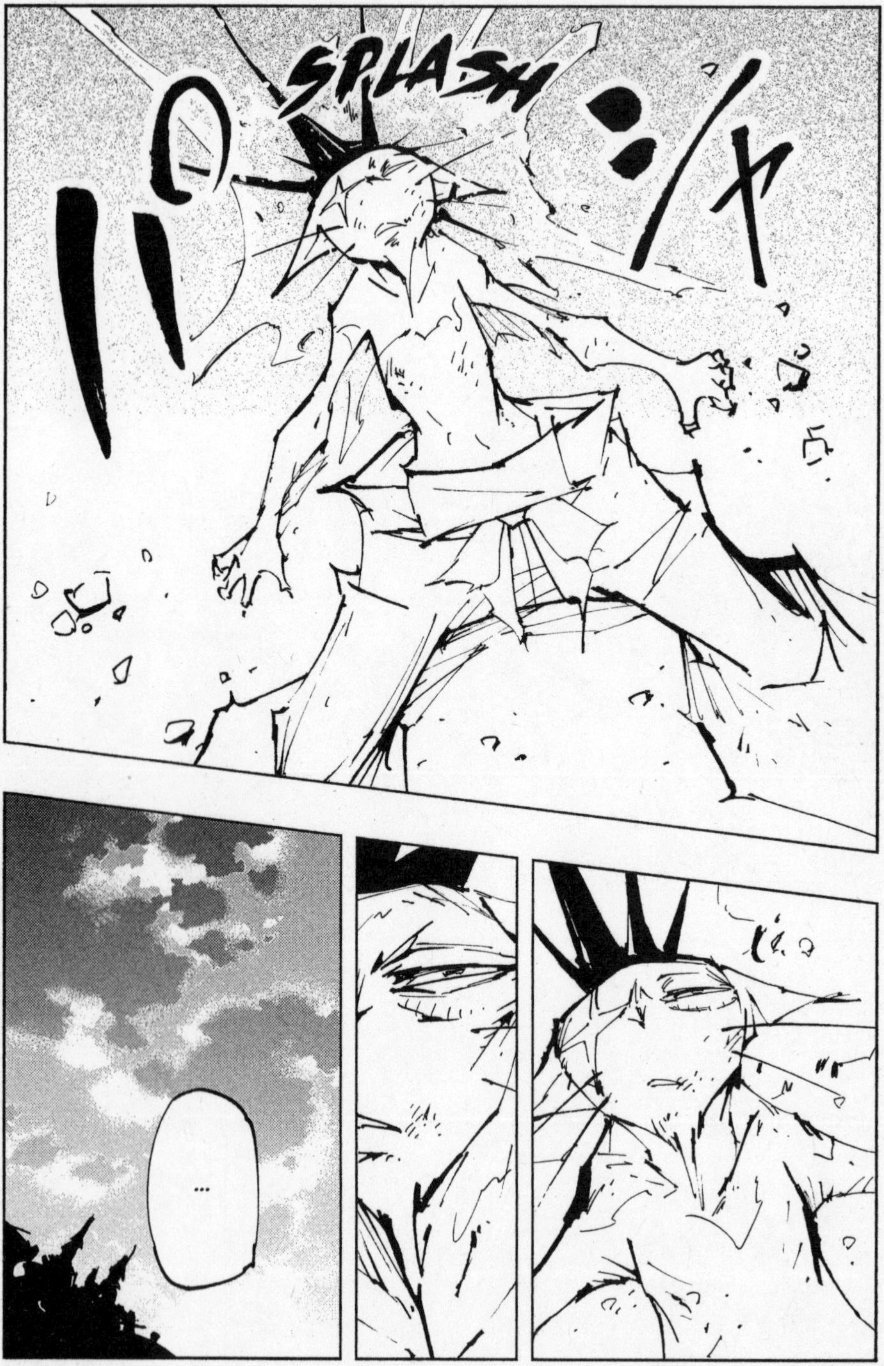
SPLASH
...

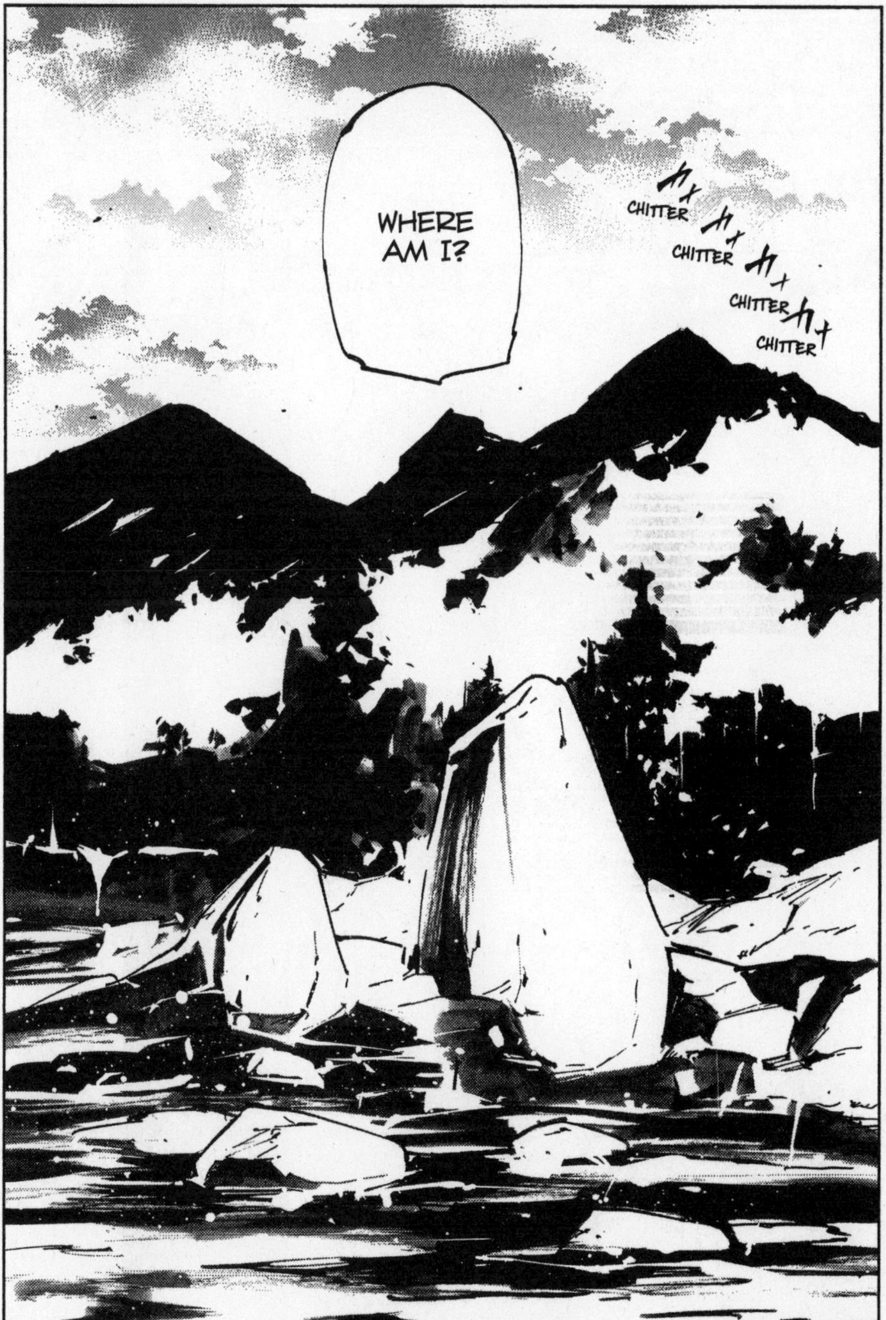
WHERE AM I?
CHITTER
CHITTER
CHITTER
CHITTER

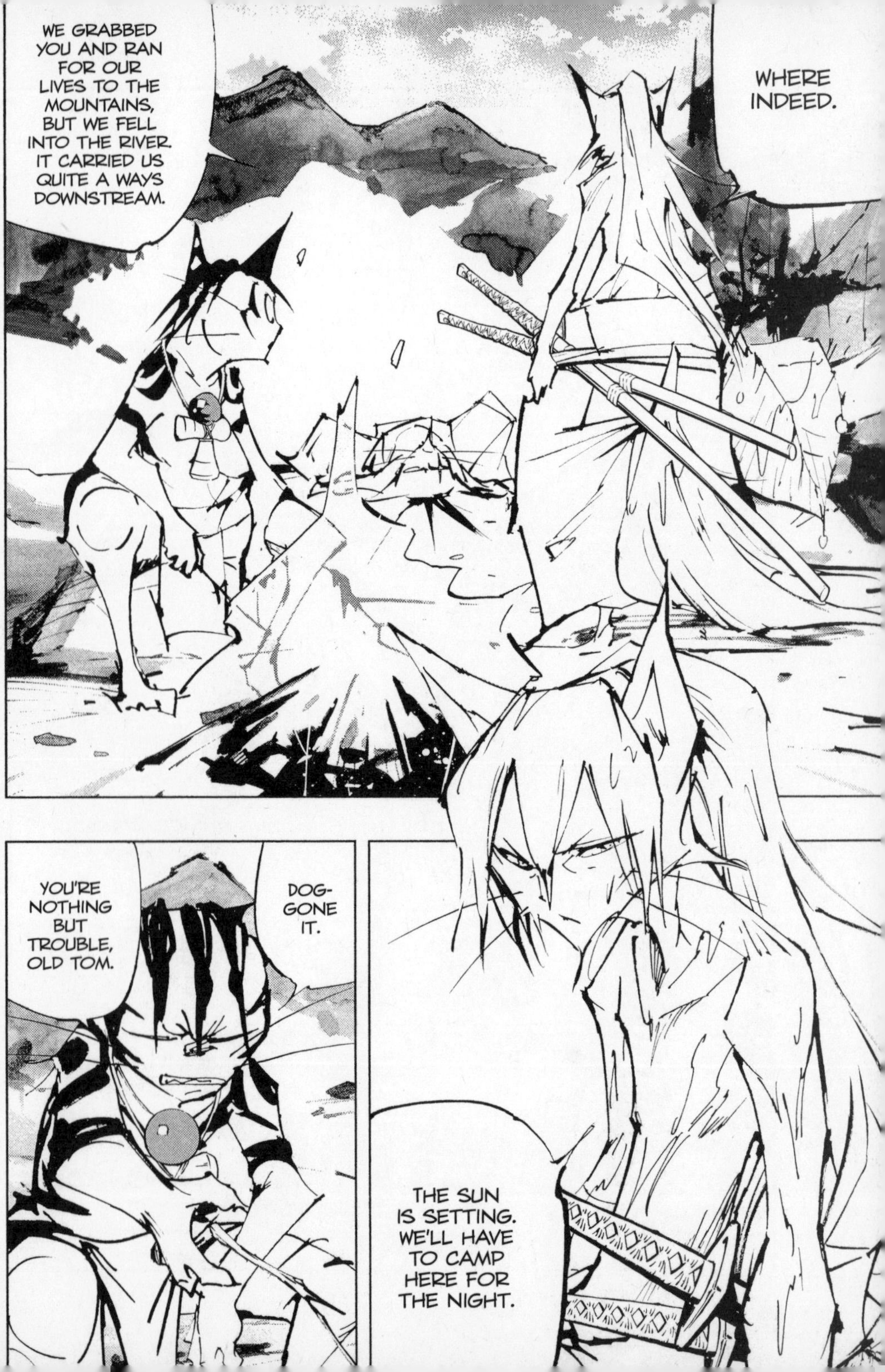
WHERE INDEED.
WE GRABBED YOU AND RAN FOR OUR LIVES TO THE MOUNTAINS, BUT WE FELL INTO THE RIVER. IT CARRIED US QUITE A WAYS DOWNSTREAM.
THE SUN IS SETTING. WE'LL HAVE TO CAMP HERE FOR THE NIGHT.
DOG-GONE IT.
YOU'RE NOTHING BUT TROUBLE, OLD TOM.

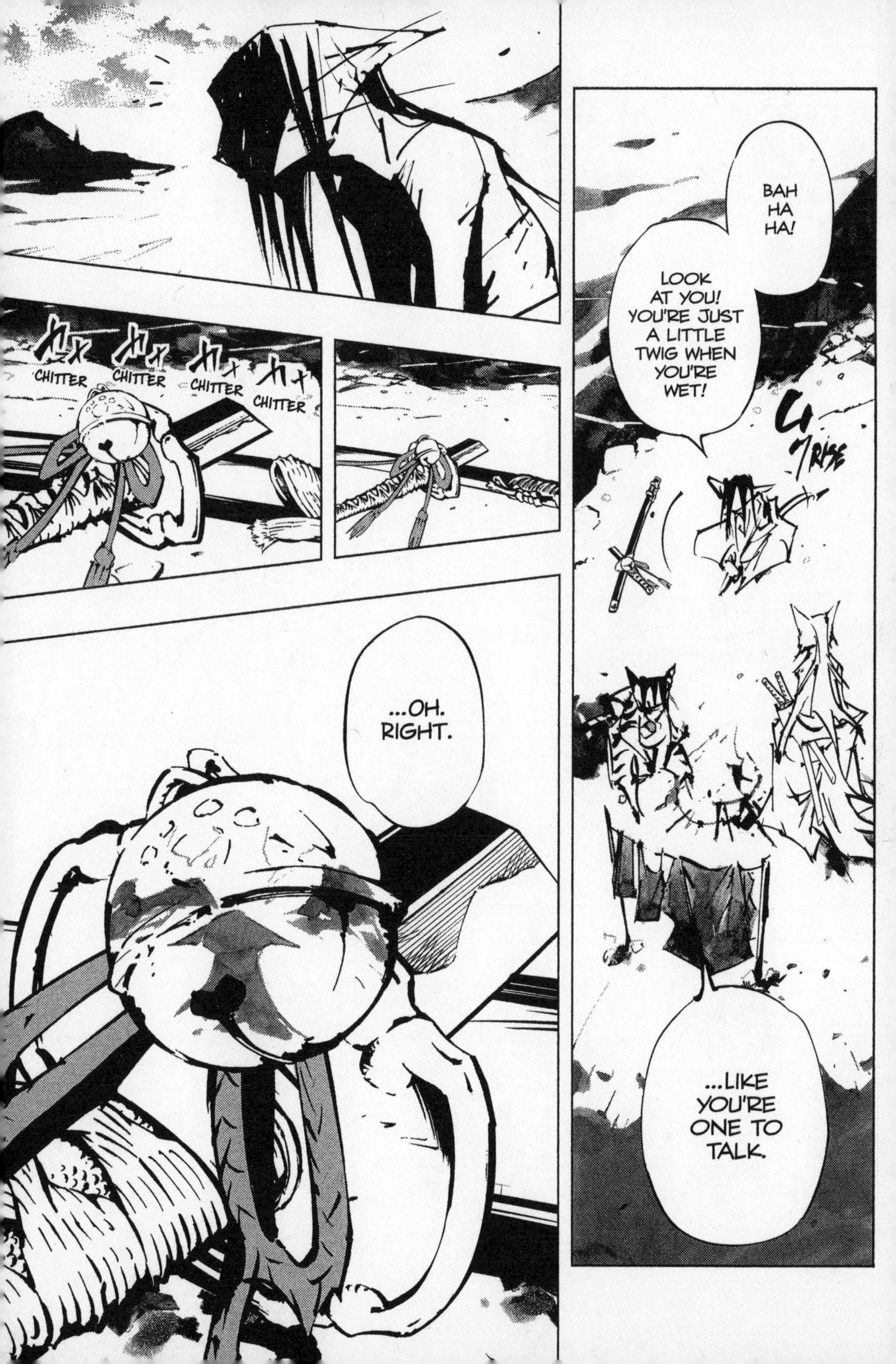
BAH HA HA!
LOOK AT YOU! YOU'RE JUST A LITTLE TWIG WHEN YOU'RE WET!
RISE
...LIKE YOU'RE ONE TO TALK.
CHITTER
CHITTER
CHITTER
CHITTER
...OH. RIGHT.

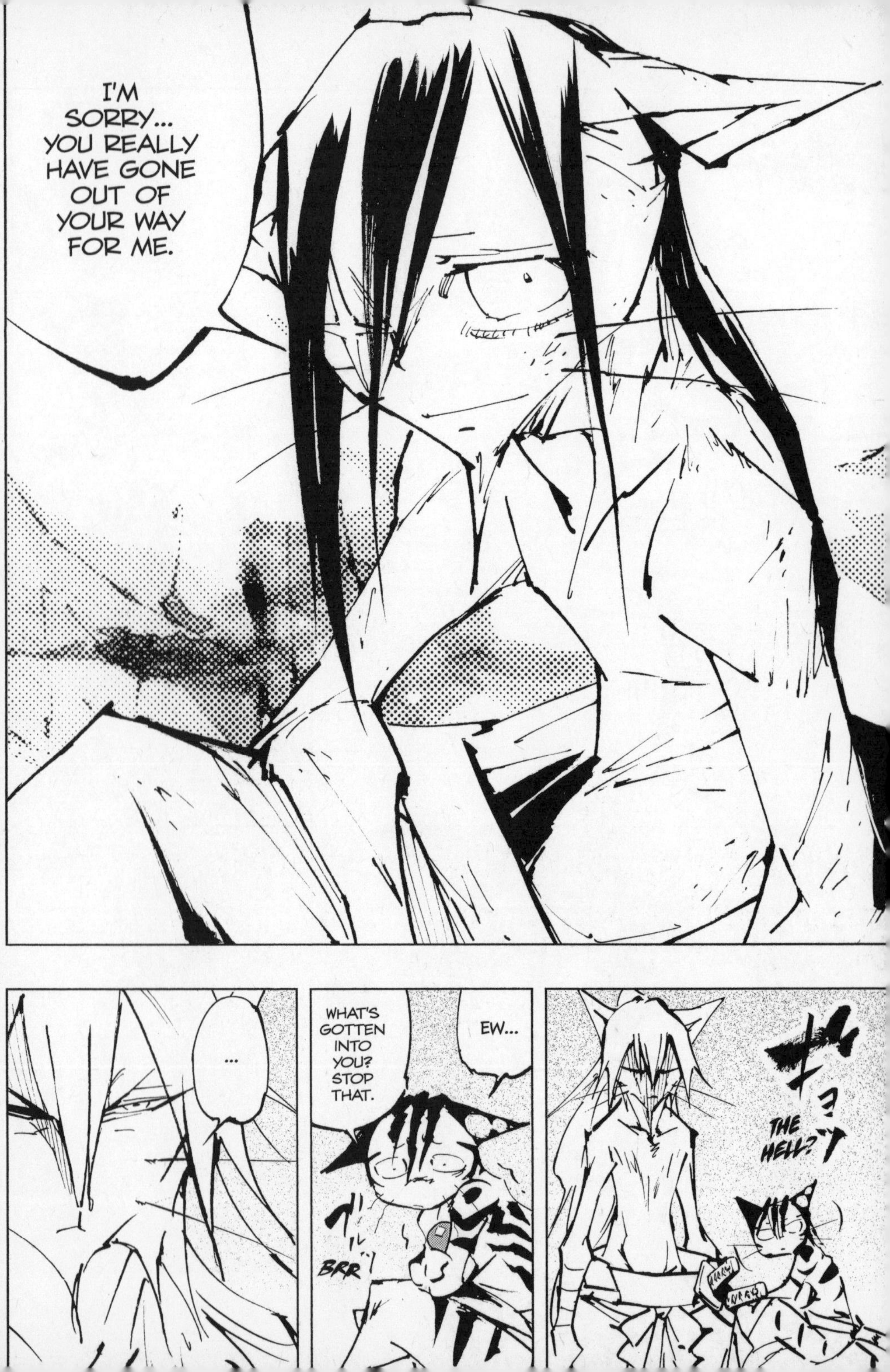
I'M SORRY... YOU REALLY HAVE GONE OUT OF YOUR WAY FOR ME.
THE HELL?
EW...
WHAT'S GOTTEN INTO YOU? STOP THAT.
BRR
...

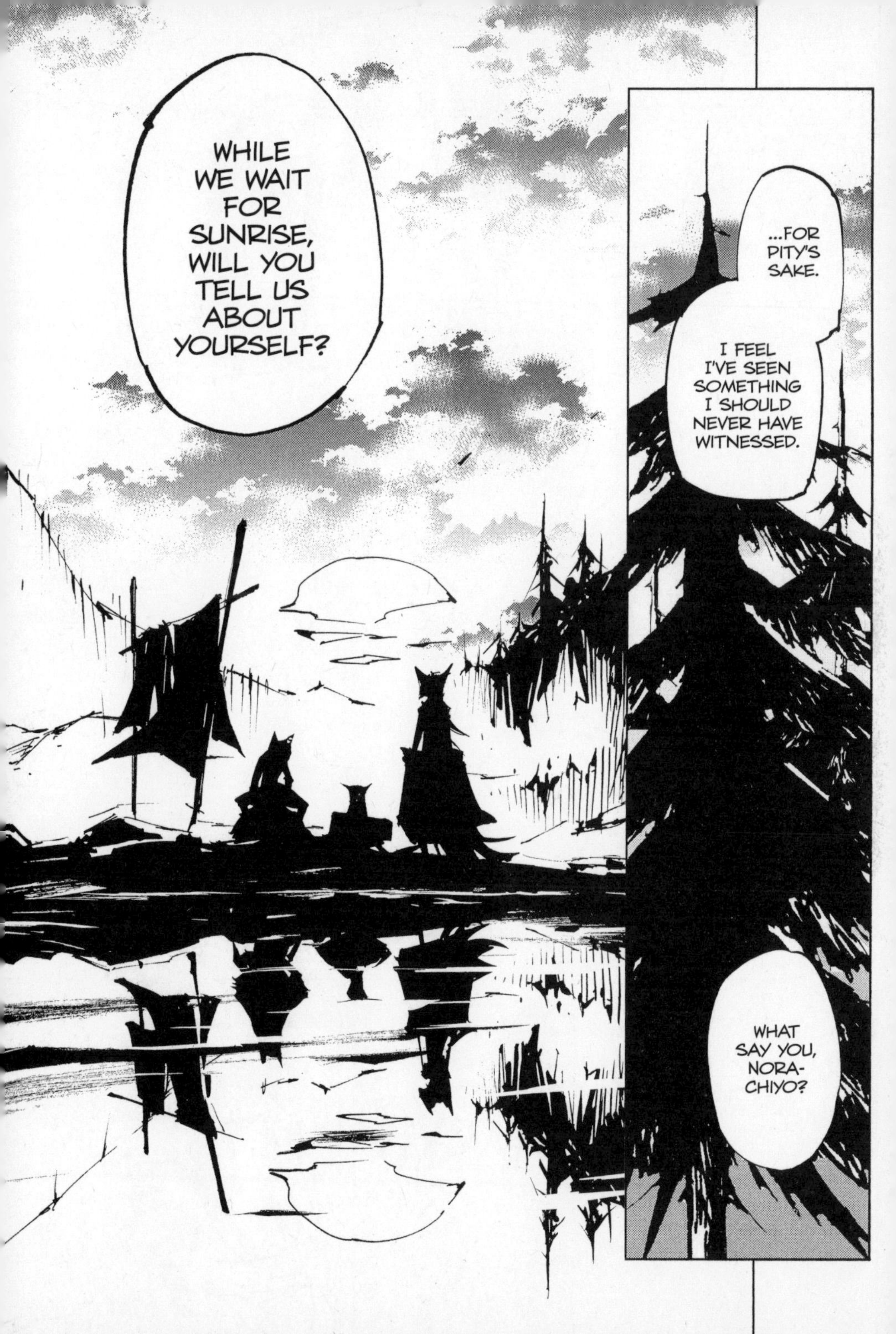
...FOR PITY'S SAKE.
I FEEL I'VE SEEN SOMETHING I SHOULD NEVER HAVE WITNESSED.
WHAT SAY YOU, NORA-CHIYO?
WHILE WE WAIT FOR SUNRISE, WILL YOU TELL US ABOUT YOURSELF?

猫ヶ原

ネコガハラ

NeKoGaHaRa

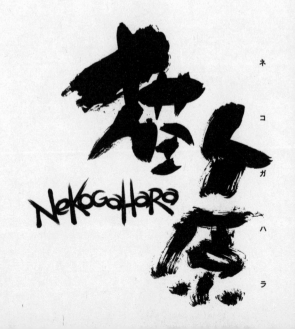

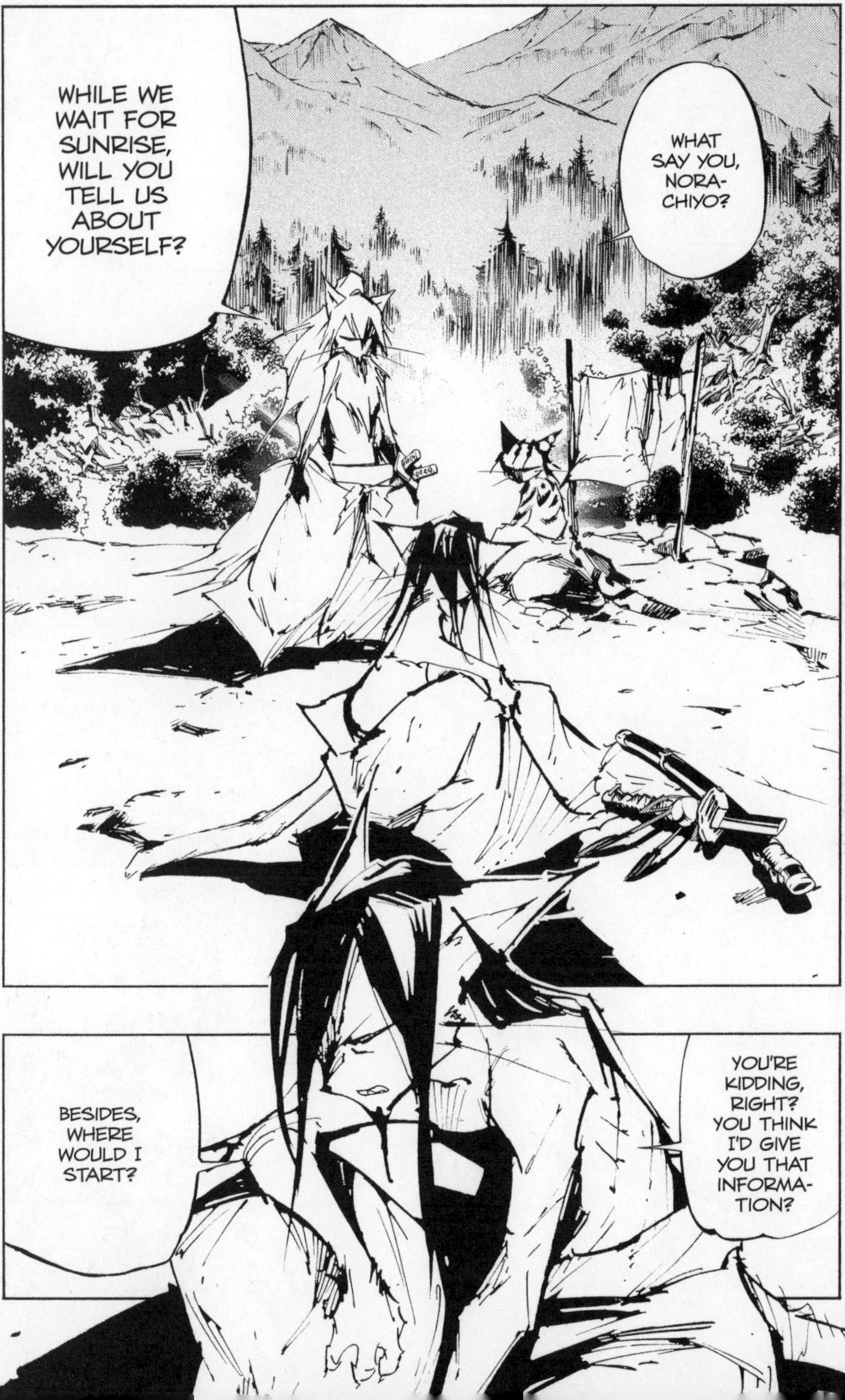
WHILE WE WAIT FOR SUNRISE, WILL YOU TELL US ABOUT YOURSELF?
WHAT SAY YOU, NORA-CHIYO?
YOU'RE KIDDING, RIGHT? YOU THINK I'D GIVE YOU THAT INFORMATION?
BESIDES, WHERE WOULD I START?

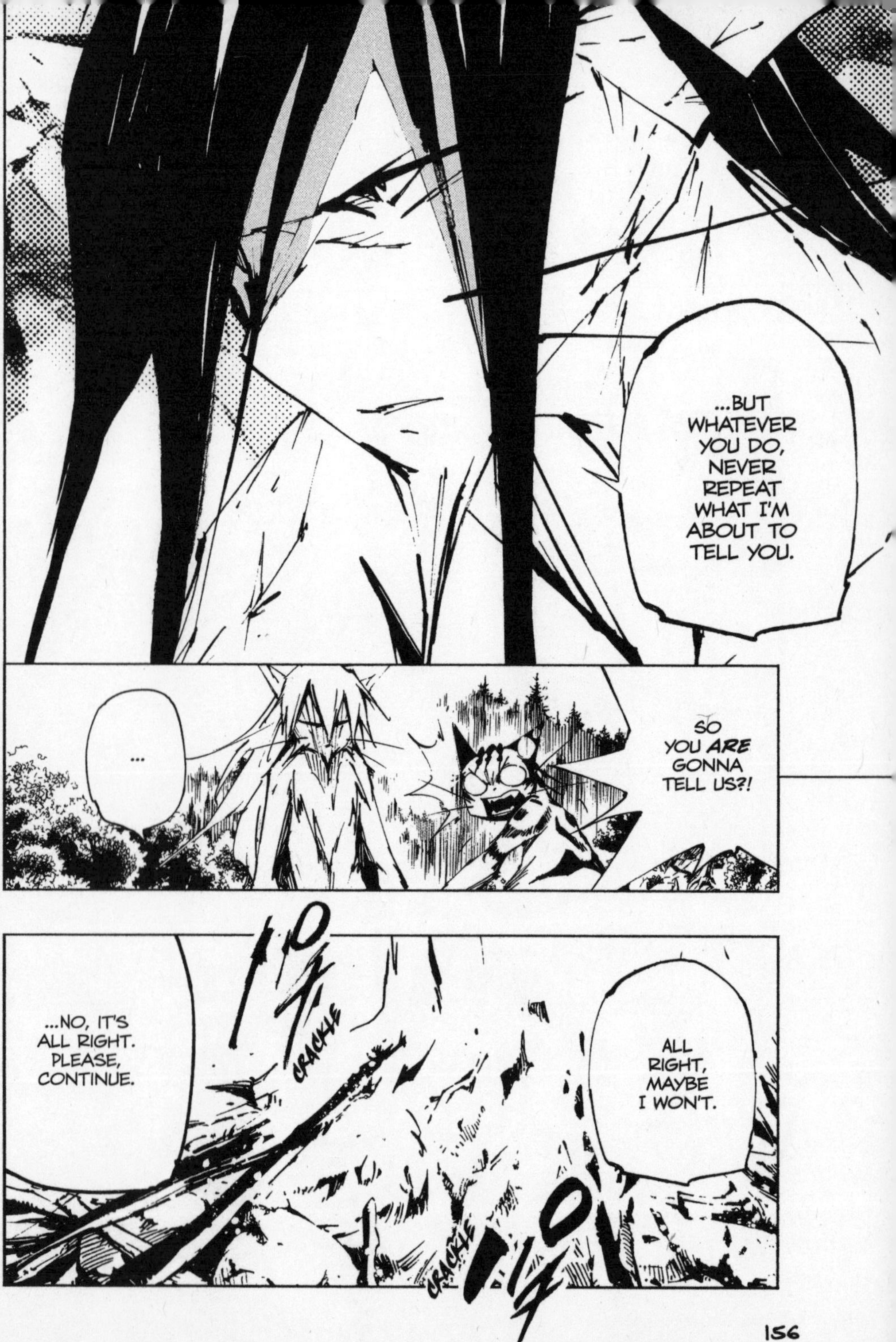
...BUT WHATEVER YOU DO, NEVER REPEAT WHAT I'M ABOUT TO TELL YOU.
SO YOU **ARE** GONNA TELL US?!
...
ALL RIGHT, MAYBE I WON'T.
CRACKLE
...NO, IT'S ALL RIGHT. PLEASE, CONTINUE.
CRACKLE

Nekogahara

CHAPTER 19:
HI LONE KITTY,
PART 1

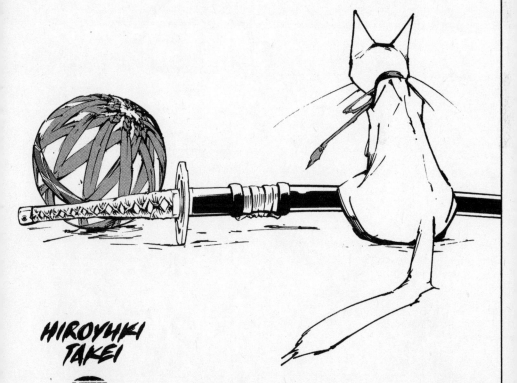

HIROYUKI
TAKEI

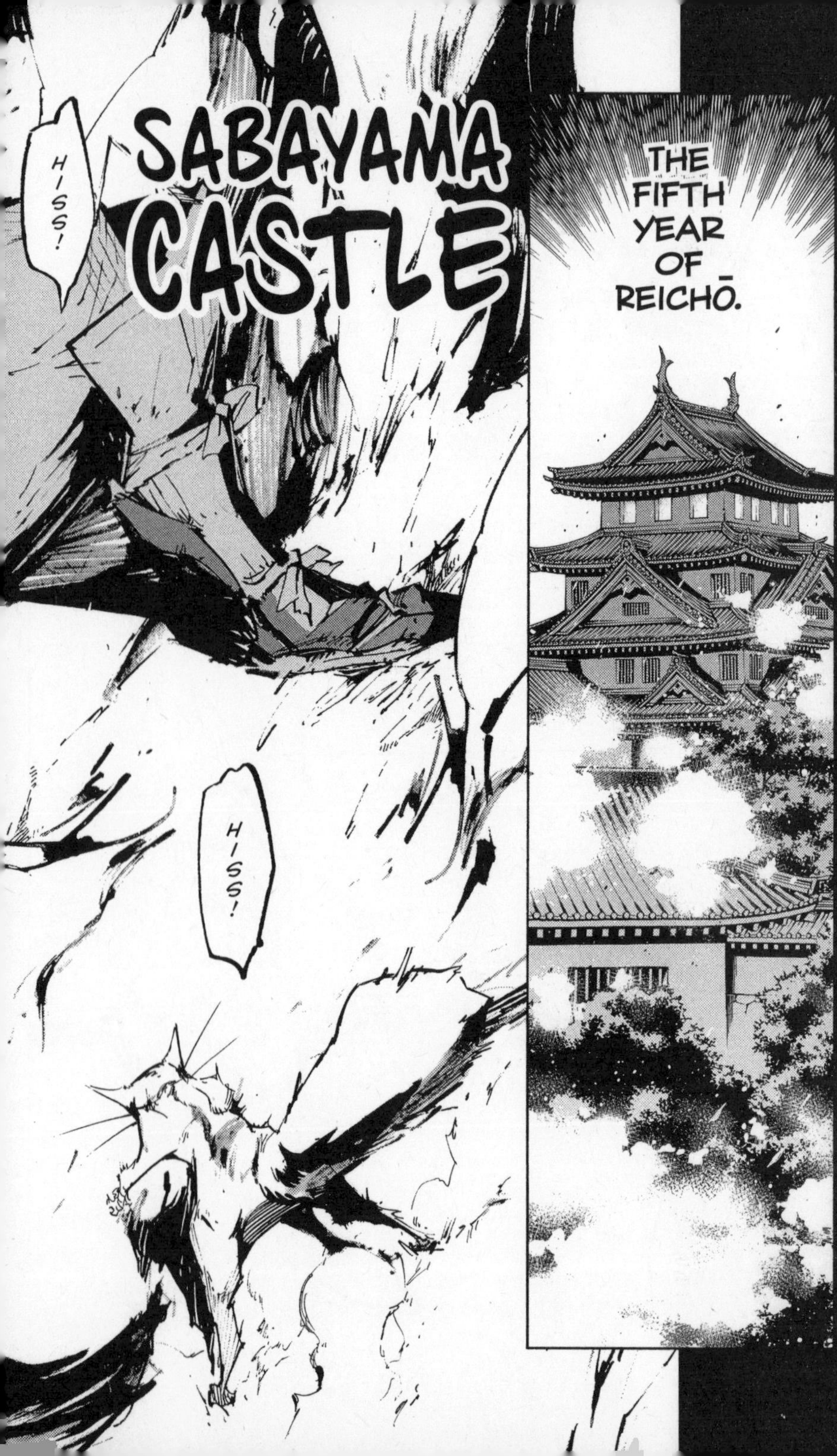
THE FIFTH YEAR OF REICHŌ.
SABAYAMA CASTLE
HISS!
HISS!

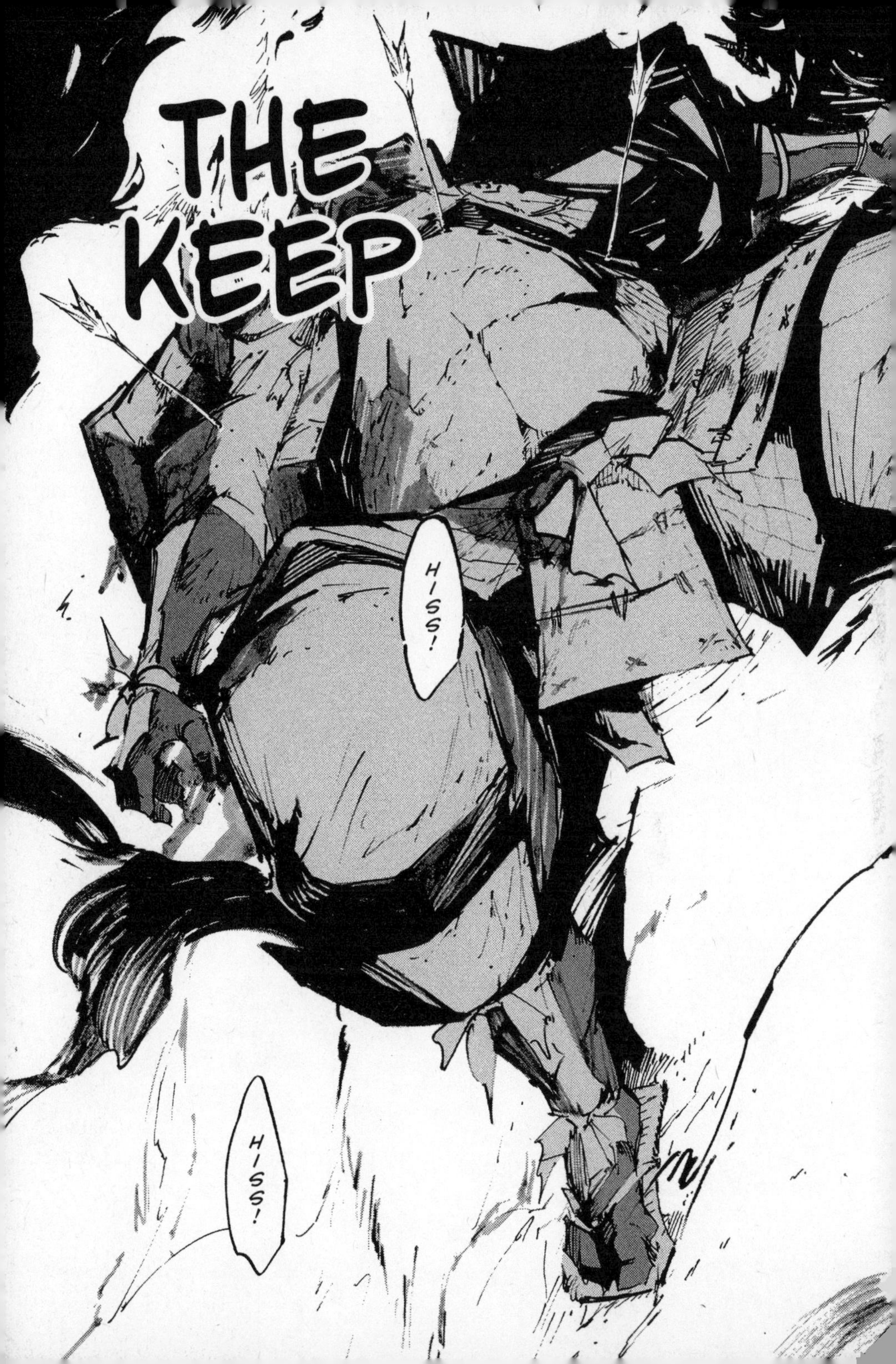
THE KEEP
HISS!
HISS!

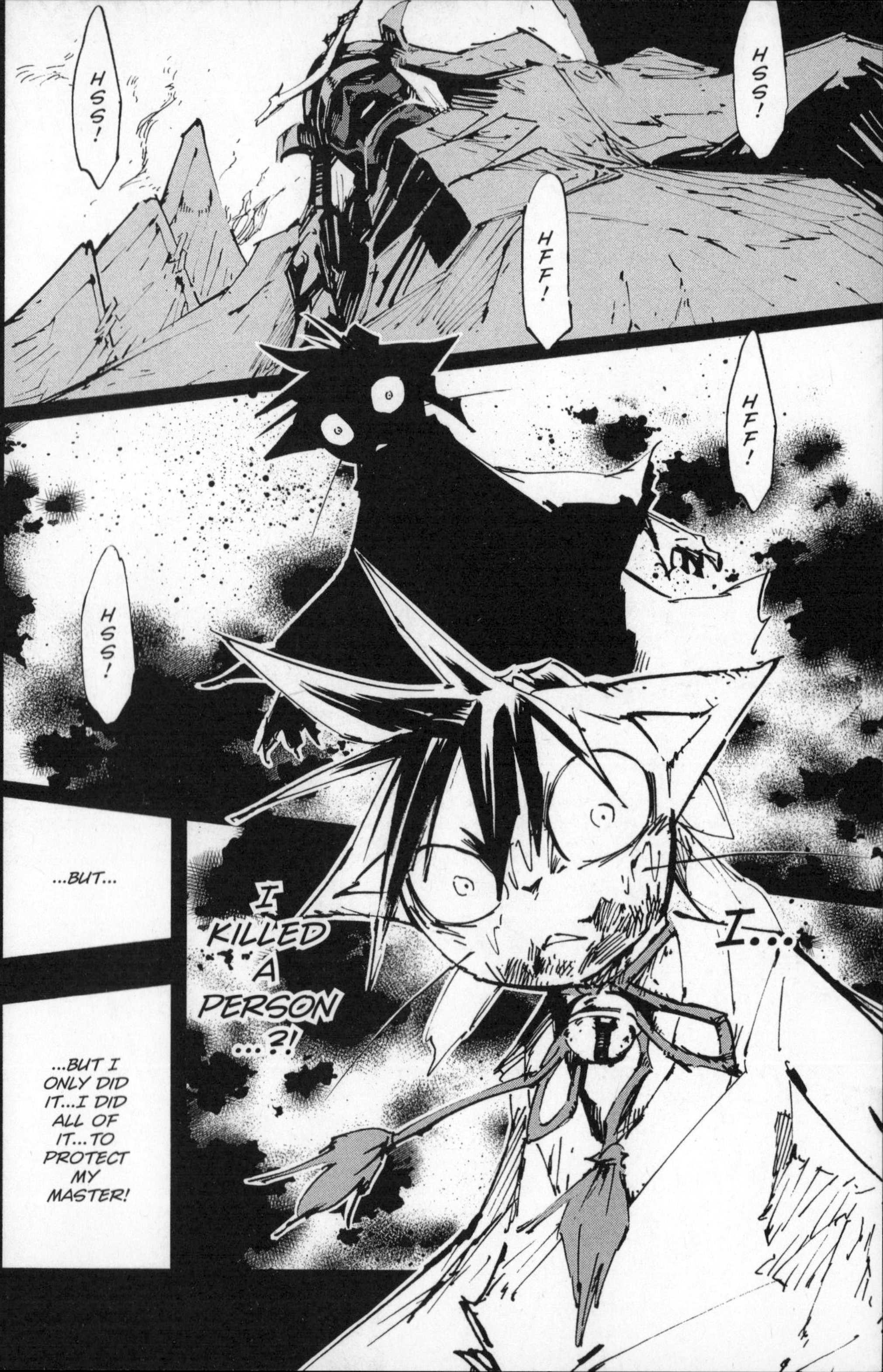
HSS!
HFF!
HSS!
HFF!
HSS!
I...
I KILLED A PERSON ...?!
...BUT...
...BUT I ONLY DID IT...I DID ALL OF IT...TO PROTECT MY MASTER!

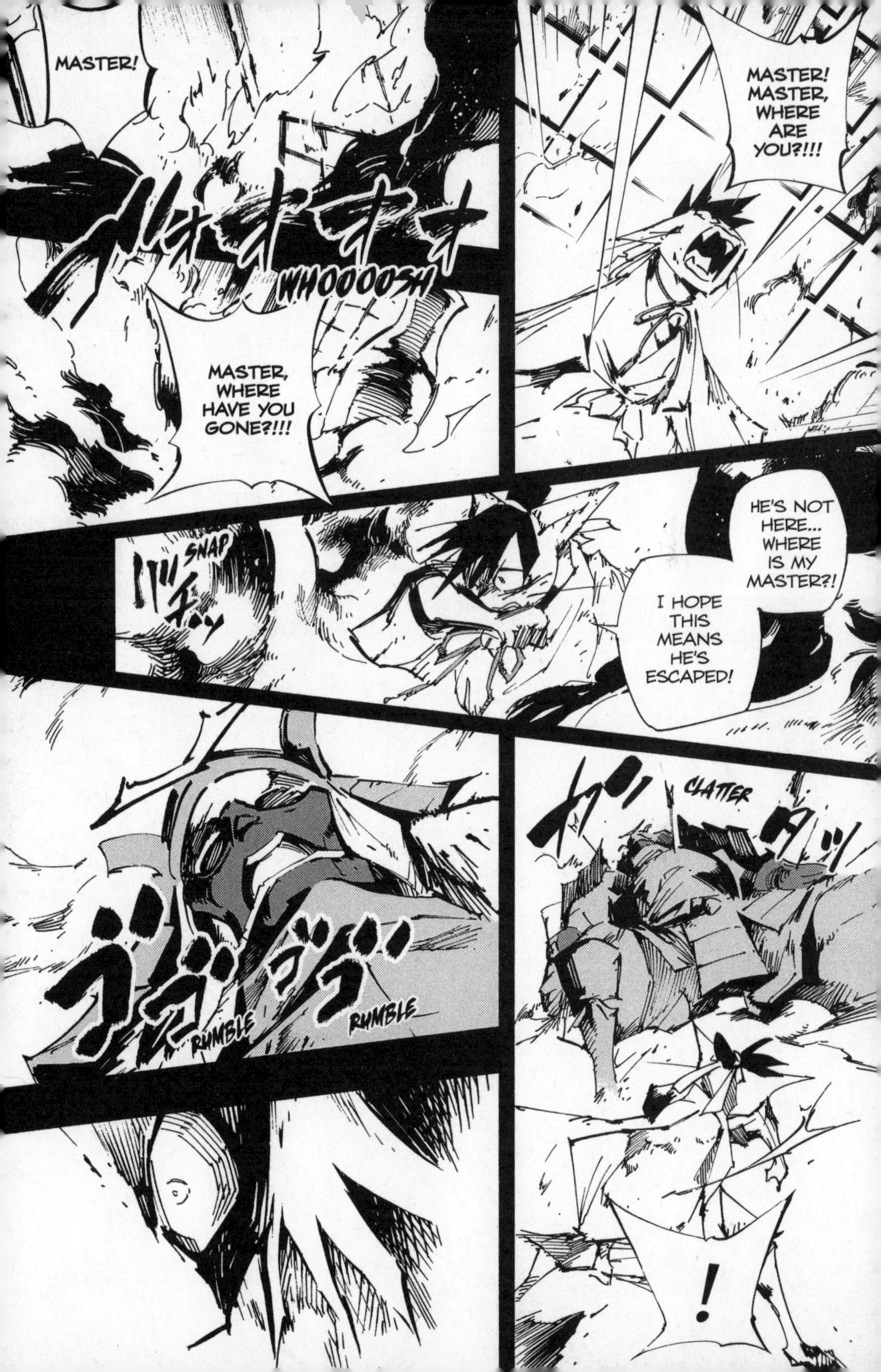
MASTER! MASTER, WHERE ARE YOU?!!!
MASTER!
WHOOOOSH
MASTER, WHERE HAVE YOU GONE?!!!
HE'S NOT HERE... WHERE IS MY MASTER?!
I HOPE THIS MEANS HE'S ESCAPED!
SNAP
CLATTER
!
RUMBLE
RUMBLE

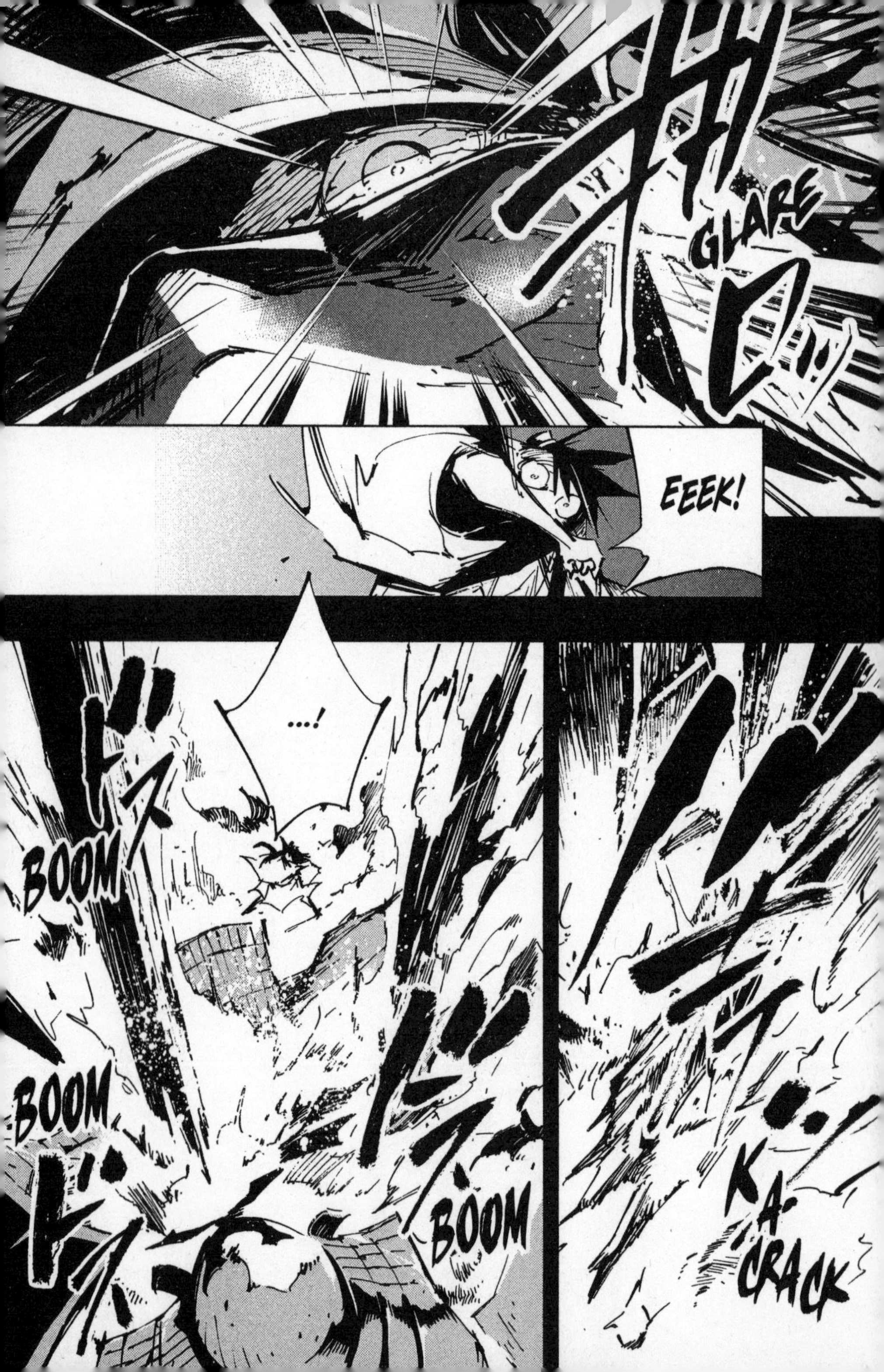
GLARE
EEEK!
KA-CRACK
...!
BOOM
BOOM
BOOM

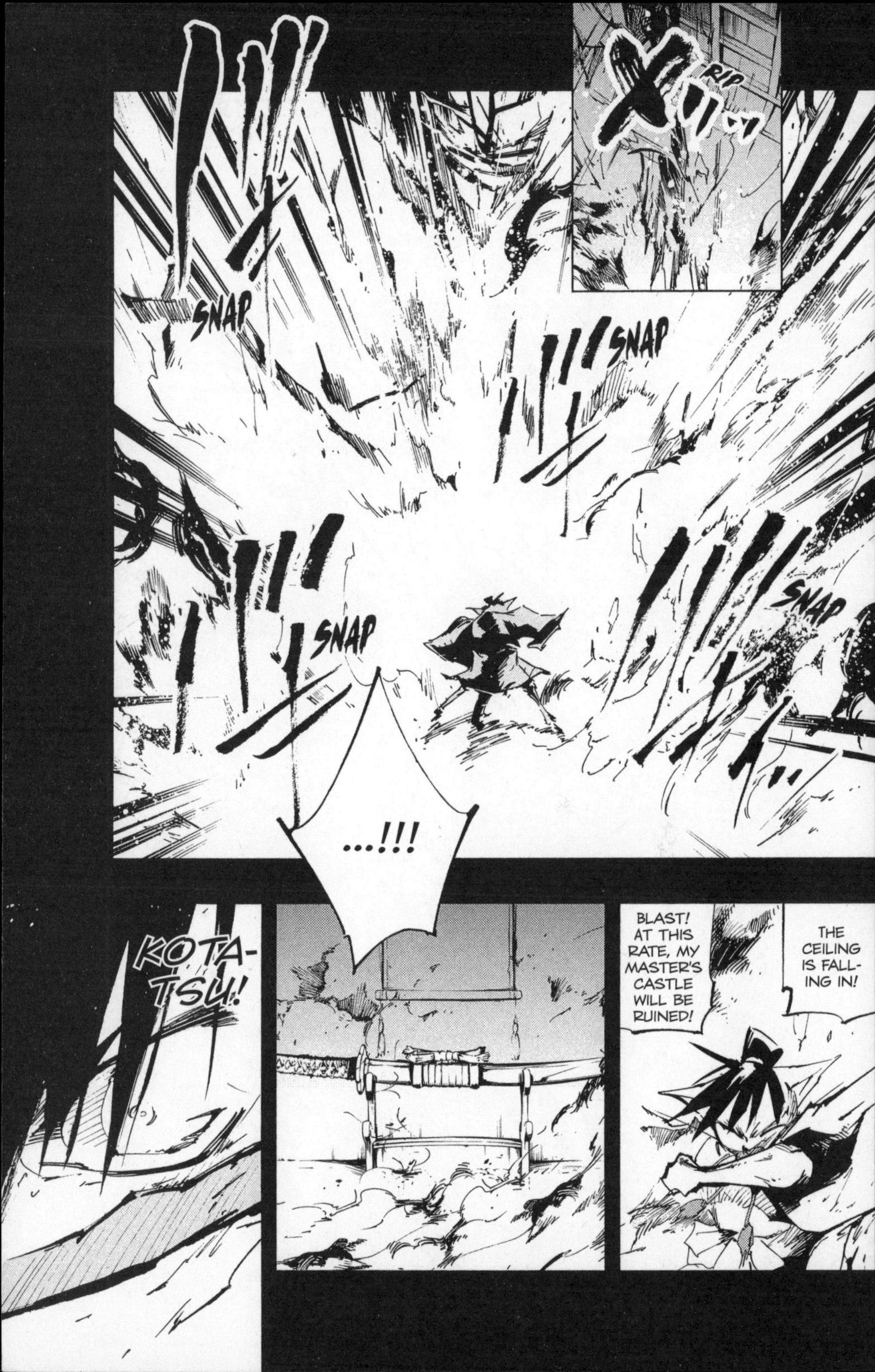
RIP
SNAP
SNAP
SNAP
SNAP
...!!!
THE CEILING IS FALL-ING IN!
BLAST! AT THIS RATE, MY MASTER'S CASTLE WILL BE RUINED!
KOTA-TSU!

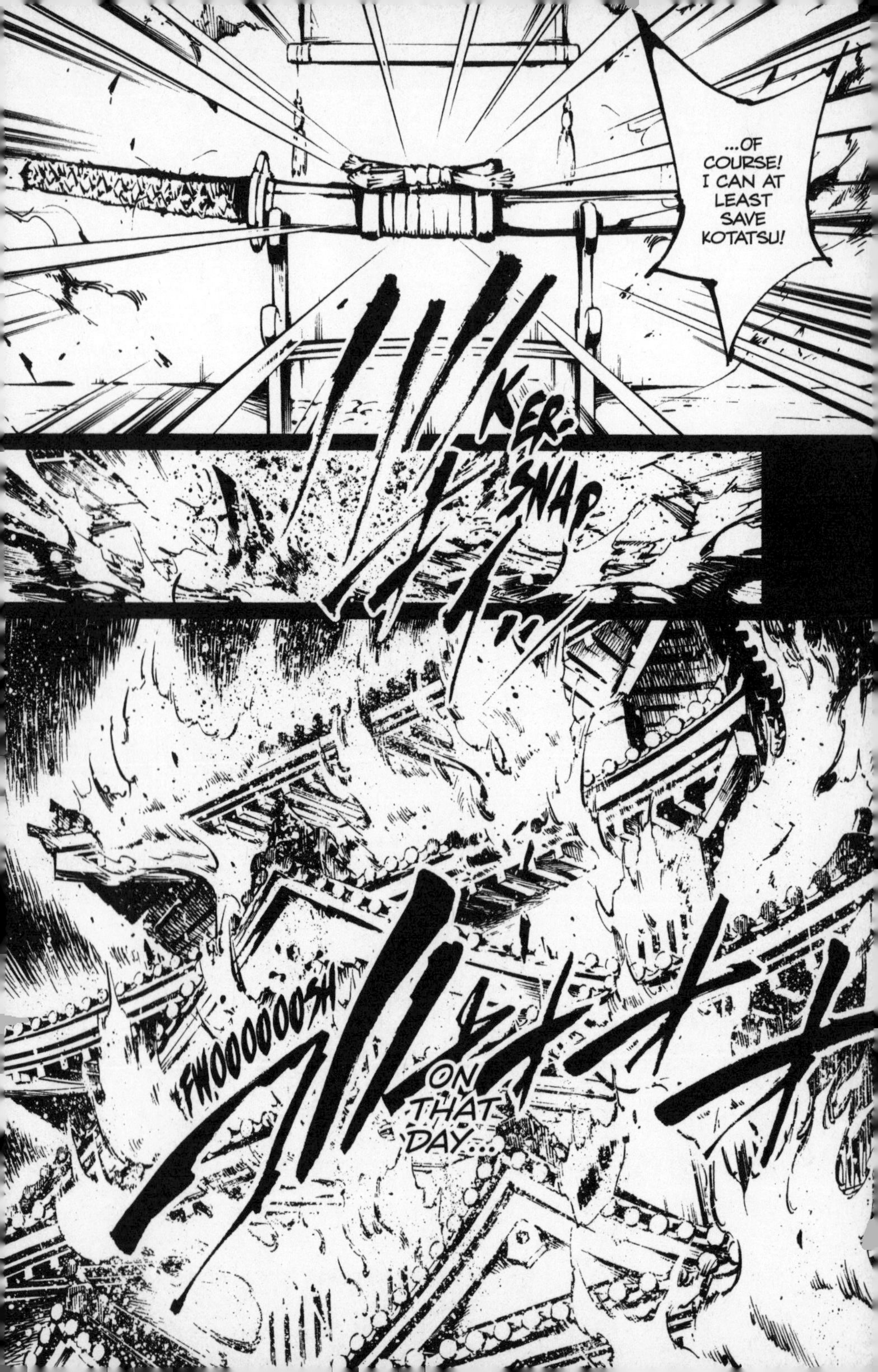
...OF COURSE! I CAN AT LEAST SAVE KOTATSU!
KER-SNAP
FWOOOOOOSH
ON THAT DAY...

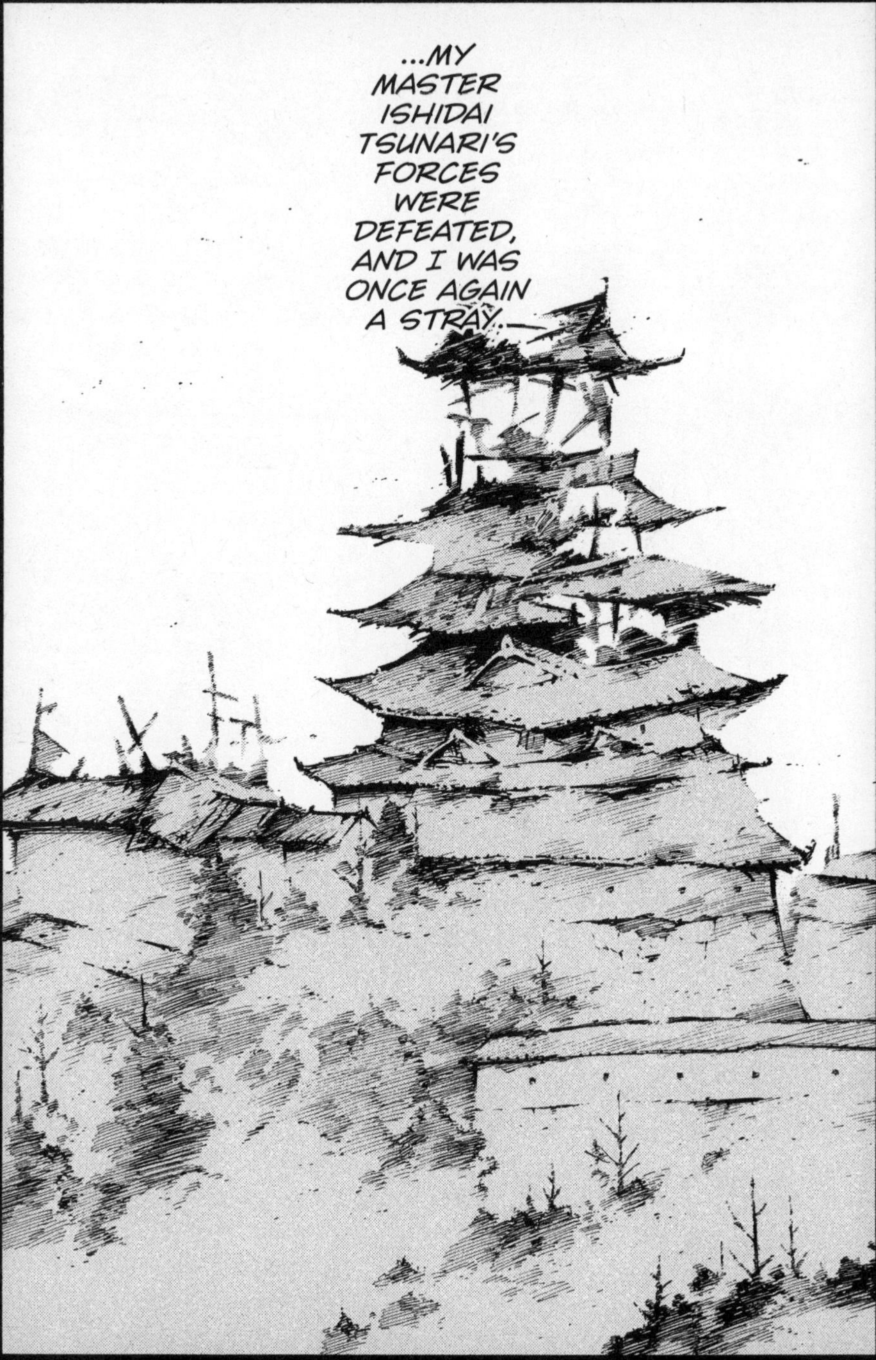
...MY MASTER ISHIDAI TSUNARI'S FORCES WERE DEFEATED, AND I WAS ONCE AGAIN A STRAY.

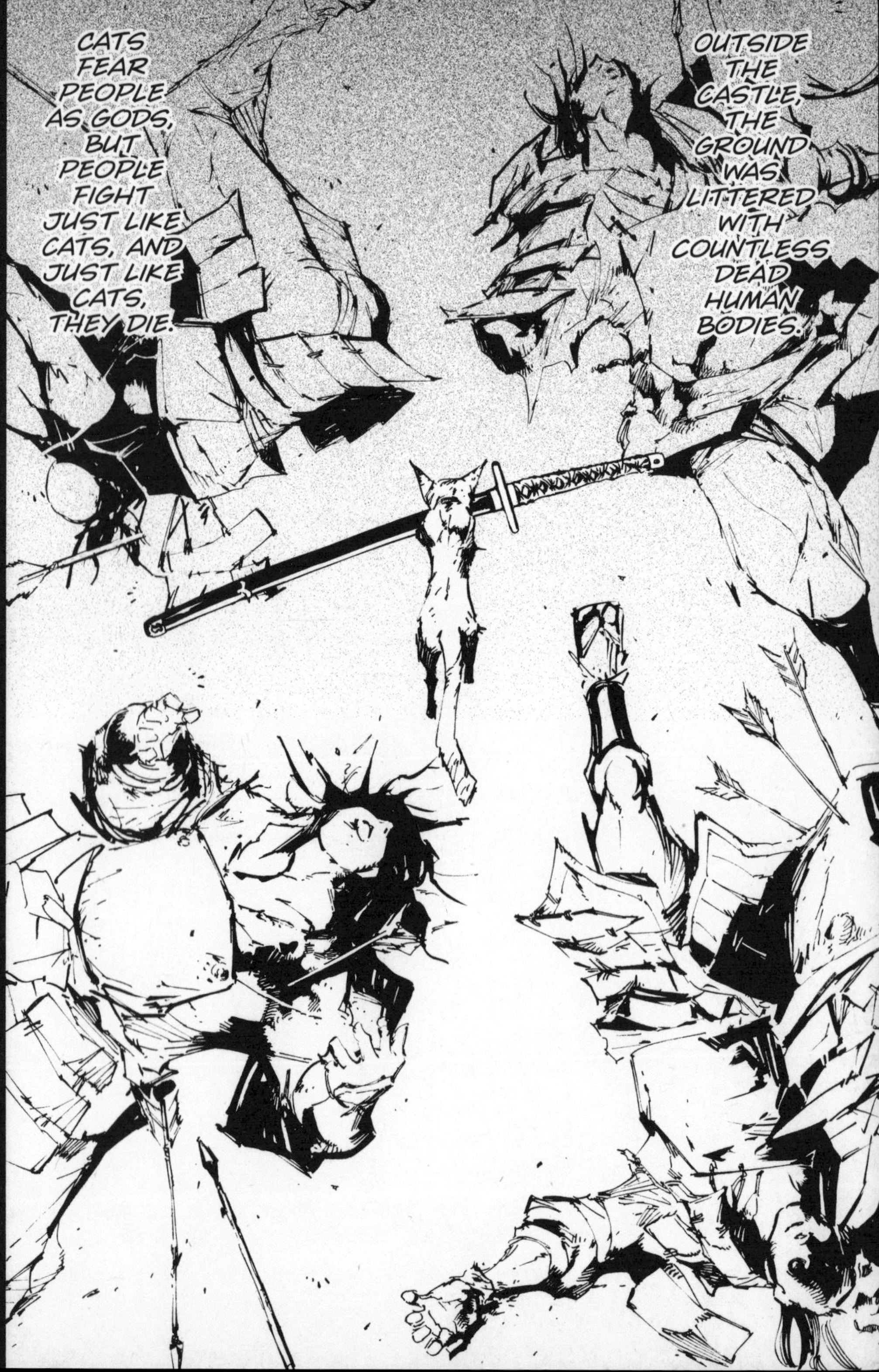
OUTSIDE THE CASTLE, THE GROUND WAS LITTERED WITH COUNTLESS DEAD HUMAN BODIES.
CATS FEAR PEOPLE AS GODS, BUT PEOPLE FIGHT JUST LIKE CATS, AND JUST LIKE CATS, THEY DIE.

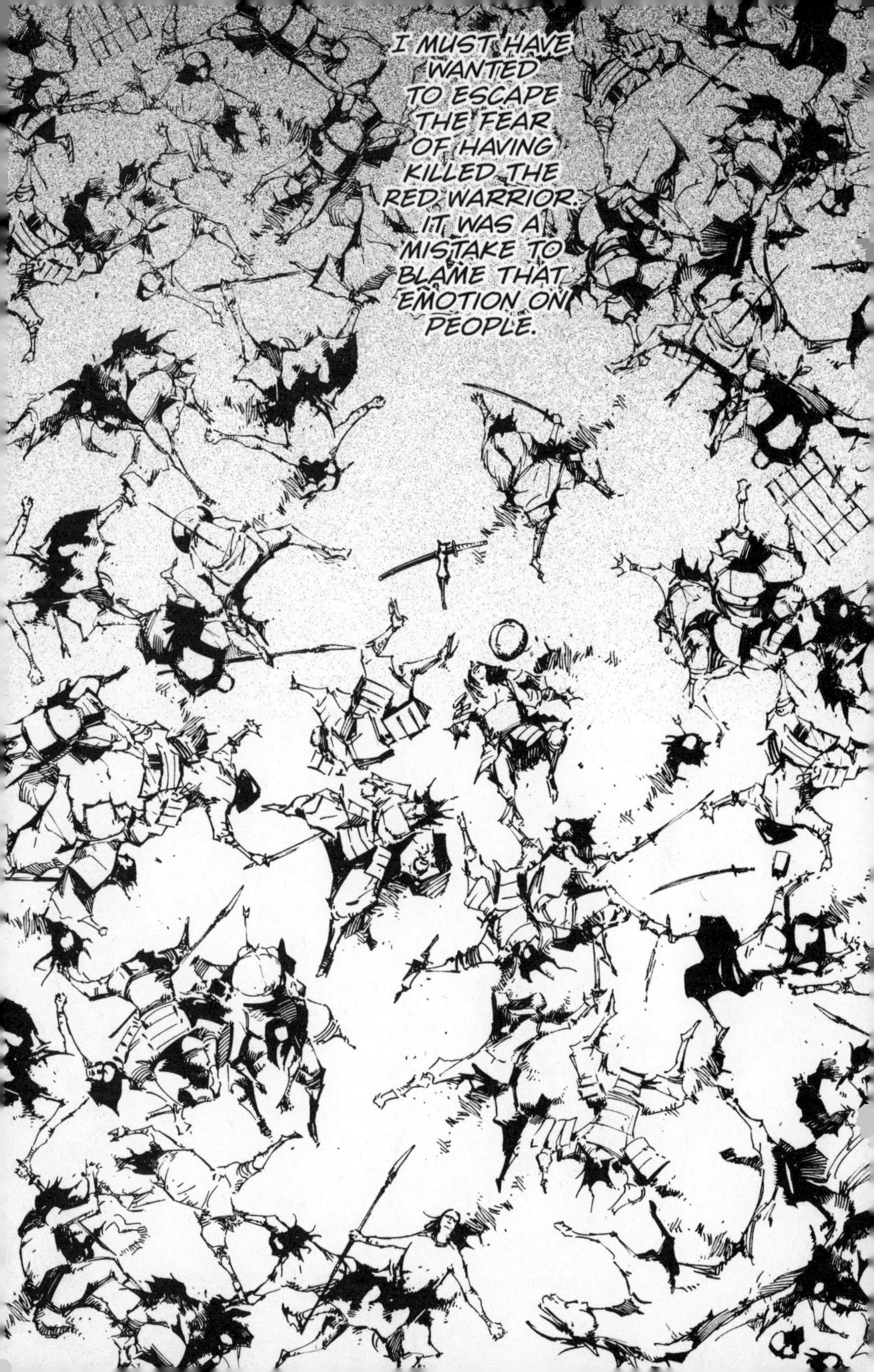
I MUST HAVE WANTED TO ESCAPE THE FEAR OF HAVING KILLED THE RED WARRIOR. IT WAS A MISTAKE TO BLAME THAT EMOTION ON PEOPLE.

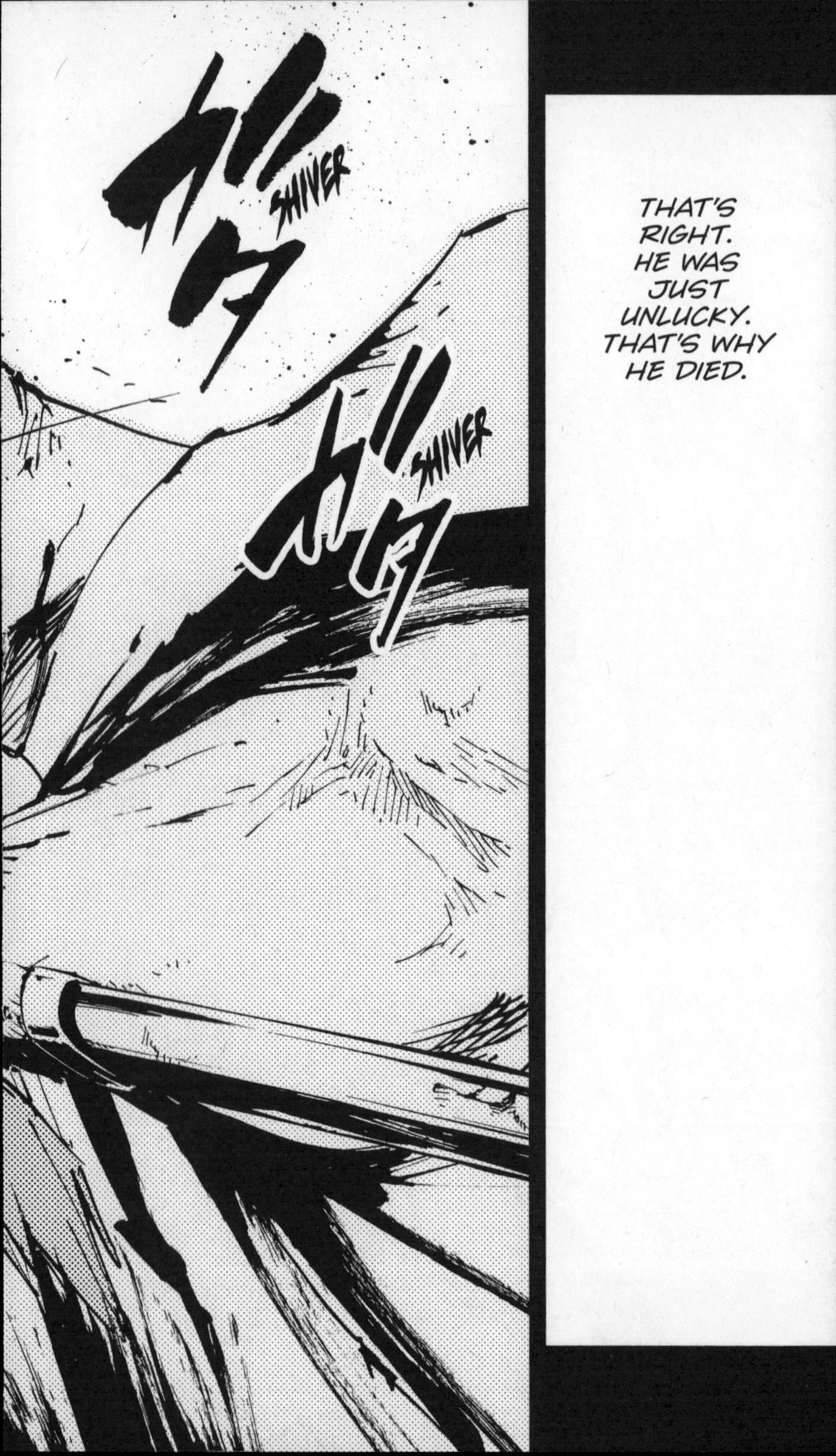
THAT'S RIGHT. HE WAS JUST UNLUCKY. THAT'S WHY HE DIED.
SHIVER
SHIVER

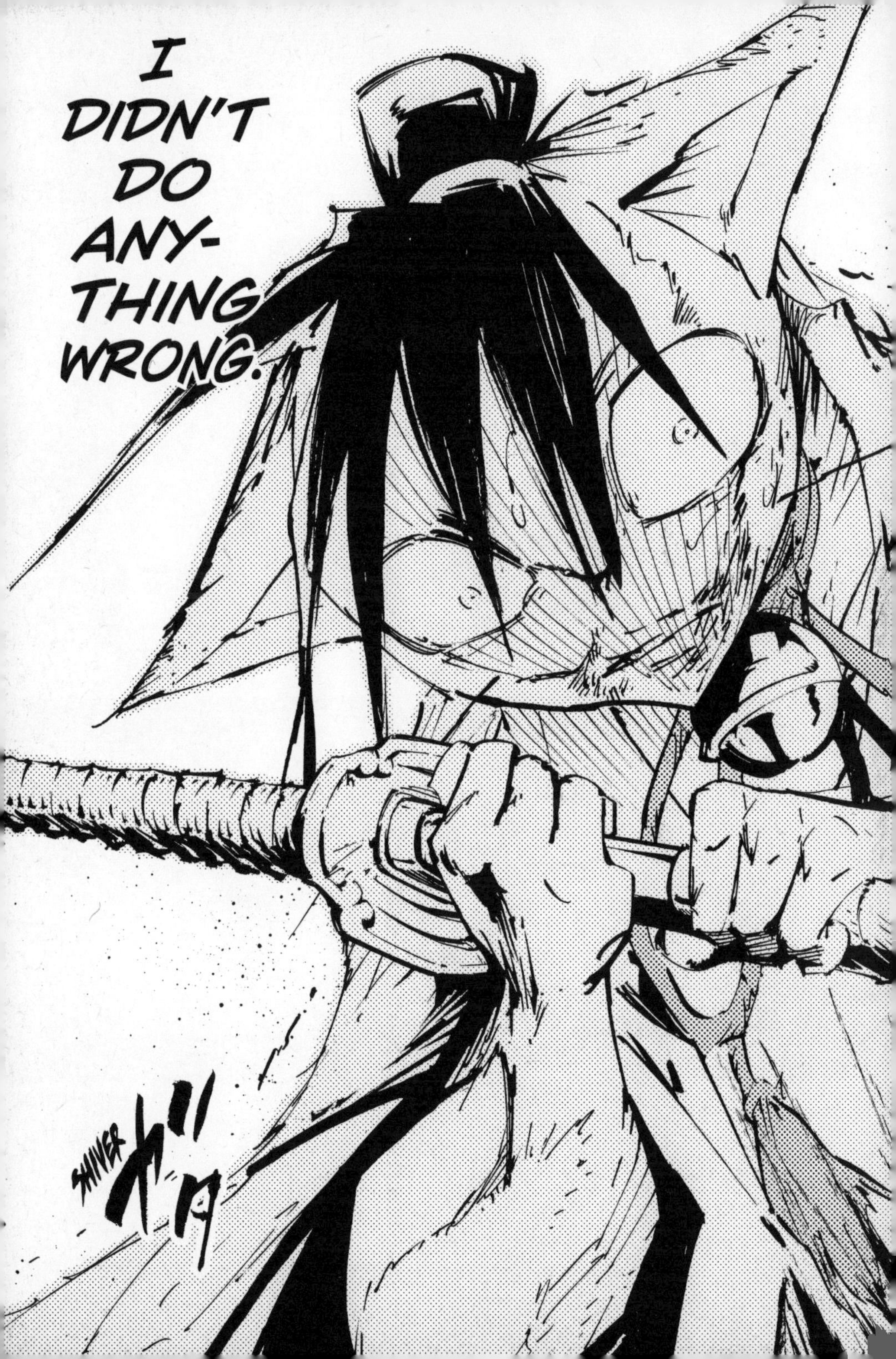
I DIDN'T DO ANY-THING WRONG.
SHIVER

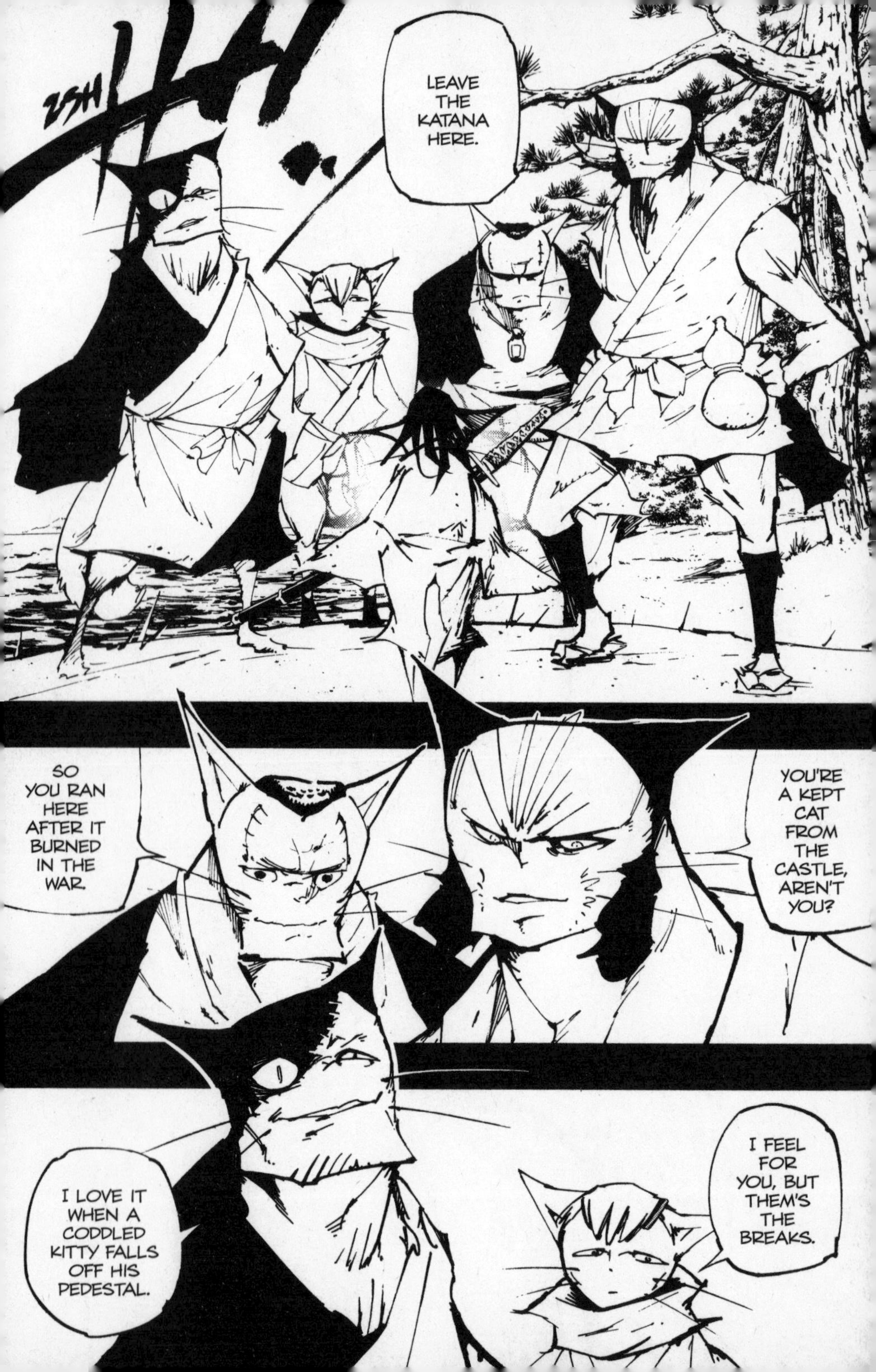
LEAVE THE KATANA HERE.
ZSH
YOU'RE A KEPT CAT FROM THE CASTLE, AREN'T YOU?
SO YOU RAN HERE AFTER IT BURNED IN THE WAR.
I FEEL FOR YOU, BUT THEM'S THE BREAKS.
I LOVE IT WHEN A CODDLED KITTY FALLS OFF HIS PEDESTAL.

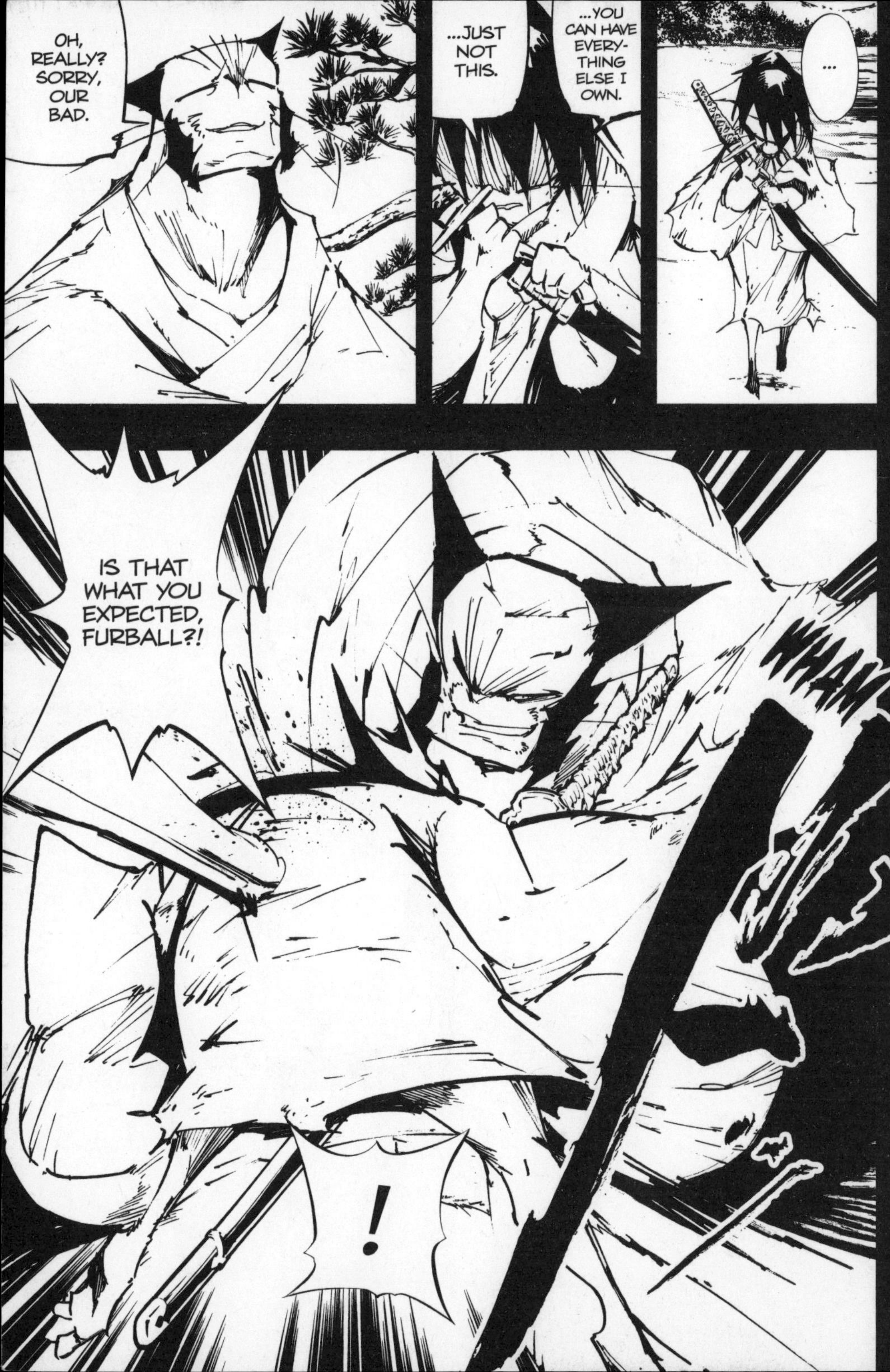
...
...YOU CAN HAVE EVERYTHING ELSE I OWN.
...JUST NOT THIS.
OH, REALLY? SORRY, OUR BAD.
IS THAT WHAT YOU EXPECTED, FURBALL?!
WHAM
!

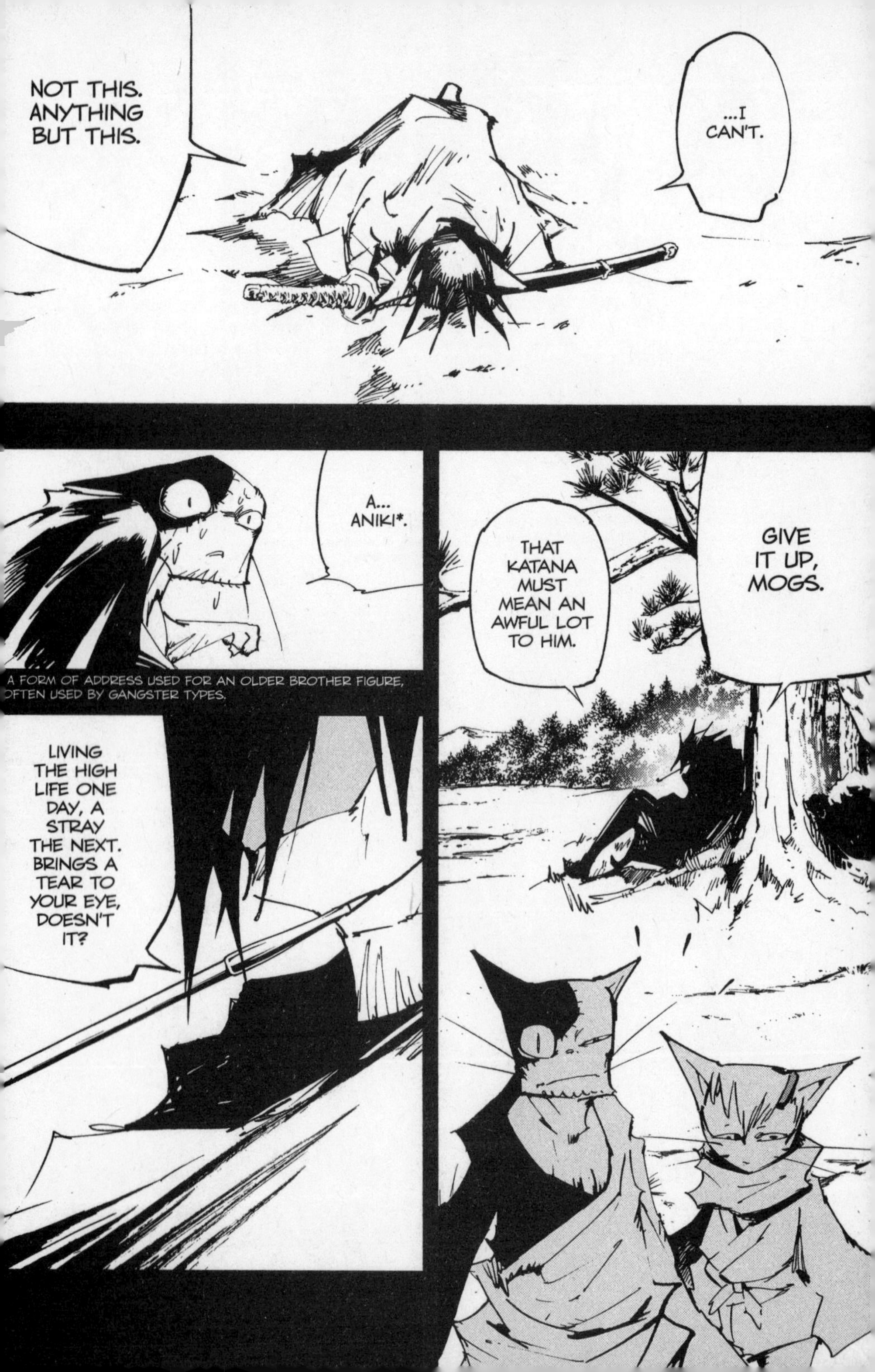
...I CAN'T.
NOT THIS. ANYTHING BUT THIS.
GIVE IT UP, MOGS.
THAT KATANA MUST MEAN AN AWFUL LOT TO HIM.
A... ANIKI*.
*A FORM OF ADDRESS USED FOR AN OLDER BROTHER FIGURE, OFTEN USED BY GANGSTER TYPES.
LIVING THE HIGH LIFE ONE DAY, A STRAY THE NEXT. BRINGS A TEAR TO YOUR EYE, DOESN'T IT?

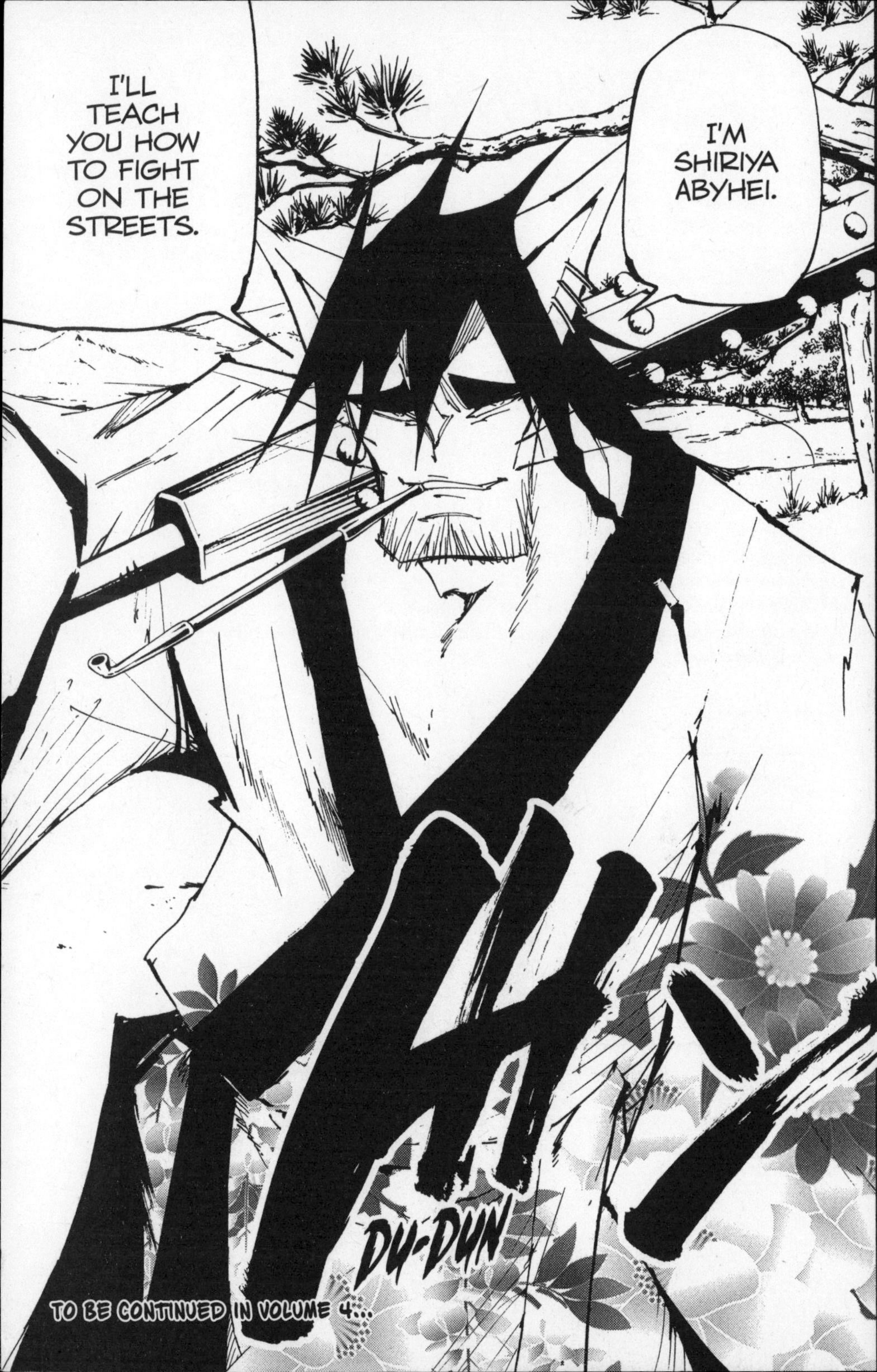
I'M SHIRIYA ABYHEI.
I'LL TEACH YOU HOW TO FIGHT ON THE STREETS.
DU-DUN
TO BE CONTINUED IN VOLUME 4...

TRANSLATION NOTES

Three Grown Kittens, page 2

The translators took a bit of a liberty with the chapter title. Also, there was a poem included with the magazine publication of this chapter, which influenced the translators' choice of chapter title. The poem was:

Two grown kittens,
tattered and torn
all lazy and listless
in light fur adorned.

The Japanese chapter title is *Sanbiki ga Kiru!*, which means "Three [Animals] Wear [Clothing]!". The "wear" part of the title is likely a reference to the fact that Norachiyo has finally put on some clothes. Written another way, it is the title of a Japanese historical drama which has been translated as "Three for the Kill!" To make the chapter title more relatable to readers who are unfamiliar with the TV show, the translators chose to use a cat connection rather than a historical drama connection, and alluded to the nursery rhyme "Three Little Kittens". As for the poem, the original Japanese has a list of three words that sound very similar—*kizudarake*, *kedaruge*, and *kedarake*—which roughly mean "covered in injuries," "listless," and "covered in fur."

Don'cha know, page 7

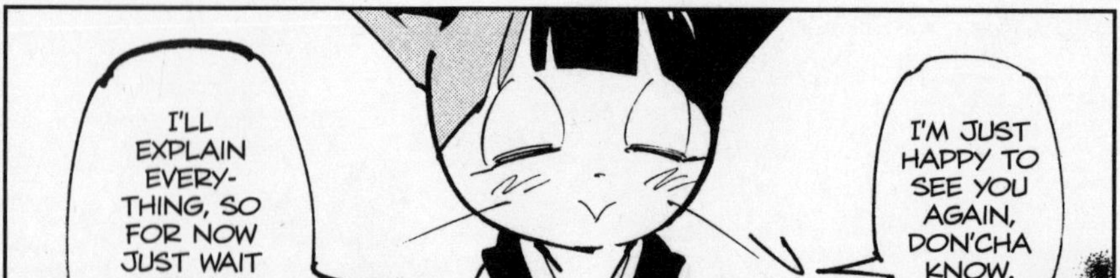
I'M JUST HAPPY TO SEE YOU AGAIN, DON'CHA KNOW.
I'LL EXPLAIN EVERY-THING, SO FOR NOW JUST WAIT HERE AND HAVE SOME TEA.

When Omike spoke to Norachiyo in the first chapter, she mostly uses *teineigo*, or polite speech. Now that she and Norachiyo are on somewhat closer terms, she drops the formalities and lets her accent come through. She speaks in the dialect of the Yamagata region, which is quite some distance from Norachiyo's home in Ōmeow. It may be a little anachronistic, but the translators have chosen to represent the Yamagata dialect with the Minnesota dialect of the United States.

The young lion, page 27

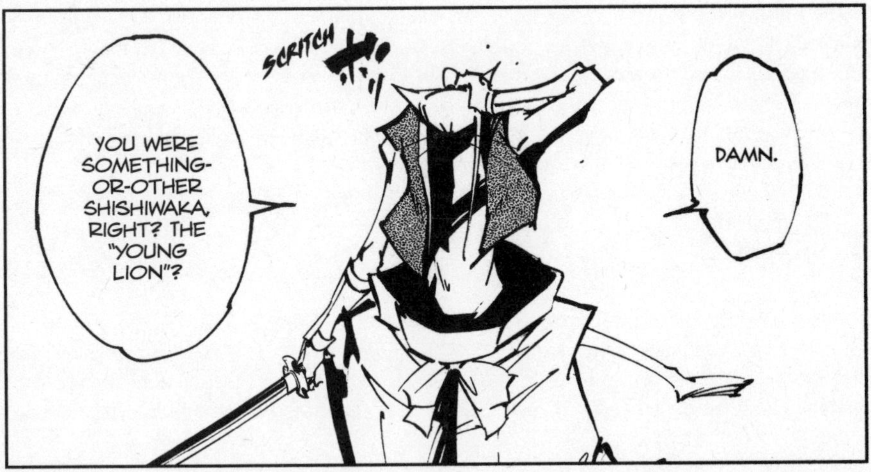
DAMN.
SCRITCH
YOU WERE SOMETHING-OR-OTHER SHISHIWAKA, RIGHT? THE "YOUNG LION"?

The translators asked Kurogane to do them a favor and translate Shishiwaka's name, for the benefit of our English-speaking readers. Shishiwaka is Japanese for "lion youth," so of course Kurogane knows that any time he says the name, he is in effect calling the cat a young lion.

Stover's Steamcloud, page 56

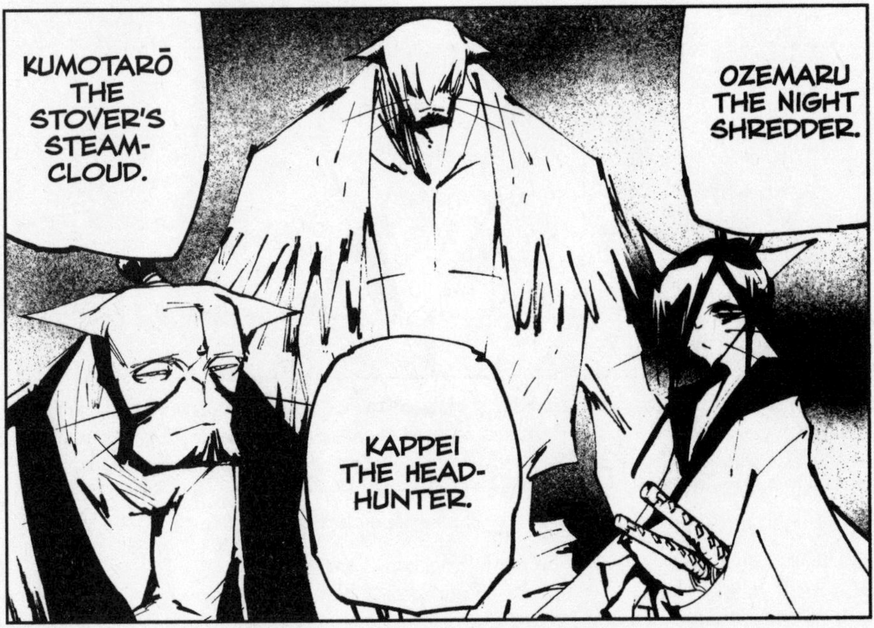
OZEMARU THE NIGHT SHREDDER.
KUMOTARŌ THE STOVER'S STEAM-CLOUD.
KAPPEI THE HEAD-HUNTER.

Kumotarō's epithet, *Tōge no Kamamushi* translates literally to "pot-steam of the mountain pass," but more importantly, it is a play on words. Although the translators cannot be sure yet why Kumotarō was given this nickname, it sounds similar to a famous style of *ekiben*, or "train station lunch," known as *Tōge no Kamameshi*, or "the pot-cooked meal of the mountain pass." It was invented for travelers on the go, who were sick and tired of the limited options available to eat at train stations along their journey. The translators hoped to create a similar connection by invoking the American brand of frozen prepared foods, Stouffer's. The reader may rest assured that stoves called *kamado* did exist in Japan at the time this series takes place. The "cloud" part comes from Kumotarō's actual name, meaning roughly "cloud boy."

His Nick Name, page 87

The title of this chapter is a reference to the international hit anime movie, *Your Name*., or *Kimi no Na wa*, in Japanese. The chapter title is *Yatsu no Nawa*, which literally means "his rope," specifically the sort of rope used to tie up arrested persons. The translators attempted to maintain both the reference to the movie and idea of capturing someone by adding "nick," which is slang for "arrest."

Jumanji, page 126

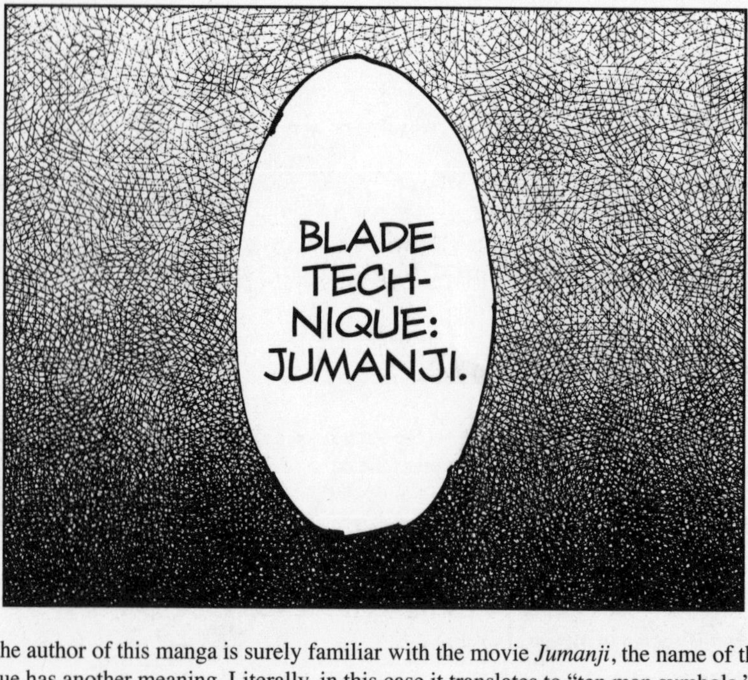
BLADE TECH- NIQUE: JUMANJI.

While the author of this manga is surely familiar with the movie *Jumanji*, the name of this technique has another meaning. Literally, in this case it translates to "ten man symbols." The man symbol, or swastika, is an auspicious religious symbol in Buddhism, where it represents the footprints of Buddha. In Chinese and Japanese art, it has been used to represent a repeating pattern, and very occasionally it has been used to represent ninja. The "ten" likely comes from the type of weapon Abyhei is using—a *jitte*, whose name means "ten hands." This weapon was common among police officers in the Edo Era, who were not allowed to carry swords.

Unsafe Cracker, page 127

It should come as no surprise to the reader that this chapter title is based on more wordplay. The original Japanese for this portion of it is *ore ore sagi*, which usually refers to a type of phone fraud called "me me fraud," where a crook will call an unsuspecting victim and, claiming to be a relative, say, "It's me, it's me. I got in trouble and need some money." In this case, however, the phrase is given kanji characters that mean "Break! Break, heron!" As there are no avian creatures anywhere to be seen in this chapter, the translators believe the "heron" was only there for the wordplay, and chose to replace the pun with an English one that focused on the "break" aspect of the phrase.

CHITTER CHITTER, page 149

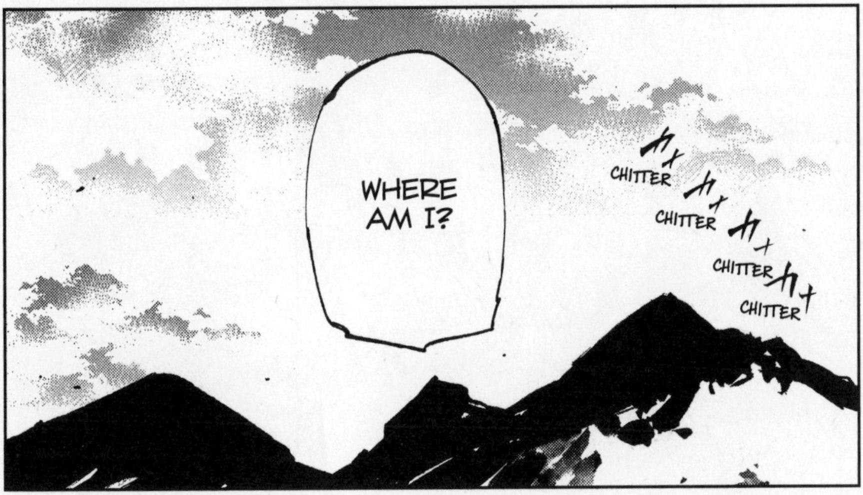
WHERE AM I?
CHITTER
CHITTER
CHITTER
CHITTER

In English, one of the few ways to express the sound of a cicada is CHITTER CHITTER, but in Japanese, there are specific ways to express the calls of different species of cicada. In this case, the original Japanese used was KANA KANA KANA KANA, which is the sound of *higurashi* (EN: evening cicada). The sound of cicadas is one of many ways to give life to a scene and place it in a specific season or time. The evening cicada is often active in between September-October, so it's most likely the fall season. A type of cicada that is more common in Japan is active in summer, and its call (MIIN MIIN MIIN in Japanese) is normally used to depict summer scenes in manga and anime.

Reichō, page 158

Because these events take place before Japan adopted the Western calendar, time was not marked with the same years. Prior to the Meiji Era, a new era began whenever the emperor decided something significant enough to mark the beginning of an era had occurred. Norachiyo's story begins in the fifth year of the Reichō Era, which is a feline era that corresponds with the human Keichō Era that began in 1596 (making the fifth year 1600). Incidentally, *reichō* can mean "superior" or "primate," likely referring to the humans who reign supreme.

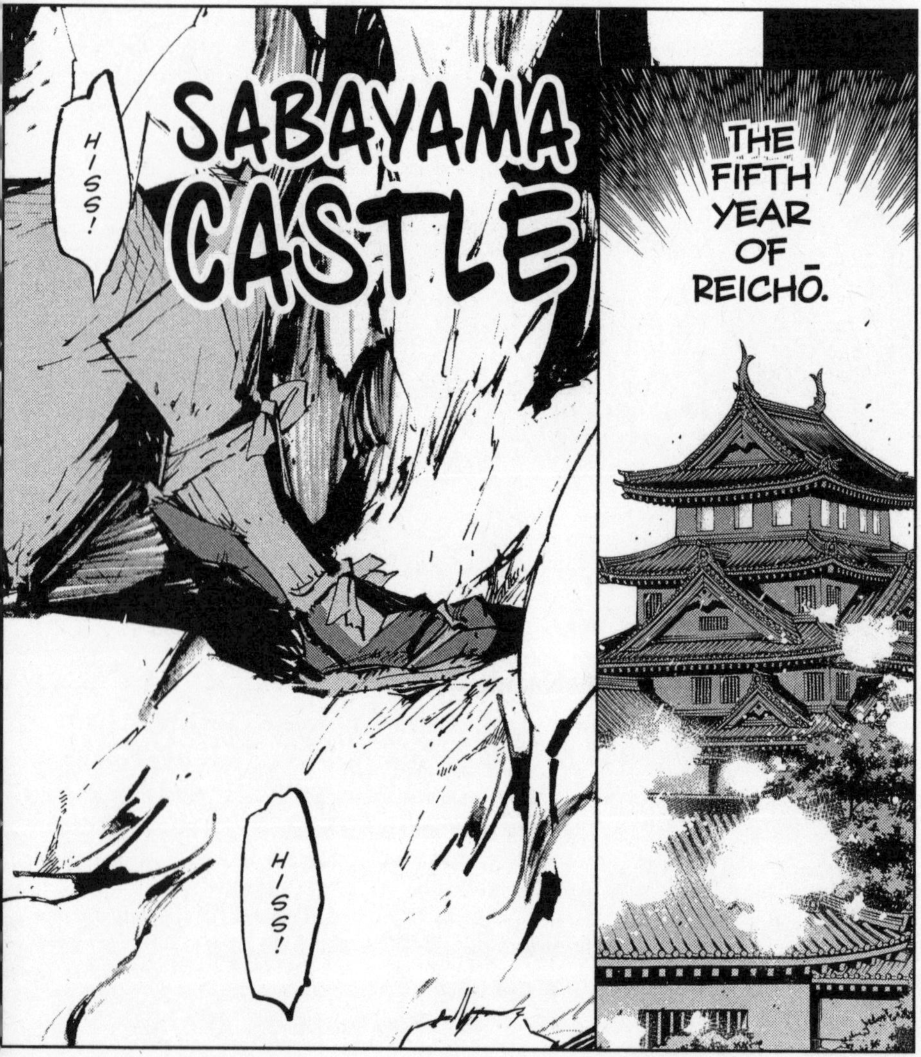
THE FIFTH YEAR OF REICHŌ.
SABAYAMA CASTLE
HISS!
HISS!

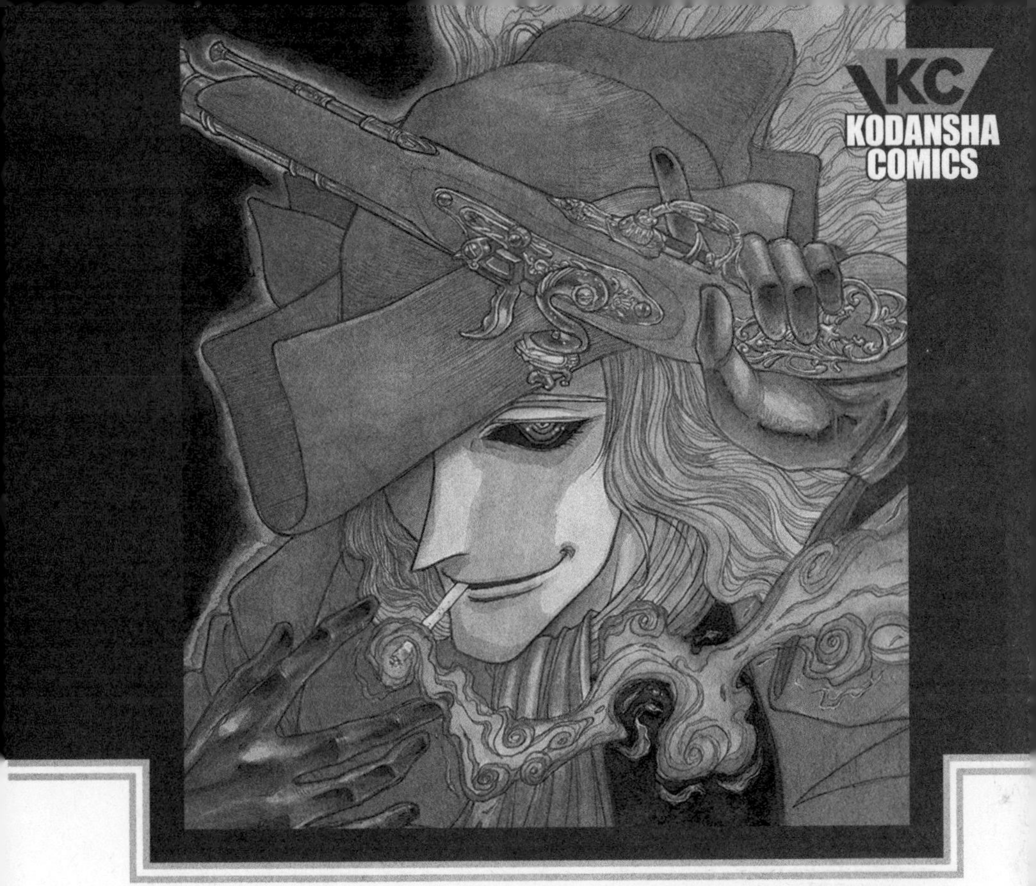
KC
KODANSHA COMICS

The Black Museum: The Ghost and the Lady

By Kazuhiro Fujita

Deep in Scotland Yard in London sits an evidence room dedicated to the greatest mysteries of British history. In this "Black Museum" sits a misshapen hunk of lead—two bullets fused together—the key to a wartime encounter between Florence Nightingale, the mother of modern nursing, and a supernatural Man in Grey. This story is unknown to most scholars of history, but a special guest of the museum will tell the tale of The Ghost and the Lady...

Praise for Kazuhiro Fujita's *Ushio and Tora*

"A charming revival that combines a classic look with modern depth and pacing... **Essential viewing both for curmudgeons and new fans alike.**" — Anime News Network

"**GREAT!** The first episode of Ushio and Tora captures the essence of '90s anime." — IGN

Nekogahara: Stray Cat Samurai volume 3 is a work of fiction. Names, characters, places, and incidents are the products of the author's imagination or are used fictitiously. Any resemblance to actual events, locales, or persons, living or dead, is entirely coincidental.

A Kodansha Comics Trade Paperback Original.

Published in the United States by Kodansha Comics,
an imprint of Kodansha USA Publishing, LLC, New York.

Publication rights for this English edition arranged through Kodansha Ltd., Tokyo.

First published in Japan in 2017 by Kodansha Ltd., Tokyo, as *Nekogahara* volume 3.

ISBN 978-1-63236-397-8

Printed in the United States of America.

www.kodanshacomics.com

9 8 7 6 5 4 3 2 1

Translation: Alethea Nibley & Athena Nibley
Lettering: Scott O. Brown
Editing: Ajani Oloye
Kodansha Comics edition cover design: Phil Balsman